BEHIND THE SCENES IN
American Government

Peter Woll   BRANDEIS UNIVERSITY

BEHIND THE SCENES IN

American Government

Personalities and Politics

Eighth Edition

HarperCollins*Publishers*

Sponsoring Editor: Lauren Silverman
Project Editor: Claire M. Caterer
Art Direction: Teresa Delgado
Text Design Adaptation: North 7 Atelier, Ltd.
Cover Design: Ben Arrington
Cover Illustration/Photo: Erikson-Dillon Art Services Inc.
Production: Jeffrey Taub
Compositor: ComCom Division of Haddon Craftsmen, Inc.
Printer and Binder: R. R. Donnelley & Sons Company
Cover Printer: The Lehigh Press, Inc.

Behind the Scenes in American Government, Eighth Edition

Library of Congress Cataloging-in-Publication Data
Behind the scenes in American government: personalities and politics
   / [compiled by] Peter Woll.—8th ed.
        p.   cm.
     1. United States—Politics and government—20th century.
  I. Woll, Peter, 1933–
  JK271.B533   1991   90-49629
  320.973—dc20   CIP

ISBN 0-673-52028-5 (student edition)
ISBN 0-673-52154-0 (teacher edition)

91 92 93 94 9 8 7 6 5 4 3 2 1

FOR ELAINE HERRMANN,
who worked behind the scenes
to make this book possible.

CONTENTS

Preface   xv

Chapter One
Political Parties and Politicians   **1**

1   Randall Rothenberg
In Search of George Bush   **3**

*Once known as a charismatic politician, Vice President George
Bush had an image problem as he campaigned for the
presidency. Personal politics defined his political style, often
pushing issues to the background.*

2   Garry Wills
Late Bloomer   **15**

*Dan Quayle seemed to add little to the Republican ticket in
1988 except youth and enthusiasm. The butt of jokes and
political satire from coast to coast, Quayle's character and
politics are in many ways quite different from the press and
media portrayals of him as a highly conservative, inept, and
inexperienced politician. Nevertheless, disturbing questions
remain about his leadership capabilities.*

3   Marjorie Williams
The Bad Boy of American Politics   **24**

*Lee Atwater worked behind the scenes of the 1988 Bush
presidential campaign, forging a successful but controversial
strategy that his opponents labeled "dirty tricks."*

4   Garry Wills
Making History with Silo Sam   **36**

*Bold, charismatic, dedicated, driven, and flamboyant are among
the adjectives that describe Jesse Jackson. His emotional*

*political style contrasted sharply with that of his party's
presidential nominee in 1988.*

5   Howard Fineman
The New Black Politics   42

*Black politicians like Douglas Wilder and David Dinkins have
increasingly found that avoiding political extremes and
appealing to the center is a formula for success.*

6   Jill Alper and Gabriel Kaplan
**Hard Counts: Behind the Scenes of the '89 Virginia
Gubernatorial Race**   47

*Two young staffers on Douglas Wilder's campaign trail give a
lively account of how they helped to elect the first black
governor of Virginia since the Reconstruction.*

7   John Homans
The Lure of the Political Road   58

*Behind the scenes of every presidential campaign are staffers
who often battle more among themselves than with opposing
candidates. To many political professionals the excitement of
campaigning becomes an end in itself, regardless of who wins
or loses.*

8   Mike Royko
The Boss   65

*This excerpt from the best-selling exposé of city politics depicts
the inner workings of one of the last big-city machines and its
powerful boss, Chicago Mayor Richard J. Daley.*

Chapter Two
Pressure Groups and Lobbyists   81

9   Evan Thomas
Influence Peddling in Washington   82

*Hordes of lobbyists swarm over the nation's capital and prowl
its corridors of power, as described in this colorful* Time

magazine cover story. The hired guns of special interests
include many former congressmen, staffers, and administration
officials who have turned their positions of public trust into
private gain.

10

Haynes Johnson
When Money Talks, Washington Listens   98

Top government officials obtain valuable experience and
contacts that can put them in good stead later in the private
sector. Many former public servants obtain highly lucrative
jobs, turning their experience into profit.

11

Chuck Alston
PACs and the Battle for Clean Air   104

An unusually broad alliance of PACs (Political Action
Committees) attempted unsuccessfully to defeat clean air
legislation, illustrating that Congress cannot, in the words of
its critics, simply be described as "the best that money can
buy."

12

Tom Watson
PAC Pilgrimage Becomes Candidates' Ritual   112

Congressional candidates increasingly rely upon PAC (Political
Action Committee) money to finance their campaigns.
Incumbents receive the lion's share of PAC contributions, but
they and challengers alike must make periodic pilgrimages to
solicit PAC support.

Chapter Three
The Media and Political Consultants   **123**

13

Larry J. Sabato
How Political Consultants Choose Candidates   126

Campaigning has become big business, and professional
political consultants play a leading role. Consultants are not
simply hired guns but often carefully choose candidate-clients
to fulfill their political objectives as much as the candidates hire
them to win elections.

14 Lois Romano
Pat Caddell: Down, but Never Out   **136**

*Consultants as well as candidates have their ups and downs as
political winds shift. A* Washington Post *reporter portrays a
leading political consultant who continues to inject his own
personality and values into the political process.*

15 Jonathan Alter
The Media and Campaigning—'88 Style   **144**

*A leading Washington writer and political insider gives a lively
account of the media's vital role in every aspect of presidential
campaigning.*

16 Joseph Napolitan
**Negative Campaigning: What It Is, How to Use It,
How to Defend Against It**   **148**

*In modern campaigns politicians must be prepared to respond
to negative attacks. Above all, they do not want to "do a
Dukakis"—in other words, to passively ignore an opponent's
attack.*

17 Jody Powell
The Right to Lie   **155**

*A former presidential press secretary reveals, in a selection
taken from his provocative book* The Other Side of the Story,
*how he manipulated the media to protect the national interest
and individual lives during the Iranian hostage crisis.*

Chapter Four
The Presidency   **169**

18 James David Barber
Presidential Character, Style, and Performance   **171**

*Presidential character often determines White House
performance. The political scientist who predicted in advance
how President Richard M. Nixon's character would result in a
White House debacle that turned out to be the Watergate affair
analyzes how different presidential characteristics affect
performance.*

19 Fred Barnes
Fearless Leader: Bush in the White House 182

President George Bush's nonconfrontational political style more than his stand on issues seemed to account for his unusual popularity after his first year in office, a time when most presidents suffer a decline in their approval ratings.

20 George E. Reedy
The White House Staff: A Personal Account 187

An old Washington hand and one of Lyndon B. Johnson's most astute staffers depicts the rarefied atmosphere of the White House and its impact upon the president's aides. This selection is from the author's provocative book The Twilight of the Presidency.

21 David Hoffman and Ann Devroy
The White House Tough Guy 192

When President-elect George Bush chose New Hampshire Governor John H. Sununu to be his White House chief of staff he both paid off a political debt and made a like-minded conservative the head of his political team. Sununu lived up to his reputation for being a strong-willed and take-charge person.

22 Peggy Noonan
Confessions of a White House Speechwriter 200

A speechwriter for Ronald Reagan and George Bush gives a rare account of what it is like to be a woman on the White House staff engaged in an activity that many of her colleagues deemed of only minor importance.

Chapter Five
The Congress 213

23 David Rogers
Man of Capitol 217

Michigan congressman John Dingell, who "muscles, questions and regulates," has played an effective power game on Capitol

Hill that has made him one of the most influential members of the House.

24 Mark G. Michaelsen
My Life as a Congressional Candidate 222

Running for Congress is challenging and exhilarating even in the face of almost certain defeat.

25 Rowland Evans and Robert Novak
The Johnson System 228

In their masterly book Lyndon B. Johnson: The Exercise of Power, *Evans and Novak picture Johnson as a consummate politician who, as majority leader, ruled the Senate with an iron hand. His overwhelming personality and highly individualistic style made a lasting imprint on friends and foes alike.*

26 Laurence Leamer
Robert Byrd and Edward Kennedy: Two Stories of the Senate 234

Edward Kennedy is a star and Robert Byrd is a tactician. Kennedy's individualistic style is in sharp contrast to Byrd's emphasis on collegiality. Both, in different ways, achieved power and status in the Senate, as described in this selection from Laurence Leamer's book on leading Washington personalities, Playing for Keeps.

27 Jackie Calmes
From Majority Leader to Committee Chairman: How Robert Byrd Wields Power in the Senate 243

When he stepped down as party chief to become chairman of the powerful Senate Appropriations Committee, West Virginia Senator Robert Byrd shifted objectives and strategies but maintained and in some ways even enhanced his power on Capitol Hill.

28 Julie Rovner
Rockefeller's Path to Senate Power 251

The scion of a rich and famous family, West Virginia Senator John D. Rockefeller IV has gained power on Capitol Hill by paying careful attention to Senate norms and customs. He gained influence the "old-fashioned way," which means with hard work, respect for colleagues, and a reputation as a policy expert.

Chapter Six
The Courts
259

29 Bob Woodward and Scott Armstrong
The Brethren and the Abortion Decision 262

Clashing personalities and intrigue on the Supreme Court may affect the outcome of important cases that have a nationwide impact. In their best-selling book The Brethren, *Bob Woodward and Scott Armstrong write about the impact of personalities on the Court's decision to guarantee women the right to obtain abortions.*

30 Lynn Rosellini
Justice William Brennan, Jr.: The Most Powerful Liberal in America 281

Before he stepped down in 1990, Supreme Court Justice William J. Brennan, Jr.'s firm commitment, keen mind, and ingratiating style made a lasting imprint on the Court and constitutional law.

31 Joan Biskupic
Justice Antonin Scalia: Dynamo on the Court 287

Ideological commitment, brilliance, wit, and energy have made Justice Antonin Scalia the Supreme Court's most powerful conservative.

Chapter Seven
The Bureaucracy
297

32 Sanford J. Ungar
The King: J. Edgar Hoover 301

The bulldog face of J. Edgar Hoover was not a facade. The man behind the mask had an iron will and a quick temper, as

Sanford J. Ungar vividly illustrates in this selection from his
definitive book F.B.I.

33   Jonathan Alter
The Powers That Stay   323

Top-level bureaucrats must be skillful politicians to maintain
their power. Many of the most successful, such as Admiral
Hyman Rickover and J. Edgar Hoover, were political
entrepreneurs. Others, such as Defense Secretary Frank
Carlucci, learned to serve and often manipulate many masters.
This entertaining selection from the Washington Monthly
describes the games that bureaucrats play.

34   David Stockman
The Triumph of Politics   335

A left-wing liberal in college, David Stockman changed his
stripes and as Ronald Reagan's budget director led the
conservative attack on government spending and taxes. In a
selection from his best-selling book, he describes how he
became, in effect, a surrogate president.

PREFACE

This book is designed to be an exciting supplementary text for introductory American government courses. It is politics through the eyes of participants, focusing upon the personalities who shape the way the political game is played and who, more often than is commonly thought, place their individual imprints upon public policies. The text can also be used to complement a wide range of courses that analyze parties and political campaigning, interest groups and lobbyists, the media and political consultants, the presidency, Congress, the courts, and the bureaucracy.

Politics is, by any measure, fascinating. But this fascination is not often conveyed to students because many books and courses concentrate on structures and processes at the expense of the individuals who constitute the lifeblood of politics. And it is, after all, the people in politics who shape its character, just as they themselves are shaped by it. This book illustrates how character and personality influence politics, and the ways in which political institutions and processes such as the presidency and political campaigning affect the personalities and actions of those who are directly, and sometimes indirectly, involved. Vignettes of famous politicians, pressure group leaders, journalists and political consultants, members of Congress, White House staffers and presidential advisers, Supreme Court justices, and top-level bureaucrats make up the book. By introducing students to the colorful and powerful personalities who are found in politics, I hope to make American government the lively subject that it should be.

WHAT'S OLD, WHAT'S NEW

The eighth edition of *Behind the Scenes in American Government* portrays the leading and upcoming political personalities that are shaping the politics of the 1990s. In Chapter One, "Political Parties and Politicians," the text retains the popular portrayals of President George Bush and perennial political candidate Jesse Jackson, as well as the riveting Mike Royko account of former Chicago Mayor Richard Daley's personality cult and leadership style. New to the eighth edition is Gary Wills's *Time* cover story, which takes a probing look at Vice President Dan Quayle, rising above the clichés and jokes that have characterized him to suggest he is a far more serious politician than his popular image portrays. Other selections added to the eighth edition in Chapter One include a lively account of how Lee Atwater's political style helped him to rise to power and prominence in the Republican party from relatively obscure roots; a fasci-

nating description of the new black politics and politicians that gained prominence as the decade of the 1990s began; and a fascinating look behind the
scenes of Douglas Wilder's successful race for governor of Virginia, written by
two young political staffers who helped to forge his campaign and were instrumental in his success.

Chapter Two on pressure groups and lobbyists continues the popular selection on influence peddling in Washington from a *Time* cover story, and *Washington Post* reporter Haynes Johnson's account of the power of money in the
nation's capital. *Congressional Quarterly* writer Chuck Alston adds a fascinating
account of the role of PACs in the battle for clean air, a piece that profiles a
variety of political personalities and is full of flavor.

Chapter Three, "The Media and Political Consultants," has retained the
classic and popular selections by Larry J. Sabato on political consultants, Lois
Romano on political consultant Pat Caddell, Jonathan Alter on the media and
their role in political campaigning, and Jody Powell on "The Right to Lie," a
description of the often trying times of a presidential press secretary. New to the
eighth edition is a political consultant's firsthand description of negative campaigning, which focuses on political candidates' alleged personality weaknesses
and misdeeds in modern elections and which offers advice to candidates on
how to cope with it.

New readings in Chapter Four on the presidency include Fred Barnes's profile
of President Bush in office, focusing on his leadership style. Veteran *Washington
Post* journalists and Washington insiders add a lively profile of White House
Chief of Staff John H. Sununu, entitled "The White House Tough Guy." Reagan
speechwriter Peggy Noonan contributes an exciting behind-the-scenes account
of how a talented speechwriter coped with a detached president and often
overbearing White House staff.

Turning to Chapter Five, on the Congress, the eighth edition of *Scenes* takes
into account major upheavals on Capitol Hill that occurred in the late 1980s and
early 1990s as power shifts occurred among congressional leaders. The chapter
retains the classic selections by Rowland Evans and Robert Novak, "The Johnson
System," and by Laurence Leamer on the contrasting Senate styles of Robert
Byrd of West Virginia and Edward Kennedy of Massachusetts. New in the eighth
edition is an in-depth *Wall Street Journal* profile of Michigan congressman John
Dingell, who wields wide power as the chairman of the influential House Energy
and Commerce Committee. Another new and timely piece describes how West
Virginia Senator Robert Byrd changed his style in the Senate as he stepped down
from being majority leader to become chairman of the influential Appropriations
Committee. Internal Senate power is also the subject of a new profile of West
Virginia Senator John D. Rockefeller IV, who adopted an "old-fashioned" Senate
style to gain influence. Finally, students should be particularly fascinated with
a fresh selection written by a young congressional candidate who challenged an
incumbent, which describes his life as a congressional candidate.

Chapter Six, "The Courts," has kept the popular Bob Woodward and Scott

Armstrong selection from their best-selling book *The Brethren,* which gives a behind-the-scenes account of how the personalities and styles of individual justices played an important role in making the historic abortion decision in *Roe v. Wade* (1973). For the eighth edition there are new portrayals of justices William J. Brennan, Jr., who led the Court's liberal wing from his first day as a justice until his resignation in 1990, and Antonin Scalia, who has become the Court's leading conservative.

Chapter Seven, "The Bureaucracy," keeps the classic selections by Sanford J. Ungar on "The King"—J. Edgar Hoover—and by Jonathan Alter on "The Powers That Stay." Added to the chapter is the popular piece by David Stockman, drawn from his best-seller *The Triumph of Politics,* giving a firsthand account of his critical role as budget director in the Reagan presidency. Stockman also highlights the crucial role bureaucrats often play in making important government decisions.

ACKNOWLEDGMENTS

I am especially indebted to Elaine Herrmann, who has assisted me over the years with this and other projects. Her extraordinary skills and especially her good humor in the face of the many pressures that always accompany writing and publishing a book have saved many a day for me. I would also like to thank my editors, Lauren Silverman and Claire Caterer, with whom it has been a delight to work. Their professional competence improved the book and smoothly guided it through the intricate publishing process.

Peter Woll

POLITICAL PARTIES AND POLITICIANS

Chapter

One

In classical democratic theory, political parties are supposed to bridge the gap between people and government. They are to be the principal policy-makers, presenting contrasting choices to the electorate so that, by voting, people can participate in the choice of government programs. It is important that a political party have control over its candidates and office holders, because a party that has a majority in the legislature and controls the executive branch will then be able to carry out its platform.

Although political parties in an ideal situation are suited to presenting meaningful and realistic policy choices for the electorate, they also serve the personal goals of their active members, which may have nothing at all to do with implementing one public policy instead of another. Roberto Michels draws from the great German sociologist Max Weber to define the political party as:

> A spontaneous society of propaganda and of agitation seeking to acquire power, in order to procure thereby for its active militant adherents chances, ideal and material, for realization of either objective aims or of *personal advantages,* or of both. Consequently, the general orientation of the political party, whether in its personal or impersonal aspect, is that of *machtstreben* (striving to power).[1]

In this chapter we will be concerned with the personal motives of active party members. These motives affect the organization and orientation of political parties at national, state, and local levels. The drive for power may completely overshadow party policy. American party leaders will often shape their policy promises in accordance with the wishes of the majority of the electorate. And, in the absence of any clear electoral desires, which is a common situation, party leaders themselves must determine their actions, which are usually directed toward expanding their power and status in both the party and government. Their personalities often determine the kinds of decisions they will make, and the way in which they conduct their offices. At the lower levels of parties, particularly in city party machines, the orientation of adherents is often economic security as much as a drive for power. Policy is almost completely irrelevant at these lower echelons.

[1]Alfred D. Grazia, trans., Roberto Michels's *First Lectures in Political Sociology* (Minneapolis: University of Minnesota Press, 1949), p. 134. Italics added.

COMMONLY REFERRED TO BY the media as "wimp," Vice President George Bush proved the image to be far from the truth as he readily captured the 1988 Republican presidential nomination and went on to campaign vigorously for his place in history as president of the United States. Bush brought to his campaign leadership skills that were known to the public and of little interest to a media apparently obsessed with George Bush's alleged Irangate mistake in not vigorously opposing President Reagan's plan to sell arms to Iran in exchange for hostages. Nor did Bush, if he knew of it, apparently oppose the even more serious White House debacle, engineered by the president's staff, that secretly and in violation of federal law transferred arms sales' funds to the Nicaraguan contras.

But Vice President Bush, like his predecessors, had to play second fiddle to the president. The vice president's office by its very nature is low-key. No president wants a vice president to upstage him. It was impossible for "the real George Bush" to emerge from a White House dominated by "the Great Communicator," Ronald Reagan.

However, Bush, like many former vice presidents, used the office to gain the support of Republican organizations throughout the nation. Richard Nixon had done the same in the late 1950s. Bush, like Nixon before him, generously gave his time to party fund-raisers and organizational meetings. He seemed the natural *party* heir to Ronald Reagan, although not necessarily Reagan's ideological equivalent.

Bush built his presidential campaign on an effective organization and loyalty to Ronald Reagan. Ironically, public opinion polls suggested that Bush's party rival for the nomination, Kansas Senator Robert Dole, would be more likely to win against Michael Dukakis, the leading contender for his party's nomination. But Dole's organization could not match that of Bush. Internal bickering and staff fights crippled the Kansan's organization, and Dole's leadership style, drawn from the legislative rather than the executive arena, appeared to be hesitant and uncertain. Whether Bush won by default or by design will remain a question for political historians to decide. But after Bush swept the critical Southern primary on March 8, 1988, that encompassed all of the southern states, including Florida and Texas, there was no doubt he was on his way to the nomination.

The Bush campaign, however, did not seem to illuminate much about the candidate himself, neither his personality nor what issues, except in the vaguest of terms, he considered to be most important. The author of the following selection goes in search of George Bush, and in the process sheds light on his character and style, which, as political scientist James David Barber has pointed out, are always important ingredients of presidential performance.[1]

---

[1]James David Barber, *The Presidential Character,* 3rd ed. (Englewood Cliffs, N.J.: Prentice-Hall, 1986).

1 Randall Rothenberg
IN SEARCH OF
GEORGE BUSH

A crackling fire warmed the White House office of the Vice President this raw winter day, complementing the deep wood tones, the rich Oriental rugs and the family photographs. Sprawled in a chair, George Bush contemplated a question: How would his leadership differ from that of his chief rival for the Republican presidential nomination, Senator Robert J. Dole of Kansas?

"Can't talk about Bob Dole's leadership," Bush said of the man who humiliated him in the Iowa caucuses and whom, in turn, he defeated in the bitterly contended New Hampshire primary. Then, immediately, Bush caught himself. "I can work well with people," he added. "I can effect change without brutalizing people."

A simple response to a simple question, but telling in what was omitted. After seven years as deputy in the most ideologically charged Administration in this century, and in the midst of the political fight of his life, George Bush's credo remains intact: all politics is personal.

He has strewn handwritten epistles by the thousands along the path of his political career ("George Bush is a fiend for writing personal notes," says a former White House official). On the stump, he seems to delight less in being recognized than in recognizing. "Hey, my main man!" he says to a high school student he greets by name in Ames, Iowa. He spots a fellow back in a crowd in Iowa City. "Hey, how's Shirl? Back in Marshalltown?" After his Iowa drubbing, he attacked New Hampshire not with policies but with *politesse*—offering help to locals whose cars had stalled, shaking hands at factory gates, tossing snowballs with reporters.

But ideas? "I'm not what you call your basic intellectual," said Bush during a break in a campaign whose next test comes two days hence, in the agglomeration of Southern primaries dubbed "Super Tuesday." He grew insistent: "Be what you are in life. Don't try to be everything just because you're running for president."

The statement rings with irony, for if any man in American politics has *been* everything, it is 63-year-old George Herbert Walker Bush. Yet his résumé is the paradox of his public existence.

Throughout his rapid ascension from job to appointive job, Bush has left in his wake respect and deep affection. He is credited with building the Texas Republican party, keeping the G.O.P. together when Watergate ripped its fabric, and restoring morale at a Central Intelligence Agency critically damaged by Congressional investigations.

Yet his political legacy is as ephemeral as the good will is substantial. One former White House aide calls him "the invisible man"—an apt description of him throughout much of his career. Two months of interviews with more than 60 of his colleagues, family and close observers from across his history leave an impression of George Bush as a man who has willingly sublimated ego and ideology to the values of the institutions he has served, rarely probing, seldom questioning, never reaching.

Eddie Mahe, Jr., the political director of the Republican Committee when Bush was its chairman in the early 1970's, is an admirer of the Vice President's honesty and tenacity. Nonetheless, Mahe, now a Washington political consultant unaffiliated with any presidential candidate, says of Bush, "He's not a deep person."

What is more, adds Mahe, "He doesn't have the courage of his convictions."

"Let me tell you something," George Bush said to a high school student's query not long ago. "The latest thing in politics is to stretch you out on some kind of psychoanalytical couch to figure out what makes you tick."

His own motivations, he continued, were quite basic: "I've always said that I have respect for my Dad because he believed in public service. *I* believe in public service."

Prescott Sheldon Bush, a managing partner at the investment banking firm of Brown Brothers, Harriman, personified noblesse oblige, serving on sundry public boards and committees and later becoming a United States Senator. But he was an imposing man who had little time for his children. "Everyone was afraid of him," recalls his son Jonathan Bush, 56. "He was a man on a mission, and he had mother to raise us." Dorothy Walker Bush, now 86, bred into her five children rules to buttress the sense of service instilled by their father. During childhood summers at Walker's point, the family's waterfront retreat in Kennebunkport, Me., and on the lawn of their nine-bedroom Victorian house in Greenwich, Conn., they learned competitiveness—"the zeitgeist of the time," according to her youngest child, William "Bucky" Bush, 49.

Whatever the game, the best at it was her second son, George. Yet "Poppy," as he was called, played ball with such grace that the others couldn't begin to be jealous. "He was too big a hero, too big a star," says Jonathan. "You were just too anxious to get close to him."

For all the competitiveness, Dorothy Bush absolutely forbade bragging. Even the slightest hint of self-aggrandizement, according to Bucky Bush, would be met by her firm statement: "We've heard enough of the 'Great I Am.'"

Dorothy Bush also taught her children loyalty. George Warren, a childhood friend of George Bush's, recalls how as a young adult he rushed to his parents' house in Greenwich the day his father was killed in an accident. When he got there, he found Dorothy waiting on the lawn.

"I hadn't seen her in years, and the two families very seldom saw each other socially," says Warren, now a retired teacher. "And she took it upon herself to come to our house to tell me. It shows tremendous loyalty. And you'll find that quality in George Bush as well."

Loyalty, modesty, competitiveness—the qualities are George Bush's strengths. But they haunt him. Preternaturally disposed to team play at any cost, he is loathe to rise above his surroundings. When he says, as he did in 1984, "I'm for Mr. Reagan—blindly," he doesn't understand the sophisticates' snickers.

One duty few young American men questioned in 1942, the year George Bush graduated from high school, was going to war. On June 12, his 18th birthday, he joined the Navy, his mathematics courses at Andover qualifying him to become a torpedo bomber pilot.

Bush became the Navy's youngest flier, shipping out to the South Pacific on the carrier San Jacinto. Leo Nadeau, his gunner, painted "Barbara" on the cowling of their Grumman Avenger in inch-high white letters. George had met Barbara Pierce—the daughter of the publisher of McCall's Magazine— during a prep-school Christmas dance.

On Sept. 2, 1944, flying cover for an invasion of Chichi-Jima, Bush felt a jolt. The cockpit filled with smoke. After delivering four bombs to the target, he bailed out of his burning plane. His two mates didn't make it.

He was picked up by an American submarine and after several months of recuperation asked to be reassigned to combat, eventually flying a total of 1,228 hours. There were no more close calls, but for his heroism on that mission, Bush was awarded the Distinguished Flying Cross.

He breezed through Yale, a young married man in a hurry, gaining the captaincy of the baseball team, membership in the exclusive secret society Skull and Bones, an economics degree, a Phi Beta Kappa key and a baby son.

A family friend, Neil Mallon, a man who "could charm the fangs off a snake," according to Bucky Bush, offered George a bottom-of-the-ladder job in Midland, Tex., at Dresser Industries, his large oil company. After two years, Bush joined with a neighbor to create a firm that would purchase royalty rights from small landowners if a driller found oil on the land. Several years later, he formed another company to locate and buy oil-producing properties. His uncle, Herbert Walker, found $800,000 through Eastern investors to help get the firms started.

But the exhilaration was marred by tragedy. In March 1953, the Bushes' second child, Robin, was diagnosed as having leukemia. After six months of grueling commuting between Texas and New York's Memorial Hospital, George and Barbara Bush saw their 3-year-old daughter die.

By the early 1960's, something began to gnaw at Bush. Although a father of five and a millionaire, neither the family sense of noblesse oblige nor his own desire for recognition were being served. So in 1962 Bush, then living in Houston, ran for the chairmanship of the Harris County Republican Party.

If George Bush has been caught in a political vise for his entire career, squeezed between a right wing suspicious of his moderation and centrists who believe he too readily accommodates extremists, it was in Houston that his ideological travails began.

The Republican Party was in its nascent stages in Texas in the early 1960's; for a time, only two Republicans sat in the Texas Legislature. Even so, the party was being torn apart by battles between establishment Republicans and the more militant members of the John Birch Society. Bush won the chairmanship race, and immediately began drawing in people from both factions, identifying with one or the other as the occasion warranted.

When he ran for the Senate in 1964 against the liberal Democratic incumbent, Ralph Yarborough, Bush termed himself a "Goldwater Republican" and opposed both the Nuclear Test Ban Treaty and much of the Civil Rights Act. But he still managed to antagonize the right.

"The rumor ran rampant through the Goldwater organization that the Bush people had damaged Goldwater's race because they had been getting voters to the polls who were going to vote for Johnson" but who split their ticket and voted for Bush, recalls Congressman Bill Archer, a nine-term Republican veteran from Houston. True or not, says Archer, "these were the seeds" of the right wing's discontent with Bush.

The seeds sprouted after he lost the Senate race. Within a year, his wing of the Republican party was known as the "Bush Faction" and was considered "an extension of the Eisenhower-Scranton-Rockefeller-Romney wing," according to Archer. When Bush ran for Congress in 1966 in west Houston, he campaigned actively in black neighborhoods, sponsored a black girls' softball team and spoke of the need for "equal opportunity." He won handily, against a law-and-order Democrat widely considered more conservative.

"Young Bush," as he was known, became an immediate presence in Washington, gaining a coveted seat on the House Ways and Means Committee. Back home, he was a power. A 1968 *Houston Chronicle* editorial maintained that "Bush has become so politically formidable nobody cares to take him on."

Not only was he powerful, he was independent. He voted for an open-housing bill that was vehemently opposed in most of Texas. Political calculation probably entered into the vote; according to an aide to a longtime Texas Congressman, "Anybody who was considering a Senate race" in 1970, as Bush was, "would have voted that way, because his eye would have been on the vast south Texas vote," much of it Hispanic.

But it took courage to cast that vote, for in Houston, "it was like the world came unglued," recalls Bill Archer. "I can't think of an issue that's come along since then that's been as explosive emotionally."

A meeting was called at Memorial High School in Houston for constituents to discuss open-housing. Hundreds of people filled the auditorium and the atmosphere was charged. The young Congressman talked about the black Vietnam veteran. "A man should not have a door slammed in his face because he is a Negro or speaks with a Latin American accent," affirmed Bush. He received a standing ovation.

That summer, the night he was nominated for the presidency, Richard M. Nixon convened a meeting in his hotel room to discuss Vice Presidential possibilities. George Bush's name came up several times. "I've heard nothing but good about George," said Nixon. Nevertheless, he felt Bush was too young for the post.

Bush entered the 1970 Texas Senate race with a strong shot at unseating Ralph Yarborough. But then Lloyd Bentsen, like Bush a businessman and World War II pilot, defeated Yarborough in the Democratic primary. Although he was expected to benefit from defections by liberals, Bush lost. Yet he ended his electoral career with his popularity undiminished.

"He was considered back at the time one of the most charismatic people ever elected to public office in the history of Texas," says Bill Archer. "That charisma, people talked about it over and over again."

What happened? Did Bush change or did our perceptions of leadership change? Probably some of both. He is a child of the war years, when charisma and courtliness coincided. He came of age intellectually when politicians believed in the "end of ideology." How quaint both notions seem, now that personal and ideological passion are measures of political charisma.

President Nixon had promised to take care of him if he lost his Senate race, and Bush knew what he wanted. After the election, his friend Potter Stewart called a top White House aide and said, "This may surprise you, but George would like to be more involved in foreign policy. He'd like to be Ambassador to the United Nations."

Bush recognized from the start that the United Nations post was "a ceremonial thing," in the words of a former aide. He assiduously pursued the Administration's official "two-China" policy—admitting mainland China to the world body without jettisoning Taiwan—ignoring the fact that Henry A. Kissinger, the national security adviser, was already in the process of dismissing Taiwan from Administration thinking.

Considered "loyal," according to a former Nixon aide, Bush was the President's natural choice to replace the irreverent and independent Bob Dole as chairman of the Republican National Committee. But he quickly adapted to the reigning culture of the committee. He considered himself a party man, not a servant of the White House. And when Watergate became a burning issue, about six months into his tenure, Bush made it clear that his loyalty was to the state chairmen. He was a traveling preacher of Republicanism. In his first year as party chairman, he jetted 124,000 miles, gave 118 speeches and conducted 84 press conferences, strenuously attacking any implication that the G.O.P. was connected to Watergate.

But Bush was tormented by the increasingly debilitating situation. According to his brother Prescott, Nixon at one point told him directly, "There's absolutely nothing to these accusations. I'm telling the truth and there's nothing hidden." Bush believed him, and although he privately vented his despair to White House aides, he also displayed what Eddie Mahe, the Republican committee's political director at the time, calls "a toughness that is not generally seen as being part of George Bush."

After Gerald R. Ford succeeded Nixon in the Oval Office, Bush lobbied hard for the Vice Presidency. He was in Maine, at his beloved Walker's Point, with Peter Roussel, a longtime aide, when he received the call telling him that President Ford had chosen Nelson A. Rockefeller for the post.

Bush returned stoically to the porch where the two men had been sitting. Shortly thereafter, a television news crew from Portland arrived. "You don't look too broken up about this," the reporter told Bush.

"You can't see what's on the inside," he replied.

Demanding an audience, Bush told the president he was quitting the national committee. Ford soon countered with an offer to make Bush the chief of the United States liaison office in Beijing.

In China, Bush courted the image of the regular guy who eschewed diplomatic formalities in order to bicycle everywhere and understand the native ways. A different view of his 16 months in China slipped out shortly after he returned. The historian Barbara Tuchman recalls appearing with him at a forum sponsored by a church in Connecticut. After Bush spoke about his experiences in the Far East, someone asked whether he'd had a chance to meet any of the local people. According to Mrs. Tuchman, Bush replied: "Oh yes. They gave us a boy to play tennis with."

At the Central Intelligence Agency—which Ford offered to him in a 1975 Administration shakeup termed the "Halloween Massacre"—Bush again aggressively sought to portray himself empathetically within the agency. Intelligence veterans, already scarred by ongoing Congressional investigations of past agency practices, viewed the appointment of this quintessential political animal with alarm.

But within days, according to several former intelligence officials, Bush had turned sentiment around. He "became one of the boys," in the words of one. He not only mastered superficial symbolism—taking the employees' elevator to his seventh-floor office rather than the director's private elevator—but would also bring one of his subordinates to National Security Council meetings and, after a few words of introduction, turn and say, "I've brought my brains along, let's listen to him."

Yet that same amiability may also have been responsible for the one substantive controversy during his tenure at the C.I.A., the "Team B Affair."

For years, many in the intelligence community had been disturbed by discrepancies between the agency's estimates of Soviet strategic capabilities and what later events proved to be true. Conservatives on the President's Foreign Intelligence Advisory Board wanted to create a group of outside experts—"Team B"—who would review the same information as did the agency's intelligence officers and assemble a competing set of estimates. Bush agreed to the exercise.

But Team B, in the eyes of several intelligence veterans, was packed with conservative ideologues. Ray Cline, a deputy director of the agency before Bush's arrival and a strong Bush supporter, says that its members "were clearly people who had a more alarmist view about Soviet strength than was being expressed in the intelligence community at the time." Agency staffers pleaded in vain with Bush not to allow Team B to be stacked with such conservative figures as professor Richard Pipes of Harvard.

The study's conclusion—that the Russians were seeking military superiority over the United States, rather than mere parity—lent support to hard-liners who opposed arms control. As Director of Central Intelligence, Bush, ironically, helped to empower conservatives who still consider him weak on defense policy.

But more telling was his allowing the Team B episode in the first place. It was widely viewed, in the words of one intelligence veteran, as "a bad idea that he permitted in the interests of getting along with everybody."

George Bush is a man of rules and institutional values. He operates superbly within established parameters—chairing meetings, carrying diplomatic messages to foreign friends and foes. "He's such a good listener," says a top Administration national security official. But when the rules change—when ideologues try to force their agenda or when the Iran-contra affair bypasses established national-security procedures—Bush can be caught off guard.

A turning point of his 1980 presidential campaign came in Nashua, N.H., at a planned two-man debate between Bush and Ronald Reagan, jointly sponsored by the *Nashua Telegraph* and by Reagan. Just before the event, Reagan's staff opened the debate to the other contenders. Bush refused to agree to the open forum. He sat mutely on stage while Reagan and the newspaper's editor argued over the new format. When the editor, Jon Breen, threatened to shut down the sound system, Reagan shouted, "I paid for this microphone!" Even though the two-man debate proceeded as planned, Bush's recalcitrance left an indelible impression.

That night, after the debate, as they were returning to his hotel, Reagan said to James H. Lake, one of his campaign aides: "I don't understand it. How would this guy deal with the Russians?" Reagan was not questioning Bush's mettle, according to Lake, but his "wisdom." Bush "failed to understand that in order to win this game he would have been better served by being more flexible," he says.

Bush's apparent lack of an ideological base may account for his remarkable malleability. In 1980, running as a self-described "moderate conservative," he could call Ronald Reagan "as far to the right as you can get." But "the minute they accepted the Vice Presidency, the Bushes forgot about the past and became Reagan people," says Nancy Clark Reynolds, a Washington public affairs executive and a longtime friend of Nancy and Ronald Reagan.

One former Administration official who wants to remain anonymous calls Bush "a neutral political functionary" who would "come to a lot of Cabinet Council meetings, listen for a while, raise a few points, and say, 'Why can't we overcome this problem? What's the solution?' He had this sense that there was a disembodied solution out there that involved no political or ideological position." Bush is reminiscent of the small-town civic leader in the late sociologist C. Wright Mills's study of America's ruling classes, "The Power Elite," who said: "We do not engage in loose talk about the 'ideals' of the situation and all that other stuff. We get right down to the problem."

Bush replaces ideology with what might be called a cult of courtesy. Stretched out in Air Force II recently, his gray suit jacket replaced by a blue flight jacket with his name threaded vertically up the zipper, his tie loosened, he bridled at the mention of the name of a prominent liberal activist. It wasn't the man's politics that disturbed the Vice President; it was that he had once disparaged Bush in front of one of Bush's sons.

"Can you imagine that—to a man's son!" he said, munching on a beef stick. "Now, what kinda thing is that to say?"

But the graciousness and civility also make Bush a potential captive of what the author Christopher Buckley, a former Bush speechwriter, calls "the gentle man phenomenon: it's good to be liked, better to be loved." Indeed, the drive for accommodation seems to lie behind many of Bush's celebrated gaffes over the years, among them his 1981 toast to Philippine dictator Ferdinand E. Marcos that "we love your adherence to democratic principles," his 1984 gloat to New Jersey longshoremen that he had to "kick a little ass" in his campaign debate with Geraldine Ferraro, and his enthusiastic comment in Europe last fall that when Russian mechanics "run out of work in the Soviet Union, send them to Detroit, because we could use that kind of ability."

"George Bush wants to see himself as a regular guy," says a former state Republican chairman who was wooed ardently by Bush in preparation for the 1988 election. Bush's brother Prescott agrees: "With the dock workers, he probably felt, 'I'm one of you and I can talk the way you talk.' " He seems to refuse to acknowledge that his upbringing effectively prevents him from identifying fully with many of those whom he would court. "It's when he tries to be Everyman that he sounds false," says Jim Lake, the former Reagan aide.

Bush's desire to appeal to people on their terms, rather than his, often looks like capitulation, and this is the root of his widely discussed "toughness" problem. During the 1988 campaign, he has been obsessed with proving his strength, not only in contrived confrontations with television newscasters, but in interviews, where, without provocation, he will cite his "toughness."

"I avoid sometimes the manifestations of my toughness," he said in one recent conversation. At another point, he added: "I don't have to go out and beat my chest like Tarzan . . . and assert toughness by being brutal to people."

But it is not his physical, or even his emotional, toughness that is in question—through World War II and personal tragedies he's exhibited ample quantities of both, and his set-to with Dan Rather and his strident anti-Dole commercials in New Hampshire betokened a willingness to hit hard. The doubts concern his intellectual independence.

Bush had explicitly pledged his loyalty to Ronald Reagan when he was offered the Vice Presidency. After the 1980 election, he made that oath the center of his political existence. Not only would he never be seen or heard disagreeing with President Reagan on any matter, but he also would never publicly offer any substantive opinions of his own.

All modern Vice Presidents have been immensely frustrated in their jobs, to be sure. But none felt completely constrained from at least offering opinions within the confines of the White House. Richard Nixon and Nelson Rockefeller both spoke their minds in National Security Council meetings. Walter F. Mondale was President Carter's faithful soldier, but differed with him over MX missile deployment, the Soviet grain embargo and the sale of F-15 fighter-plane equipment to Saudi Arabia, among other matters.

Bush's loyalty to President Reagan may be the strongest asset he carries into the pro-Reagan south on Tuesday. But, because of the way he has exercised his fealty, no one knows for certain how Bush has influenced the President on policy, nor can anyone—including his closest advisers—point definitely to areas where Bush has attempted to make an impact.

Bush, as have other Vice Presidents, chaired several task forces in the White House that he cites often in his campaign speeches. Their success has been mixed. His staff estimates that his Task Force on Regulatory Reform will save the government $150 billion in regulatory costs during the coming decade. But conservatives in the White House, among others, have criticized it for serving as little more than a "reporting mechanism" on the costs of regulation.

The South Florida Task Force, formed in 1982 to deal with the marked increase in cocaine and marijuana smuggled into the Sunshine State, was successful in uniting several competing government bureaucracies in the cause of drug interdiction. But during the task force's existence, cocaine imports increased, its price dropped and marijuana smugglers shifted their operations to domestic cultivation. And the Vice President's Task Force on Combatting Terrorism, whose final report aptly summarized the conventional wisdom on antiterrorism policy, had its key recommendation—"The U.S. Government will make no concessions to terrorists"—violated by the Iranian arms-for-hostages trade.

Beyond the task forces, one can only collect impressions about Bush's White House activities. For example, he supposedly played a role in softening President Reagan's "evil empire" rhetoric about the Soviet Union and in opening a dialogue with Moscow after Korean Air Lines Flight 007 was downed by the Russians. And scuttlebutt inside the White House had it that he was responsible for convincing the President to withdraw American troops from Beirut after the 1983 bombing of the marine barracks there.

How fully his whispers in President Reagan's ear contributed to these moves is unknown. "He did not, as other Vice Presidents did, speak up in National Security Council meetings," says a national security aide who has served in several Republican Administrations.

A number of his own aides declare flatly that Bush, in 1985 and 1986, interceded with the President to resolve a dispute between Attorney General Edwin Meese III and then Labor Secretary Bill Brock over Meese's desire to eliminate an executive order requiring certain affirmative action standards in Federal hiring.

But another former Administration official familiar with the Meese-Brock contretemps says that Bush's role is "just something I'm not aware of. . . . [Then chief of staff] Don Regan took the viewpoint that as long as there was disagreement in the Cabinet Council, then it wouldn't go to the President. That was what wore people down."

It is impossible to coax details about these or other incidents from either Bush or his aides. Whatever he and President Reagan speak about in their private, weekly Mexican-food lunches in the Oval Office remains locked in their hearts. The Vice President virtually taunts those who would question his involvement in White House decisions.

"There are just many examples in my mind that I'm not gonna share with you, where I know I've shaped what happens," Bush said in a White House interview. "You can't point to three things, I take that on the chin, because it's offset by the fact that I know I've been loyal."

More telling, perhaps, than Bush's apparently meager involvement in policy formulation is the perception that he actively backed away if the slightest controversy was involved. "There was sort of a fail-safe strategy that he and his people employed," says one former official.

Eventually, many in the Administration simply wrote him off as a player. Although some senior officials would, throughout the two terms, continue to try to use Bush as a conduit to the president, others gave up. Says one national security aide: "It became known that you didn't go to George Bush to get the president to do something."

Even after the reelection landslide in 1984, Bush apparently refused to step into the foreground. In late 1984 and early 1985, he rejected David Stockman's pleas for help in convincing the President to cut the deficit. A year later, according to several sources, he spurned repeated appeals from leading Republicans to intervene with the President to dismiss Donald T. Regan as chief of staff.

A year later, Bush was absent from the scene during the battle to confirm Robert H. Bork as an associate justice on the Supreme Court. One former aide says that members of Bush's staff said they wanted "to get out front on Bork" but "it never materialized."

Given the Vice President's penchant for noninvolvement, we can perhaps see more clearly his role in the Iran-contra affair, an issue that will continue to hound Bush, if not in the rest of the primaries then certainly in a general election campaign. Bush attended at least thirty meetings at which the Iranian arms sale was discussed, beginning in the summer of 1985. Moreover, Bush's staff had information that might have led them to question Lieutenant Colonel Oliver L. North's relationship with the contras: the Vice President's national security adviser, Donald P. Gregg, a former C.I.A. station chief, was told in August 1986 that North was involved in Central America with associates of the renegade C.I.A. agent Edwin Wilson.

Yet Bush has consistently maintained that he was "out of the loop" on the arms sale, that he was "deliberately excluded" from key meetings on the subject, and that he was completely unaware of the diversion of funds to the contras.

In a White House interview, Bush grew testy when the subject was pursued: "I've said all I really want to say on this subject. . . . To rehash all this and then, frankly, play into the hands of political opponents is not in my interest.

But the question remains: How could he *not* have known?

The most frequent response from those who have worked with him is that the Vice President was ill-served by his and the White House staff. "Somebody screwed him," says Admiral Daniel J. Murphy, Bush's former chief of staff. "I'm sure it was the N.S.C. staff." While Murphy singles out North and the former national security adviser, Rear Admiral John Poindexter, others point to Don Gregg, who declined to transmit to Bush the news about North's involvement with intelligence agency apostates. Gregg told Congressional investigators that he did not consider the information "Vice Presidential." (Bush said recently that "ex post factor, maybe" he should have been told about North's escapade.)

Criticisms of Bush's staff occur with startling frequency. "There's a feeling he deserves to be better served," says a senior Administration foreign policy official. "He has a weak national security staff," echoes another official. "They don't have an impact on policy, and they don't have a grasp of the issues involved."

There are indications that Bush purposely chose a lackluster Vice Presidential staff in order to fit in to the Reagan White House. According to one former campaign adviser, Bush said that he felt a high-powered staff could create contention rather than harmony with the President's staff.

The Vice President grew angry in a recent interview when told of criticisms of his staff. "I just deny that. I don't agree with that. I think it's wrong," he said. He maintains his own code of loyalty and forgiveness. "I'll be damned if I'm gonna let the pressure in the newspapers compel me to fire Don Gregg," he said heatedly. "That's not fair and that's not right and I'm not gonna do that!"

Still, his professed lack of knowledge about the Iran-contra affair indicates an unwillingness or inability to draw on all available resources for intelligence and enlightenment.

In his classic 1960 study on leadership, "Presidential Power," the Harvard political scientist Richard E. Neustadt noted that a successful executive must actively seek information.

"It is not information of a general sort that helps a president see personal stakes," wrote Neustadt. "It is the odds and ends of tangible detail that, pieced together in his mind, illuminate the underside of issues put before him. To help himself he must reach out as widely as he can for every scrap of fact, opinion, gossip, bearing on his own interests and relationships as President."

In the Iran-contra matter, this Bush did not do.

Can one predict, from his handling of the Iran-contra matter—or, indeed, from his handling of the Vice Presidency—how George Bush would lead as President of the United States? Difficult to say. His innate moderation shines through in a few specific proposals he has made on the Presidential campaign trail.

He wants a line-item veto to balance the budget and a cut in capital-gains taxes—eminently conservative ideas, yet far from right-wing. But he opposes the concept of an across-the-board freeze on Government spending, because he wants to be able to spend money on AIDS research, drug interdiction and tax-free savings accounts for college education. He has said time and again that he wants to be known as "the education President," employing "the bully pulpit, using the Presidency, to promote the kind of excellence we want."

Beyond these proposals, he adds little to the debate over post-Reagan politics. In the twilight months of the Reagan Presidency, this man who has blended in so well is still leery to call too much attention to himself and his thoughts.

Yet there is a calm that pervades him. Sitting in his White House office recently, George Bush pondered whether life would have been different had he "stopped to smell the roses."

"I sometimes think about that now," he said. "But how many people that pause to find themselves, wondering who they were, uncertain of themselves, have the blessings that I have that come from strength of family?"

He admitted that he would love to spend more time reading, or fishing at Walker's Point, especially when he thinks how "adversarial and denigrating" politics has become. "But do I have a certain self-assurance that I'm on the right track and that I'm lifted up by friends and family?" he asked. "Yeah."

"You see, I know who I am," he said. "I know exactly where I want to go. How to take this country there."

And if he didn't make it? "I'd be a good grandfather," answered the Vice President of the United States.

W HEN THEN REPUBLICAN presidential nominee George Bush selected the youthful Indiana Senator Dan Quayle to be his running mate in 1988, many party regulars, to say the least, were surprised. Quayle appeared to add little to the ticket except youth and youthful enthusiasm. No sooner had Bush made his announcement than investigative reporters turned up all sorts of questions about Quayle's past, most of which focused upon his alleged use of family influence to gain admission to law school and to obtain an appointment to the National Guard over others to avoid the draft. As the following selection points out, however, Quayle's character and politics are quite different from press and media portrayals of him as a highly conservative, inept, and inexperienced politician.

2 Garry Wills

LATE BLOOMER

Can one, at this point, disentangle Dan Quayle from Dan Quayle jokes? He seems to induce a short attention span in others, leaving them stunned with a serene vacancy. The *New Republic* has penalized with mock awards people who are foolhardy enough to speak well of him. Can anyone be taken seriously who takes Quayle seriously? As the polls show, Quayle has not recovered from the way he was shoved into the public arena under a rain of blows. Gallup reported last month that 54 percent of the public—including 43 percent of Republicans—said he is not qualified to be President; 49 percent thought Bush should pick a new running mate for 1992. "My skills," Bush said recently, "have always been in negotiating and conciliating." That sounds like wishful thinking from a man so long under assault, including the deadly assault of laughter. Like Charlie Chaplin in the ring, what can he do but crouch behind the referee and wave his gloves in vague call-it-off gestures? Yet he practiced conciliation even before he stood so badly in need of it.

When he was elected to the Senate in 1980, Quayle told political scientist Richard Fenno, "I know one committee I don't want—Judiciary. They are going to be dealing with all those issues like abortion, busing, voting rights, prayer. I'm not interested in those issues, and I want to stay as far away from them as I can." Yet Quayle was not raised among people who shied from extremes. He is the coeval of the cold war: the year of his birth, 1947, also gave us the CIA, the attorney general's list of subversives and the internal-security program. When Quayle was five years old, Dwight Eisenhower

From *Time*, April 23, 1990. Copyright 1990 The Time Inc. Magazine Company. Reprinted by permission.

carried Indiana with the help of Quayle's grandfather, publisher Eugene Pulliam, and William Jenner, who were, respectively, the right and the far right of the state Republican Party. When the John Birch Society was set up in 1958 with the thesis that Eisenhower had collaborated with communism, Quayle's parents became enthusiastic supporters of it. James Quayle compared Birch Society founder Robert Welch to the legendary prophet Nostradamus.

When Dan Quayle was starting high school in Arizona, his neighbor Barry Goldwater was beginning his race for the presidency. When Richard Nixon ran for reelection in 1972, Quayle's father decided that Nixon, like Eisenhower, had betrayed the conservative movement—so Quayle pere supported the insurgent Republican right-wing candidate John Ashbrook. When Quayle entered the Senate, it was as the beneficiary of a conservative political-action-committee blitz that knocked off five liberal Senators that year (including his opponent, Birch Bayh of Indiana). Quayle's whole (short) adult life was spent cocooned in the modern conservative movement. He should have spread his butterfly wings as an ideologue, yet he came out talking compromise. That is the most striking thing about his intellectual formation.

If he seemed for much of his life unaffected by the world around him, that may have been an advantage, considering the world he lived in. He avoided the Vietnam War, but he also ignored much that led to Vietnam. Inattentiveness is sometimes a survival skill. Quayle's pugnacious father did not always agree with Quayle's more famous grandfather, Eugene Pulliam, and among Pulliams it matters from which wife of Eugene one is descended (he had three). When the 17-year-old Quayle thought of siding with his father against his grandfather on behalf of family friend Barry Goldwater, his mother Corinne (a daughter of Pulliam's second wife) told him, "Don't start any more trouble in the family. We already have enough problems." Quayle's father, James—an ex-Marine who named his son for a friend, James A. Danforth, a World War II hero killed in action in Germany—was gung-ho for Vietnam. J. Danforth Quayle was, famously, not. Considering the other enthusiasms of his father's, from Nostradamus to Fundamentalist preacher "Colonel" Robert Thieme, there is something to be said for the son's reluctance to join his father's battles. Quayle grew up golfing with his imperious grandfather and camping (gun in hand) with his volatile father, an opinionated owner-editor whose Indiana newspaper is known to its local critics as the Huntington Herald "Suppress." Young Danny kept his head down, his eye on the ball.

One of Quayle's college professors has an indelible memory of trying to make a point with Quayle, and talking into air. "I looked into those blue eyes, and I might as well have been looking out the window," says William Cavanaugh. But he was the teacher of Quayle's freshman composition course; he had differed with his student over the prose of Wittaker Chambers. *Witness,* Chambers's portentously anticommunist book, was a kind of

bible in the Quayle family. Quayle's tactical incomprehension with Professor Cavanaugh may have been the response of one who knows where ideological conflict goes when it is pushed. Attending law school in Indianapolis, Quayle lived outside town with his grandmother, the divorced second
wife, while a son of the first wife edited the Indianapolis paper, and the
third wife was active in the Pulliam chain. Quayle kept peace all around.
He may not know much, but he seems to have self-knowledge when he
calls himself accommodating.

Is Quayle serene merely because he is vacuous, preferring drift to ideology? That view obliges one to explain how, in politics, he drifted often and
early to the top. Even his friends admit that his success was not by any blaze
of intellect. Says M. Stanton Evans, the ex-editor of the Indianapolis News,
who helped Quayle get his first political appointment: "There is a cycle in all
of his offices. When he comes in, he is underestimated—too young, too
inexperienced—and then he surpasses people's expectations." In other words,
Quayle first gets the job and then gets qualified for it. But for a politician,
getting the job is the primal qualification. How did he succeed at that? The
only answer his critics have been able to come up with is a false one—family
influence.

Influence should have counted at DePauw University, an old Methodist
school in northern Indiana with loyal alumni and great institutional pride.
Quayle was a third-generation Pulliam at the school, a member of the same
fraternity (Delta Kappa Epsilon) to which his grandfather, father and uncle
had belonged. His grandfather founded the national journalism fraternity
Sigma Delta Chi at DePauw, gave the school many bequests, and served on
its board. There was a Pulliam Chair in History until just before Dan's arrival
on campus. "If I had known he was a Pulliam," says Ted Katula, the athletic
director who was Quayle's golf coach, "that would have impressed me. Pulliams are big here. I didn't learn he was one till he was running for Congress."
Yet Katula was the member of the university staff Quayle saw the most. Little
was made of Quayle's being a Pulliam because few people knew it. He did
not bring the subject up. In his experience, family ties were as much a source
of division as advantage.

Quayle got special treatment at DePauw in one provable case: he graduated with a major in politics without taking the required course in political
theory. When he flunked the theoretical parts of the final exam, he was given
a special exam without those parts. He was one of two students for whom
this was done that year, and the common denominator in their cases is not
family (the other man was not a Pulliam) but a quarrel between the department head and the teacher of political theory over the size and kind of
assignments given in the course. The two students had dropped the class
when there were protests that the teacher, newly arrived from Harvard, had
too long a reading list, protests the department head, energetically backed. If
other teachers went easy on Quayle, it was because he is the kind of person

for whom people like to do favors. They were just doing what George Bush would later do on a colossal scale.

Quayle, who has refused to release his college and law school transcripts, was certainly no student at DePauw. The teachers who disliked him did so because he was good at getting by on charm. He was serious only about golf, a family passion instilled in him during the long Arizona days of his adolescence. His father, who has a unilaterally disarming candor, admits overstating it when he said of Dan's major, "If he's anything like his old man, it was probably booze and broads." But the minutes of Quayle's fraternity have this entry: "A petition was submitted to have Bro. Quayle censured for his violation of house security. It was moved he be: (1) fined $25, (2) removed from all house offices, (3) warned that his pin will be lifted if he does it again. A motion was accepted to table the petition's motion." Violating house security means having unauthorized persons in one's room.

There had not been much war protest on the DePauw campus by the time Quayle graduated in 1969. Quayle's father was writing editorials backing the war in Viet Nam, but his son was not paying attention. As graduation approached, Quayle had to do some shopping around to find an opening in the National Guard. (In 1988 he said he meant to go to law school, but he had not applied to one.) He asked people he knew about the Guard, whom to call, but it is unlikely they did or could rig things for him. His grandfather was semiretired in Arizona; his father was not a natural ally in this effort. He had the advantage of knowing where to go, but not of fixing what the response would be.

During his service in the Guard through much of the academic year 1969–1970, Quayle decided he did indeed want to study the law. Admission would not be easy after his admittedly poor academic performance at DePauw, but here a personal contact was helpful. He knew the admissions director of the Indiana University law school in Indianapolis—through his family, as he knew most older people. This admissions director, Kent Frandsen, was a judge in the little of Lebanon, outside Indianapolis. Another prominent citizen there was Quayle's grandmother, Martha Pulliam, who was given the Lebanon paper as her own in the divorce. (She was the one Quayle would live with.) Frandsen gave Quayle a break, something he was doing for many others at the time. The night school was expanding its enrollment—it would move into a new and larger building in 1970—and Frandsen had a summer program to try out marginal cases. Quayle, out of school for a year, went into that program.

Frandsen did him another favor when he called in Quayle and another student, Frank Pope, and asked them to start a student newspaper for the night school. Before, there had been just a mimeographed sheet. Frandsen wanted to begin life in the new building with a real paper, and he allotted money to the project. Quayle became editor of the journal he and Pope called the *Barrister*. It is unlikely Frandsen would have asked Quayle to do this if he doubted he could manage the newspaper along with courses at night and work during the day.

Daytime work was expected of Quayle (he had waited on tables in De-Pauw), and his father suggested working in the office of Indianapolis Mayor Richard Lugar. The father called his friend, fellow Pulliam editor Stan Evans. According to Evans, "Jim asked me to lunch with Dan. I did most of the talking and learned for the first time that he wanted to go to law school. I said I thought it would be better to work in the [state] attorney general's office than in the city government, since I knew that many of the people who worked there were in law school."

Evans knew about the young Republicans in the statehouse, since they were involved with him in conservative causes. As he said of Quayle's performance, "He was not as ideological as the other people in the A.C.'s office. He was certainly not out at Ashbrook rallies." (Evans, a friend of Quayle's father's, agreed with him on the need for a third-party candidate in 1972.)

It was normal that those working in the state government should have political connections of some sort. In the Lieutenant Governor's office were Daniel Manion, son of the John Birch Society's Clarence Manion, and Frank Pope, whose family was so close to William Jenner that he grew up calling him Uncle Bill. In the budget agency was Judy Palmer, who was the personal assistant to Edgar Whitcomb's wife during Whitcomb's 1968 campaign for Governor; in the prosecutor's office Vicki Ursalkis. All these people were students at the night school, only a few blocks from the statehouse, but they saw more of each other during their daytime tasks, in the balconies ringing the rotunda, than in the school, even though Quayle, Pope, Ursalkis, and Palmer made up a study group for their law classes. According to Pope, the women carried the men in these preparations. "Dan and I wouldn't have done what we did in law school without Vicki and Judy." Quayle dated Vicky before he met Marilyn.

Most of these Republicans had past ties to the Jenner organization, which Quayle's grandfather had opposed for years, but that did not trouble Quayle's relations with them. Quayle liked to ask Pope's mother, when he played bridge at her house, about old Jenner wars she relished as a party organizer. He took this in without much comment, and certainly without reciprocal revelations. "There was one thing Dan Quayle never talked about," Frank Pope says now, "and that was his family."

The statehouse was a den of young activists, among whom Quayle seemed almost apolitical. Pope says Manion "dragged" Quayle and him to a meeting or two of the Young Americans for Freedom, but "Dan [Manion] was so far right he scared Danny and me." Certainly there were young activists in Quayle's circle who shared his father's zeal for Ashbrook. But Quayle did his work at the attorney general's office and in class, and went home to his grandmother's house in Lebanon.

Marilyn Tucker was as bright as the women in Quayle's study group, and her uncle, the Indiana secretary of state, was a Jenner man. She and Quayle were sure of each other from the start and were married in 1972 by the friend of both their families, Kent Frandsen. It was a fine political marriage by Indiana standards, but after passing the bar exam in 1974 Quayle went back to Huntington, to his father's small paper, without announced political ambitions.

The myth now firmly established is that some Fort Wayne party men chose Quayle because of his looks for the thankless task of running against eight-term Democratic Congressman Ed Roush in 1976. Quayle was recently introduced to a board meeting of the Hoover Institution as one who volunteered to "fall on the sword" in that 1976 campaign. But Walter Helmke, the G.O.P. candidate in 1974, says that the idea of Roush's invincibility is nonsense. "He only beat me by 8,000 votes, and that was in the post-Watergate election when Republicans did badly. When Dan ran against Roush, Gerald Ford swept Indiana for the Republicans. Ford carried Dan."

The idea of Quayle's passive role in this beauty-queen audition is also overstated. Helmke remembers that Quayle was out in his journalist's role observing his own campaign and Richard Lugar's unsuccessful run against Birch Bayh in the 1974 Senate race. Helmke was surprised when Quayle asked foreign policy questions in those local races. And two years later, when Helmke showed around Roush's district, they were not looking for swords to fall on.

Nor did talent scouts have to prod Quayle into his 1980 campaign against Birch Bayh. He aggressively sought a conflict in which the odds were longer against him than they had been four years earlier with Roush. When golf coach Katula asked why he would risk a safe House seat on such a race, Quayle told him "Coach, we're just going to have to work harder."

He campaigned in all 92 counties of the state. He defused the age issue by saying, over and over, "Birch Bayh was almost the same age when he beat Homer Capehart." (This ploy would backfire when Quayle used a similar line about John Kennedy in 1988.) When Bah accused him of extremism, Quayle distanced himself from the ads being run against Bayh by the National Conservative Political Action Committee, telling the Washington lobbyists, "Your negative campaign will allow him [Bayh] to allege that outsiders are trying to tell the people of Indiana how to vote." Quayle resigned from the Committee for the Survival of a Free Congress because it was trying to purge third-party presidential candidate John Anderson from the Republican party. He ran an ideological campaign but with just enough touches of pragmatism.

Quayle is not interested in lost causes. (Maybe it was fitting that he not go to Viet Nam?) In this he resembles his grandfather, who constantly frustrated his conservative editors. Eugene Pulliam, says Stan Evans, "was a seat-of-the-pants guy, unpredictable." Jameson Campaigne, Jr., whose father edited the Indianapolis *Star* for Pulliam, says, "He [Pulliam] was not a conservative; he was a Methodist—a good government type. That is why he opposed Jenner and the corrupt Republicans in Indiana."

Pulliam bought 51 newspapers in his career, but most of them were small-town papers, and he had a small-town approach to government. It is not surprising that he settled in Lebanon, a little community that is almost an annex to its golf course. Pulliam believed in paternalistic civic improvement, where business, politics and journalism unite to clean up a town and run it for its own good. He clashed early in his career with the Klan, lax liquor laws and prostitution.

When he got involved in national politics, it was as a pragmatist. He joined Eisenhower in 1952 against the Taft conservatives. He joined Lyndon Johnson in 1964 against Goldwater, whom he had helped draw into politics in order to "clean up" Phoenix. He went back to the Republicans in 1968 and stuck with Nixon. Quayle's father rebelled against both Eisenhower and Nixon by supporting Birch and Ashbrook—lost causes. Pulliam had no more use for the Birchers than for Klansmen.

Some mistook Pulliam for an ideologue because his pragmatic political stands mattered as much to him as the papers' income. He defied advertisers over matters like liquor licensing and a Phoenix beltway, favored by the business establishment, which he helped defeat. He was prickly about his independence and about his family and loved institutions. He resigned from the board of DePauw when the school refused to turn down federal money with strings attached. His own children and heirs were expected to work; the money he left is tied up, dependent on their performance on the newspapers.

Pulliam gave the readiest daily sign of his competitiveness on the golf course. He learned in Lebanon how to talk with the city establishment on the links, and he set a Quayle pattern of buying homes that overlook the fairways. He liked year-round golfing, so he left Lebanon in the winter, first for Florida, then for Phoenix. He was an advocate of improvement, tourism, and more golf courses for Phoenix long before he bought his paper there. The Phoenix course on which Quayle learned to play is nestled among a dozen or so clubs, their bright green carpets dramatic against the pebbly desert.

Quayle was such a natural golfer that his grandfather soon liked having him for a partner. The Pulliams read character on the golf course. The De-Pauw coach admires the nerve, even the courage, of Quayle's game. "He likes the heat of battle." He claims that Quayle rises to challenge, takes chances but keeps his head. Could Quayle beat his old coach, who stays in shape and plays constantly? "By the 16th hole, conversation would be at a minimum."

Quayle's competitiveness appealed to Roger Ailes, who handled him in his 1986 reelection race for the Senate. Quayle's record in debates was good until he met Lloyd Bentsen. He debated Roush five times in 1976 and Bayh once in 1980. The general view was that both men underestimated him and were beaten by him. Dan Evans, Quayle's 1980 manager, says he was effective against Bayh because he was not being "handled," as in 1988—the Nancy

Reagan excuse about debate "overpreparation." But Quayle needed help in 1988, when he was on the defensive from the outset. Indiana reporters say that even now he has not regained the confidence and ease he showed in his earlier campaigns.

Quayle starts from a conservative base but tries to keep the freedom to maneuver away from it. In 1976 he suggested that marijuana be decriminalized, a view too radical to be repeated before his constituents. Dan Coats, who now holds Quayle's Senate, is a born-again Christian who as Quayle's aide helped him win votes from the religious right; but Richard Fenno, the political scientist who observed his 1980 race, noticed that Quayle kept his commitments to a minimum in this part of his campaign. In the Senate, Quayle avoided the social issues and sought expertise in defense, specializing in SDI. His staff emphasizes the way he could cooperate "even with Teddy Kennedy" to pass the job-training act. This kind of paternalistic program, involving business, that his grandfather supported in towns he "looked after." Quayle's pragmatism is good politics, but he seems to favor it in any case. In an editorial for the *Barrister* (the first political writing of his I can find), Quayle attacked the machine-driven convention system in Indiana, calling for open primaries—the kind of reform Eugene Pulliam always favored.

As Vice President, Quayle has established a right-wing base again, choosing a hard-line and activist staff (unlike Vice President Bush's bland low-profile aides). The number of Ph.D.s is emphasized by his press office (two for Carnes Lord, his national security aide). He recruited from the ranks of believers in the cold war, just before that war's demise, surrounding himself with those who have an investment in it. His chief of staff, William Kristol, is the son of neoconservative Irving Kristol and Gertrude Himmelfarb and is a former aide to William Bennett. Quayle is comfortable with intelligence in his vicinity.

Structurally, Quayle's position with Bush, a man never quite accepted by the right as "one of our own" is that of Nixon with Eisenhower—bridge to the right, voice of the right, pacifier of the right. In the latter role he has already been criticized by the *National Review* and conservative columnist Eric Breindel. It is a high-risk position, since reflex anticommunism is not the right-wing glue it was before Mikhail Gorbachev. Quayle has treated changes in the Soviet Union as suspect, while saying he does not differ from the President (the refrain against which all Vice Presidents must play their own tunes). Quayle is loyal to individuals, as he showed in the Senate in 1986 by his frantic efforts to win a judgeship for Daniel Manion (whose written opinions were more embarrassing than Quayle's spur-of-the-moment inanities); but he does not play to lose. If Bush wants to get rid of Quayle, he may get as little cooperation as Eisenhower got from Nixon. Kristol, who turned down other job offers in the Administration to go with Quayle, is firm for his man. Similar commitments are in the making.

During the 1988 campaign, people wondered about Quayle's actions (and even his whereabouts) in the Vietnam War. But the startling thing is that, if he inherited the Oval Office tomorrow, Quayle would be the first President since World War II who did not serve in the military during that war. Even Jimmy Carter, the U.S. President of most recent birth (1924), was a Navy cadet during the war—the first baby boomer so near the top—he is also the first man to have grown up entirely within the confines of the modern conservative movement. He was surprisingly unscarred by that (or any) experience when Bush chose him. Quayle claimed John Kennedy was just as young in 1960; but Kennedy had known prewar Europe as well as the wartime Pacific.

Stan Evans traces an arc in Quayle's career of rising (if belatedly) to expectations. The angle of the arc must now go up, dramatically. Quayle was born not only roughly a quarter-century after any preceding President; he spent another quarter-century blissfully AWOL from history. His press secretary, David Beckwith, calls the Vice President a "classic late bloomer"— which means that the first three decades or so of his life do not matter, just the last decade. That is starting late even for a faster learner than Quayle has given evidence of being. How can he "rise to expectations" when the U.S. can expect all the troubles of a world coming out of the cold war, and when the person doing the rising came in with the cold war himself? That is why, for all the jokes, we must take Dan Quayle seriously. We must do so, because Bush did not.

T HE FOLLOWING PROFILE OF A controversial political tactician illustrates how skillful political advisers can shape party as well as campaign strategies. The selection's protagonist, Lee Atwater, was credited with George Bush's victory in the 1988 presidential race. Democrats accused him of negative campaigning and dirty tricks, but no one doubted his effectiveness. Whatever may be his political reputation, as a person Atwater exudes wit and charm, making him a popular figure not only with his Republican colleagues but also with many Democrats as well. As this book goes to press Atwater is fighting a malignant brain tumor with the same determination and courage that made him a political star.

3 Marjorie Williams
THE BAD BOY OF
AMERICAN POLITICS

Lee Atwater is especially watchful now, after ten months on the job as chairman of the Republican National Committee. For he has spent much of that time trying to manage his way out of a box.

He made this box himself, of course. It was Atwater who fashioned its planks from the knotted pine of Southern politics, who hammered in the barbed nails of a relentless political technique. It was Atwater, working obsessively, who planed and sanded it; who polished the wood with his assiduous self-promotion. And it was Atwater who finished off the lid with the cheap lumber of campaign '88 and the convict labor of Massachusetts prisoner Willie Horton.

For a few months after former Bush campaign manager Lee Atwater was anointed party chairman by a grateful president-elect, it seemed he had built a pedestal, lifting himself, at 38, to a kind of national ubiquity. Within the tiny political community he thinks of as his peer group, his new post was a long-sought affirmation of his skills as a strategist, a grown-up—promotion from his old persona as Peck's Bad Boy of the tactical realm. And outside Washington, he had taken to a new level the strange evolution of his species, becoming one of the few American politicians to be widely famous, without ever having to run for or govern anything. Suddenly people stopped him on the street to ask for his autograph. His name was a question on "Jeopardy!"

With his much-hyped blues guitar and public passion for horror movies, he was the first baby-boom politician who was really *of* the baby boom. To

GOP activists—especially young ones—he had become a hero, the man who made it cool to be a Republican.

But he had aroused too much bad feeling along the way. In March, students at predominately black Howard University occupied the administration building to protest Atwater's election to the board of trustees, holding him accountable, as manager of Bush's 1988 campaign, for what the student newspaper called "the most racist strategy in a national presidential campaign in the twentieth century." Mainstream Republicans began to grumble over Atwater's avidity for the limelight, and grumbled louder when he posed for an antic photo in *Esquire* with his sweatpants pooled around his ankles. And then in June, Atwater aide Mark Goodin resigned after the RNC issued a mailing insinuating that Thomas S. Foley, the new Speaker of the House, was gay. Although Atwater denied participation, he was widely held responsible—widely denounced.

To his enemies, he represents the ascendancy of cynicism and sewer politics, the triumph of image over not only substance but also reality. They say, in the boyish vernacular of the trade, that he is chronically "over the line."

To his GOP allies, he symbolizes a voyage out of the 35-year wilderness of minority status in the House of Representatives and a permanent extension, to state level, of the party's presidential winning streak.

In neither version is Lee Atwater the only example of the phenomenon he symbolizes. But he is certainly the most vivid and most visible. And either way, whether he is seen as a guerrilla testing the limits of acceptable political warfare or a renegade who has trampled the boundaries, his career has come to define where those boundaries lie.

The concept of workaholism does not begin to describe Harvey LeRoy Atwater's single-minded pursuit of his calling. It would be more accurate to see him as a kind of idiot savant of American politics, with hyperdeveloped acuteness in this one realm.

Atwater came to politics through a summer internship in the office of South Carolina Sen. Strom Thurmond, but his discipline predated his passion for politics by a year or so. He was a dismal student in high school, but as a freshman at Newberry College, a small Methodist school 37 miles from his home town of Columbia, S.C., he underwent a dramatic conversion from pudgy, beer-guzzling fraternity guy to driven, straight-A student with grand ambitions. "It was a very distinct change, almost like throwing a switch . . . ," says Carlos Evans, an Alpha Tau Omega fraternity brother. "He made up his mind that he was going to be somebody someday. And everything he did from that point on was directed to that end."

He decided to run 50 miles a week—10 each on Saturday and Sunday, and six miles a day for the rest of the week—and to read two books every week. He stopped drinking on all but special occasions, lost weight, and began the self-teasing discipline of smoking cigarettes only on Friday. He has cut down the mileage, in deference to his aging knees, but in all other respects has pursued the regimen for 19 years.

Atwater is fond of saying that "everything's a microcosm of everything else." By which he means: Everything is like a campaign. Even retroactively, he compares or relates almost everything to this central activity of his life.

Was it hard on him to move around, he asked, when his father's job as an insurance adjuster involved frequent transfers before the family settled in Columbia? No, he says, because "it was very good for me politically. . . . We moved to the key, critical political points of the state: Charleston, Aiken, Columbia, and Spartanburg. So I had a good understanding of the state because of the places I'd lived." He is talking about events that took place before he was 10.

He is asked about the household accident that killed his 3-year-old brother, Joe, when Lee was 5. Lee was in the next room playing with his toy soldiers one afternoon as Joe was watching their mother deep-fry doughnuts. Stepping down from the wastebasket he was standing on to watch the cooking, the little boy pulled the pot of bubbling fat down on top of him and was fatally burned. Lee witnessed his brother's suffering. "It had a big impact on me, there's no question about it," he says. "I can close my eyes and see it." But he declines to answer questions about what that impact was, contenting himself with this observation: "Well, to the extent you go into anybody's life, there's a few defining events, just as there are in campaigns. You can go back and analyze."

Seeing the world through this lens, he must necessarily greet people as potential constituents, susceptible to a variety of appeals. "I don't know how many layers you have to peel back to get to the real Lee Atwater, or whether the layers *are* the real Lee Atwater," says one former colleague from the Bush campaign.

It makes him a strangely isolated extrovert. He has always been socially popular, a lover of crowds. He keeps up with many friends from boyhood and college, ranging from bankers to bar owners, inviting them by threes and fours to family weekends at the Atwaters' cabin in the Shenandoahs. These old friends—the only ones with whom he drinks alcohol—are the friends who can help him relax. "Because there's no angle," he says. "There's no angle."

But according to Sally Atwater, even these weekends have political meaning for her husband. "He talks to 'em, he'll talk about their daily life, that kind of thing—where their goals are. So he's always doing the politics."

The year after Atwater found politics, he became a record-setting recruiter for the South Carolina College Republicans. First he persuaded his best-looking fraternity brothers to drive them to local women's colleges to recruit new members, who would be enlisted, in turn, to recruit at all-male schools. When the guys set out for Winthrop College, an hour and a half away, Atwater would equip them with three pens—one red, one blue, and one black—and instructions to rate the girls as date material while they were at it, for the benefit of the whole fraternity. "The red were the best-looking girls, the blue were the mediocre, and the black were 'Don't call,' " remembers fraternity brother Evans. "That was 90 percent of the incentive. Why else would a group of guys take time to drive to Winthrop College?"

Motivation and reward: Atwater has always been fascinated by the leverage inherent in knowing what people need and want—or can be induced to want.

As a junior at A.C. Flora High School, he invented a sort of alternative newspaper—really a single-page, mimeographed bulletin that was his own running challenge to the rules of high school social structure. Called "Big A's Comedy Ratings," it offered a changing list of the funniest students in the school; because Atwater was a popular student, admired for his wit, the "ratings" evolved into a certification of popularity. The fun of it, Atwater's friends remember, was that he often anointed the unlikeliest people he could think of, simply to sit back and enjoy the social anxiety that would result.

"After a couple of issues, people would do stupid things just to get on this rating," says a classmate, Warren Tompkins. "He told me later that that's when he first learned the power of the press—that you could manipulate people's thought processes by something you printed."

As early as junior high school, he was fascinated by all-star wrestling, with its bellowed insults and theatrical aggression. He calls it "the only honest game in town" and has often spoken of its application to politics, telling Dossier, a Washington society magazine, that he sometimes advises candidates to tune in to one of the choreographed festivals of mutual abuse that constitute prefight interviews: "It's a caricature of a politician's press conference," he says.

Which makes the audience a parody of the citizenry. And Atwater's interest in the audience is what college fraternity brother Eddie Gunn remembers best. "We enjoyed watching the matches," he says, "but we especially enjoyed watching the fans. They took it so seriously, like they thought it was real."

Over the years, Atwater would learn to codify such knowledge as this: He earned a master's degree in mass communications, then did years of field training in the whole apparatus of modern opinion molding—the polling and the focus groups, and how you mix paid media (which is advertising) with "earned" media (which is surrounding your candidate with 100 members of the Boston police department for a shot that will make network news).

But none of this formal training has ever been more valuable than what he had already taught himself about the people who believe all-star wrestling is real and buy fat remedies from the back pages of the National Enquirer.

Atwater's reputation as a bare-knuckle tactician has tended to obscure how much he contributes to the campaigns he works for. Beneath all the smoke is a very intelligent man, with a political mind of great dexterity.

It's commonly said that Atwater can see around corners. Says South Carolina Governor Carroll Campbell, perhaps Atwater's closest political ally, "He's got a sixth sense about what's around that corner that you'd better be ready for."

"When you cut away all the theater and all the drama and all the mystiques," says Janet Mullins, media director for the 1988 campaign, "you've got someone who really is that good at getting someone elected. . . . He's far and away much smarter than most other people in this business."

He is more committed to his business than most, for one thing. He cut his teeth as a Columbia political consultant in a decade of managing local races, down to the mayoral and county council level, in South Carolina and neighboring states. He has never missed an election cycle; even in 1982, as a White House operative, he was careful to stay closely involved in a handful of House races.

The Atwaters live in an unpretentious brick house in the District of Columbia, and their two daughters, Sara Lee and Ashley Page, attend public schools. Atwater is generously paid, of course: He makes $125,300 at the RNC and gives occasional paid speeches for as much as $15,000 a throw. But the finances of this game have been so distended that in Republican political circles in Washington, in 1989, these numbers lend some credence to his claim that he is not motivated by money.

Friends say Atwater is anxious for recognition as a big-picture man, and piqued when his trickster reputation gets in the way. "The one uncompleted mission of his, in terms of his communicating to the world who he is, is the sense that he's a larger political thinker than just someone who can figure out how to spook an opponent before he goes into a debate," says John Buckley, spokesman for the National Republican Congressional Committee.

And yet Atwater is best known for that whiff of brimstone that follows him from one campaign to another. To understand his talents and the controversy that has followed him, you need to understand two things about Southern politics.

The first is that as recently as 25 years ago, the Republican Party scarcely existed in the South. "Republicans in the South could not win elections simply by showing various issues and talking about various issues," Atwater has said. "You had to make the case that the other guy, the other candidate, is a bad guy."

In other words, you had to go negative. So Atwater mastered the art of making the voter pull the lever against the other guy. Bush's campaign against Michael Dukakis—hitting hard on such issues as gun control, the Pledge of Allegiance and the Massachusetts furlough program that turned lifer Willie Horton loose—was, of course, a textbook example of driving up the opponent's negatives.

The furlough issue also drew on the second major theme of Southern GOP politics in the past 25 years: race. The rise of the party in that time has been largely among Southern whites alienated by the Democrats' embrace of civil rights—especially in such heavily black states as South Carolina, which today has some of the most racially polarized election returns in the country.

Race and negativism meet at the "wedge" issue, the kind of emotionally laden topic that splits off elements of the traditional Democratic coalition. Wedge issues might include such things as school prayer, the death penalty, laws governing pornography. Atwater is the master of this art.

A negative campaign, of course, is not the same thing as a dirty campaign. But often, when it is not to a candidate's advantage to be seen going negative, the inflammatory issues are raised covertly. This is the essence of the worst of the stories that follow Atwater.

The demonology always includes the 1980 South Carolina congressional race in which he did some polling for Rep. Floyd Spence. Spence's opponent, Tom Turnipseed, alleges that selected white voters received calls from telephone pollsters pointedly informing them, in the course of one question, that Turnipseed belonged to the NAACP. In the course of campaign spatting over this and other contentious issues, Atwater revived the issue of Turnipseed's treatment, as a teenager, with electroshock therapy: "I'm not going to respond to that guy," he said. "In college, I understand they hooked him up to jumper cables."

Atwater denies raising the question of Turnipseed's NAACP membership, and has repented of the ugly remark. He "feels terrible" about it, he told the *New York Times.* Which is pretty much the same thing he said six years later in apologizing to a Jewish businessman in Columbia, Samuel Tenenbaum, for referring to him as "a Gestapo-type politician."

Tenenbaum, a Democratic fund-raiser, had been trying for years to tag Atwater with a story from 1978, when Carroll Campbell, then a state senator and a longtime Atwater client, was running for the U.S. House of Representatives against Max Heller, the popular Jewish mayor of Greenville. It is one of the most serious counts raised against Atwater, surrounded by some of the most tantalizing evidence; it is also a tale no one has ever shown to be true.

In brief, it is alleged that the Campbell campaign enlisted a third-party candidate to inject antisemitism into the race, passing to him a poll showing that Heller could be defeated if voters were told that he did not believe in Jesus Christ. The third candidate hammered this point home, Heller's support fell, and Campbell won the election. Both Campbell and Atwater vehemently deny the story—indeed, Atwater denies all involvement in the campaign; reporters have picked over and over the incident without proving it.

Atwater expresses anger that these and other incidents are hashed over in every history of his career. But according to friends and colleagues, the man most responsible for promoting the down-and-dirty Atwater persona has long been Lee Atwater. Many people tell of Atwater's boasting to them of campaign exploits.

William Carrick, a Democratic consultant who shares roots in South Carolina, says that it was part of Atwater's service to his clients to project himself as "the bad guy, the Machiavellian, back-room, behind-the-scenes operative who does things that are sort of somehow independent of the candidate's oversight." It boosted his gunslinger's reputation, and for years, no one cared enough who Lee Atwater was to make his tactics an issue in subsequent campaigns.

Atwater's biggest problem is that he and Willie Horton became household names together. The Horton case was the perfect weapon in the Bush campaign's effort to paint Dukakis as a pointy-headed Massachusetts liberal out of touch with plain common sense: Horton, under life sentence for murder, had been allowed out of prison for weekends under a state furlough program and had terrorized a Maryland couple, torturing and stabbing the man and raping the woman.

Horton is black, the couple is white, and the campaign was accused of using the issue as an unsubtle pitch to America's worst racial fears and prejudices. Atwater and others have protested that Horton's race was incidental to the furlough issue and that the campaign itself never used Horton's photograph—promptly denounced any state parties or independent groups that did.

But at a party meeting in July 1988, Atwater delivered a damning monologue that marked the Horton issue as a classic instance of Southern-style racial politics.

"There is a story about a fellow named Willie Horton, who, for all I know, may end up being Dukakis's running mate. . . . The guy [Dukakis] was on TV about a month ago, and he said, 'You'll never see me standing in the driveway of my house talking to these [vice presidential] candidates.' And guess what? Monday, I saw in his driveway of his home Jesse Jackson. So anyway, maybe he [Dukakis] will put this Willie Horton on the ticket after all is said and done."

After the election, Bush's campaign managers were quick to distance themselves from Willie Horton—or from "the furlough issue," as they are careful always to call it. Some have succeeded better than others: rarely, for example, do Bush or Secretary of State James A. Baker III, who was the campaign's chairman, come in for a full share of the discredit. That Atwater is most frequently blamed is due in part to his eagerness to take credit for the campaign. But it is also because Atwater is a product of the Southern GOP.

"He plays a very subtle game in the politics of race," says Earl Black, a former graduate school professor of Atwater's at the University of South Carolina and an expert on Southern Politics. With blacks voting solidly for Democrats, the challenge to Republicans has been to scoop up disaffected, traditionally Democratic white voters who are revolting against the pace of change in the South—without appearing to appeal to bigotry. "You have to avoid overt appeals to race," continues Black, a Democrat. "But that doesn't rule out other means of achieving the desired result."

Atwater's three major allies in South Carolina politics all have charged histories in the area of race; two were pioneers in building the Southern GOP through racial politics. The first, Harry Dent, was the sharp Dixie pol largely responsible for crafting Richard Nixon's so-called "Southern Strategy" in 1968. That year Nixon, with crucial support from Thurmond, managed to win enough white Democratic votes in the peripheral South to neutralize both George Wallace and Hubert Humphrey—largely through such means as publicizing Nixon's opposition to busing schoolchildren and his support for "freedom of choice" plans, which were often a subterfuge to evade desegregation orders. Atwater has called that "a model campaign," saying, "I've used that as a blueprint for everything I've done in the South since then."

The second mentor was Thurmond himself, the Dixiecrat who led a third-party presidential campaign in 1948 on a states-rights platform, saying "There's not enough troops in the army to break down segregation and admit the Negro into our homes, our eating places, our swimming pools and our theaters." He called the 1964 Civil Rights Act "extreme to the point of being revolutionary," and in that year switched from the Democratic to the Republican Party to support Barry Goldwater.

Atwater's third major influence, as much ally as mentor, is South Carolina Gov. Campbell. At 49, Campbell is widely cited as an exemplar of New South Republicanism. Atwater has supported his career since 1974, when he ran unsuccessfully for lieutenant governor, and most recently helped him win a narrow victory for the governorship in 1986. Campbell's roots in racial politics have a more modern look than Thurmond's, but they date back to 1970, when he led a group called the Citizens Committee to Prevent Busing.

Southern politics has changed radically in the past 20 years, and all of these mentors have taken more moderate public stances in that time, enabling Atwater to argue that they represent the progressive strain of the Southern GOP.

Since he became party chairman, he has made minority outreach his most visible priority. But skeptics abound.

Democrats have argued that Atwater hopes to kill at least four birds with the one stone of minority outreach: (1) it will make Democrats spend time and effort defending their most faithful base; the more visibly they can be made to do this, identifying themselves more and more with blacks in the eyes of conservative whites, the better; (2) it will assuage the misgivings of moderate-to-liberal Republicans, especially in the North and Midwest, who are alarmed by racial polarization of the two parties; (3) it may at least lower black animus against the GOP, so that it is more difficult to mobilize minorities against Republican candidates—an especially important goal in Southern state and local races, where black turnout has been a major Democratic advantage in recent years; and (4) if the GOP should actually happen to pick up some votes, so much the better.

Democrat Carrick, who has known Atwater for years, says, "I don't think

Atwater's racist himself. He's not personally a bigot. . . . I read Willie Horton in the light of, these guys had their backs up against the wall and they were looking for wedge issues, and the ultimate wedge issue for the 1980s and 1990s is race, and they used it."

Atwater seems genuinely startled to find himself, at this late date, hand-cuffed to Willie Horton. He is working at minority outreach the way he works at everything he undertakes: hard and systematically. And very publicly. Speaking on the occasion of what would have been Martin Luther King, Jr.'s 60th birthday last January, at King's Ebenezer Baptist Church in Atlanta, he said, "I was too young to appreciate the significance of his life, the bravery of his work, or the tragedy of his death. . . . But I know now. I know that Martin Luther King, Jr., is a towering giant in our history. . . . I share his dream of a united America and a brotherhood of man."

Lee Atwater has ideological beliefs of a kind: conservative. Somewhat libertarian, though he isn't at pains to spell out where this puts him on various social issues dear to the far-right wing of the GOP. "I've had two criteria" in selecting candidates, he says. "They've got to be a good person . . . and they've got to be conservative."

But government interests him only as the end that enables the means. A passion for waging politics over policy hardly makes Atwater unique among campaign technicians; but he is remarkable for his disdain of the kingdom to which he holds the keys. "He has a large measure of distrust—even a con-tempt—for large institutions," says a onetime Atwater associate. And he sees most of what goes on in Washington as a circus of self-interest.

Atwater decided a year or so out of college that he would never be a candidate for office. "I made a conscious decision not to try to acquire [power] for myself," he says. When it is suggested that he now holds considerable power, he answers, "But not power in the sense that I'm not governing. . . . The ultimate power in this country resides in the hands of those who are elected, and who are governing. And I'm very conscious about that, and that's one of the reasons I don't lobby. I would be getting out of the role I've established for myself. Because then I would be, in effect, participating in the process of governing."

It is, of course, preposterous to suppose that this chief political adviser to the president is not "participating in the process of governing." Atwater talks to the president at least twice a week and to White House chief of staff John Sununu "every day, for one reason or another," according to Sununu's execu-tive assistant, former Atwater aid Ed Rogers.

But he is, he insists, simply a political operative. And whatever advice he offers—on personnel, on managing the press, or on the politics of the capital gains tax—seems to have no reality to him beyond the political.

The job of RNC chairman was to be the job in which he could have it all: affirmation as an important player. Power and publicity, without the respon-sibilities of office. The enticement of new political games to be learned with the big new toy that is the national party. And the chance to marry more closely than ever a united party and a White House political operation.

"Lee has had a plan to get to where he is today for about 10 years," says National Republican Congressional Committee Co-chairman Ed Rollins. "And this is a town where long-range planning is lunch."

But somewhere he miscalculated, and today he finds himself, instead, in his box.

It is one of those soupy July evenings in Washington, above 100 degrees—the kind of night when nothing but passion or duty could compel souls out of doors. Accordingly, only a few dozen people have come to sit in the bleachers of the Democratic Party, while a beautiful young throng fills the Republican side. They're here to cheer on the RNC softball team, coached by Atwater, against the Democratic National Committee team coached by Chairman Ron Brown.

GOP team members sport newly minted, numbered T-shirts on which the Republican elephant, wearing sunglasses, plays guitar—a reference to the chairman's favorite hobby. Many fans wear T-shirts with the legend "Lee Atwater's Red, Hot and Blue Revue, 1989 World Tour," which refers both to the Arlington, Va., rib joint of which he owns a small part, and a series of concerts listed on the T-shirt's back. A select few people, at the top of the status hierarchy, stalk the sidelines with shirts saying "Atwater's Cast Party, Presidential Inaugural," which dates back to the rhythm-and-blues concert he arranged last January.

It is all part and parcel of his efforts to peddle the other, more palatable side of the Atwater myth: the blues-pickin', bad old good old boy, the Southern lad who made it in the big city by saluting the flag, speaking his mind and never letting the bastards get him down.

This is Atwater the performer, about whom old friends reminisce with astonishing unanimity, describing an exhibitionism that was held in relative check for the 15 years of Atwater's career as a behind-the-scenes operative—and that in January burst back into full flower.

Even before the Foley incident, several close political advisers had told Atwater that he should lower his profile. After that controversy, with his fame clearly shading into notoriety, he began turning down interviews about anything more personal or flamboyant than the RNC's candidate recruitment program.

But even now, after months of good behavior, he remains a prisoner of his past success: Having advertised himself for years as the baddest political operative in America, he must now persuade the world that he doesn't deserve the ruthless reputation he cultivated so tirelessly.

His most immediate problem, the one that follows him to work every day, is his potential to be a problem. Bush has been careful to demonstrate his confidence in Atwater, but in the wake of so much controversy, the chairman is inescapably a potential liability to the White House. No adviser is brilliant or useful enough to justify a president's having to answer for him more than once at a nationally televised press conference, as Bush was forced to do in the wake of the RNC attack on Tom Foley.

After these months of good behavior, many of Atwater's allies are baffled that he continues to be demonized. In the words of one friend, "Lee Atwater didn't create negative campaigning; he's just someone who has been real good at it. That environment has been the ambient noise of every campaign for the last 12 years."

Atwater may not have invented the science, his enemies reply, but he is unique in the ruthlessness he has brought to politics on the national level.

Both sides are partly correct: He is singular, and he is one of many. He is a freak of political nature, but one who could never have flowered so well as in this place and time. Yet both sides also miss a larger point. American politics has changed so fast, and the ambient noise has grown so loud, that in a sense Lee Atwater has become the indispensable man. As the designated villain of American politics, he has quieted fears that his brand of cynicism may be the universal currency of elections today.

Never mind that the empty, read-my-lips politics of flag preservation and no-tax pledges have already crept from elections into governance. Never mind that races this November in Virginia, New Jersey and New York City degenerated into charges of lying and pandering, tax dodging and rapist coddling without any visible leadership from the chairman of the RNC. As long as one man can be said to embody all the problems of American politics, they will seem limited problems.

As long as Lee Atwater is locked in his box, we may cherish an illusion that the line marking the outer frontier of acceptable politics is, at least for now, standing still.

BOLD, *CHARISMATIC, DEDI-cated, driven,* and *flamboyant* are among the adjectives that describe Jesse Jackson. He stands before black crowds, and, in his 1988 quest for the presidency, before white crowds as well, asking them to repeat after him, "I am somebody!" His campaigns for the Democratic presidential nomination in 1984 and 1988 mobilized blacks in unprecedented numbers, making their voice heard in party politics as it had never been before. Many successful black politicians had preceded him at the local level, but Jackson was the first black candidate to make a serious run for the presidency.

Jesse Jackson's political roots are in the 1960s. He participated and led sit-ins and protest marches while attending the all-black North Carolina Agricultural and Technical State University in Greensboro. Clearly adept at politics, he became president of the student body.

Although politics became his chosen profession, Jackson might well have gone in another direction. A talented athlete, he became a star three-letter man at the all-black Sterling High School in Greenville, South Carolina. Desegregation began in Greenville the year after Jackson graduated.

Both the New York Giants and the Chicago White Sox recruited Jackson, the Giants outbidding the Sox with an offer of $6000. Jackson was chagrined, however, that the Giants offered the star white player from one of the town's two white high schools $95,000. Jackson refused the Giant's offer and accepted instead an athletic scholarship to the University of Illinois. There the football coach told him that blacks were supposed to be linemen, not quarterbacks. Characteristically Jackson would have none of that, and after his freshman year, he transferred to Greensboro, where he soon became the quarterback of the football team.

Jackson decided to be a minister in 1965, a year after graduating from college. Black ministers traditionally have been political as well as religious leaders, shaping both the content and style of black politics. Jackson soon became a protégé of the Reverend Martin Luther King, Jr., and an active participant in the 1960s civil rights movement. He accompanied King on the famous Selma, Alabama, march and was with him in Memphis when King was assassinated three years later.

Finally Jackson settled in Chicago, where his extraordinary activity and success in leading the black community provided him with the political base to establish Operation PUSH (People United to Serve Humanity) to boost the education and job opportunities of ghetto children.

Throughout his political career, Jackson has always been a master of the media, a consummate stylist who knows how to attract public attention. Even in high school "Jackson and his friends were the athletic, social and academic stars of Sterling High School. . . . They seem to peer out of almost every picture in the 1959 'Torch,' their senior yearbook."[1] Long before he ran for the presidency, his name was a household word in the white as well as the black community.

While Jackson headed PUSH, one

---

[1]*Greenville News,* October 13, 1983. I am indebted to Joyce Trammell of Greenville, South Carolina, for providing information on Jackson's high school career.

journalist wrote, "Jesse Jackson's staged entrances into page-one politics are small masterpieces of showmanship. In the Middle East, at Camp David, wherever photojournalists gather he descends as if on wires deus ex video. He stays just long enough to spin off a few provocative quotes, in self-contained twenty-second snippets, shrewdly timed to accommodate the editors in the cutting room. Then he is up and away back to his Chicago base."[2]

Jackson made his most serious presidential quest in 1988. His charismatic style and emotionally charged messages—"Down with dope, up with hope!"; "We don't need welfare, we need fair share!"—galvanized a black community and appealed to many white voters as well. By the middle of the primary season, he led other Democratic contenders in the popular vote and had only somewhat fewer delegates than the leader, Massachusetts governor Michael Dukakis. For the first time in history it seemed possible that a black man would become the nominee of a major party. The following selection profiles the candidate and his extraordinarily successful campaign.

4 Garry Wills
MAKING HISTORY WITH SILO SAM

Standing over my seat in the airplane, he shadowboxes with the empty aisle just darkened for takeoff: "It's like a fighter who's got his guard up high, looking over at 'the Bear' "—his head periscopes over his hands—"and you expose yourself to these terrible body blows. Drugs." His midsection abruptly gives under the imagined punch, but the hands stay up. "Debt." He buckles again. "The purchasing of America. Energy." It is Jesse Jackson's analysis of the gut dismay he finds in contemporary America. He is an ecumenical collector of dismays.

"I start my policy toward Russia from here, from the hurt"—he holds his aching fighter's sides—"and move on out toward them." Protecting against the body blows, he argues, will make America stronger against the Russian Bear. "We've been leading with our left, with our left"—he jabs, repeated, automatic. "Always military first, not economic, not diplomatic."

His aides complain that reporters cover his style, not his message. But he is remarkably successful in phrasing a message that others understand— "keepin' the grass down where the goats can get at it," in the famous advice George Wallace gave him. ("We can't have no goats jumpin' in the air after

[2]Clarence Page, "Jesse Jackson—'I am somebody!' . . . but who?," Washington Monthly, February 1980, p. 26.

grass," Jackson says.) Certainly his rivals have grasped his message, especially Richard Gephardt, who dramatized his anticorporate populism in a series of ads that led Michael Dukakis to say "That's Jesse's line." Jackson, picking up on that in a Des Moines debate, said he could not afford the slick ads, but sure enough, "That's my line. That's my line."

One aspect of Jackson's populism is not imitated by others—certainly not by Gephardt with his xenophobic pitch. Jackson can establish emotional ties with the troubled, with dispossessed farmers, striking workers, the sick and the elderly. This empathy with white misfortune was the surprise in Iowa, where his flamboyant gentleness disarmed farmers and won improbable allies. More than any other candidate, he sends people away from his speeches happy, proud that they are somebody.

His populism can keep itself in motion without the prods of rancor. Even the villains of his moral fables—the barracudas who devour little fish of all sorts ("barracudas swim very deep, where it's very dark; they can't even tell whether they are swallowing white fish or black fish")—are not so much evil in their own waters, but mainly when they swim back at us from Taiwan. GE is attacked for selling goods made overseas with jobs the company took from America in the first place. Jackson's solution is to keep GE at home with a combination of tax penalties and tax incentives.

Purists of the left attack Jackson for his readiness to deal with capitalists (even, in the past, to adopt president Reagan's idea of enterprise zones). He is voraciously inclusive, and thinks no one should go away from a party without his or her piece of the cake. "Let's make a deal" is the constant offer of this hyperactive opportunist and optimist. His original civil rights project, Operation Breadbasket, began as a demand for higher black employment by corporations, but Jackson added "What can we do for you?" and established "covenants" endorsing firms for black consumers. On that basis he made further demands for blacks in managerial positions, in what looks to some like economic coercion but is thought of by Jackson as economic statesmanship. Everybody gets something—bosses get cooperation and customers; workers get some control over their working conditions.

Jackson is an includer, not an excluder. He likes to be liked; he hates to lose any audience (which makes him run perpetually late, lingering with every group to complete his sale). Jackson is a performer, and, like Reagan, to whom he bears some unexpected resemblances, he is a master at wrapping a deeply felt conviction inside a one-liner. And he is bad at firing anyone. His receptiveness to anybody who will join him can be ludicrous, as when he took a wrestler named "Silo Sam," who claims to be seven-foot-seven, along on several stops the day after he met him, accepting Silo's public endorsement at a Teamsters' meeting, along with Billy Carter's, as a sign of his support from "ordinary people."

Despite his alacrity for inclusion, he has been rebuffed by repeated exclusions in the past. Ann Lewis, the Democratic strategist, remembers one of her first endeavors with Jackson. They were at the Japanese embassy in Washington, part of a delegation to protest racially condescending remarks made by Premier Nakasone. "Before we went out to meet the press," she recalls, "Jesse gathered us together and said, 'We cannot contribute to any further racism. These people do not know how much trouble they are in, and we must not add to the flames by our remarks.' " Then, as Jackson drove Lewis home, he complained of a party-sponsored dinner in 1986 that had included all the former Democratic presidential candidates yet pointedly excluded him. "He was hurt by that," says Lewis. "But I said he could not let them define themselves as the party. We are all the party."

Back in the '60s, Jackson was treated as a Johnny-come-lately to the civil rights movement, given minor and thankless tasks. As a result of David Garrow's important book *Bearing the Cross,* we now know that the civil rights movement was internally riven by the time Jackson joined it. The Southern Christian Leadership Conference was being shoved out of its original nest in Atlanta and was meeting resistance from established black preachers in Chicago. Jackson, who was not even a minister yet (and therefore less of a threat) was given Operation Breadbasket to operate on indeterminate territory partway between SDCLC and Chicago's local pastors. The group met, as its successor, Operation PUSH, still does, on Saturday mornings, so as not to invade the sacred turf of the Sunday preachers. Jackson was "included out" from the beginning.

Yet when Andrew Young got up to speak to the San Francisco convention about the platform, he was booed by younger delegates loyal to Jackson. At a black caucus, summoned to calm black delegates' angers, Coretta King was booed when she spoke for Young. "That was yesterday," some delegates called up to her. "What have you done for us today?" Young slipped out the back door. Only when Jackson arrived and made an emotional plea for unity did all those onstage lock arms and sing "We Shall Overcome." Jackson rebuked his followers: "When I think about the roads I've walked with Andy, and the leadership of Mrs. King—her home bombed, her husband assassinated, her children raised by a widow—she deserves to be heard." Those who talk about a "changed" Jackson in this campaign, less strident and more conciliatory, were not watching that tense moment in the 1984 campaign.

During the 1970s, while other movement leaders went into local politics or burned themselves out, Jackson became the only national black leader. He alone traveled the length of the nation, addressing a new generation in school after school, attacking drugs, calling for academic excellence, preaching self-discipline (a message that had few allies then, with the embarrassing exception of the Black Muslims).

The charge against Jackson in those days was that he was inspiring, he gave good speeches, but he had no follow-through. (The same charge, Garrow reminds us, dogged Dr. King all his days.) Yet Operation Breadbasket, that orphaned program, was expanded into Operation PUSH, and that turned into the "rainbow coalition," which became the 1984 campaign and has led on to Jackson's strong showing in the current presidential race. The argument that Jackson is not a builder masks the fact that he has found new ways to build a movement, going beyond the civil rights organizations (which, in their day, departed from older political structures).

Jackson is forming a movement to go beyond civil rights toward economic justice, which means going beyond black and white politics. It is true that the worst domestic crises that afflict America—unemployment, debt, blighted inner cities, drugs, fatherless children, AIDS—are especially wounding to black citizens. Jackson speaks for these victims but not exclusively for them. Blacks and whites must participate in the solution to problems they both created. The trick, as Bert Lance puts it in Southern terms, is to "combine a minority of the majority vote with a majority of the minority vote"—as happened in the 1986 election of Southern Democratic Senators, following on Jackson's campaign and registration efforts of 1984. Those elections, giving the Democrats control of the Senate, made possible the rejection of [Supreme Court nominee] Robert Bork. "We did it under the [Judiciary Committee] chairmanship of Senator Biden," Jackson says. "We couldn't have done it under the chairmanship of Senator Thurmond."

In 1986 young black voters reversed a historic pattern and turned out in greater numbers than young whites. When Jackson went to visit Alabama's Senator Howell Heflin on the Bork nomination, Heflin said he did not want to do anything to discourage the "new voters," and thus opposed Bork. Jackson, solemn in the meeting, chuckles afterward at the circumlocution: "The 'new votuhs'! Don't you just love it?" But it was more than black voters who stood in Bork's way. The combination that defeated him—minorities, women's groups, civil liberties activists—looked like the rainbow coalition.

Jackson sees his campaigns as part of an ongoing process that is changing American politics: "It is important to watch what happens in elections at the county level, all over the nation. The impact of this election is going to be felt in the elections of 1990, when the census is taken, and in 1991, when reapportionment takes place." He wants to build from the consensus established to defeat Bork: "There were fears about letting new people into the process, whether we could handle all these women, or 18-year-olds, or blacks, or homosexuals. But they have all proved to be just as American as earlier voters. We have to redefine *we.*" Inclusively.

After his shadowboxing in the airplane's aisle, Jackson, still standing up during takeoff, told me, "President Reagan said something that should have got more attention from the press. He said the last 40 years had not been good for the West. These last 40 years have been the most exciting and liberating for the world. Whole empires have fallen, new nations been created, people taken charge of their own lives. What Reagan meant is that all those little s——s in the UN have been beating up on us for 40 years—us, Somoza, us, Batista, us, Marcos. We've got to redefine *us.*"

When asked about his lack of experience in office, Jackson says, "I've dealt with more world leaders than any of the candidates, and I met them when they were living [a dig at Bush's errands to funerals of foreign dignitaries]. Take all the Democratic candidates, blindfold us, drop us anywhere in the world with a dollar in our pockets, and who do you think would lead the others out?

"If we can have relations with Russia and China, certainly we can expand our influence in Latin America by negotiating with Castro. The Israelis and the Palestinians are in a death grip. They have their arms around each other and a knife at each other's back. They are hollowing each other out, afraid to let go for fear of being knifed in the face. They must be pried a-loose." The week Jackson said this, the Israeli journalist Wolf Blitzer wrote a long article in the Jerusalem *Post*, concluding, "Israel and its friends in the American Jewish community clearly have an important self-interest in establishing as decent a relationship with him as possible."

Whether Jackson poses a threat or offers therapy to his party, he constitutes something of an intelligence test for America. With his unashamed assertion of who he is, he flirts with prejudice, daring it out of its cave. He is the only presidential candidate who can say *ain't* without being considered ignorant except by the ignorant: "We makin' what ain't nobody buyin'." More than most politicians, he has a sense of the absurd in a campaign, and cannot resist making jokes as well as history (as he proved during his surreal day with Silo Sam). Though he has resolved not to criticize other Democrats, an occasional mocking touch comes through. At last year's Congressional Black Caucus, the master of ceremonies did an elaborate dance to slip a little platform in front of the microphone each time Governor Dukakis came up to it to answer a question. Jackson eyed the platform quizzically, stepped onto it for a moment, towering above the adjusted microphone, and softly said, "I've waited years for equal standing."

George Will, in the spirit of old crackers giving voting quizzes to blacks when they tried to register earlier this year asked Jackson on television, "As a President, would you support measures such as the G-7 measures and the Louvre Accords?" (Like the redneck quizzers, Will got the trick question slightly wrong—the Louvre Accord was a G-7 measure.) Jackson has survived cleverer ploys of exclusion than that, but can the rest of the country continue to indulge them?

Jackson likes to end speeches with the story of his grandmother, who took odds and ends of cloth ("not hardly fit to wipe your shoes with, some of them") and stitched them into a quilt that kept him warm as a child. Then, referring to different minorities or excluded parts of his audience, he tells farmers, or strikers, or Hispanics, that "you're right, but your patch ain't big enough." The minorities must unite to extend their influence. He does not reach the real conclusion of his parable—that the white patch ain't big enough either; the majority cannot solve the nation's problems. If blacks do not participate in the solution to this country's difficulties, there will be no solution. It is going to take a thorough interweaving of minorities within majorities and majorities within minorities to deal with crime and drugs and jobs and health. So far, the most energetic piecer-together of the component strips of such an electoral quilt is Jesse Jackson, rhetorical, ecumenical, opportunistic, making history, making jokes.

SINCE THE BLACK-REGISTRA-tion drives of the 1960s and the Voting Rights Act of 1965, blacks have become a significant political force. Cities with large black voter registrations, such as Atlanta and Detroit, have elected black mayors, as have many other cities where blacks constitute a significant proportion of the vote. Successful black candidates, especially in gubernatorial elections, have also attracted a large proportion of white votes. For example, when Los Angeles mayor Tom Bradley ran for governor of California in 1982, he received 48 percent of the vote in a state that was only 7 percent black. Virginia governor Douglas Wilder captured 50 percent of his state's vote in his successful 1989 race in a state that was only 19 percent black. The following selection describes the new political style of black politicians who more and more are stressing mainstream values to broaden their electoral appeal.

Howard Fineman
5 THE NEW BLACK POLITICS

Douglas Wilder is an equal-opportunity joiner: a gregarious black man who likes being admitted to institutions that bestow power and social acceptance in mainstream America. In 1951 he was among the first soldiers in the newly integrated Army and won a Bronze Star in Korea. He proudly wears his "33rd Degree" Masonic ring, denoting his top rank in that ancient order. In his hometown of Richmond, Va., he even wanted to join the Commonwealth Club, sanctum of the state's political aristocracy. In 1982, a rising star in politics, Wilder insisted on being taken to lunch there by Democratic Party allies. They rode to the club with him but then decided they couldn't ask him in. It was an all-white club and they weren't ready to risk the members' wrath. Wilder, seething with anger, drove away as his eyes welled up with tears.

Now Wilder can join the club if he wants to. The tradition is to offer a membership to the governor. Last week, by a wispy 7,000-vote margin, the people of Virginia chose Wilder to be their next governor. [He became] the first African-American ever elected governor in any state. The Commonwealth Club story stands as a revealing episode about the man Virginia picked. It was hardly surprising that he was turned away. But it was no surprise at all that he wanted to get in. It was the traditional place where Virginia does its deals.

Wilder's story typifies the outlook of the other black politicians who won historic victories [in 1989]. From New York to Seattle, voters in majority-white jurisdictions elected a new wave of black Democrats who, like Wilder, seek acceptance rather than confrontation—and don't mind paying dues if there are reasonable odds of eventual success. Insiders all, they have risen through integrating institutions—the military, professional schools, party politics—while hearing and benefiting from the inspirational message of the civil rights movement. They form a new elite moving in tandem, but not in lockstep, with the "Movement" and with figures who got their start in it, such as Jesse Jackson. "We're seeing the emergence of what I call a New Black Politics," says Howard University professor Ronald Walters. "These are black politicians who benefited from the civil rights movement. But they don't come out of it. They are the wave of the future, as more blacks run in white districts."

Four-step maneuver: With shrewdness and caution, the new black candidates executed a neat, four-step maneuver. They sold themselves as competent, experienced politicians in the cultural mainstream. They capitalized, in varying degrees, on a growing aura of racial tolerance—what Jesse Jackson last week called "the maturing of white America." At the same time the new black candidates held onto the near-total support of black voters, who evidently were unwilling to consider voting for a white candidate.

The candidates also managed—barely—to avoid running aground on white voters' hidden racial fears, revealed at the last moment by exit polls. In New York, a city with a 5-to-1 Democratic edge, Republican Rudolph Giuliani drew an extraordinary 70 percent of the white vote. That made Democrat David Dinkins's victory bittersweet. Dinkins supporters say the huge turnout in Staten Island, Queens, and parts of Brooklyn clearly was racially motivated. "Racism is too gentle a word," argues Dinkins adviser Wilbert Tatum, editor of the *New York Amsterdam News.* "This was a pure antiblack vote."

Even so, the result was an impressive sweep for the new breed of black politicians—breakthrough victories in Virginia and in cities which blacks had never won or seriously contested: Dinkins in New York, John Daniels in New Haven, Conn., Chester Jenkins in Durham, N.C., and Norman Rice in Seattle, Wash. The racial equation was different but the trend was as evident in Cleveland, Ohio, which featured a heated contest between black candidates. There, Michael White won by offering himself to white and black voters alike as a calm and competent antidote to the abrasive city council president, George Forbes.

These milestones were reached by candidates whose résumés and styles linked them to universal American values. "These black Democrats have learned what white liberals need to learn," said Democratic polltaker Geoffrey Garin. "Out of necessity, they've had to carefully figure out how to connect with people's values." Wilder's ads reminded everyone of his wartime heroics. Dinkins, mild-mannered though he was, touted his Marine Corps service. White started in politics in the classic way: the student-body presidency at Ohio State University. Hands-on business experience was another claim to the cultural center: Rice, in Seattle, had been a commercial banker; Jenkins, in Durham, is a senior marketing analyst for GTE Corp. Even sports was middle ground. Daniels of New Haven, a football star in high school and at Villanova University, is a college football referee.

Each man is also a party stalwart. Dinkins had been president of the Board of Elections and city clerk before winning the office of Manhattan borough president. Wilder was Virginia's first black state senator since the Reconstruction Era. Elected lieutenant governor in 1985, he was the first black to hold statewide office in the old Confederacy in modern times. Ads pointedly pictured him presiding over the state Senate, gavel in hand. In New Haven, Daniels had more than twenty years of officeholding to his name; even White, at 38 years old, had been in politics for 14 years. He said he had been dreaming of being mayor of Cleveland since the age of 14. Few doubted his account.

A moderate approach: Their campaigns moved to the middle, too—or certainly away from specially "black" issues. Wilder cleverly used his pro-choice position on abortion to identify himself with Virginia's Jeffersonian distrust for government. That allowed him to paint his opponent, Republican Marshall Coleman, as a right-to-life extremist. In Durham Jenkins sided with slow-growth groups, portraying his foe as ravenously pro-development. In Seattle, where busing was controversial, Rice, late in the campaign, took a more moderate approach in calling for an eventual end to the practice. In overwhelmingly Democratic New York, Dinkins hammered away at Giuliani by calling him a "Reagan Republican." "A lot of these guys were able to do to us what we did to them in 1988," said a ruefully admiring Lee Atwater, chairman of the Republican National Committee. "They seized the middle, and pushed our guys out of the mainstream."

The election victors will have to continue their balancing acts to succeed in office. The effort of combining roles of ethnic leader and pol-for-all could prove painfully difficult over the long haul. In most cases, for instance, the candidates relied on financial support from local business and development interests—whose low-tax goals could clash with demands for social services from core black constituencies.

The new black politicians didn't make things easier by running campaigns that were, for the most part, short on fiscal specifics in cities with budget problems. Yet no one had the temerity to campaign on the need for higher revenues. Like President George Bush, they have no particular mandate to do anything other than attack the twin evils of crime and drugs. Wilder, in an interview with *Newsweek,* seemed most inclined to rely, in part, on his reputation for Reaganesque charm. "They referred to me as the Teflon Candidate," he laughed. "And I thought that was something Ronald Reagan patented!"

Array of heroes: Now the very term "black politics" needs reexamining, says Walters of Howard. "What does that term mean if black politicians aren't looking to meet an agenda of black concerns?" he asks. Jackson is sure to prod the new politicians into focusing on such an "agenda." And black pols may be vulnerable to pressure from him; they need one very big tree," said Democratic insider Robert Beckel. On the other hand, Beckel said, Dinkins, Wilder and the others give blacks a wider array of leaders to follow. The newly elected leaders will be called on to play that role, and yet presumably will want to encourage blacks—and whites, for that matter—to dismiss race, once and for all, as a factor in public life.

For the new leaders, and for the Democratic party they belong to, the biggest challenge is the most obvious: to govern well. The party still is seen as too hung up on the process of doling out chunks of power to constituencies, says Democratic polltaker Garin, and not enough on solving problems of the nation as a whole. "In the short term, all this obsessive focus on race and the Democratic Party isn't very helpful," says Garin. "In the long term, it can be helpful to us—if these folks do well. There's an awful lot riding on this new crop of leaders." For them, it seems, the real challenge has only begun.

U NTIL 1989 JESSE JACKSON dominated black politics at the national level. Jackson's charismatic personality and left-of-center politics appealed to the black community and to many whites as well, giving him a broad constituency but one that was far from a national majority. After the elections of 1989, as the previous selection points out, a new black politics emerged that stressed competence over charisma, and modern mainstream ideas more than the liberalism of the past.

In the 1989 Virginia gubernatorial race, the black Democratic candidate, former Lieutenant Governor Douglas Wilder, won over the white Republican candidate, former State Attorney General J. Marshall Coleman, by a razor-slim margin of less than six thousand votes.[1] Race was an unspoken issue throughout the campaign in a state that had not elected a black governor since Reconstruction days. Abortion was also a major issue, Wilder taking the pro-choice view while Coleman stood with the right-to-life constituency opposing abortion. While race almost lost Wilder the election, many observers believed that his pro-choice position was a major factor in his victory. Wilder discounted race as a factor in the final vote tally, but he ran well behind his two white Democratic ticket mates, Donald S. Beyer, Jr., who captured the lieutenant governor's office with 54 percent of the vote, and Mary Sue Terry, who won the state attorney's general office with 63 percent of the vote.

Often acrimonious exchanges between the two candidates marked the campaign. Coleman turned to strong negative campaigning in the final weeks of the contest, and accused the media as well of a "double standard" by favoring Wilder over him.

Although race, abortion, and other issues clearly affected the outcome of Wilder's campaign, behind the scenes two young staffers, one who had worked in Dukakis's presidential campaign and one who had worked in Simon's, were working feverishly to put together an effective organization to persuade voters and to get out the vote. That organization was called the Joint Campaign, and it was run out of the Headquarters of the state Party.

The *Washington Post* described Jill Alper, one of the authors of the following selection, as "a twenty-four-year-old Democratic Party organizer, [who] has spent weeks supervising the mailing of a million letters, the dialing of countless telephone calls and the work of a twelve-member staff, most of whom have been deployed in Democratic neighborhoods around the state. She has raised and spent about $750,000, none of which is subject to Virginia's campaign finance disclosure laws. And until now, only a few political strategists paid any attention."[2] On election eve, commented the *Washington Post,* "tomorrow belongs to relatively anonymous activists such as Alper."[3]

The Joint Campaign also helped the Democratic candidates to present a coor-

---

[1]Wilder received 896,283 votes (50.15%) to Coleman's 890,750 votes (49.85%).

[2]*Washington Post,* November 6, 1989, p. 1: Metro.

[3]Ibid.

dinated message. Gabe Kaplan worked as the press secretary, working with groups that endorsed the ticket, rebutting Republican attacks on the candidates, and organizing the Democratic contact with the media.

The following is their firsthand account of the campaign.

6 Jill Alper and Gabriel Kaplan
HARD COUNTS: BEHIND THE SCENES OF THE '89 VIRGINIA GUBERNATORIAL RACE

Maybe once you wanted to change the world, but now you would settle for just changing the number of precincts captains posted on the wall. You have always loved politics, followed it religiously since you were little. Perhaps you were once involved in student government and never lost the taste for it. Or maybe you just love the excitement of being associated with the candidate. Now, however, it is 2:00 A.M. You are running on four hours' sleep, and the Chinese food you ate a few hours ago just moved. Or maybe that was your head accelerating toward the desk. You remember once thinking this process was utterly absurd and wonder why you are once again involved in what can sometimes be only best described as an ordeal.

Why indeed? Is it perhaps because working on a campaign can be the most exhausting, hectic, anxiety-filled experience of your life, and for some people, this constitutes living? Or is it because you are most alive at those moments when the bombs of political salvos burst around you, when the excitement most others are only aware of when they glance briefly at the evening news actually courses through you and involves you completely like an electrical charge from a wet toaster.

Getting Involved

It was the summer of 1989. We and most of our friends were finally recovered from the long string of Presidential primaries, caucuses, and the culminating, crushing blow that was the devastating Presidential loss of Governor Michael S. Dukakis. For us, restlessness had set in; Washington was hot and humid, like a sauna run amok in a low-class health club. It was time to get out, to stop staring aimlessly at the White House and to get back into the field and direct our vengeance at some unsuspecting Republican candidate.

In Virginia lay a chance to make history. Lt. Governor Douglas Wilder was running against pro-life Republican candidate J. Marshall Coleman and hoping to become the first black governor since just after the Civil War. The *Webster* decision had made this election a key test of the willingness of states

Reprinted by permission of Gabriel Kaplan.

to go back on their protection of a woman's right to choose whether or not to have an abortion. For the Democrats, it was a chance to test a new concept, the coordinated campaign: an attempt to combine the field operations of the entire Democratic ticket in order to maximize the resources of time, money, and people.

To complete the grassroots activities of phonebanking, door-to-door canvassing, direct mail, and get-out-the-vote they needed a campaign director. Will Robinson, the consultant to what would be called the Virginia Joint Campaign, called Jill and took her out to lunch.

"They need someone to run the coordinated campaign in Virginia," he said. "Why don't you do it?"

Jill thought briefly, looked back at Will, and asked, "When do I leave?"

After two weeks in Virginia, Will and Jill saw that the state party could serve as a vehicle to respond to negative media attacks and rebut Republican charges. They needed to create a press operation. Seven hundred miles away, an unemployed Gabe Kaplan had just quit a campaign in New Jersey and was sick in bed with mono. When he got better, he would need something to do before starting a job in Washington in November. He called Will, who asked, "How quickly can you get down here?"

A Day in the Life

The daily routine passed, in Virginia, like any daily campaign routine. We would get up at 7:30 after the usual six-hour sleep, or more often, when our will failed, 8:30. We would drag ourselves into the office and use as much of the first few quiet moments to read the paper and catch up on campaign developments.

Soon the phones would start to ring and we were all thrown into action, responding to the latest crisis in the Democratic ranks or to the latest attack from the other side. Either a Democratic Party county chair was resisting our efforts to organize the campaign in a particular area or was offending key parts of our constituency. Maybe the bus company mistakenly had shipped our important voter contact lists to New York. Perhaps a field worker was just too tired and could no longer put up with the frustrations of the job. After too many short nights and dazed by the little cooperation she received from her fellow Democrats, she was at her wits' end, spinning helplessly in her headquarters.

Late every night we would drag ourselves back to the campaign crash pad, a place unaffectionately referred to as the "roach motel." Forced to call in an exterminator twice during the campaign, the marks of his effectiveness lay feet up across the floor, littered the kitchen, and occasionally fell from our toilet kits. Sparse was barely the word for the decor. Our furnishings consisted of one rug, two futons, and three beds. As is usual in a campaign, we had insisted that a place to sleep be included in our work agreement. Yet the best the campaign could come up with was to rent, from a Democratic landlord, this ramshackle set of old rooms that we suspected had once, in better days, served as a crack house.

Gabe's first night in the place, still a little feverish from mono, he woke up before sunrise, sweating in the sweltering August night and pulled some sort of sluglike thing from his neck. Reluctant to discover its true character, he simply lay back on the bed and listened to the roar of traffic outside the window. Drifting back to sleep was never easy once you woke up. Occasionally you would be startled by the hollering of some neighbors who passed the evening suspiciously perched on their front porch and who, every now and then, flagged down the slow-moving vehicles that passed.

The Campaign Staff

The tender age of the campaign's staff had attracted a great deal of press attention. One reporter dubbed the Wilder campaign the "Kiddie Crusade." The Wilder staff had responded by printing up T-shirts with a silk-screened drawing of a baby wearing a Wilder T-shirt and boasting the most vicious quotes thrown at the staff. "Wildly unprofessional" read one T-shirt line.

The staff was young. Wilder's press secretary was 24 and had taken a leave from Yale Divinity School to assist the campaign. The trip director was the same age. The scheduler, the person charged with handling all aspects of the candidate's scheduling strategy, offering advice on choosing events to attend and sending regrets to those Wilder would miss, was 23. The top fund-raiser, who successfully raised the then unheard-of sum of $6.7 million and kept the Wilder paid media effort alive, was 25. Over at the Joint Campaign, the situation was similar. Jill and Gabe were both 24.

The Strategy

Based on the electoral history of the state, we knew we would need 750,000 votes to win the Governor's race. Our job with the Joint Campaign was to identify these Wilder voters and then make sure we got them to the polls on election day. This task became our one focus; to get the "hard count," our arsenal of supporters motivated every minute of the staff's time.

A sophisticated set of targeting data was compiled to tell us where to direct our efforts at finding these voters. The campaign focused on those precincts which were not traditionally Democratic and which contained voters who would "split their ticket," shifting their Party allegiance from year to year or office to office. Within these precincts, our field staff organized phonebanks and door-to-door canvasses and we sent out thousands of pieces of mail to contact those voters identified from our polling as "ticket splitters."

Generally, we targeted men and women under the age of 45. Throughout the state we delivered to these voters the message that the Democrats believed in a woman's freedom to choose, and we delivered this message over and over again. Only in the southwest part of the state, where we stressed economic development, did we vary. We had to win the younger voters who did not conform to traditional voting patterns.

Attack-Counterattack

We also spent a great deal of our time reacting to Republican negative tactics, and often, a morning attack would lead us to drop our planned events and switch over to quick responses aimed at defusing the offensive and turning the tables on the other side. The statewide campaigns often used the Joint Campaign to respond to negative attacks and to launch political counteroffensives. This maneuver allowed their candidates to stay above the fray of a negative campaign. The press rarely made the distinction between the Joint Campaign we ran on behalf of the Democratic candidates and the candidates themselves. Polls showed that in the public's eye, the Democrats had been much less negative than the Republicans.

Persuading the Voters

In poll after poll, one truth became obvious: Republican attacks were failing to move voters. A September poll by Mason-Dixon duplicated one done in July; Coleman led in both polls by about 44 to 38 percent, with everyone else undecided. Despite a series of attacks on Wilder's handling of his personal finances and commercials which claimed Wilder was soft on crime because he at one time opposed the death penalty, voters were unmoved.

The Coleman campaign had fallen into an early pattern that revealed their strategy. They used voter concern about crime and drugs to paint Wilder as a "soft Liberal." They resurrected past complications in his financial affairs to question his character. Although the media gave a great deal of attention that summer and fall to the crime problem and the war on drugs, the electorate would vote based on other concerns.

Making Choice the Choice

The key issues in the Virginia election proved to be prosperity under the last eight years of Democratic Governors Chuck Robb and Gerald Baliles, abortion, and race. The polls began to change and Wilder began creeping past the Republican only after the debut of Wilder's ad pointing out Coleman's unpopular position on abortion. The impact of the message was that Coleman would take Virginia backward.

Wilder's ads, perhaps better than any other campaign tool, framed the

Choice issue best. In the wake of the summer's *Webster* decision, the electorate had realized that the constitutional privilege awarded by the court in 1973 was in jeopardy of being taken away by state legislatures. A voter who had not seen abortion as a political issue but as a constitutional right was now motivated to decide that her personal choice in matters of family planning was not an area with which Government could tamper. She, and often he, would single-mindedly refuse to support a candidate who felt Government had a role in such matters. Wilder's organization presented Choice as a conservative, antigovernment position. After *Webster,* the rhetoric of the Reagan years came back to haunt the Republican right-wing.

The New Mainstream

The campaign forged a message that Wilder represented a "new mainstream," something developed over the preceding eight years under Democratic Governors Chuck Robb and Gerald Baliles. Wilder peppered his speeches with phrases such as "We've come too far to turn back now," or "We must look forward, not backward," or "Virginia can never look back." By the end of the campaign, we could all repeat his speeches word for word.

The Wilder campaign characterized Coleman as a conservative extremist, out of step with Virginia values, who wanted to take the state back to a darker, less prosperous time. For many voters, the abortion issue validated this message, convincing them that Coleman was backward, did not share their values, was less able than Wilder to continue the prosperity begun under the Democrats, and wanted to tamper with success. In these voters' eyes, even though the abortion issue was not their only concern, it proved that Wilder was the rightful heir to the governorship. Winning votes with this message was Doug Wilder's greatest triumph.

Tuning the Message

One week before the election we had leads that ranged from three points to eleven points in published and private polls. The Coleman campaign was struggling to understand what was going wrong, desperately trying to find itself. We were cautiously optimistic but also concerned. We had always felt the election would be very close. We had assembled a team of lawyers to handle election irregularities and prepare for a potential recount. In the summer, our media consultant had said that our final Get-Out-the-Vote effort would be crucial. He said he could get us close, but the field organization would have to win it. At this point, the numbers looked perfect, but we knew that the potential for slippage was very great.

Behind the rosy picture of the published polls lay a gloomier reality. The real fight, the effort to win over the "ticket splitters," those who would decide the election, was much closer. Watching the day-to-day numbers of our identified ticket splitters was like watching a finely tuned scale tip off balance to one side, and then to the other. Two weeks before election day, Wilder had finally drawn even with Coleman among ticket-splitting voters. The Republican's lead, which at one time had been up to 13 percent, had disappeared and Wilder crept ahead by about one percentage point.

We had made a quarter of a million phone calls to the voters who we thought would decide the race, and still we were practically tied. Even more worrisome, over a quarter of the people we called had refused to answer our questions. This was five times greater than normal. We were at a loss to explain the discrepancy. We could not tell how 63,000 people would vote on election day.

The freedom-of-choice message had by this point completely saturated the persuasion targets, and tracking polls showed no further movement. The field operation opted for a riskier strategy. To the campaign's surprise, senior citizens, a group we knew would turn out in large numbers to vote, were largely undecided. The Choice message had neither alienated nor converted them. Most Seniors who had made up their minds had broken for Coleman, but the larger group of undecided seniors appeared ready to support Wilder. The last seven days of the persuasion effort was spent on phoning and mailing senior-citizen voters with a message emphasizing Coleman's weakness on issues of concern to seniors.

Negative Campaigning

Toward the end of the race, the campaign decided to highlight Coleman's tactics and make them an issue. In the final days of the campaign many analysts began to deal with Coleman's excessive attacks and the irritation it was causing many voters. Coleman had already run advertising which questioned Wilder's commitment to the death penalty, his handling of his finances, his ownership of a run-down house in a poor neighborhood, and his practices as an attorney. One advertisement seemed an attempt to use the crime issue to win back women who had moved to Wilder because of his position on Choice. It showed a rape victim hidden in shadow as a defense lawyer questioned her aggressively. The text of the advertisement questioned Wilder's introduction of a bill allowing defense attorneys to do just that.

Coleman had traditionally run negative campaigns, and polls revealed voters had been especially receptive to our criticism of his tactics because they knew what to expect from him. By 4 to 1 the voters thought Coleman had run a more negative campaign. Coleman had traditionally launched his most vicious attacks in the final days of a campaign and in light of his attacks so far we braced ourselves for his final onslaught.

Fighting Back

We decided to draw a line in the sand. When the Chairman of the national Republican Party came to campaign in the state two weeks before the election, state Party Chairman Larry Framme held a press conference to warn voters that a slew of negative garbage was coming their way. To make his point, he awarded the Republicans with the first-ever "Golden Trash Can Award." We had toyed with the idea of spraying a toilet plunger gold, and a number of reporters later suggested it would have been more appropriate. We, however, exercised a bit of restraint and processed with the trash can. The news coverage of the award was scattered, but when Gabe, with TV cameras in tow, delivered the trophy to Republican headquarters, an irate press secretary almost wrapped the can around his neck.

War of Attrition

We worried a great deal about voter intimidation as well. The Democratic Party has recently had to seek restraining orders against several operatives of the Republican National Committee to prevent them from engaging in what they refer to as their "Ballot Integrity Project." The aim is to discourage participation in high-performance Democratic precincts, and they usually target their efforts to minority neighborhoods. An internal RNC memo that came to light during the 1986 Louisiana U.S. Senate campaign stated that an attempt to influence the periodic purge of the voter files should "keep the black vote down considerably."

On election day, reports trickled out of the Tidewater region of the state that Democrats had allegedly received mysterious 3:00 A.M. calls reminding them to vote for Wilder and, worse, that a large number of minority voters had been called and told not to show up at the polls because they were not registered. As the campaign ended, the racial aspect of the contest was to eclipse our concern with intimidation and negative attacks.

The Mystery Tape

Shortly after the "Golden Trash Can" the National Right to Work Committee held a press conference to say they had proof that Wilder had made a secret promise to labor to undermine Virginia's sacred right-to-work law. Wilder publicly ridiculed these charges, but everyone sensed they were trying to set him up. We also surmised that if they were hoping to catch him in a lie, they knew that the right-to-work issue was not in itself potent enough make up the lost ground.

Sure enough, they hoped to make honesty the issue. The Right to Work people called Wilder a liar the next day and played a tape which they claimed revealed his secret promise. Coleman immediately jumped on the bandwagon.

The tape purported to disclose a meeting Wilder held with striking coal miners in the southwest part of the state shortly after winning the nomination. The quality of the sound was very poor. On three separate occasions Wilder clearly told the miners that he supported Virginia's right-to-work law and would not work to change it. He added that it was politically unrealistic for them to expect a candidate for Governor to do so anyway. Our opponents claimed that the tape revealed Wilder agreeing with union leader Jackie Stump that "You had to had to put the camel's head in the tent" to change right to work. It was a weak argument at best, but the press loved the sexy aspect of the audiotape. Its rich imagery evoked Watergate, Hoover's FBI, and Iran-Contra. The story ran for two days and began to peter out.

The miners' strike had been a political problem from the start. Many striking miners blamed the Democrats and particularly Governor Baliles for sending in state police. The Republicans were just waiting for a sign of sympathy to jump on Wilder as a soft-hearted Liberal indebted to the unions. Wilder needed the traditionally strong Democratic base out of the Southwest coalfields to turn out on election day. Between the two sides he had to walk a fine political line.

The Last Gasp

In the end, the tape probably had little impact on the election's outcome but it provided the lead-in for the last desperate attempt of the Coleman campaign to salvage their effort. Coleman challenged Wilder to meet him on the steps of the state Capital to debate the issue and answer the charges. Wilder did not show up and it rained on the lonely Republican. That hardly mattered to Coleman. He quickly launched into a tirade against the media for what he claimed was their unfair treatment of him and their coddling of Wilder. He singled out the *Washington Post,* claiming it was a liberal newspaper. But his most spectacular charge was of a "double standard." Many reporters wrote that Coleman seemed to imply the media favored Wilder because he was black. The United Press International observed, "In heated terms, Coleman argued the media was too kind to Wilder and suggested the Democrat benefitted from a double standard because he was black" (UPI, November 4, 1989).

Of course, the Coleman campaign will never discuss the rationale behind the attack, but the outburst seemed calculated. The campaign had been remarkably free of the racial issue. Both candidates had gone to great lengths to avoid it. Now, Coleman was ten points down in the polls. His words focused attention on the racial aspect of the contest.

The final stories of the campaign chronicled Coleman's repeated claims of a "double standard." Voters heard little about abortion as the campaign drew to an end. Attention focused on Coleman's charges and on Wilder's race. Throughout the last weekend of the campaign, Coleman repeated his charge. "I have been complaining for some time that there is one standard for my opponent and another standard for me" (UPI, November 4, 1989).

Democrats could not respond for to do so would only allow Coleman to shift attention away from the issues which Wilder had so successfully developed. Wilder dismissed the attack, but the press was too overwhelmed by the implication of Coleman's words to include anything else in their campaign coverage.

Victory

When the dust cleared around 4:00 A.M. Wednesday morning and we trudged home after putting in 24 hours of election-day work, we knew we had won. We were pretty sure that we would have a recount. We could only wonder what role Coleman's final charges had played in the narrow outcome.

At 7:00 P.M. the exit polls had Wilder up by 9 points. They showed that underdog Democratic candidate for Lieutenant Governor, Don Beyer, whose best preelection poll showing had him down by 10 points, had won by 10 points. Clearly something was wrong. We had thought Wilder's coattails might carry Beyer. Instead, he had outperformed Wilder.

As the night stretched on, Wilder's exit-poll margin never materialized. Gabe wandered the ballroom a little puzzled but assured the reporters that the lead would soon materialize and hold solid. We had all seen races where radical shifts occurred over the course of the evening, and we hardly doubted that this election would be different. At some point in time Wilder would take the lead and put Coleman away for good. We also knew the officials were counting Republican precincts first. But we were still down with 35 percent of the precincts reporting. We did not begin to edge ahead until 68 percent had reported. Our largest margin of the evening was two points, or 20,000 votes.

Around 11:30 the news shows flashed the numbers for the strongly Democratic city of Norfolk. Jill flashed Gabe a panicked look. Our hearts jumped. We thought, "Had we just blown the 'sure thing'?"

We were gathering off-stage, preparing the entryway for Wilder to stride in and make his victory speech. Will leaned over and whispered in Gabe's ear, "We've got a problem." We had done well in Norfolk, but we should have done better. We had racked up record turnouts in most Democratic regions, but in Norfolk turnout was down from what the Democrats had needed.

We had worked so long and hard for the moment of victory which everyone had assured us we would have. We had begun to believe in a landslide ourselves, and began to count down the days when we would no longer have to listen to Republican attacks. But now, exhausted, it felt as though we had run a marathon, struggling and gasping through the last five miles, only to be told at the finish that we now had another ten to go.

We gathered what was left of our energy, the lawyers, and the field team and raced back to Party headquarters to begin preparing for the recount and to start verifying the election-night results. We spent the rest of the evening at the state Party headquarters tracking the final returns from the outstanding precincts, and watching, with one eye on the TV, as Wilder's lead ebbed and progressed. We had to wake up weary voting registrars and asked them to confirm their tallies. As the TV stations wrapped up their coverage of the election, they had Wilder up by 3,000 votes. Our election night figures showed a margin of 8,000 votes. Our whopping victory had never materialized. The final recount held on December 21 showed Wilder had won by 6741 votes, a margin of less than three votes per precinct.

Post-mortem

Wilder had run essentially the same campaign as Beyer, his running mate for Lieutenant Governor, but he had racked up 60,000 fewer votes. Most polls had misrepresented his lead by almost ten points. Either respondents had told the pollsters they were undecided when they were not, or they had said they supported Wilder when they did not. Perhaps Coleman's negative ads and final attacks account for the discrepancy between Wilder and Beyer, yet many analysts assumed that race explains the disparity as well.

Despite the media's acclaim for a black's victory in the heart of the old confederacy, Wilder's ability to attract support from new voters who moved into Virginia from other areas of the country provided him with his winning margin. The new Virginia voters tend to be younger, upscale, and economically conservative; many had voted for Bush in the last election. Wilder's middle-of-the-road appeal, as captured in his image of the "new mainstream" attracted them when contrasted with the GOP's aggressive posture against a woman's right to choose. When an observer removes Wilder's winning margin from Northern Virginia and Tidewater, Coleman clearly wins the Governorship.

Given the importance of abortion in the race and Wilder's margin in areas that have received an influx of such voters, it is safe to say that the New South elected Doug Wilder the first black Governor. Politically, the Old South has been changed forever, and Wilder's victory is but a manifestation of greater national demographic changes over the last 20 years. Analysts make much of the conservative grip over the Sun Belt, but social and economic change in the South has opened up new areas of opportunities for Democrats.

The Wilder campaign was an opportunity for each of us to play a small role in a historic moment. We had expected to need 750,000 votes to win the election. Instead, Wilder racked up 890,000 votes. The "Kiddie Crusade," an object of jokes three months earlier, had helped elect the nation's first black governor since Reconstruction and had helped produce record turnouts. Each of us young people, trained and inspired by our experience in Virginia have gone on to play roles in Democratic races throughout the country and may probably do so into the next century. The lure of the political road is truly irresistible.

DEMOCRATIC THEORY POSTU-lates a close fit between political campaigning and governing. Campaigns are supposed to enhance democratic choice, defining issues and presenting them to the electorate.

But campaigning and governing are quite different endeavors. Candidates and their staffs may enjoy both activities, but often they have a preference for one over the other. Some candidates get emotional highs from campaigning and may run in election after election even if they do not win, simply for the pure enjoyment of campaigning. Even the gruel-ing presidential nominating process attracts a host of candidates who know their chance of winning is slim to none.

To run for office, candidates require an extensive and skilled campaign staff. Advance men, media experts, organizers, speech writers, and pollsters are among those who constitute what has become a professional campaign corps.

For many participants political campaigning is more a lure than a livelihood. The following selection describes the exhilaration of a presidential campaign from the vantage point of the mostly young staff who become involved.

7 John Homans
THE LURE OF THE POLITICAL ROAD

A presidential campaign is a moveable feast: sandwiches on the plane, a Budweiser and chocolate-chip cookies in the office, hors d'oeuvres sneaked at a fund-raiser. Lunch is nice, but there is often something more important going on.

Not long ago, before Iowa sank like Atlantis beneath the political map, Steve Murphy, the state director for the Presidential campaign of Missouri Congressman Richard A. Gephardt, had lunch on his mind. Briefly. Then CBS called. Next it was David Doak and Robert Shrum, Gephardt's media consultants, hashing out which ads to run in the next week. It was a call upon which the future of Dick Gephardt's candidacy may have rested, and in the middle of it Ed Reilly, the candidate's pollster, reinforced the pressure of the situation by getting the 36-year-old Murphy into a headlock.

Ten minutes later, at a restaurant across the street, Murphy—who has worked in Presidential politics since 1972, when he was a volunteer on the campaign of then-Senator George McGovern—was trying to explain why he does it. "A colleague of mine," he said, "Teresa Vilmain, the Iowa coordinator for Dukakis, once described me in this way: 'There are some people for whom this is a cause, and there are some for whom it's a profession. For you, it's an adventure.'"

For many of the younger people who work in politics, campaigning is a rite of passage—their Paris, their grand tour, their great adventure. For most of them, one such experience is enough. Life takes over. Jobs, commitments, marriages, all tend to get in the way of the single-minded intensity the pursuit of the Presidency requires.

There are some, however, like Murphy, who get hooked. They are likely to describe themselves as "professional political operatives," but the word *professional* seems out of place in the context of a campaign, implying a distance from the work, an ability to leave the job at the office. They also describe themselves at times as "politics junkies," a term that may get closer to the truth of the experience, its oddly bohemian feel, its obsessive nature.

Year after year, these political gypsies shift from advance work for a presidential candidate to manager of a gubernatorial campaign to consultant on a Senate race, then back to another White House contest. They profess to feel the tug of home. They talk about their futures, about starting a consulting business, about sleeping in their own beds every night. But home can wait. So can the wealth and notoriety that accrue to media consultants and White House staffers. Political gypsies put up with their bivouacs along the campaign trail—the campaign offices, unfurnished apartments and hotel rooms, one just like another—for the sake of the life, a sort of competitive circus with the Presidency as its prize.

Every primary and caucus state has one or two political watering holes—taverns, usually in the state capital—where gypsies and media people congregate to trade tales from the front. In Atlanta, they are drawn to the bar at the Omni Hotel. New Hampshire boasts the Wayfarer Hotel's bar in Bedford. In Iowa, it is the bar at the Savery Hotel in Des Moines for Democrats and the Skywalk lounge on the second floor of the Marriott Hotel for Republicans.

One night, about seven weeks ago, Jack Weeks, an advance man for the Presidential campaign of Massachusetts Governor Michael S. Dukakis, was sitting at the Savery bar, watching it fill up with members of his fraternity. There was a reunion feel in the room. Advance people are a subculture within a subculture. They are political trailblazers, moving one step ahead of the candidate to scout out the lay of the land, and so they often wind up in the same bars at the same time. A few of the other advance people—John Toohey and Steve Rabinowitz with Illinois Senator Paul Simon, Dennis Walto with former Colorado Senator Gary Hart—were Weeks's subordinates in 1984, when he worked with Hart.

This year, despite occasional sniping between Senator Albert Gore, Jr.'s and Dick Gephardt's campaign managers, it has been a relatively friendly competition among Democrats. In the bar, the political enemies fraternized easily, touting their candidates with what often seemed to be tongues in cheeks. A Simon advance man was talking with his fiancée, who does advance for Richard Gephardt. (But party lines aren't often crossed: When Tom Synhorst, Republican Senator Robert J. Dole's Iowa campaign manager, wandered into the Savery, people wondered audibly if he was lost.)

Jack Weeks has big blue-gray eyes, creased at the corners from squinting into the sun at the countless events he has organized. At the age of 35, he is the *éminence grise* of the advance world, and indeed, there's some gray in his hair, a fact that was not left unremarked-upon by the advance people from the other campaigns who saw him sitting there.

He started out in politics the old way, running errands for South Boston ward heelers in order to obtain patronage jobs in the city's parks during summer vacations from school. After Harvard and the army he worked for some local politicians. He came to the attention of one of Senator Edward M. Kennedy's operatives, who was recruiting staff for Kennedy's 1976 Senate campaign and asked Weeks to get some petitions filled with the signatures of his neighbors in Southie. The busing controversy was raging at the time and Kennedy wasn't popular there. But two days later, Weeks brought the petitions back with some 800 signatures, and his political career was launched.

Weeks has the swagger of a small man from a tough town. Indeed, he was a boxer, good enough to be Golden Gloves. Over a Heineken, he was talking about the fight game.

"You're in the ring," he said, "and there's someone over on the other side who's going to try to hurt you. You're very, very nervous. But when you win, you win."

He thinks politics is better. "Infinitely better," he said. "I'd be hard pressed to find a better business to be involved with."

He swooped his hand in a figure 8 and his voice rose. "You start going like this, like a roller coaster. Think of '84 with Hart. You finish second in Iowa, but it's a surprise finish, and all of a sudden you're on a roll. You win New Hampshire big. Maine. Mondale holds his own in the South. Illinois you lose. Things start crumbling. You lose New York, and it really starts falling apart. Crushed in Texas. People are saying, 'Get out, get out.' But you turn around and win Ohio and Indiana."

There are good rounds and there are bad rounds; there is the roar of the crowd and the flash of cameras. But, Weeks says, "There's *nothing* like winning. There's nothing like winning."

For true political gypsies, advance work supplies the political drug in its purest form. There's no room for self-doubt, no time for indecision. An advance man comes into a town cold and knows that in four days the world is going to drop out of the sky in a fleet of Lear jets and he had better have something to show it. He's got to recruit volunteers, get a site, pull together a crowd and ensure there is a place from which reporters can file their stories, which become the advance man's trophies. "The ultimate is a piece on the national news or in the *New York Times*," says Barry Wyatt, head of advance for Richard Gephardt. "It's not uncommon to find advance people, after they've been on the road for a couple of months, with a satchel full of clippings."

Perhaps the most important part of an advance man's job is to orchestrate the symbolism, to make sure the picture the press gets is the picture a campaign wants it to get.

Jack F. Kemp's people, for example, are always looking for a football the former professional quarterback can throw—a *local* football, preferably, not one of the several pigskins they carry with them. When the Buffalo, N.Y., Congressman was campaigning in Minnesota recently, Peter Sterling, 22, his deputy regional political director, found the football in a sporting goods store at a mall a couple of days before Kemp was to arrive. Sterling pressed a clerk into service as a wide receiver, mapped out his pass route and told the press the play. All that was left was for Kemp to arrive and throw. Cameras rolled and, as planned, it made the local news.

When *Time* magazine put Iowa on the cover, Jack Weeks preened a bit over the photographs inside. "Take a look at the picture of Dukakis," he said. "It's just him and people. Now look at Paul Simon in front of the tractor. See the people on either side? Staff or Secret Service. It's obvious."

That is what is known in the trade as T.M.B.S.: "Too Many Blue Suits." Occasionally, the situation is created by what is called a "clutch," a supporter or staff person who is so taken with the candidate's light that he or she won't move away, even when the cameras begin to click.

When a candidate is courting the members of a particular union, and the owner of a company with whom the workers are fighting walks out of his plant and grabs the candidate's hand, and a photographer catches the moment on film, what results is called a "dirty picture." In 1984, Walter Mondale was standing by a factory gate trying to shake hands with employees, but the workers, to avoid the cameras, were going through another entrance. A frantic union leader, desperate to provide something for the press to see, brought out the plant's product. Before anyone could stop him, he thrust a package of toilet paper into Mondale's hands. Today, Democratic gypsies still shake their heads over the ultimate dirty picture.

Campaigns have evolved their own distinctive form of lore. These are known as war stories, but what they record are disasters. Tornados, heart attacks, lost rosary beads—all can figure in the mythology.

In 1984, Mitchell Schwartz—today a Dukakis advance man, but then doing advance for Mondale after his first candidate, Ohio Senator John Glenn, dropped out of the race—was organizing a Mondale event in Toledo, Ohio.

"Mondale was going to give a speech on the decline of trade in front of a small crowd, and the background was going to be ships in the harbor," recalled Schwartz. "I went to the harbor master, and he said there'll be no action in this area—guaranteed.

"Mondale started speaking at 1:00, and in the first minute there's a long blast on a whistle and a ship pulls out. The next day, lead story in the *New York Times,* first sentence: "In a speech frequently interrupted by passing ships. . . ." (War stories are often embellished: the article was not on the front page, nor did it open with the sound of whistling ships.) Schwartz suspected sabotage but was never able to find out for sure.

An advance person's mission is to keep his charge free of such perils. The candidate, in fact, should not have to think about anything but what he is going to say. If he wants to know where he's going, he looks at the suit in front of him; that's his advance man.

"You know how baby ducks bond with the first thing they see after they hatch?" asked a Simon advance person. "That's the way it is. Sometimes I think I could lead him into a broom closet."

Power used to be the reason people got involved in electoral politics. Parties had deep roots in the community, passing out jobs and favors, dealing in the perks as well as the politics.

The old system was stretched and ultimately broken during the 1960s by that decade's divisive issues, by the increasing sophistication of campaign technology, and by changes in the rules that opened the process and took power out of the hands of the boys in the back room. In the absence of the traditional motive, political gypsies claim universally that ideals are what draw them into the process today.

Steve Murphy, the Gephardt organizer, proudly calls himself a child of the '60s, a member of the generation that was going to change the world. He volunteered for George McGovern's campaign while he was a student at the University of Delaware. After he graduated, he worked as a VISTA volunteer, doing community organizing on New York's Lower East Side. The work satisfied his idealism, but he came to feel that changing Christie Street and changing the world were two different propositions.

"I guess I'm much too impatient," he said. "I figured out that if I wanted to have a real impact, electoral politics was the way to do it."

In 1976, he joined Jimmy Carter's campaign as a paid field organizer, corraling votes in the South and the Middle West, sacrificing the minuscule but concrete increments of change that community organizing can produce for the gamble that his man would get to the White House. He loved it. The results were measurable. "Elections have consequences," said Murphy.

But in the end, vociferous protestations to the contrary, it is not merely idealism that drives gypsies from one campaign to another. It is the adrenalin rush that comes from risking public failure, and the knowledge that successes will be advertised across the nation.

One of Murphy's fondest memories from his first professional Presidential campaign is of an event he organized in a black church in Chicago. He had committed the cardinal campaign sin of miscalculating the size of the crowd he could expect—there were 400 people in a church that seated 1,500. During the event he was close to tears, not even able to sit in the room.

"That night I was offering my resignation, out of humiliation, in Oriental fashion," he said. Murphy's colleagues rubbed his nose in his failure to draw a crowd.

The next morning, however, a picture of Carter singing in the church choir was on the morning television news and in several papers. Murphy was a campaign hero. It was a triumph of symbolism. The press had anointed the event as a step on the road to the White House.

The hot lights and cameras and microphones have a magnifying effect, turning the mundanities of campaigning into details of great import. The aura of importance is partly an illusion, based as it is on the possibility that the unknown candidate for whom one is toiling may be elected President. But prestige accrues quickly. A couple of successful campaigns on the state level can lead to a Presidential opportunity, and suddenly a young operative is at the center of the world, however briefly.

"In what other profession," asked Paul Maslin, a pollster for the Paul Simon campaign, "could a 27-year-old person be on the front page of the *New York Times* and be interviewed by all the major networks?"

Life on the road never really loses its appeal, but as gypsies get older, the real world tends to intrude. On a wall at Jack Weeks's house in Boston is a large map of the United States. His sons John, who is 3, and Christopher, 7, keep track of his progress across the country with colored pins. Weeks calls them twice a day when he's on the road, but he knows that there is no substitute for being home. "You don't have a personal life on the road," he said. "You have conversations, that's all you have."

Beginners tend to think advance is glamorous. "You're in Las Vegas one week, Texas the next, then you're somewhere else, you're all over the country," said Weeks. "The press is around, you get to see the candidate every three or four days.

"But think of it," he continued. "You're not really seeing the country. I mean, I look at the ceiling in the hotel, what kind of ceiling do I have? Then the event happens, and you're gone, you're somewhere else doing the same thing all over again.

"The loneliest thing is if you're coming in late to some town," said Mitchell Schwartz, the Dukakis advance man. "You've been on the road for two straight weeks, you're coming off the plane, lugging your bag, and everyone is meeting spouses or boyfriends or girlfriends. And you realize that no one's meeting you. The only people you see are at the Avis counter and the hotel."

Weeks is divorced, and though he says his profession didn't cause the split, he admits that a Presidential campaign can put a severe strain on even the most stable relationship. "The person at home just can't understand why it's so important," he said. Weeks preaches perspective to the younger people. "There's life after a campaign," he will say.

But that life often proves sedentary and unsatisfying. Richard Bond engineered George Bush's spectacular victory in the Iowa caucuses in 1980; he was rewarded with the position of the Vice President's deputy chief of staff. But after a year, Bond got restless. However prestigious the Washington job may have been, the autonomy he enjoyed on the campaign trail spoiled him for the bureaucratic grind of Government. "The pace in the White House didn't agree with me," says Bond. This year, he is back on the road as George Bush's national political director—well paid, but no less a gypsy.

The intensity of a race, the long hours and the isolation from friends and familiar points of reference turn a candidate's gypsy contingent into a kind of extended family. That makes losing—and sometimes even winning—a trying experience. Because one way or another, the family breaks up.

"You try to hang on to each other for as long as you can, but that doesn't necessarily hold to reality," says Arnot Walker, a former advance man who is now press secretary for New York University President John Brademas. "It's over. That's hard."

And finally, after a number of races, the intensity takes its toll. Burn-out, it's called. Political people, like athletes, begin to think about what comes next when they reach their 30s. But, also like athletes, they don't like to rule out the possibility of a triumphant comeback.

"I don't think I'll be involved in the next one," said Steve Murphy. He paused. "But I've said that before."

THE PRECEDING SELECTIONS have illustrated that increasingly at the national level candidates and their followers give an individualistic cast to parties. Each candidate has his or her own organization that exists within the broader party. Neither national party committees nor leaders can determine who will run under their party labels.

Political parties were stronger in the past, especially at local levels. Occupying an important place in party history is the urban party machine, the paradigm of which was the Daley machine in Chicago.

The following selection describes the kinds of people and personalities that controlled the political machine in Chicago, from its powerful leader Mayor Richard J. Daley to the men who helped to keep him in office, including precinct workers and captains and the city bureaucrats appointed by the mayor to serve the party. Chicago politics clearly revealed a cult of personality in operation. The organization, operations, and policies of the Democratic party in Chicago were a perfect reflection of the personality of Mayor Richard J. Daley.

8 Mike Royko
THE BOSS

KUNSTLER: Mayor Daley, do you hold a position in the Cook County Democratic Committee?
WITNESS: I surely do, and I am very proud of it. I am the leader of my party.
KUNSTLER: What was that?
WITNESS: I surely do, and I am very proud of it. I am the leader of my party in Cook County.
KUNSTLER: Your honor, I would like to strike from that answer anything about being very proud of it. I only asked whether he had a position in the Cook County Democratic party.
HOFFMAN: I will let the words "I surely do" stand. The words after those may go out and the jury may disregard the expression of the witness that he is very proud of his position.

The Hawk got his nickname because in his younger days he was the outside lookout man at a bookie joint. Then his eyes got weak, and he had to wear thick glasses, so he entered politics as a precinct worker.

He was a hustling precinct worker and brought out the vote, so he was rewarded with a patronage job. The Hawk, who had always loved uniforms

From *The Boss: Richard J. Daley of Chicago* by Mike Royko. Copyright 1971 by Mike Royko. Reprinted by permission of the publisher, Dutton, an imprint of New American Library, a division of Penguin Books USA Inc.

but had never worn one, asked his ward committeeman if he could become a member of the county sheriff's police department. They gave him a uniform, badge, and gun, and declared him to be a policeman.

But the Hawk was afraid of firearms, so he asked if he could have a job that didn't require carrying a loaded gun. They put him inside the County Building, supervising the man who operated the freight elevator. He liked the job and did such a good job supervising the man who operated the freight elevator that the Hawk was promoted to sergeant.

When a Republican won the sheriff's office, the Hawk was out of work for one day before he turned up in the office of the county treasurer, wearing the uniform of a treasurer's guard. His new job was to sit at a table near the main entrance, beneath the big sign that said "County Treasurer," and when people came in and asked if they were in the county treasurer's office, the Hawk said that indeed they were. It was a good job, and he did it well, but it wasn't what he wanted because he really wasn't a policeman. Finally his committeeman arranged for him to become a member of the secretary of state's special force of highway inspectors, and he got to wear a uniform that had three colors and gold braid.

The Hawk is a tiny piece of the Machine. He is not necessarily a typical patronage worker, but he is not unusual. With about twenty-five thousand people owing their government job to political activity or influence, nothing is typical or unusual.

The Hawk keeps his job by getting out the Democratic vote in his precinct, paying monthly dues to the ward's coffers, buying and pushing tickets to his ward boss's golf outing and $25-a-plate dinners. His reward is a job that isn't difficult, hours that aren't demanding, and as long as he brings out the vote and the party keeps winning elections, he will remain employed. If he doesn't stay in the job he has, they will find something else for him.

Some precinct captains have had more jobs than they can remember. Take Sam, who worked his first precinct forty-five years ago on the West Side.

"My first job was as a clerk over at the election board. In those days to succeed in politics you sometimes had to bash in a few heads. The Republicans in another ward heard about me and they brought me into one of their precincts where they were having trouble. I was brought in as a heavy, and I took care of the problem, so they got me a job in the state Department of Labor. The job was . . . uh . . . to tell the truth, I didn't do anything. I was a payroller. Then later I went to another ward as a Democratic precinct captain, where they were having a tough election. I did my job and I moved over to a job as a state policeman. Then later I was a city gas meter inspector, and a pipe fitter where they had to get me a union card, and an investigator for the attorney general, and when I retired I was an inspector in the Department of Weights and Measures."

The Hawk and Sam, as precinct captains, are basic parts of the Machine. There are some thirty-five hundred precincts in Chicago, and every one of them has a Democratic captain and most captains have assistant captains. They all have, or can have, jobs in government. The better the captain, the better the job. Many make upwards of fifteen thousand dollars a year as supervisors, inspectors, or minor department heads.

They aren't the lowest-ranking members of the Machine. Below them are the people who swing mops in the public buildings, dump bedpans in the County Hospital, dig ditches, and perform other menial work. They don't work precincts regularly, although they help out at election time, but they do have to vote themselves and make sure their families vote, buy the usual tickets to political dinners and in many wards, contribute about 2 percent of their salaries to the ward organization.

Above the precinct captain is that lordly figure the ward committeeman, known in local parlance as "the clout," "the Chinaman," "the guy," and "our beloved leader."

Vito Marzullo is a ward committeeman and an alderman. He was born in Italy and has an elementary school education, but for years when he arrived at political functions, a judge walked a few steps behind him, moving ahead when there was a door to be opened. Marzullo had put him on the bench. His ward, on the near Southwest Side, is a pleasant stew of working-class Italians, Poles, Mexicans, and blacks. A short, erect, tough, and likable man, he has had a Republican opponent only once in four elections to the City Council. Marzullo has about four hundred patronage jobs given to him by the Democratic Central Committee to fill. He has more jobs than some ward bosses because he has a stronger ward, with an average turnout of something like 14,500 Democrats to 1,200 Republicans. But he has fewer jobs than some other wards that are even stronger. Marzullo can tick off the jobs he fills:

"I got an assistant state's attorney, and I got an assistant attorney general, I got an electrical inspector at twelve thousand dollars a year, and I got street inspectors and surveyors, and a county highway inspector. I got an administrative assistant to the zoning board and some people in the secretary of state's office. I got fifty-nine precinct captains and they all got assistants, and they all got good jobs. The lawyers I got in jobs don't have to work precincts, but they have to come to my ward office and give free legal advice to the people in the ward."

Service and favors, the staples of the precinct captain and his ward boss. The service may be nothing more than the ordinary municipal functions the citizen is paying taxes for. But there is always the feeling that they could slip if the precinct captain wants them to, that the garbage pickup might not be as good, that the dead tree might not be cut down.

Service and favors. In earlier days, the captain could do much more. The immigrant family looked to him as more than a link with a new and strange government: He was the government. He could tell them how to fill out their papers, how to pay their taxes, how to get a license. He was the welfare agency, with a basket of food and some coal when things got tough, an entree to the crowded charity hospital. He could take care of it when one of the kids got in trouble with the police. Social welfare agencies and better times took away many of his functions, but later there were still the traffic tickets to fix, the real estate tax assessments he might lower. When a downtown office didn't provide service, he was a direct link to government, somebody to cut through the bureaucracy.

In poor parts of the city, he has the added role of a threat. Don't vote, and you might lose your public housing apartment. Don't vote, and you might be cut off welfare. Don't vote, and you might have building inspectors poking around the house.

In the affluent areas, he is, sometimes, merely an errand boy, dropping off a tax bill on the way downtown, buying a vehicle sticker at City Hall, making sure that the streets are cleaned regularly, sounding out public opinion.

The payoff is on election day, when the votes are counted. If he produced, he is safe until the next election. If he didn't, that's it. "He has to go," Marzullo says. "If a company has a man who can't deliver, who can't sell the product, wouldn't he put somebody else in who can?"

Nobody except Chairman Daley knows precisely how many jobs the Machine controls. Some patronage jobs require special skills, so the jobholder doesn't have to do political work. Some are under civil service. And when the Republicans occasionally win a county office, the jobs change hands. There were more patronage jobs under the old Kelly-Nash Machine of the thirties and forties, but civil service reform efforts hurt the Machine. Some of the damage has been undone by Daley, however, who let civil service jobs slip back into patronage by giving tests infrequently or making them so difficult that few can pass, thus making it necessary to hire "temporary" employees, who stay "temporary" for the rest of their lives. Even civil service employees are subject to political pressures in the form of unwanted transfers, withheld promotions.

On certain special occasions, it is possible to see much of the Machine's patronage army assembled and marching. The annual St. Patrick's Day parade down State Street, with Daley leading the way, is a display of might that knots the stomachs of Republicans. An even more remarkable display of patronage power is seen at the State Fair, when on "Democrat Day" thousands of city workers are loaded into buses, trains, and cars which converge on the fairgrounds outside Springfield. The highlight of the fair is when Daley proudly hoofs down the middle of the grounds' dusty racetrack in 90-degree heat with thousands of his sweating but devoted workers tramping behind him, wearing old-fashioned straw hats and derbies. The Illinois attorney general's staff of lawyers once thrilled the rustics with a crack manual of arms performance, using Daley placards instead of rifles.

Another reason the size of the patronage army is impossible to measure is that it extends beyond the twenty to twenty-five thousand government jobs. The Machine has jobs at racetracks, public utilities, private industry, and the

Chicago Transit Authority, which is the bus and subway system, and will help arrange easy union cards.

Out of the ranks of the patronage workers rise the Marzullos, fifty ward committeemen who, with thirty suburban township committeemen, sit as the Central Committee. For them the reward is more than a comfortable payroll job. If they don't prosper, it is because they are ignoring the advice of their Tammany cousin George Washington Plunkett, who said, "I seen my opportunities and I took 'em." Chicago's ward bosses take 'em, too.

Most of them hold an elective office. Many of the Daley aldermen are ward bosses. Several are county commissioners. Others hold office as county clerk, assessor, or recorder of deeds and a few are congressmen and state legislators. Those who don't hold office are given top jobs running city departments, whether they know anything about the work or not. A ward boss who was given a $28,000-a-year job as head of the city's huge sewer system was asked what his experience was. "About twenty years ago I was a house drain inspector." "Did you ever work in the sewers?" "No, but many a time I lifted a lid to see if they were flowing." "Do you have an engineering background?" "Sort of. I took some independent courses at a school I forget the name of, and in 1932 I was a plumber's helper." His background was adequate: his ward usually carries by fifteen thousand to three thousand votes.

The elective offices and jobs provide the status, identity, and retinue of coat holders and door openers, but financially only the household money. About a third of them are lawyers, and the clients leap at them. Most of the judges came up through the Machine; many are former ward bosses themselves. This doesn't mean cases are always rigged, but one cannot underestimate the power of sentimentality. The political lawyers are greatly in demand for zoning disputes, big real estate ventures, and anything else that brings a company into contact with city agencies. When a New York corporation decided to bid for a lucrative Chicago cable TV franchise, they promptly tried to retain the former head of the city's legal department to represent them.

Those who don't have the advantage of a law degree turn to the old reliable, insurance. To be a success in the insurance field, a ward boss needs only two things: an office with his name on it and somebody in the office who knows how to write policies. All stores and businesses need insurance. Why not force the premium on the friendly ward boss? As Marzullo says, everybody needs favors.

One of the most successful political insurance firms is operated by party ancient Joe Gill. Gill gets a big slice of the city's insurance on public properties, like the Civic Center and O'Hare Airport. There are no negotiations or competitive bidding. The policies are given to him because he is Joe Gill. How many votes does Prudential Life deliver? The city's premiums are about $500,000 a year, giving Gill's firm a yearly profit of as much as $100,000.

Another firm, founded by the late Al Horan, and later operated by his heirs and County Assessor P. J. Cullerton gets $100,000 a year in premiums from the city's park district. Since Cullerton is the man who sets the taxable value of all property in Cook County, it is likely that some big property owners would feel more secure being protected by his insurance.

When the city's sprawling lakefront convention hall was built, the insurance business was tossed at the insurance firm founded by George Dunne, a ward boss and County Board president.

Another old-line firm is operated by John D'Arco, the crime syndicate's man in the Central Committee. He represents the First Ward, which includes the Loop, a gold mine of insurable property. D'Arco has never bothered to deny that he is a political appendage of the Mafia, probably because he knows that nobody would believe him. A denial would sound strained in light of his bad habit of being seen with Mafia bosses in public. Besides, the First Ward was controlled by the Mafia long before D'Arco became alderman and ward committeeman.

D'Arco's presence in the Central Committee has sometimes been an embarrassment to Chairman Daley. Despite D'Arco's understandable efforts to be discreet, he can't avoid personal publicity because the FBI is always following the people with whom he associates. When D'Arco announced that he was leaving the City Council because of poor health, while remaining ward committeeman, the FBI leaked the fact that Mafia chief Sam Giancana had ordered him out of the council in a pique over something or other. Giancana could do that, because it is his ward; D'Arco only watches it for him. One of Giancana's relatives has turned up as an aide to a First Ward congressman. Another Giancana relative was elected to the state senate. At Daley's urging, the First Ward organization made an effort to improve its image by running a young banker for alderman. But the banker finally resigned from the council, saying that being the First Ward's alderman was ruining his reputation.

When he is asked about the First Ward, Daley retreats to the democratic position that the people elect D'Arco and their other representatives, and who is he to argue with the people? He has the authority, as party chairman, to strip the First Ward, or any ward, of its patronage, and there are times when he surely must want to do so. Raids on Syndicate gambling houses sometimes turn up city workers, usually sponsored by the First Ward organization. While he has the authority to take away the jobs, it would cause delight in the press and put him in the position of confirming the Mafia's participation in the Machine. He prefers to suffer quietly through the periodic flaps.

The question is often raised whether he actually has the power, in addition to the authority, to politically disable the Mafia. It has been in city government longer than he has, and has graduated its political lackeys to judgeships, the various legislative bodies, and positions throughout government. While it no longer is the controlling force it was in Thompson's administration, or as arrogantly obvious as it was under Kelly-Nash, it remains a part of the Machine, and so long as it doesn't challenge him but is satisfied with its limited share, Daley can live with it, just as he lives with the rascals in Springfield.

Ward bosses are men of ambition, so when they aren't busy with politics or their outside professions, they are on the alert for "deals." At any given moment, a group of them, and their followers, are either planning a deal, hatching a deal, or looking for a deal.

Assessor Cullerton and a circle of his friends have gone in for buying up stretches of exurban land for golf courses, resorts, and the like. Others hold interests in racetracks, which depend on political goodwill for additional racing dates.

The city's dramatic physical redevelopment has been a boon to the political world as well as the private investors. There are so many deals involving ranking members of the Machine that it has been suggested that the city slogan be changed from Urbs in Horto, which means "City in a Garden," to *Ubi Est Mea,* which means "Where's mine?"

From where Daley sits, alone atop the Machine, he sees all the parts, and his job is to keep them functioning properly. One part that has been brought into perfect synchronization is organized labor—perhaps the single biggest factor in the unique survival of the big city organization in Chicago. Labor provides Daley with his strongest personal support and contributes great sums to his campaigns. Daley's roots are deep in organized labor. His father was an organizer of his sheet-metal workers' local, and Bridgeport was always a union neighborhood. With politics and the priesthood, union activity was one of the more heavily traveled roads to success. Daley grew up with Steve Bailey, who became head of the Plumbers' Union, and as Daley developed politically, Bailey brought him into contact with other labor leaders.

Thousands of trade union men are employed by local government. Unlike the federal government and many other cities, Chicago always pays the top construction rate, rather than the lower maintenance scale, although most of the work is maintenance. Daley's massive public works projects, gilded with overtime pay in his rush to cut ribbons before elections, are another major source of union jobs.

His policy is that a labor leader be appointed to every policymaking city board or committee. In recent years, it has worked out this way: The head of the Janitors' Union was on the police board, the park board, the Public Buildings Commission, and several others. The head of the Plumbers' Union was on the Board of Health and ran the St. Patrick's Day parade. The head of the Electricians' Union was vice president of the Board of Education. The Clothing Workers' Union had a man on the library board. The Municipal Employees' Union boss was on the Chicago Housing Authority, which runs the city's public housing projects. The head of the Chicago Federation of Labor and somebody from the Teamsters' Union were helping run the poverty program. And the sons of union officials find the door to City Hall open if they decide on a career in politics.

The third major part of the Machine is money. Once again, only Daley knows how much it has and how it is spent. As party chairman, he controls its treasury. The spending is lavish. Even when running against a listless nobody, Daley may spend a million dollars. The amount used for "precinct money," which is handed out to the precinct captains and used in any way that helps bring out the Democratic vote, can exceed the entire Republican campaign outlay. This can mean paying out a couple of dollars or a couple of chickens to voters in poor neighborhoods, or bottles of cheap wine in the Skid Row areas. Republicans claim that the Democrats will spend as much as $300,000 in precinct money alone for a city election. To retain a crucial office, such as that of county assessor, hundreds of thousands have been spent on billboard advertising alone. Add to that the TV and radio saturation, and the spending for local campaigning exceeds by far the cost-per-vote level of national campaigning.

The money comes from countless sources. From the patronage army, it goes into the ward offices as dues, and part of it is turned over to party headquarters. Every ward leader throws his annual $25-a-head golf days, corned beef dinners, and picnics. The ticket books are thrust at the patronage workers and they either sell them or, as they say, "eat them," bearing the cost themselves.

There are "ward books," with page after page of advertising, sold by precinct workers to local businesses and other favor-seekers. Alderman Marzullo puts out a 350-page ad book every year, at one hundred dollars a page. There are no blank pages in his book. The ward organizations keep what they need to function, and the rest is funneled to party headquarters.

Contractors may be the best of all contributors. Daley's works program has poured billions into their pockets, and they in turn have given millions back to the party in contributions. Much of it comes from contractors who are favored, despite the seemingly fair system of competitive bidding. In some fields, only a handful of contractors ever bid, and they manage to arrange things so that at the end of the year each has received about the same amount of work and the same profit. A contractor who is not part of this "brotherhood" refrains from bidding on governmental work. If he tries to push his way in by submitting a reasonable bid, which would assure him of being the successful low bidder, he may suddenly find that the unions are unable to supply him with the workers he needs.

Even Republican businessmen contribute money to the Machine, more than they give to Republican candidates. Republicans can't do anything for them, but Daley can.

The Machine's vast resources have made it nearly impossible for Republicans to offer more than a fluttering fight in city elections. Daley, to flaunt his strength and to keep his organization in trim, will crank out four hundred thousand primary votes for himself running unopposed. His opponent will be lucky to get seventy thousand Republicans interested enough to cast a primary vote.

Unlike New York, Lost Angeles, and other major cities, Chicago has no independent parties or candidates jumping in to threaten, or at least pull votes away from the leaders. It is no accident. Illinois election laws are stacked against an independent's ever getting his name on a voting machine.

In New York, a regular party candidate needs five thousand signatures on his nominating petitions, and an independent must have seventy-five hundred. With any kind of volunteer organization, an independent can get the names, which is why New York will have half a dozen candidates for mayor.

The requirements are even less demanding in Los Angeles, where a candidate needs a seven-hundred-dollar filing fee and petitions bearing five hundred names. Los Angeles voters have a dozen or so candidates from which to choose.

But Chicago has never, in this century, had more than two candidates for the office of mayor. The state legislature took care of the threat from troublesome independents years ago.

When Daley files his nominating petitions, he needs about thirty-nine hundred names, a figure based on one-half of one percent of his party's vote in the previous election. Daley usually gets so many names that the petitions have to be brought in by truck. Using the same formula, his Republican opponent needs about twenty-five hundred signatures, which isn't difficult, even for a Chicago Republican.

But an independent would have to bring in about sixty to seventy thousand signatures. He needs 5 percent of the previous total vote cast. And not just anybody's signature: only legally defined independents, those who have not voted in the recent partisan primaries.

That's why there are only two candidates for mayor and the other offices in Chicago—a Republican and a Democrat. And sometimes there aren't even that many, Mayor Kelly having once handpicked his Republican opponent.

The only alternative for an independent is to run as a write-in candidate, a waste of time.

It has never happened, but if an independent somehow managed to build an organization big and enthusiastic enough to find seventy thousand independent voters who would sign his petition, he would probably need an extra thirty thousand signatures to be sure of getting past the Chicago Election Board, which runs the city's elections and rules on the validity of nominating petitions. Names can be ruled invalid for anything short of failing to dot an *i.* An illiterate's *X* might be acceptable on a Machine candidate's petition, but the Election Board is meticulous about those of anybody else.

The board used to be run by a frank old rogue, Sidney Holzman, who summed up its attitude toward the aspirations of independents, Republicans, and other foreigners: "We throw their petitions up to the ceiling, and those that stick are good."

Despite all these safeguards and its lopsided superiority over local opposition, the Machine never fails to run scared. For this reason, or maybe out of habit, it never misses a chance to steal a certain number of votes and trample all over the voting laws. Most of it goes on in the wards where the voters are lower middle class, black, poor white, or on the bottle. To assure party loyalty, the precinct captains merely accompany the voter into the voting machine. They aren't supposed to be sticking their heads in, but that's the only way they can be sure the person votes Democratic. They get away with it because the election judges, who are citizens hired to supervise each polling place, don't protest. The Democratic election judges don't mind, and the Republican election judges are probably Democrats. The Republicans assign poll watchers to combat fraud but they never have enough people to cover all of the precincts. If they prevented the common practices, imaginative precinct captains would merely turn to others. In some wards, politically obligated doctors sign stacks of blank affidavits, attesting to the illness of people they have never seen, thus permitting the precinct captain to vote the people in their homes as absentee voters for reasons of illness. And several investigations have established that death does not always keep a person's vote from being cast.

The aforementioned Holzman was always philosophical about vote fraud, conceding that it occurred, and even saying that "a good precinct captain will always find a way to steal votes," but asserting: "In city elections, we don't have to steal to win. And in statewide elections, the Republicans are stealing so much downstate, that all we do is balance it out."

Out of this vast amalgam of patronage, money, special interests, restrictive election laws, and organizational discipline emerge a handful of candidates, and they are what it is supposed to be all about.

Most of them come up through the system, as Daley did, beginning as doorbell ringers, working in the jobs their sponsors got for them, pushing the ward book, buying the tickets, doing the favors, holding the coats, opening the doors, putting in the fix, and inching their way up the organizational ladder, waiting for somebody to die and the chance to go to the legislature, into the City Council, and maybe someday something even bigger.

As hard as a party member may try, and as bright and presentable as he may be, he probably won't make it if he isn't from a strong ward with an influential ward boss. A loyal, hardworking City Hall lawyer can become a judge, if his ward brings in the vote and his sponsor pushes him, while in another ward, where the Republicans dominate and the ward boss just hangs on, the City Hall lawyer can only dream of his black robe.

Judge Wexler, Daley's night school classmate, lived with this problem. Wexler had worked feverishly as the city's chief prosecutor of slum cases, dragging landlords into court, reaping publicity for the mayor's administration, while deftly avoiding the toes of slum landlords who had political connections. For years he trotted into Daley's office with his news clippings. But when slate-making time came around, other people got to be judges.

"My ward committeeman was so weak, he couldn't do anything. I used to ask him for a letter to the Central Committee sponsoring me for a judgeship.

You have to have a sponsoring letter. And he'd say: 'A letter for you? I want to be a judge myself, and I'm not getting anywhere.' I would have never made it if it hadn't been for Daley and knowing him from night school. He did it for me personally." Wexler was fortunate. For the others with ambitions, it is either a strong committeeman and advancement, or an obscure job with nothing to put in the scrapbook.

Only one other shortcut exists, and it is part of the system of the Machine: nepotism. A Chicago Rip Van Winkle could awaken to the political news columns and, reading the names, think that time had stood still.

There was Otto Kerner, Cermak's confidante and a federal judge, and he begat Otto Kerner, governor, federal judge, and husband of Cermak's daughter; John Clark, ward boss and assessor, begat William Clark, attorney general and 1968 U.S. Senate candidate; Adlai Stevenson, governor and presidential candidate, begat Adlai Stevenson, U.S. senator; Dan Ryan, ward boss and county board president, begat Dan Ryan, ward boss and county board president; Edward Dunne, mayor, begat Robert Jerome Dunne, judge; John J. Touhy, ward boss and holder of many offices, begat John M. Touhy, Illinois House Speaker; Joe Rostenkowski, ward boss, begat Daniel Rostenkowski, congressman; Arthur Elrod, ward boss and county commissioner, begat Richard Elrod, sheriff; John Toman, ward boss and sheriff, begat Andrew Toman, county coroner; Thomas Keane, ward boss and alderman, begat Thomas Keane, ward boss and alderman; Joe Burke, ward boss and alderman, begat Edward Burke, ward boss and alderman; Paul Sheridan, ward boss and alderman, begat Paul Sheridan, alderman; Theodore Swinarski, ward boss, begat Donald Swinarski, alderman; David Hartigan, alderman, begat Neil Hartigan, ward boss and chief park district attorney; Louis Garippo, ward boss, begat Louis Garippo, judge; Michael Igoe, federal judge, begat Michael Igoe, county board secretary; Daniel McNamara, union leader, begat Daniel McNamara, judge; Thomas Murray, union leader and school board member, begat James Murray, congressman and alderman; Peter Shannon, businessman and friend of Daley, begat Dan Shannon, Park District president; Morgan Murphy, Sr., business executive and friend of Daley, begat Morgan Murphy, Jr., congressman; William Downes, real estate expert and friend of Daley, begat a daughter, who married a young man named David Stahl, who became deputy mayor; James Conlisk, police captain and City Hall favorite, begat James Conlisk, police superintendent; Daniel Coman, ward boss and city forestry chief, begat Daniel Coman, head of the state's attorney's civil division.

They are their brothers' keepers, too.

Alderman Keane keeps his brother on the powerful board of real estate tax appeals; Assessor Cullerton keeps his brother in the city council and his brother-in-law as his chief deputy assessor; Alderman Harry Sain kept his brother as city jail warden when sheriff; and County Board president Dunne keeps his brother as boss of O'Hare and Midway airports, and Congressman John Kluczynski keeps his brother on the state Supreme Court.

Nobody in the Machine is more family conscious than Chairman Daley. Cousin John Daley became a ward committeeman and served several terms in the state legislature, where his remarkable resemblance to the mayor sometimes unnerved his associates. Uncle Martin Daley had a well-paying job in county government that he did so skillfully he seldom had to leave his home. Cousin Richard Curry heads the city's legal department. Daley's four sons are just finishing law school, so their public careers have not yet been launched, but the eldest, Richard, at twenty-seven, was a candidate for delegate from his district to the state constitutional convention. He piled up the biggest vote in the state. The people in Bridgeport recognize talent. And the sons have been judge's clerks while going through school. When one of the mayor's daughters married, Daley promptly found a city executive job for the father of his new son-in-law.

Daley didn't come from a big family but he married into one, and so Eleanor Guilfoyle's parents might well have said that they did not lose a daughter, they gained an employment agency. Mrs. Daley's nephew has been in several key jobs. Her sister's husband became a police captain. A brother is an engineer in the school system. Stories about the number of Guilfoyles, and cousins and in-laws of Guilfoyles, in the patronage army have taken on legendary tones.

There are exceptions to the rules of party apprenticeship and nepotism. A few independent Democrats have been dogged enough to defeat weak Machine candidates in primaries for alderman, or, as happened once in the Daley years, for a seat in Congress. But it is never easy, and the strain leaves most independents so exhausted that most of them eventually embrace the Machine, at least gently, to avoid recurring primary struggles.

In theory, anybody can walk right into party headquarters at slate-making time, go before the ward bosses who make up the committee, and present themselves as prospective candidates. One political hanger-on, a disc jockey, even caught them in a mirthful mood, and when he actually got down on his knees and begged, they let him run for a minor office. But even the slate makers do not kid themselves into thinking they are deciding who the candidates will be. They listen to the applicants, push their favorites, the men from their wards, and wait for Chairman Daley to make up his mind. Some of the men on the slate-making committee have been surprised to find that they themselves were slated to run for offices they hadn't even sought. It is a one-man show, and they know it. This vignette illustrates it:

In 1968, slate makers were putting together their county ticket. They listened to the applicants, talked it over, then Daley and a couple of the party ancients came out of another room with the list.

Daley had decided that the strongest candidate for the crucial office of state's attorney, the county's prosecutor, would be Edward Hanrahan, a former federal prosecutor. It is a "must" office because a Republican would use it to investigate City Hall. Hanrahan was the strongest candidate because his Republican opponent also had an Irish name.

But slating Hanrahan required that the incumbent, John Stamos, who had been appointed to fill a vacancy, be shifted to something else. Stamos, a diligent and skilled young prosecutor, was Greek; Greeks were a small voting bloc, and Stamos was just professional and aloof enough to make some party elders nervous. Daley had decided to let Stamos run for the office of Illinois attorney general, which has prestige but less power and challenge. That completed the ticket.

Their decision made for them, the slate makers filed out of the conference room to go downstairs and meet the news media. As they came out, one of them saw Stamos and said, "Congratulations, John, you're going for attorney general."

"Bullshit," Stamos said, adding, "I won't go for it." Daley reasoned, but Stamos repeated, "Bullshit." And left the hotel.

While the slate makers stood around looking confused, Daley told a secretary to call Frank Lorenz, an obedient party regular who was between elective offices. She got him on the phone and Daley said, "Come on over, Frank, you're the candidate for attorney general."

One of the slate makers later said: "If Lorenz had stepped out to take a piss, he would have missed out, and the next guy Daley thought of would have got it, if he answered his phone. That's the way things are run sometimes, and everybody says we're so goddamn well organized."

A minute or two later, it was all resolved. Normally, Stamos would have been punished. But for party unity and to avoid alienating big Greek financial contributors, he was elevated to the state appellate court.

"You never know what in the hell is going to happen in there," a ward boss said. "He moves us around like a bunch of chess pieces. He knows why he's doing it because he's like a Russian with a ten-year plan, but we never know. I think his idea is to slate people who aren't going to try to rival him or add to someone else's strength. Look at how Cullerton got to be assessor. First he was a nothing alderman. He was a real nothing. But Daley put him in as finance chairman so he could have somebody who wouldn't get out of line. Then he put him in as assessor. Keane wanted assessor for his brother George. George would have loved it. Funny how people love to be assessor, haw! But Daley wasn't about to give Tom Keane the assessor's office, so he looked around and there was faithful Parky Cullerton.

"When he had to pick a chief judge, who were the logical guys? Neil Harrington, but he couldn't give it to Neil because he used to be part of the old South Side faction, and Daley wouldn't trust him. Harold Ward? He is independent, he might tell Daley to go screw himself or something.

"So he gave it to John Boyle, because he knew he'd have Boyle's complete loyalty. Why? Because Boyle had that scandal when he was state's attorney years ago and after that he couldn't get elected dogcatcher. He was a whipped dog, so he was perfect for Daley.

"And there's this thing he has with old people. Jesus, we've reslated people who were so senile they didn't even know what office they were running for. When it gets to that point, you know it has got to be something more than him being soft-hearted. There were some we could have just told them they were being reslated, and they would never have known the difference. He does it because then he doesn't have to worry about them. They'll sit there on the county board or wherever they are and do just what they're told.

"It's one-man rule, absolutely. It used to be that if Kelly got mad at you, there were seven or eight guys you could go to and get it squared. The same thing with Nash, and when Arvey was chairman. But there's only one Daley. You're dead if he doesn't like you. There's no point in going to someone to try to get it squared because they can't, and they won't even try because they're afraid it'll get him mad at them. He's a friend of mine, but he can be a mean prick."

Just how mean, and how subtle, was discovered by Arnold Maremont, a millionaire industrialist and art collector who decided he wanted to go into politics and to start at the top.

Daley does not dislike millionaires. He lets them contribute to the party, serve on advisory boards, take on time-consuming appointments, and help elect Machine Democrats to office.

Maremont had done it all. He contributed money, worked in Governor Kerner's campaign, led a campaign to pass a $150 million bond issue that revitalized the state's mental health program, and pitched in on numerous liberal causes and mental health and welfare programs.

His dream was to be a U.S. senator, and in early 1961 he went to Daley's office and told him that he'd like to run against Senator Everett Dirksen. He made it clear that he wanted to do it properly and not jump into the primary as a maverick. The party's blessing was what he was after.

Daley showed interest, but said he had certain reservations: mainly he wasn't sure if downstate county chairmen would support a Jew. He suggested that Maremont tour the state, talk to the county chairmen, and he indicated strongly that if Maremont made a good showing, he'd be Daley's man.

Maremont pushed aside his business and civic work and spent most of the early summer barnstorming through Illinois. A spunky, brash man, he'd walk into a bar in a tiny southern Illinois town—grits and gravy country—and announce: "My name's Arnold Maremont. I want to run for the Senate and I'm a Jew." People seemed to like him, as he wolfed down chicken-and-peas dinners at the county meetings, charming little old ladies and picking up support from the chairmen. All the while, he sent back regular reports to Daley: They will go for a Jew! Elated, he headed back to Chicago, ready to give Daley his final report and the good news. He got back to town just in time to pick up that day's papers and read that Daley had, indeed, decided to slate a Jewish senatorial candidate: Congressman Sidney Yates, a party regular.

That ended Maremont's political ambitions. Furious, he was convinced that Daley had merely used him to conduct a free one-man survey of downstate Illinois. He wouldn't have even tried had he ever heard Daley explain why he is so dedicated a party man: "The party permits ordinary people to get ahead. Without the party, I couldn't be mayor. The rich guys can get elected on their money, but somebody like me, an ordinary person, needs the party. Without the party, only the rich would be elected to office."

If Daley's one-man rule bothers the men who sit on the Central Committee, they are careful to keep it to themselves. The meetings take on the mood of a religious service, with the committeemen chanting their praise of his leadership. "It has been . . . my pleasure and honor . . . to give him my advice. . . . The greatest mayor . . . in the country . . . the world . . . the history of the world. . . ."

Only once in recent years has anybody stood up and talked back, and he was one of the suburban committeemen, generally referred to around party headquarters as "a bunch of meatheads."

The suburban committeeman, Lynn Williams, a wealthy manufacturer and probably the most liberal member of the Central Committee, had been angered by Daley's attacks on liberals after the 1968 Democratic convention. Daley had been making speeches lambasting pseudoliberals, liberal-intellectuals, suburban liberals, suburban liberal-intellectuals, and pseudoliberal-intellectual suburbanites. He had been shouting: "Who in the hell do those people think they are? Who are they to tell us how to run our party?"

Williams, a strong supporter of young Adlai Stevenson, who had angered Daley with an attack on "feudal" politics, stood up, finally, at a Central Committee meeting and delivered a scathing rebuttal to Daley, saying that without liberal participation the party would be nothing but a skeleton, its only goal, power. As he talked, the committeemen's heads swiveled as if they were watching a tennis game, wonder and fear on their faces. They had never heard such talk, and wondered what Chairman Daley would do. Strike him with lightning. Throw the bum out?

When Williams finished, Daley, in a surprisingly soft voice, said, "I've always been a liberal myself."

Other committeemen joined in his defense, recalling countless liberal acts by Daley. One man shouted at Williams, "Perhaps you didn't know, but this happens to be a very liberal outfit."

The shock of the committeemen at the sound of somebody criticizing Daley didn't surprise Williams. He has said: "Most of them are mediocrities at best, and not very intelligent. The more successful demonstrate cunning. Most are in need of slavery—their own—and they want to follow a strong leader."

In March 1970, the committeemen met for the purpose of reelecting Daley chairman. Alderman Keane nominated him and eighteen other committeemen made lengthy speeches seconding the nomination. One of them recited, "R, you're rare; I, you're important; C, you're courageous; H, you're heavenly; A, you're able; R, you're renowned; D, you're Democratic; J, is for your being a joy to know; D, you're diligent; A, you're adorable; L, you're loyal; E, you're energetic; and Y, you're youthful."

Once again Lynn Williams stood, but not to criticize. He, too, joined in the praise and made one of the seconding speeches. Daley had since slated young Adlai Stevenson III, whom Williams had supported, for the U.S. Senate. Daley and Williams even exchanged handshakes. In a way, Williams seemed to emphasize his own point about the committee's need to follow a strong leader.

PRESSURE GROUPS
AND LOBBYISTS

Chapter

Two

Since the publication of David Truman's classic, *The Governmental Process,* in 1951, many political scientists have become enamored of the "group theory" of politics.[1] Although the origins of group theory date back at least as far as John C. Calhoun, who stated its premises and implications in his posthumously published work, *A Disquisition on Government,* in 1853, real acceptance of the group theory did not come until the twentieth century. There are two essential premises of group theory: (1) individuals function in the political process only through groups; (2) the interaction of political interest groups produces the national interest. Today, group theory is not as widely accepted as it once was. Theodore Lowi, in particular, has led an attack on the group theorists' second assumption.[2] But the idea that politics is essentially a group process, rather than an individual process, remains largely unchallenged. The extreme expression of this view treats groups anthropomorphically, that is, as if they were persons. But groups are not mystical entities that can exist apart from the individuals who act as their leaders and members, or from the important intermediaries, such as the Washington lawyers, between pressure groups and government.

Individual character, personality, and style affect the ways in which pressure groups interact with government. The selections in this chapter have been chosen to demonstrate the personal dimension of the group process.

[1]David B. Truman, *The Governmental Process* (New York: Alfred A. Knopf, 1951).

[2]Theodore J. Lowi, *The End of Liberalism,* 2nd ed. (New York: W.W. Norton, 1979).

T HE PRACTICE OF LOBBYING IS as old as government itself. Lobbying styles and techniques have changed over the years in response to different political environments. The crasser forms of influence peddling in the nineteenth century, which often included outright bribery of state and national legislators, have given way to subtler techniques. A vast lobbying corps continues to roam the capital's corridors of power, seeking to influence legislators and other government officials. But laws as well as social and political customs circumscribe, at least to some degree, their freedom to act. They certainly cannot, for example, do what railroad tycoon Jay Gould did in attempting to influence the Albany legislature in his competition with railroad magnate Cornelius Vanderbilt in the late nineteenth century. Gould arrived in the state's capital with a valise stuffed with $500,000 in greenbacks with the obvious intention of bribing the lawmakers. His behavior, in the words of one of the time's chroniclers, had "the most frenzying and over-stimulating effect . . . which it would take many years of disciplined machine leadership to eliminate."[1]

While modern-day lobbying may be less crude than in the past, the Washington lobbying corps has expanded in numbers and power. Many individuals have turned positions of public trust into private gain as former congressmen, staffers, and administration officials become high-paid lobbyists. The following depiction of lobbying in the 1980s highlights the personalities, styles, and techniques that are involved. Also discussed is the perennial question of what, if any, limits should be placed upon lobbying.

9 Evan Thomas
INFLUENCE PEDDLING IN WASHINGTON

The hallway is known as "Gucci Gulch," after the expensive Italian shoes they wear. At tax-writing time, the Washington lobbyists line up by the hundreds in the corridor outside the House Ways and Means Committee room, ever vigilant against the attempts of lawmakers to close their prized loopholes. Over near the House and Senate chambers, Congressmen must run a gauntlet of lobbyists who sometimes express their views on legislation by pointing their thumbs up or down. Not long ago, Senator John Danforth, chairman of the Senate Commerce Committee, could be seen on the Capitol steps trying to wrench his hand from the grip of a lobbyist for the textile

[1]Quoted in Edgar Lane, *Lobbying and the Law* (Berkeley and Los Angeles: University of California Press, 1964), p. 24.

From *Time,* March 3, 1986. Copyright 1986 Time Inc. Reprinted by permission.

industry seeking new protectionist legislation. Though Danforth himself wants help for the shoe, auto, and agricultural industries in his native Missouri, the Senator—an ordained Episcopal minister—rolled his eyes heavenward and mumbled, "Save me from these people."

There have been lobbyists in Washington for as long as there have been lobbies. But never before have they been so numerous or quite so brazen. What used to be, back in the days of Bobby Baker, a somewhat shady and disreputable trade has burst into the open with a determined show of respectability. Tempted by the staggering fees lobbyists can command, lawmakers and their aides are quitting in droves to cash in on their connections. For many, public service has become a mere internship for a lucrative career as a hired gun for special interests.

With so many lobbyists pulling strings, they may sometimes seem to cancel one another out. But at the very least, they have the power to obstruct, and their overall effect can be corrosive. At times the halls of power are so glutted with special pleaders that government itself seems to be gagging. As Congress and the administration begin working this month to apportion the deepest spending cuts in America's history and to sort out the most far-reaching reform of the tax laws since World War II, the interests of the common citizen seem to stand no chance against the onslaught of lobbyists. Indeed, the tax bill that emerged from the House already bears their distinctive Gucci prints, and the budget is still filled with programs they have been able to protect.

Of course, the common citizen often benefits from various "special interest" breaks (for example, a deduction for home mortgages or state and local taxes). One man's loophole is another man's socially useful allowance, and one man's lobbyist is another man's righteous advocate. Nonetheless, the voices most likely to be heard are often the ones that can afford the best-connected access brokers.

As the legislative year cranks up, the whine of special pleaders resonates throughout the Capitol:

In the Senate Finance Committee, heavy industries like steel and autos, led by Veteran Lobbyist Charles Walker, are working to restore tax breaks for investment in new equipment that were whittled down last fall by the House Ways and Means Committee.

In the House and Senate Armed Services Committees, lobbyists for weapons manufacturers are fanning out to make sure that lawmakers do not trim their pet projects from the defense budget.

In the Senate Commerce Committee, business lobbyists are pressing for legislation to limit liability for defective products. They face fierce opposition from consumer groups and personal-injury lawyers.

Throughout the House and Senate, lobbyists for interests ranging from com-
mercial-waterway users to child-nutrition advocates are laboring to
spare their favorite federal subsidies from the exigencies of deficit reduction.

A superlobbyist like Robert Gray, a former minor official in the Eisenhower administration who parlayed his promotional genius and friendship
with the Reagans into a $20 million-a-year PR and lobbying outfit, is in the
papers more than most congressional committee chairmen. He would have his
clients believe that he is at least as powerful. "In the old days, lobbyists never
got any publicity," says Veteran Lobbyist Maurice Rosenblatt, who has
prowled the halls of Congress for several decades. "Congressmen didn't want
to be seen with notorious bagmen. But now," he shrugs, "the so-called best
lobbyists get the most publicity."

Influence peddling, says Jack Valenti, head of the Motion Picture Association and no mean practitioner of the craft, "is the biggest growth industry
around." The number of registered domestic lobbyists has more than doubled since 1976, from 3,420 to 8,800. That figure is understated, however,
since reporting requirements under a toothless 1946 law, are notoriously
lax. Most experts put the influence-peddling population at about 20,000—
or more than 30 for every member of Congress. Registered lobbyists reported expenditures of $50 million last year, twice as much as a decade ago,
but the true figure is estimated at upwards of $1.5 billion, including cam-
paign contributions.

What does the money buy? "Everybody needs a Washington representative to protect their hindsides, even foreign governments," says Senator Paul
Laxalt. "So the constituency for these people is the entire free-world economy." Joseph Canzeri, a former Reagan aide who calls himself a Washington
"facilitator," notes, "It's a competitive business. There are a lot of wolves out
there. But there are a lot of caribou in government too."

In the amoral revolving-door world of Washington, it has become just as
respectable to lobby as to be lobbied. Ronald Reagan may have come to
Washington to pare down the size of the Federal Government, but many of
his former top aides have quit to profit off Big Government as influence
peddlers. None has been more successful more swiftly than Reagan's former
deputy chief of staff Michael Deaver, who may multiply his White House
income sixfold in his first year out of government by offering the nebulous
blend of access, influence, and advice that has become so valued in Washington. Other Reaganauts now prowling Gucci Gulch include ex-Congressional
Liaison Kenneth Duberstein and two former White House political directors,
Lyn Nofziger and Ed Rollins. "I spent a lot of years doing things for love. Now
I'm going to do things for money," Rollins told the *Washington Post* after he
left the White House. By representing clients like the Teamsters Union,

Rollins, who never earned more than $75,000 a year in government, boasts that he can earn ten times as much.

Former administration officials are often paid millions of dollars by special interests to oppose policies they once ardently promoted. This is particularly true in the area of foreign trade, as documented by the *Washington Post* a week ago. For example, Reagan has ordered an investigation into the unfair trade practices of South Korea. That country will pay former Reagan aide Deaver $1.2 million over three years to "protect, manage and expand trade and economic interests" of the nation's industry. Deaver refuses to say exactly what he will do to earn his fee, but he has hired Doral Cooper, a former deputy trade representative in the Reagan administration, as a lobbyist for his firm. Japanese semiconductor and machine-tool firms are also charged by the administration with engaging in unfair trade practices. They have hired Stanton Anderson, who had served as director of economic affairs for the administration's 1980 transition team.

Foreign governments are particularly eager to retain savvy Washington insiders to guide them through the bureaucratic and congressional maze, and polish their sometimes unsavory images in the U.S. The Marcos government in the Philippines has retained the well-connected lobbying firm of Black, Manafort & Stone for a reported fee of $900,000. Another Black, Manafort client is Angolan rebel Jonas Savimbi. Not to be outdone, the Marxist regime of Angola hired Bob Gray's firm to front for it in Washington. Two years ago, Gray told *Time* that he checks with his "good friend," CIA Director William Casey, before taking on clients who might be inimical to U.S. interests. It is unclear just what Casey could have said this time, since the CIA is currently funneling $15 million in covert aid to Savimbi to help his rebellion against the Angolan regime. Last week outraged Savimbi backers chained themselves to a railing in Gray's posh offices in Georgetown and had to be forcibly removed by local police.

Lobbyists call themselves lawyers, government-affairs specialists, public relations consultants, sometimes even lobbyists. They offer a wide array or increasingly sophisticated services, from drafting legislation to creating slick advertisements and direct-mail campaigns. But what enables the big-time influence peddlers to demand upwards of $400 an hour is their connections. "I'll tell you what we're selling," says Lobbyist Frank Mankiewicz. "The returned phone call."

Old-time fixers such as Tommy "the Cork" Corcoran and Clark Clifford were not merely practiced lawyers but had some genuine legislative expertise to offer. Lately, however, Washington has seen the rise of a new breed of influence peddler, whose real value is measured by his friends in high places—particularly in the White House. Clifford prospered no matter who was in office; after the Reagans go home to California, it is hard to believe that Deaver or Gray will remain quite such hot commodities.

There is, and has long been, a strong whiff of scam about the influence-peddling business. Its practitioners like to imply that they have more clout than they truly do. In the post-Watergate era, power has been fractionated on Capitol Hill. Where a few powerful committee chairmen once held sway, Congress has become a loose federation of 535 little fiefdoms. This has made a lobbyist's job more difficult, but it hardly means that Congress has been liberated from the thrall of special interests. Well-intentioned congressional reform has been subverted over the years by the proliferation of lobbyists and the spiraling cost of election campaigns, two trends that go together like a hand and a pocket. The result has often been institutional paralysis. The very fact that Congress and the White House felt compelled to enact the Gramm-Rudman measure, requiring automatic spending cuts, is a monument to the inability of weak-willed legislators to say no to the lobbyists who buzz around them.

President Reagan has tried to sell his tax-reform bill as the supreme test of the public interest vs. the special interests. In pitching his campaign to the public, he has accused special interests of "swarming like ants through every nook and cranny of Congress," overlooking, perhaps, that many of the most prominent ants are his former aides. Few lobbyists, however, seem especially offended by his rhetoric, and certainly their livelihoods are not threatened. Indeed, many lobbyists candidly admit that true tax reform would actually mean more business for them, since they would have a fresh slate upon which to write new loopholes.

The way lobbyists have feasted on the president's tax-reform bill illustrates why the bill is known in the law firms and lobbying shops of K Street as the "Lobbyists' Full Employment Act." The 408-page proposal first drafted by the Treasury Department 16 months ago, known as Treasury I, was called a model of simplicity and fairness. It would have swept the tax code virtually clean of loopholes for the few in order to cut tax rates sharply for the many. But the 1,363-page tax bill sent by the House to the Senate last December is so riddled with exemptions and exceptions that the goal of fairness was seriously compromised, and simplicity abandoned altogether.

The lobbyists wasted no time biting into Treasury I. Insurance executives calculated that such loophole closings as taxing employer-paid life insurance and other fringe benefits would cost the industry about $100 billion over five years. Led by Richard Schweiker, who was President Reagan's Secretary of Health and Human Services before becoming head of the American Council of Life Insurance, the industry launched a $5 million lobbying campaign that can only be described as state of the art.

Even before the Treasury had finished drafting its original plan, the insurers were showing 30-second spots on TV that depicted a bird nibbling away at a loaf of bread labeled "employee benefits." An actress in the role of frightened housewife exclaimed, "We shouldn't have to pay taxes for protecting our family!" Life insurance agents around the country were revved up by a twelve-minute film entitled *The Worst Little Horror Story in Taxes.* In the film, Senate Finance Chairman Robert Packwood, a strong advocate of preserving tax breaks for fringe benefits, was shown urging the public to write their Congressmen. The insurers also mounted a direct-mail campaign that inundated Congress last year with 7 million preprinted, postage-paid cards. The campaign was successful: by the time the bill passed the House of Representatives last December, the insurance lobby figured that it had managed to restore about $80 billion of the $100 billion in tax breaks cut out by Treasury I. The insurers hope to win back most of the rest when the bill is reported out by the Senate Finance Committee this spring.

Threats to close a single loophole can bring scores of lobbyists rallying round. The original Treasury proposal sought to eliminate Section 936 of the U.S. Tax Code, which gives tax breaks worth some $600 million to companies that invest in Puerto Rico. Treasury Department officials conceded that the tax break helped create jobs by luring business to the island, but figured that each new job was costing the U.S. Treasury about $22,000. To defend Section 936, a coalition of some 75 U.S. companies with factories on the island formed a million-dollar "Puerto Rico-U.S.A. Foundation" and hired more than a dozen lobbyists, including Deaver. Last fall Section 936 advocates flew some fifty Congressmen and staffers to Puerto Rico on fact-finding trips.

Deaver, meanwhile, coordinated a lobbying campaign aimed at National Security staffers and officials in the State, Commerce, and Defense Departments. The strategy was to cast Section 936 as a way to revive the president's moribund Caribbean Basin Initiative and erect a bulwark against Communism in the region. Some two dozen companies with plants in Puerto Rico promised that if Section 936 was retained, they would reinvest their profits in new factories on other Caribbean islands. During a tense moment in the negotiations with the administration, Deaver even managed to place a ground-to-air call to Air Force I as it flew to the Geneva Summit last November. He wanted to alert Secretary of State George Shultz to stand fast against the maneuverings of tax reformers at the Treasury. Not surprisingly, the Treasury gnomes were overwhelmed. Later that month the administration committed itself to preserving Section 936.

The fabled "three-martini lunch," threatened by the Treasury Department's proposal to end tax deductions for business entertainment, was preserved as at least a two-martini lunch after heavy lobbying by the hotel and restaurant industry. In the House-passed bill, 80 percent of the cost of a business lunch can still be deducted. The oil-and-gas lobby managed to restore over half the tax breaks for well drilling removed by the original Treasury bill. Lawyers, doctors, and accountants won an exemption from more stringent new accounting rules. The lobbying by lawyers was a bit crude: Congressmen received letters that were supposedly written by partners of different law firms but were all signed by the same hand. No matter. Though congressional etiquette demands that each constituent's letter be answered personally, "We just let our word processors talk to their word processors," shrugged a congressional staffer.

The real deal making was done over so-called transition rules, which postpone or eliminate new taxes for certain individual businesses. The House-passed bill is studded with some 200 transition rules, which have been written to protect pet projects in a Congressman's district or large industries with particular clout on the Hill. Drafted behind closed doors, these rules are written in language designed to make it difficult to identify the real beneficiaries. One transition rule, for instance, waives the cutbacks on investment tax credits and depreciation for the fiberoptic networks of telecommunications companies that have committed a certain number of dollars for construction by a certain date. It turns out that just two companies profit from the exception: AT&T and United Telecom.

Not every lobbyist made out in the wheeling and dealing, by any means. Some were a little too greedy. The banking lobby pushed an amendment that would actually *increase* its tax breaks for bad-debt reserves. The lobbyists figured that they were just making an opening bid; their real aim was to protect existing tax breaks. To their surprise, however, the amendment passed in the confusion of an early Ways and Means Committee drafting session. When jubilant banking lobbyists began shouting "We won! We won!" outside the hearing room, some Congressmen became angry. Giving more tax breaks to the already well-sheltered banking industry was no way to sell voters on tax reform. The amendment was repealed.

Despite the predations of lobbyists, a tax-reform bill may be signed into law this year. But it must first survive the Senate, and already the advocates are queuing up to be heard. "I wish there were a secret elevator into the committee room," laments Senator David Pryor of Arkansas, a member of the Finance Committee. "Whenever I go there to vote, I try to walk fast and be reading something."

Some Congressmen may try to avoid lobbyists, but many have come to depend on them. "God love 'em," quips Vermont Senator Patrick Leahy. "Without them we would have to decide how to vote on our own." Sarcasm aside, lobbyists do serve a useful purpose by showing busy legislators the virtues and pitfalls of complex legislation. "There's a need here," says Anne Wexler, a former Carter administration aide turned lobbyist. "Government officials are not comfortable making these complicated decisions by themselves." Says Lobbyist Van Boyette, a former aide to Senator Russell Long of Louisiana: "We're a two-way street. Congress often legislates on issues without realizing that the marketplace has changed. We tell Congress what business is up to, and the other way around."

Lobbyists and government officials alike are quick to point out that lobbying is cleaner than in earlier eras, when railroad barons bought Senators as if they were so much rolling stock. "It's an open process now," says Jack Albertine, president of the American Business Conference, a trade association of medium-size, high-growth companies. "All sides are represented, the contributions are reported, and the trade-offs are known to everybody. In the old days you never knew who got what until a waterway project suddenly appeared in someone's district."

In some ways the growth of interest groups is healthy. Capitol Hill at times seems like a huge First Amendment jamboree, where Americans of all persuasions clamor to be heard. Movie stars plead on behalf of disease prevention, Catholic clerics inveigh against abortion, farmers in overalls ask for extended credit, and Wall Street financiers extol the virtues of lower capital-gains taxes. No single group dominates. When the steel, auto, and rubber industries saw the Reagan administration as an opening to weaken the Clean Air and Clean Water acts, the "Green Lobby," a coalition of environmental groups, was able to stop them.

But not every voter has a lobby in Washington, "Sometimes I think the only people not represented up here are the middle class," says Democratic Congressman Barney Frank of Massachusetts. "The average folks—that's what bothers me." Of course, that is not entirely true; many ordinary citizens are represented by such lobbies as the National Association of Retired Persons and Common Cause.

Lobbyists cannot afford to rely solely on well-reasoned arguments and sober facts and figures to make their case. In the scramble to win a hearing, they have developed all manner of stratagems designed to ingratiate themselves and collect IOUs.

Helping Congressmen get reelected is an increasingly popular device. Veteran Washington Lobbyist Thomas Hale Boggs, Jr., is on no fewer than 50 "steering committees" set up to raise money for congressional election campaigns. By night, "Good Ole Boy" Boggs can be found shmoozing at Capitol Hill fund raisers, where lobbyists drop off envelopes containing checks from political action committees at the door before digging into the hors d'oeuvres. By day, Boggs lobbies Congressmen, often the same ones for whom he has raised money the night before. Lately high-power political consulting firms such as Black, Manafort & Stone have taken not only to raising money for candidates but actually to running their campaigns: planning strategy, buying media, and polling. These firms get paid by the candidates for electioneering services, and then paid by private clients to lobby the Congressmen they have helped elect. In the trade this cozy arrangement is known as "double dipping."

Special-interest giving to federal candidates has shot up eightfold since 1974, from $12.5 million to more than $100 million by the 1984 election. Nonetheless, PACs can give no more than $5,000 to a single campaign, and all contributions are publicly filed with the Federal Election Commission. "Elections are so expensive that the idea of a PAC's having inordinate influence is ridiculous," says Boggs.

Some Congressmen are not so sure. "Somewhere there may be a race of humans who will take $1,000 from perfect strangers and be unaffected by it," dryly notes Congressman Frank. Says Congressman Leon Panetta of California: "There's a danger that we're putting ourselves on the auction block every election. It's now tough to hear the voices of the citizens in your district. Sometimes the only things you can hear are the loud voices in three-piece suits carrying a PAC check."

Even the most reputable influence peddlers use their political connections to build leverage. As director of the 1984 GOP Convention, Lobbyist William Timmons, a quietly genial man who represents such blue-chippers as Boeing, Chrysler, ABC, and Anheuser-Busch, controlled access to the podium. GOP Senators lobbied him for prime-time appearances. A *Wall Street Journal* reporter described Senator Pete Domenici of New Mexico, who was running for reelection in the fall of 1984, thanking Timmons a bit too effusively for allotting time for him to address the convention. "You told me you'd give me a shot," gushed Domenici. "So I appreciate it, Brother."

Family ties help open doors. Tommy Boggs's mother, Lindy, is a Congresswoman from Louisiana; his father, the late Hale Boggs, was House majority leader. Other congressional progeny who as lobbyists have traded on their names for various interests: Speaker Tip O'Neill's son Kip (sugar, beer, cruise ships); Senate Majority Leader Robert Dole's daughter Robin (Century 21 real estate); Senator Paul Laxalt's daughter Michelle (oil, Wall Street, Hollywood); and House Appropriations Committee Chairman Jamie Whitten's son Jamie Jr. (steel, barges, cork).

Then there is so-called soft-core (as opposed to hard-core) lobbying. Since the real business of Washington is often conducted by night, a whole cottage industry has grown up around the party-giving business. Michael Deaver's wife, Carolyn, is one of half a dozen Washington hostesses who can be hired to set up power parties, which bring top government officials together with private businessmen. "Facilitator" Canzeri puts on charitable events to burnish corporate images, like a celebrity tennis tournament that drew scores of Washington lobbyists and netted $450,000 for Nancy Reagan's antidrug campaign. Lobbyists, not surprisingly, work hard not just at reelecting Congressmen but also at befriending them. Congressman Tony Coelho of California describes the methods of William Cable, a former Carter administration aide who lobbies for Timmons & Co. "Three out of four times," says Coelho, "he talks to you not about lobbying, but about sports, or tennis—I play a lot of tennis with him—or your family. He's a friend, a sincere friend." Congressman Thomas Luken of Ohio is so chummy with lobbyists that he has been known to wave at them from the dais at committee hearings.

Congressmen often find themselves being lobbied by their former colleagues. More than 200 ex-Congressmen have stayed on in the capital to represent interest groups, sometimes lobbying on the same legislation they helped draft while serving in office. Former Congressmen are free to go onto the floor of Congress and into the cloakrooms, though they are not supposed to lobby there. "Well, they don't call it lobbying," shrugs Senator Pryor. "They call it visiting. But you know exactly what they're there for."

Congressional staffers also cash in by selling their expertise and connections. Indeed, members of the House Ways and Means Committee were concerned that the president's tax-reform bill would provoke an exodus of staffers into the lobbying ranks. Their fears were not unfounded: the committee's chief counsel, John Salmon, quit to work as a lobbyist for the law firm of Dewey, Ballantine; James Healey, former aide to Committee Chairman Dan Rostenkowski, quit to join Black, Manafort.

As Congressmen became more independent of committee chairmen and party chieftains, they have tended to listen more to the folks back home. Predictably, however, lobbyists have skillfully found ways to manipulate so-called grass-roots support. Direct-mail outfits, armed with computer banks that are stocked with targeting groups, can create "instant constituencies" for special-interest bills. To repeal a 1982 provision requiring tax withholding on dividends and interest, the small banks and thrifts hired a mass-mailing firm to launch a letter-writing campaign that flooded congressional offices with some 22 million pieces of mail. The bankers' scare tactics were dubious—they managed to convince their depositors that the withholding provision was a tax hike, when in fact it was set up merely to make people pay taxes that they legally owed. But the onslaught worked. Over the objections of President Reagan and most of the congressional leadership Congress voted overwhelmingly in 1983 to repeal withholding.

Onetime liberal activists who learned grass-roots organizing for such causes as opposition to the Vietnam War now employ these same techniques on behalf of business clients. Robert Beckel, Walter Mondale's campaign manager in 1984, has set up an organization with the grandiose title of the Alliance to Save the Ocean. Its aim is to stop the burning of toxic wastes at sea. Beckel's fee is being paid by Rollins Environmental Services, a waste-disposal company that burns toxic waste on land.

Grass-roots organizations sometimes collide. Lobbyist Jack Albertine recently established the Coalition to Encourage Privatization. Its public policy purpose: to enable private enterprise to run services now performed by the government. Its more immediate goal: to persuade Congress to sell Conrail to the Norfolk Southern Railroad. In the meantime, Anne Wexler has been building the Coalition for a Competitive Conrail, a farm-dominated group pushing for Morgan Guaranty as the prospective purchaser.

Booze, broads, and bribes—what nineteenth-century congressional correspondent Edward Winslow Martin called "the levers of lust"—are no longer the tools of the trade. This is not to say, however, that lobbyists have stopped wining and dining Congressmen and their staffs. Public records indicate that Ways and Means Chairman Rostenkowski spends about as much time playing golf as the guest of lobbyists at posh resorts as he does holding hearings in Washington.

Though it has become more difficult to slip a special-interest bill through Congress in the dead of night, it is not impossible. In 1981, when a group of commodity traders began lobbying for a tax loophole worth $300 million, then Senate Finance Chairman Dole poked fun at the commodity traders on the Senate floor. "They are great contributors. They haven't missed a fund-raiser. If you do not pay any taxes, you can afford to go to all the fund-raisers." But then commodity PACs and individual traders increased their contributions to Dole's own political action committee from $11,000 in 1981–1982 to $70,500 in 1983–1984. Dole, engaged in a campaign to become Senate majority leader, badly needed the money (his PAC contributed some $300,000 to 47 of the Senate's 53 Republicans). In a late-night tax-writing session in the summer of 1984, Dole quietly dropped his opposition to the tax break for the commodity traders, and it became law.

Such victories inspire other loophole-seeking businessmen to hire guides through the congressional maze, at any price. There is no shortage of hungry lobbyists ready to relieve them of their money. "You get hustlers in Washington who get hooked up with hustlers outside of Washington, and the money moves very quickly," says Peter Teeley, former press aide to Vice President George Bush and now a Washington PR man. "Some people are getting ripped off." Says Senator Pryor: "Businessmen are very, very naive. It's amazing what they pay these lobbyists. The businessmen panic. They really don't understand Washington."

As one of the most successful lobbyists in town, Bob Gray naturally has his detractors, and they accuse him of overselling businessmen on his ability to solve all their Washington problems with a few phone calls. "Gray is so overrated it's unbelievable," says one U.S. Senator. "He makes a big splash at parties, but his clients aren't getting a lot for their money." Gray insists that he never promises more than he can deliver. But his own clients sometimes grumble that, for a fat fee, they get little more than a handshake from a Cabinet member at a cocktail party.

When the big lobbying guns line up on opposite sides of an issue, they tend to cancel each other out. Threatened with a takeover by Mobil Oil in 1981, Marathon Oil hired Tommy Boggs's firm to push a congressional bill that would block the merger. The firm managed to get the bill through the House by using a little-known procedural rule at a late-night session. In the Senate, however, Mobil—represented by former Carter aide Stuart Eizenstat—was able to stop the bill when Senator Howell Heflin of Alabama blocked consideration on the Senate floor. Heflin is a friend of Mobil Chairman Rawleigh Warner.

"We're getting to the point of lobbylock now," says Lobbyist Carl Nordberg. "There are so many lobbyists here pushing and pulling in so many different directions that, at times, nothing seems to go anywhere." The most pernicious effect of the influence-peddling game may simply be that it consumes so much of a Congressman's working day. Every time a Congressman takes a PAC check, he is obliged at least to grant the contributor an audience. The IOUs mount up. "Time management is a serious problem," says Frank. "I find myself screening out people who just want to bill their clients for talking to a Congressman." The lobbyists are not unmindful of congressional impatience. Lobbyist Dan Dutko, for instance, has a "five-second rule"—all background documents must be simple enough to be absorbed by a Congress-man at the rate of five seconds per page. It is no wonder that Congress rarely takes the time to debate such crucial national security questions as whether the U.S. really needs to build a 600-ship Navy, as the Reagan administration contends; most Congressmen are too preoccupied listening to lobbyists for defense contractors telling them how many jobs building new ships will create back in the district.

In theory at least, there is a partial cure to the growing power of the influence-peddling pack: further limits on campaign expenditures and public financing of elections. But Congress is not likely to vote for these reforms any time soon, in large part because as incumbents they can almost always raise more money than challengers can. Certainly, most Congressmen have become wearily resigned to living with lobbyists. They are sources of money, political savvy, even friendship. In the jaded culture of Washington, influence ped-dlers are more envied than disdained. Indeed, to lawmakers on the Hill and policymakers throughout the Executive Branch, the feeling increasingly seems to be: well, if you can't beat 'em, join 'em.

Cashing In on Top Connections

After former White House Deputy Chief of Staff Michael Deaver quit last May to become a "public affairs consultant," he drove about town for a while in a dark blue Dodge, very much like the limousines that transport top Executive Branch officials. The car served to get Deaver where he was going in more ways than one: in status-conscious Washington, it was a not-so-subtle reminder of his White House connections. Now Deaver has given up the status symbol of public power for one of private wealth. These days he rides in a chauffeur-driven Jaguar XJ6 equipped with a car phone that keeps him plugged in to some of the highest offices in the land.

The onetime California PR man who followed Ronald Reagan to Washing-ton five years ago has cashed in. As a White House official, he had to moon-light by writing a diet book, while his wife Carolyn went to work for a PR outfit, throwing parties on behalf of private clients. But now a dozen corpora-tions and foreign countries, including CBS, TWA, South Korea, Singapore, and Canada, pay him annual retainers that are, he says, "in the six figures." This year he should take home around $400,000—at the White House, his top salary was $70,200.

What makes Deaver so valuable? "There's no question I've got as good access as anybody in town," says Deaver, as he reclines on a couch in his tastefully appointed office overlooking the Lincoln Memorial. Alone among departing White House aides, Deaver was permitted to keep his White House pass. He also still chats regularly on the phone with Nancy Reagan. But Deaver insists that he never discusses his clients' problems with the first lady or the president. Actually, Deaver says, he does not do much lobbying. Nor does he do any public relations work, or legislative drafting, or direct mail, or polling, or any of the sorts of services performed by most high-powered influence shops. So what exactly does he do?

"Strategic planning," he says somewhat airily. His clients tell him "where they want to be vis-à-vis Washington in three to five years, and I help them develop a plan to get there." In fact, although Deaver is a relative newcomer to Washington, it is hard to think of a lobbyist who has a better sense of how the Reagan administration works or who has more clout among the Reaganauts. And in a city where perception is often reality, Deaver is known as a master imagemaker who kept Reagan's profile high and bright. It is not hard to see why the government of South Korea, under fire for unfair trade practices abroad and repression of political dissidents at home, would want to hire him, even at Deaver's asking price of $1.2 million for a three-year contract. "There's a new breed in Washington," says Canadian Ambassador Allan Gotlieb. "Consultants about consultants." Canada hired Deaver—at $105,000 a year—for "his unique knowledge of how this government works from the inside," says Gotlieb.

There are some who think that Canada got more than gossip and advice from Deaver. Though the former deputy chief of staff was rarely involved in policy details at the White House, the *Washington Post* reports that before he left, he showed surprising interest in the debate over acid rain. It was Deaver who is believed to have persuaded Reagan to accede to the request of the Canadian government for a special commission to investigate the problem and make recommendations. The commission's report, issued in January, called for much stronger measures to reduce acid rain than the administration had previously sought.

Canada was one of the first clients signed up by Deaver. Acting on complaints from Democratic Congressman John Dingell of Michigan, the General Accounting Office is now investigating Deaver's role for possible conflict of interest. The public official turned private sage dismisses the charges, noting that while he played a role in creating the acid-rain commission, he had nothing to do with its report. "What I did at the White House was part of my public responsibilities. If I'd gone back there after leaving and tried to influence the acid-rain study, that would be a different story. But I really can't understand what the conflict is."

Under the Ethics in Government Act, Deaver is legally barred from discussing private business matters with anyone in the White House for a period of one year after leaving office. "I can't ask the president or anyone in the

White House for anything now," he shrugs. Then, brightening, he adds, "I can, starting in May, though."

The Slickest Shop in Town

A lobbyist can perform no greater favor for a lawmaker than to help get him elected. It is the ultimate political IOU, and it can be cashed in again and again. No other firm holds more of this precious currency than the Washington shop known as Black, Manafort.

Legally, there are two firms. Black, Manafort, Stone & Kelly, a lobbying operation, represents Bethlehem Steel, the Tobacco Institute, Herba-life, Angolan "Freedom Fighter" Jonas Savimbi, and the governments of the Bahamas and the Philippines. Black, Manafort, Stone & Atwater, a political-consulting firm, has helped elect such powerful Republican politicians as Senator Phil Gramm of Texas and Senate Agriculture Committee Chairman Jesse Helms.

The political credentials of the partners are imposing. Charles Black, 38, was a top aide to Senator Robert Dole and the senior strategist for President Reagan's reelection campaign in 1984. Paul Manafort, 36, was the political director of the 1984 GOP national convention. Roger Stone, 33, was the Eastern regional campaign director for Reagan in 1984 and is now one of Congressman Jack Kemp's chief political advisers. Peter Kelly, 48, was finance chairman of the Democratic National Committee from 1981 to 1985. Lee Atwater, 34, was Reagan's deputy campaign manager in 1984 and is now Vice President George Bush's chief political adviser. Alone among the firm's partners, Atwater sticks to advising electoral candidates and does not lobby.

The partners of Black, Manafort say that the lobbying and political-consulting functions are kept separate. "It's like a grocery store and a hardware store," insists Black. "You can't buy eggs at a hardware store and you can't buy tires at the grocery." Yet these are but fine distinctions in Washington, where the firm is considered one of the most ambidextrous in the business, the ultimate supermarket of influence peddling. "You are someone's political adviser, then you sell yourself to a corporation by saying you have a special relationship with Congress," says Democratic Media Consultant Robert Squier, who does no lobbying himself. Is it proper to get a politician elected, then turn around and lobby him? "It's a gray area," sidesteps Squier. Charges Fred Wertheimer, president of the public-interest lobbying group Common Cause: "It's institutionalized conflict of interest."

It certainly is good for business. The partners charge six-figure fees to lobby and six-figure fees to manage election campaigns. As a result, they take home six-figure salaries. (Their stated aim is to make $450,000 apiece each year; they are assumed to have achieved it last year.) They unabashedly peddle their access to the Reagan administration. The firm's proposal soliciting the Bahamas as a client, for instance, touted the "personal relationships between State Department officials and Black, Manafort & Stone" that could be "utilized to upgrade a backchannel relationship in the economic and foreign policy spheres."

When Savimbi came to Washington last month to seek support for his guerrilla organization, UNITA, in its struggle against the Marxist regime in Angola, he hired Black, Manafort. What the firm achieved was quickly dubbed "Savimbi chic." Doors swung open all over town for the guerrilla leader, who was dapperly attired in a Nehru suit and ferried about in a stretch limousine. Dole had shown only general interest in Savimbi's cause until Black, the Senate majority leader's former aide, approached him on his client's behalf. Dole promptly introduced a congressional resolution backing UNITA's insurgency and sent a letter to the State Department urging that the U.S. supply it with heavy arms. The firm's fee for such services was reportedly $600,000.

The Black, Manafort partners have woven such an intricate web of connections that the strands become entangled at times. Lobbyist Kelly served as finance chairman of the National Democratic Institute, a public-interest organization established by Congress to promote democracy in underdeveloped countries. The institute recently sent observers to try to ensure a fair election in the Philippines. Yet Kelly's firm, for a reported $900,000 fee, represents Philippine President Ferdinand Marcos, who stands accused of having stolen the vote. Manafort for one sees no conflict. He points out that the firm urged Marcos to try to make the elections more credible to American observers. "What we've tried to do is make it more of a Chicago-style election and not Mexico's," he explained.

As a political firm, Black, Manafort represents Democrats and Republicans alike—and sometimes candidates running for the same seat. Kelly, for instance, is doing some fund raising for Democratic Senate candidates John Breaux in Louisiana, Bob Graham in Florida, and Patrick Leahy in Vermont. Atwater and Black are consultants for the Republican opponents in these contests. In the race for the 1988 Republican presidential nomination, Atwater advises Bush, while Stone advises Kemp. Stone and Atwater's offices are right across the hall from each other, prompting one congressional aide to ask facetiously, "Why have primaries for the nomination? Why not have the candidates go over to Black, Manafort & Stone and argue it out?"

Stone and Atwater present a contrast in styles. Stone, who practices the hardball politics he first learned as an aide to convicted Watergate co-conspirator Charles Colson, fancies $400 suits and lawn parties. With his heavy-lidded eyes and frosty demeanor, he openly derides Atwater's client, Vice President Bush, as a "weenie." Atwater, an impish "good ole boy" from South Carolina, wears jeans and twangs an electric guitar. Both, however, drive Mercedes.

For all its diverse interests, the firm remains "loyal to the president," says Black. "We would never lobby against Star Wars, for example." The firm has nonetheless attacked the president's tax-reform bill on behalf of corporate clients seeking to preserve their loopholes, and it did not hesitate to lobby for quotas on shoe imports on behalf of the Footwear Industries of America, even though Reagan strongly opposed the bill as protectionist. And at times the firm does show some selectivity. A few years back, it turned down Libya's Muammar Qaddafi as a client.

T HE FOLLOWING SELECTION continues the theme of the preceding one, stressing that a major way in which money talks in Washington is to hold out the lure to public servants that once they leave government they will be able to profit from their experience by obtaining lucrative jobs. Top government officials obtain valuable experience and contacts that can put them in good stead later in the private sector. But ethics laws constrain what public officials can do for a period of time after they leave office; they cannot, over the short term, profit from their prior government experience. However, the possibility always exists that at least some officials while still in office, with a view toward their private sector future, may bend what they are supposed to do in the public interest in the direction of special interest demands.

10 Haynes Johnson
WHEN MONEY TALKS, WASHINGTON LISTENS

Joseph A. Califano, Washington insider, examined the invitations he had received in the morning mail: To attend a breakfast honoring a congressman—and contribute $250. To another breakfast for a congressman—and another $250. To a kickoff breakfast for a political campaign committee—and $1,000. To black tie dinners for Democratic candidates—and $1,000 each. To an event honoring a congressional committee chairman too busy with Washington duties to campaign in his home district—and $250. To a dinner honoring the years of public service of a retiring U.S. senator—another $1,000. To separate functions for three other members of Congress—and contributions of $250 to $350 apiece.

"For the last year I've kept all the invitations to fund-raisers I've received," said Califano, a Washington lawyer, former Cabinet officer and presidential adviser. "It's mind-blowing. In just a year I've got well over a couple of thousand invitations to fund-raisers of one kind or another, from both parties."

Other participants in Washington's political circus say they receive the same inundation of requests for money—one of every three pieces of mail he receives, according to one prominent lawyer.

Of course, Califano and others like him are being asked for money partly because they are making so much themselves. Colleagues say Califano earns nearly $1 million a year providing advice and legal counsel based in part on

From *Washington Post National Weekly Edition,* May 12, 1986. Copyright 1986 *The Washington Post.* Reprinted by permission.

experience gained during his years as a White House aide and as secretary of Health, Education and Welfare.

Money plays a vastly greater role in the political life of the capital than it did a generation ago, according to many involved then and now. There is more of it to be made, they say, and more people seeking to make it more openly, and more blatantly, than ever. That is the first point many of them make about what might be called the "Deaver Syndrome," the rush of former government officials to profit from private dealings with the government they just served.

Not that the relationship between money and politics presents a new phenomenon in Washington. Money continues to be the "mother's milk of politics," the common denominator of the democratic system.

There is nothing new, either, about the city's recurrent seizures of conscience over the state of capital ethics like the one provoked recently by questions growing from the Washington dealings of Michael K. Deaver. This trusted adviser and public relations counselor to Ronald Reagan instantly translated his government contacts and access to high places into a multimillion-dollar business when he left the White House last May.

Since the days of George Washington, former high government officials have offered to sell their valued expertise and access to policymakers and legislators in Washington. Since then, too, tales of capital corruption have repeatedly scandalized or titillated the nation.

But today's capital ethics do seem new. Old-style corruption—venal politicians exchanging votes and favors for cash, vicuna coats and Persian rugs—is for the most part a thing of the past. At least that is the belief of a score of prominent, longtime Washingtonians interviewed about the present ethical climate of the nation's capital, many of whom agreed to speak about what one called "this sensitive subject" only if their names were not used.

In place of the old venality, many of those interviewed say, is a new prevailing attitude, symbolized now by the Deaver case—an attitude of insensitivity to the appearance of conflicts of interest.

"What's different is very clear," says Fred Wertheimer of Common Cause, the self-described citizens' lobby. "As a given, there's always been influence peddling, inside dealing . . . ranging from activities that might fit the definition of acceptable conduct to improprieties to ethical violations to statutory violations to criminal violations. This administration does not recognize this area as an issue. It is a nonissue, a nonreality, and I question whether you could find any presidential statement [from Reagan] explaining why it's important to have honesty and integrity in government, why you need standards of public service. . . .

"There is no message coming out of this administration that anything is wrong about all this. Now that's different. In the past, the key to influence peddling was that it was secret, private, people didn't know about it. Why?

Because it was considered wrong. Not necessarily by the people who did it, but ultimately it was judged wrong in the public arena. When it came out on the table, it lost. Now blatant public influence peddling is fine. . . .

"I have this image that I play around with of an administration that rode in from the West to tame the evil government, and rode in with the fresh air of the West to clean up this polluted air center, and now they're moving in, they're running around town like classic Washington insiders and they are feeding off the government."

That may be an exaggeration, but different attitudes about the lines between public and private life in Washington do seem to be reflected at top levels of the Reagan administration. An incident at the White House underscored this.

The president had invited members of the committee appointed to oversee his presidential library to a dinner. As one person who was there recalled:

"He had a big breakfast the next day in the White House and the head of the Hoover Institution [Dr. W. Glenn Campbell], who's head of the Reagan library committee, got up and said two things which showed how really insensitive some of these people are to this problem. He said, 'You know we have the tremendous advantage of raising money for this library while there's a sitting president.' Two, he says, 'You notice we have Mrs. Weinberger on this committee [Defense Secretary Caspar's wife]. Oh, boy, when Mrs. Weinberger goes to those defense contractors.' He said that. Just totally insensitive. But that's what this is all about. That's the story."

Asked about that incident, Campbell says, "I may or may not have said something close to that. The fact that we have a sitting president is self-evident, isn't it? There's no question about that. Now Mrs. Weinberger is a member of the Board of Governors and I may have said something like that as a joke, and only as a joke. To the best of my knowledge Mrs. Weinberger would never approach defense contractors. She has too much good sense to do so, and I have not and would not ever ask her to do so. This teaches me again that in Washington you cannot even make a joke without someone misinterpreting it as a serious remark."

Reagan met with key backers of his library project in Los Angeles just before leaving on his trip to Asia. Campbell said there that he hopes to raise $80 million to $100 million, but added that the list of donors will not be released.

For much of its history, Washington has attracted ambitious people seeking power and profit as well as opportunities to serve the public. And for much of its history, the making of deals and trading of influence was an accepted staple of Washington life.

It is said, for instance, that when Congress was debating whether to grant federal land to the railroads, the lobbyists literally "camped in brigades around the Capitol building." In the Ulysses S. Grant administration, when lobbyists bought and sold congressmen like sacks of potatoes and influence peddling became enshrined as a political device, Mark Twain captured the corruption in Washington during what he called "The Gilded Age." A decade later, Henry Adams, scion of presidents and social arbiter of Washington manners and morals, also turned to fiction to describe in his *Democracy* the story of a "political society full of corruption, irresponsible ambition, and stupidity."

That kind of climate, perhaps always exaggerated, continued into this century, producing scandals from Teapot Dome to Watergate that reinforced the public impression of Washington as a center of corruption. At the same time, each scandal brought a reaction and, over time, new laws, ethical codes of conduct for government, and greater public awareness and scrutiny, especially in the so-called post-Watergate era.

Public scrutiny, public disclosure, whistle-blowing, and increasing use of leaks from within government about wrongdoing have exerted a powerful check on corruption, longtime Washingtonians agree. The new rules have made it much easier to expose cases of malfeasance, a fact that may contribute to the large numbers of Reagan administration officials caught in embarrassing situations since 1981.

Today's corruption, if such a word applies, stems more from changing attitudes that make "cashing in" more acceptable, from the proliferation of lobbying groups and political action committees and from the greater amounts of money to be made.

More people appear to be drawn to government not as a career, but as a means to cash in on their public service as quickly and profitably as possible, according to lawyers and lobbyists. One observer describes this as the desire "to do two years and then come out and make a big hit. They all think that they're going to be able to be bigger earners, bigger hitters, than they were before they went in. I'm not sure it works, but that's the mythology, that's the legend, and they do come [to town] with that in mind."

At the same time, the number of jobs in which people are paid to try to influence policy in Washington has mushroomed, in private business and in the "public interest" sector. For example, the files of the Foundation for Public Affairs include the names of about 2,500 public interest organizations representing almost every conceivable political viewpoint—and all involved in the legislative or lobbying process.

Add these to the public relations firms such as that founded by Deaver after leaving the White House, the growing number of law firms, consulting groups, corporate and union offices, and firms dealing with foreign governments, and one has an enormously expanding world of people seeking to influence the government.

But according to many Washington insiders, the results these "fixers" achieve often are negligible. Obviously, special interest lobbying can produce tangible results in the form of tens of millions of dollars for clients on such major congressional legislation as the 1981 tax bill. Still, the view is widely held that much "rainmaking" is as fraudulent as . . . well, as attempts to make rain.

"My judgment has been that most of the time the people who are taking the huge fees are guilty of false pretenses," says one person intimately involved with the lobbying process. "Not in the criminal sense that you could prosecute them for it, but they're total charlatans because they can't do anything. In a sense, they're really stealing from a bunch of scoundrels. And the con men out there who are coming in here to create the fix, you know, are the biggest patsies in the world. So it's just a bunch of con men working on each other and I don't think they affect the result.

"It's a rarity when you see an important decision in government affected by an old school tie or an attempt to influence the official. I don't really think there is the kind of corruption or venality in government that the existence of all these fixers suggests. The principal corruption is the corruption of the pretenses *they* make as to what they can do when they lift these gargantuan fees off these hicks when they come to Washington. They come in, you know, with shoes and they go out without shoes."

Those involved in the process of representing clients who deal with the government resent being tagged as "influence peddlers," and see much of the news media as naively preoccupied with the occasional scandal while missing the larger picture of the way the process works.

Leonard Garment, who served in the Nixon White House and now practices law in Washington, says, "I don't think this city could work without lobbyists. Nor would the Constitution actually be a live enterprise without lobbies because that's the way one petitions for the redress of grievances.

"This is a country that is so large that the federal notion of representative government saturates our life, and that's very much the case with lobbying. Is it different now than it has been in an earlier time that I'm familiar with? Yes, but everything is bigger. . . .

"And a lot more of people who had nothing to do with government. They come here not to be part of the public life experience. They come here to be lobbyists. It's like becoming a periodontal surgeon without going to dental school. They're working on the patients without much in the way of real experience. . . .

"And everybody's got a lobbyist. It's like private businesses having jet aircraft. The accoutrements of modern life. . . . The general impression is that unless you have somebody representing you, you're in trouble. It's clumsy but roughly correct that they are like a lot of blind people groping in a closet. They know they should have somebody to explain the jargon, to read the hieroglyphics of this mysterious pre-Mayan culture called Washington. And they're told that there are this whole group of special guys that you find at the headwaters of the Potomac and if you say the right words they'll put you in a canoe and take you up there and help you find your way into the mysterious culture."

"I'll tell you what's different about Washington now," says a lobbyist for a major trade association who for years was a key congressional aide. "Money. It's just more pervasive. This proliferation of the PACs [political action committees], these around-the-clock fund-raisers. . . . All for money. Everyone expects it. It has to be done. You have to raise that money—'hitting the drum,' as they say—and you have to give it.

"Unless you hit the drum, you're not in the game. Unless you give your 'max' [a PAC can contribute a maximum of $5,000 per election to a candidate, and an individual citizen can give up to $1,000 per candidate], unless you lay out your $5,000 at a fund-raiser, you don't have access. Now that only buys a return call. I'll give you a concrete example of what money buys. I can take out of my pocket right now and show you a line in the proposed tax legislation that, if deleted, will cost my industry billions of dollars—billions, that is. Now this afternoon, three lobbyists—big, big contributors—are meeting with Sen. X on the tax bill. Others can't get in the front door. So the question is which one gets to tell his message directly. And if you don't go to those fund-raisers, if you don't hit the drum, if you don't 'max out,' you don't get in the door. They don't even return your phone calls."

To Califano, the new importance of money has had an adverse effect on the political system: "The influence of money has turned Congress into an institution that resembles the state legislatures in the days of Lincoln Steffens."

To others, such as former senator J. William Fulbright, the Arkansas Democrat whose congressional hearings on corruption at the end of the Truman administration led him then to decry "the moral deterioration of democracy," today's climate makes the past seem almost innocent. "We never even had fund-raisers here when I was in the Senate," says Fulbright, now a Washington lawyer. "They were all held in Arkansas."

The new flood of money, coupled with the flow of people from government into private practice in Washington, leads some to fear that the situation is bound to grow worse. One lobbyist speaks darkly about a "return to the Robber Baron era," when the "special interests" were virtually able to dictate legislation.

Most interviewed, however, were far less pessimistic. Many argue that a rigorous application of existing rules and guidelines would head off a new era of venality.

"There happens to be, in my view, a good set of rules about ethical conduct on the books . . . " Common Cause's Wertheimer says. "But ethical conduct is a combination of things. It's rules and guidelines. It's attitudes and atmosphere. It's oversight and enforcement. So we have the rules and the guidelines to a good degree. We have neither the attitudes and atmosphere nor the enforcement. And it all goes back to the tone established by this administration."

P OLITICAL ACTION COMMIT-
tees (PACs) have become a major
force in American politics. Corporations, labor unions, trade and professional associations, and political groups
of all kinds form PACs to channel money
into political causes. Ironically, the campaign finance laws of the 1970s that were
designed to limit the influence of money
in political campaigning encouraged the
formation of PACs by explicitly providing
for their establishment and defining the
ways in which they could contribute to
and spend in behalf of political candidates and causes.

First Amendment freedoms of association and expression prohibit governmental interference with group formation
and, under the doctrine of *Buckley v.
Valeo* (1976), prevent the government
from limiting *indirect* group expenditures
in behalf of political candidates. At the
same time, however, the Buckley case
upheld limits on *direct* individual and
group *contributions* to political candidates. It is always important to keep in
mind that PACs are perfectly legitimate
organizations and PAC activity in behalf
of political candidates is constitutionally
protected political expression. Nevertheless attacks upon "special interest" politics that PACs represent is commonplace.
Even members of Congress who receive
large PAC contributions do not hesitate
to criticize PACs publicly, a tactic they
find politically profitable and one which
the PACs themselves ignore as an understandable part of campaigning. In the
meantime, as the following case study illustrates, PACs continue to pressure
powerful members of Congress through
campaign donations and direct lobbying
to protect their interests.

11 Chuck Alston
PACS AND THE BATTLE
FOR CLEAN AIR

Industries fighting over clean-air legislation contributed nearly $612,000 to
the campaigns of House Energy and Commerce Committee members in
1989—the year barriers that had blocked committee action on air pollution
for 12 years began to fall.

Auto, steel, chemical, oil, natural gas, coal, and electric utility interests
gave Rep. Philip R. Sharp, D-Ind., who chairs the Energy and Power Subcommittee, 21 cents of every dollar he raised last year—$36,025 in all. These same
interests supplied Rep. Joe L. Barton, a junior Republican from Texas and
former oil company engineer, with $28,000, or 33 cents of every dollar he took
in from political action committees (PACs).

By contrast, Rep. Henry A. Waxman, D-Calif., who tried to push strong
environmental amendments through his Health and the Environment Sub-

From *Congressional Quarterly Weekly Report,* March 17, 1990, pp. 811–817. Copyright
1990 by Congressional Quarterly, Inc. Reprinted by permission.

committee, got stiffed. He took in just $4,000, most of it from hometown interests.

In all, nearly a nickel of every dollar that committee members raised in 1989—an average of about $15,000 each—came from one of 154 PACs *Congressional Quarterly* identified as having a significant stake in the outcome of the clean-air bill. The tally is based on Federal Election Commission (FEC) reports filed by the candidates and the PACs.

The Bottom Line
- Total 1989 contributions to House Energy and Commerce members from political action committees with a major interest in clean-air legislation—$611,945
  - Number of PACs—154
  - Average per member—$14,570
  - Percentage of members' PAC contributions—7.6%
  - Percentage of members' total contributions—5.2%

The biggest PACs—the 17 whose spending topped $10,000—clearly stepped up their efforts in 1989. Their donations increased 55 percent to $223,125 in 1989, compared with 1987, the last nonelection year. "There is more money available to an industry when they have something hot," says Rep. Al Swift, D-Wash.

Clean-air legislation is by no means the sole concern of an electric utility, a natural-gas distributor, an oil refiner or an automaker, particularly in a committee given wide berth to regulate the nation's commerce. Just last year, for instance, the committee handled legislation eliminating natural-gas price controls. These PACs' 1989 contributions, moreover, represent only a fraction of the tens of millions of dollars their industries have spent for political donations to members of Congress over the past decade. The campaign for reelection money has escalated to the point where lobbyists and members can dismiss tens of thousands of dollars as insignificant.

"It's not a lot of money in the overall scheme of things," says Thomas Dennis, a Washington-based regional vice president of Southern California Edison Co., and electric utility. Kansas Republican Bob Whittaker, a committee member who plans to leave Congress after this year, says: "$15,000 doesn't sound like that much, although it was a nonelection year. The average committee member can raise $25,000 from PACs."

Even so, the industry contributions to Energy and Commerce members shed light on the political economy of legislation in the House's "money committees." And what is unmistakable is the financial embrace of the regulators and the regulated, a relationship under increasing scrutiny as Congress grapples with campaign-finance issues.

The Energy and Commerce Committee tends to the nation's rails, trucks and airwaves, its environment, health and telephones. It oversees Hollywood, Wall Street and the Oil Patch. A seat on the committee makes raising campaign money as easy as licking the stamps for invitations to fund-raisers.

Few inside the process contend that PACs try to buy votes outright. Rather, the spending reflects the cost of doing business in Washington. Companies, unions, and trade associations want to make sure their voices are heard clearly in a committee where decisions worth millions in profits are frequently decided by one or two votes. Donations also ensure that like-thinking candidates enjoy a well-stocked war chest to face reelection.

"There is so damn much money out there that anybody who gives anybody anything for it is an idiot," Swift says. "If you can't get it from the oil guys, you can get it from the natural-gas guys. If you can't get it from the communication guys, you can get it from the rail guys."

Columbia Gas Gets Competitive

Business and labor PACs gave $136 million to congressional candidates for the 1988 elections, one-third of all the money candidates raise, according to FEC records. About $11.9 million of this came from industries interested in clean-air legislation, according to the Center for Responsive Politics, a Washington-based organization that studies Congress.

The recent history of the Columbia Gas System, a Wilmington, Del.-based natural-gas producer, transmitter and distributor, illustrates the extent to which PACs have become an essential adjunct to a Washington lobbying operation.

The $3 billion company sells natural gas primarily in Northeast and mid-Atlantic states. Add in its pipelines and wells, and Columbia's operations sprawl across 20 states and 90 congressional districts. Rick Casali, vice president in charge of the Washington office, says that while the company is one of the industry's largest, its PACs operation was among the smallest—until 1989.

"We had some adverse decisions that came out of federal regulatory agencies," Casali says. "That caused us to have to make some very serious decisions, cutting our dividend, things that employees really felt. We pointed out that Columbia's PAC was smaller than it should be. So we got major increases in the number of dollars and members in our PAC. That gave us a larger resource base to stay competitive with other industries."

Columbia's PACs spent $89,360 on contributions to federal candidates last year, close to the $116,325 they spent during the entire 1987–1988 election cycle.

Energy and Commerce members were among the chief beneficiaries. The Columbia Gas Employees Fund, the largest of the company's three federal PACs, increased contributions to committee members nearly fivefold to $12,275 in 1989, compared with 1987. Two smaller Columbia PACs chipped in another $10,325, for a total of $22,600. In all, one-fourth of its donations to federal candidates went to Energy and Commerce members.

"That's really our bread-and-butter committee in the House," Casali says, "because it handles so many issues that have an impact on our operations and our future business: natural-gas decontrol, legislation impacting the Public Utilities Holding Company Act, the Clean Air Act."

All of this sounds familiar to Joe Hillings, vice president for federal government affairs for Enron Corp. Like Casali, he makes the rounds of members' Capitol Hill cocktail parties where the entry fee is $250 and up and has been rising. Subcommittee chairmen charge as much as $650 a ticket.

Houston-based Enron, which operates more miles of pipeline than any other natural-gas company, uses typical criteria to decide which parties Hillings will attend. The PAC supports members representing its areas of service or operation, members on committees with relevant jurisdiction, pro-energy members and pro-business members. Of late it also has considered their stand on natural-gas decontrol.

Enron's contributions to committee members increased 43 percent to $12,000 in 1989, compared with 1987. A new arrival at Energy and Commerce in the 101st Congress, Alex McMillan, R-N.C., the former president of a grocery chain, was a first-time recipient of Enron money.

"He is now very much involved in our issues," Hillings says. "We want to have somewhat of a relationship."

Enron was not unique. After McMillan moved from the Banking Committee, the money he raised from PACs interested in clean-air legislation rose to $16,350 in 1989, compared with $5,700 in 1987. PACs sponsored by Alabama Power Co., Baltimore Gas & Electric Co., Atlantic Richfield Co., the Edison Electric Institute, the National Coal Association, Philadelphia Electric Co., Texas Utilities Co. and Virginia Electric & Power Co. took note of his arrival by giving to him for the first time.

"Because I had been in business 20 years, there seems to be a natural affinity," McMillan says. "My own impression is that support tends to follow interest, and not vice versa."

Like McMillan, Democrat Thomas J. Manton of New York moved to Energy and Commerce from Banking as the 101st Congress began. His contributions from industries interested in clean-air legislation surged 231 percent to $12,250 in 1989, compared with 1987. He collected more contributions from these industries, 26 compared with 12, and their average size increased to $471 from $308.

The Southern Co.: $7.5 Billion

The contributions pale in comparison with the money at risk in clean-air legislation itself. The cost to industry is expected to reach $20 billion or more annually. Much of it will be passed along to consumers through higher prices for gasoline, cars and electricity.

Consider the Southern Co., an Atlanta-based holding company that sells electricity to most of Georgia and Alabama and large sections of Florida and

Mississippi. Coal-fired plants generate 80 percent of its electricity. Most of them burn high-sulfur coal, a leading cause of acid rain. Southern tells lawmakers that installing what are known as scrubbers and bag houses at its plants to meet new emission standards for air toxics and acid rain would cost $7.5 billion in today's dollars and could force rate increases of 25 percent.

One way Southern's management has responded is to increase PAC contributions to committee members. At one of its subsidiaries, Alabama Power Co., the Employees Federal PAC doubled contributions to $12,450 in 1989, compared with 1987. Sister PACs at Georgia Power Co., Southern Co., Mississippi Power Co., and Gulf States Power Co. kicked in another $15,950, bringing the total to $28,400.

"Utilities are heavily regulated, and what Congress does can have a major impact on the company," Southern spokesman John Hutchinson says. "Our employees realize that."

Southern and Columbia are not alone in their multiple-PAC arrangement. Texas Utilities Co., the parent company of Dallas Power & Light and Texas Power & Light, maintains four PACs that together gave $12,500 to committee members.

It is no surprise that Sharp, the chief ally on the committee for coal-burning utilities has been one of the prime recipients of electric utility and coal money. The Midwestern utilities he speaks for would bear the brunt of acid-rain provisions. Sharp is one of the few Energy members who continually faces tough reelection battles.

Three times in the 1980s voters returned Sharp with less than 55 percent of the vote. He raised about two-thirds of the $444,422 he spent on his 1988 campaign from PACs, and his Republican opponent made an issue of it.

In 1989, $36,025, or 21 percent, of the money Sharp raised came from industries with a stake in clean-air legislation. Of this, $16,750 came from coal and electric utility interests.

Another Midwesterner, Republican Tom Tauke of Iowa, led the committee in clean-air fund raising, garnering $50,800. Tauke is running for the Senate, increasing his need for money. He expects to spend at least $5 million for his Senate race.

More than one-fifth of what Tauke raised came from makers of off-road construction and farm equipment. Caterpillar Tractor Co., Deere and Co. and Navistar International Corp. together contributed $11,000. Deere is a major employer in Iowa. A member of the Environment Subcommittee, Tauke was instrumental in negotiating a deal for a study of the air pollution caused by off-road vehicles before the government takes any action.

Choosing Among Members

Committee Chairman John D. Dingell's Michigan district is a microcosm of the nation's industrial heartland. It is home to Ford Motor Co. and a sprawling collection of auto factories, steel mills, foundries and chemical plants.

For years, he has been the chief defender of industry interests in the clean-air debate and a key reason legislation hasn't moved. One reason committee members do so well with these interests is that Dingell has used his clout to make sure recent Democratic appointments reflect his views.

Nonetheless, the chairman ranked fourth among committee members in this fund raising, with $31,750. Because his seat is safe and his war chest well armed ($268,707 at year's end), most Washington lobbyists consider his fund-raising demands modest. He holds but one Washington fund-raiser a year.

Three relatively junior committee members ranked just behind Dingell in fund raising even though they do not hold leadership positions, a fact best explained by geography. Democrat Ralph M. Hall and Republicans Barton and Jack Fields represent the Lone Star State, and their toughest moments come when they must make a Texan's choice between Mom and apple pie—oil and natural gas.

Fields and Hall were the chief sponsors of an amendment adopted 12–10 in the Health and the Environment Subcommittee in October 1989 that stirred a controversy when its adoption was portrayed as gutting a key portion of the Bush administration's clean-air legislation (HR 3030). The amendment weakened a provision that would have forced greater use in automobiles of alternative fuels such as natural gas. Oil companies and automakers—and, after considerable pressure from members and other lobbies to fall in line, even natural-gas interests—backed the Hall Fields amendment *(1989 Weekly Report,* p. 2700).

Texas's natural-gas interests carried no grudges. "We consider everyone in the Texas delegation pro-energy and extremely important," natural-gas lobbyist Hillings says.

Such sentiment helped Barton, Hall and Fields each surpass the $24,000 mark. A fourth Texan, Democrat John Bryant, raised $10,650, a figure that does not reflect his entire fund-raising effort in 1989. He spent most of the year raising money for a state campaign for attorney general, a race he abandoned late in the year.

Republicans fared better than Democrats. The 17 Republican members raised $17,278 each. The 25 Democrats on the committee as of Feb. 15 raised $12,729 each.

The bottom end of the fund-raising totem pole was filled with liberals, lame ducks and members who for various reasons avoid PACs. Consistent environmental votes such as Democrats James H. Scheuer of New York, Gerry Sikorski of Minnesota, Cardiss Collins of Illinois and Jim Bates of California fared poorly.

Jim Cooper, who raised $1,300, falls in the category of those who eschew PACs, a relatively new stance for the moderate Tennessee Democrat made possible in part by a peaceful district and inherited wealth. In years past, Cooper turned almost exclusively to PACs to retire the large debt he piled up in winning his seat in 1982. In the 1987–1988 election cycle, for example, he raised $292,770 from PACs of all stripes.

"I feel uncomfortable with how few PACs give you money for good-government reasons, with how many give you money when there is a hot issue before the committee," he says now. "I raised a lot of money from PACs in the past, and if I had to rely on good-government contributions . . . ." He completes the thought with a wan chuckle.

A ban on PAC contributions, though, does not translate into freedom from special-interest fund raising. Democrats Edward J. Markey of Massachusetts and Mike Synar of Oklahoma shun PAC money but not money from the executives who run them.

Synar, for example, comes from a district with substantial oil and gas interests. He received at least $16,375 from officials of companies, mostly in the energy industry, with a stake in clean-air legislation, according to FEC reports.

"Not Just a Single Vote"

The vote on the Hall/Fields amendment in October 1989 raised once more the chicken and egg question of political fund raising: Does money determine a lawmaker's position? Or does it merely reflect it?

Once natural-gas interests signed off on the critical amendment, and the Bush administration turned neutral, the battle became a test of strength between the oil and auto lobbies and Waxman. Detroit faced the prospect of building cars it feared it couldn't sell. Oil companies faced the loss of gasoline sales to alternative fuels.

With Dingell at the fore, the subcommittee sided 12-0 with the auto industry. And whether the chicken or the egg came first, the vote broke down largely along money lines.

The 12 members who voted yes raised $72,250 in 1989 from auto and oil interests, an average of $2,755 each. Three who voted no—Tauke and Democrats Bill Richardson of New Mexico and Ron Wyden of Oregon—accounted for all but $1,250 of that. Five of the no votes raised nothing.

Detroit's biggest spenders, General Motors Corp. and Ford, taken together raised their contributions to the committee by 55 percent to $36,600 in 1989, compared with 1987.

"We do look closely at the people who have our future in their hands," GM spokesman Grey Terry says. But he added that the company "doesn't try to PAC the committee" and couldn't buy votes if it wanted to.

Dennis, the Southern California Edison lobbyist, says: "A contribution doesn't sway a member's vote. It just does not work that way. Anyone who draws that black-or-white inference is not an effective student of the way the Congress works."

So what does a PAC tell members?

"They tell me they are interested only in good government," Swift says. "You don't look them in the face and call them a liar."

What, then, do PACs want?

"There are a lot of fish to fry with members," says Dennis, whose PAC gave Swift $1,000 in 1989. "It's not just a single vote. They are in it for the long term, and so are political action committees."

Republican Whittaker of Kansas, who cast a yes vote on the crucial Hall/Fields amendment, represents an oil- and gas-producing district. "I think in my case the chicken follows the egg," he says. "I have always been convinced my support follows a very conservative philosophy."

Whittaker says he has never studied his list of contributors, a luxury he attributes to a safe seat and service on lucrative Energy and Commerce. After six terms he has decided not to seek reelection, and he will leave with an embarrassment of riches.

At the end of 1989, with no election contest in sight, his campaign account had a cash surplus of $524,099.

T HE PROS AND CONS OF PACS have been hotly debated. Supporters argue that they are nothing more than an extension of a legitimate and healthy interest group process. The tight restriction on contributions to political candidates limits the influence of PAC money. While single contributions are small, PAC contributions collectively help to finance congressional campaigns in an era of increased costs that would otherwise place severe financial burdens on candidates.

Critics charge that PAC money corrupts the political process by giving disproportionate weight in Congress to special interests. The public interest group Common Cause has declared a "War on PACs," charging that Congress has become a special-interest outpost. Particularly sinister in the view of Common Cause leaders is the fact that PAC donations are made mostly to congressional incumbents, strengthening the political and special-interest status quo. As a result, Common Cause argues, Congress becomes an entrenched political institution, unresponsive to the people and the public interest.

The following selection describes the interplay between congressional candidates—incumbents and challengers alike—and PAC managers whose influence over campaign financing is steadily increasing.

12

Tom Watson
PAC PILGRIMAGE BECOMES CANDIDATES' RITUAL

Though congressional candidates talk passionately about someday coming to Washington, many of them are already spending a lot of time here stalking one of the capital's corridors of power—Political Action Committees (PACs).

For months now, congressional contenders from across the country have been trooping to Washington in search of PAC contributions they hope will help pave the way to victory.

This pilgrimage has become an integral part of running for Congress in recent years, as challengers and open-seat contenders have come to view PACs as vital to their political welfare.

Consultants and professional fund-raisers have helped promote the pilgrimage by peddling opportunities for access to the PAC community. They are finding an increasing number of candidates eager for their services.

Candidates make their journeys in the face of daunting odds. According to a Federal Election Commission study released last May, incumbents sopped up 72 percent of all PAC contributions made during the 1983–1984

From *Congressional Quarterly Weekly Report,* March 22, 1986, pp. 655–659. Copyright 1986 by Congressional Quarterly, Inc. Reprinted by permission.

election cycle. Challengers to incumbents attracted only 16 percent of all PAC money, while candidates for open seats netted 11 percent. Most PACs have been showing decidedly pro-incumbent tendencies for many years (Figure 1).

What little money political action committees do invest in nonincumbents often is funneled to a small coterie of top-flight contenders who are strongly favored to win. PAC managers who amass a poor won-lost record know that they will be required to account for their defeats by a hostile board of directors. As a result, they are extremely wary of taking risks.

Beating Down the Doors

But if candidates realize the problems they face in trying to tap the Washington PAC community, one would not know it from the way they behave. The number of candidates making the Washington pilgrimage seems to be growing with each election cycle, as they eagerly compete for a slice of the PAC pie.

"Nearly everybody comes through here," says Bernadette Budde, political strategist for the Business-Industry Political Action Committee (BIPAC), one of the country's most influential corporate PACs. "Sometimes even after I've told them that we have consistently supported the incumbent, they still want to come by."

Tom Baker, vice president for political affairs for the National Association of Home Builders (NAHB), concurs. "Frankly," Baker says, "it's hard to keep most of them out of town."

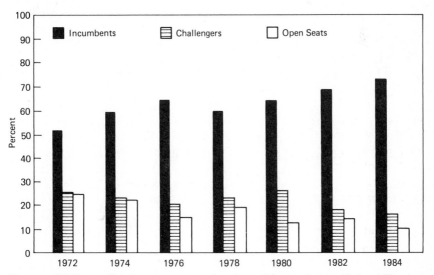

Figure 1. PAC contributions to congressional candidates. *Sources:* Federal Election Commission, Common Cause.

Candidates not only are showing up in Washington in increasing numbers; they are showing up earlier and earlier with each passing campaign. Far from being a biennial event, the Washington pilgrimage often begins immediately after Election Day for a contest two years down the road.

"We started seeing 1986 candidates in 1984," said one analyst for a health association PAC. "We view it as a two-year process. . . . It's a fulltime job."

"There's a parade that starts in September of the off-year," echoes Al Jackson, political director for the liberal-minded National Committee for an Effective Congress (NCEC). "It can be a revolving door some days."

Washington is not the only place to which candidates travel in search of PAC money. Houston and Los Angeles are prominent among the other cities that are emerging as important PAC centers. But Washington still is regarded as the symbolic and financial capital of the PAC world.

"There are PACs in other places," said Baker of the NAHB, whose Build PAC gave more money to federal candidates than all but two other political action committees during the 1983–1984 cycle. "But Washington . . . is the mecca. This is the mother lode."

"I recognize that I'm going to have to have financial help from Washington," says Indiana state Senator Jim Jontz, the likely Democratic nominee for retiring GOP Representative Elwood Hillis's House seat. "I'm committed to spending time seeking it. . . . It's a part of the process I have to pursue."

Value of the Visits

While it is clear that a desire to collect campaign cash is the major reason candidates come to Washington to visit PACs, there are other potential benefits from such journeys that may not be as apparent. The PAC pilgrimage affords candidates an opportunity to test their political appeal before a critical, seasoned audience. It also gives them valuable practice at trying to raise funds—practice that could pay off when they return home.

Some candidates feel that a trip to Washington can help them convince PAC managers they are serious about their race.

"I think making the trip shows that you're really . . . committed to your campaign," says Minnesota state Senator Collin C. Peterson, a Democrat who has decided to challenge Republican Representative Arlan Stangeland again after losing his initial bid in 1984. "If you don't go to Washington . . . it sends a negative signal. They expect you to make the trip."

Candidates also may gain an intangible sense of purpose and excitement from visiting the capital that fires their imaginations—and their campaigns.

"There may be some deep psychological reasons why a candidate has to come to Washington to feel that he is a real candidate," says BIPAC's Budde. "They may have been told by people who have been elected . . . 'Once you come and see the Capitol at night, and see your party heroes in action on the floor, you may never feel the same again.' They may need the charge that they get out of being here. The search for dollars may be secondary."

Weeding Out the Dogs

PAC managers, too, can benefit from the pilgrimage. It often provides the only chance they get to develop a firsthand feel for contenders they have known only through press clippings, poll numbers and other analysts' remarks.

"I think a lot of people in this business are like me," said David Michael Staton, a former House Republican from West Virginia (1981–1983) who now heads the political-action programs for the U.S. Chamber of Commerce. "They like to look and see and evaluate candidates from firsthand. The guy may have great numbers, but he may be a nerd." By meeting personally with a particular candidate, PAC managers say, they stand a better chance of keeping track of that contender's campaign. With a field of hundreds of candidates for federal office, that is no easy task.

"If you're a challenger, you've got to come—and more than once," says the NCEC's Jackson. "You've got to come and make sure that everyone sees your name and your face a lot . . . so that we remember who you are. There are too many races, too many candidates for us to keep track of it unless you keep your name in front of us."

"They get the challengers mixed up," echoes GOP consultant Terry Cooper, who also has worked as director of a corporate PAC. "They're going to forget whether that neat story they heard was about you in Oregon or about somebody who is running against somebody with a similar name in Missouri."

Secrets to Success

A variety of factors determine whether candidates succeed when they solicit funds from the Washington PAC community, but a surprising number of those factors are already decided before candidates arrive in town.

At a fundamental level, candidates strengthen their case if they are committed to waging a campaign before they come looking for money. A potentially strong contender arguably should face no penalty for visiting a PAC director in the course of deciding whether to run. But in practice, it often does not work out that way.

"We see some candidates who aren't even candidates," laments Budde, expressing irritation at being used as a sounding board for a prospective campaign. "I don't understand why they come to me to get my opinion about whether they should run. At the very least, they should have decided and announced. We don't like making decisions based on shadows and phantoms."

Many challengers also misuse time and resources trying to get money from PACs that have a strong record of support for the incumbents the contenders hope to unseat.

"There's no point in bringing a guy up here against an incumbent with a 90 percent voting record on our issues, the kind of guy we've mixed with," warns the NAHB's Baker. "Those records are all available. . . . That's something someone could find out in advance and save the guy a trip."

"It's not only a bad use of time," Baker continues, "it's also not good for a candidate's morale. . . . I've had guys who go through the drill with me and then ask how to get to the next association . . . where I know they're going to get exactly the same thing. My God, by the end of the day this guy is going to be totally depressed."

Primaries: Peril or Promise?

Many PAC managers also have a tendency to avoid candidates who are involved in crowded or difficult primaries. Most PACs are leery of being on the losing side of an intraparty battle, so they steer clear of primaries until one candidate emerges as the likely nominee.

Freshman Republican Representative John G. Rowland of Connecticut learned that lesson in a painful way during his 1984 challenge to Democratic Representative William R. Ratchford. "When I went down to Washington, I didn't have the nomination yet," Rowland recalls. I had 25 appointments, a poll under my arm, but no nomination. I got zero out of those visits. It was a total waste of time and money."

There is, however, an important exception to that rule. Directors of ideologically oriented PACs are much more likely than their corporate or labor colleagues to enter a primary if they find a candidate who is a clear philosophical ally.

"We use two criteria," says Jackson of the liberal NCEC. "One is that there is a clear philosophical difference between the two candidates involved. That involves both primaries and generals. The second criteria is that the race is marginal and winnable."

That policy also applies to ideological PACs on the conservative side. Jim Ellis, who until late last year worked as assistant director of the Free Congress PAC (affiliated with the Committee for the Survival of a Free Congress), said his organization also was willing to foray into a primary for an ideologically compatible candidate because "philosophical commitment for us is No. 1."

Naive Need Not Apply

Perhaps the most decisive event in a candidate's PAC pilgrimage takes place behind the PAC manager's door. There a congressional hopeful faces the same kind of pressure to make a favorable impression that is felt by an anxious applicant interviewing with a potential employer.

"You've got to know what you're talking about, and you've got to come across well . . . the simplest things you'd think a candidate would know to have," says Denis Calabrese, vice president of Southern Political Consulting, a Texas-based Republican firm. "But an amazing number of candidates walk into their first PAC meeting without having their act down."

A good performance at that meeting can help a candidate establish credibility and spread interest in his campaign throughout the PAC community. A bad showing can effectively shut a candidate out of PAC money.

"They have to convince the PAC money that they are viable," says Gary Nordlinger, head of a consulting firm that caters to a Democratic clientele. "Most of them lose it right there."

Adds Calabrese, "You've got to say, 'I'm politically sophisticated and I'm not charging at windmills here.' You've got to be able to go in there and talk about streets and counties. You can buy yourself so many points if you're not naive."

"Just the Facts, Mister"

PAC managers also agree that political naiveté on the part of the candidates is a recurrent problem that damages their chances of establishing credibility. Too often contenders cite broad partisan trends and offer shallow political complaints in lieu of a developed case for their candidacy.

"If you come in and say, 'I could beat Teddy Kennedy because he has not voted the way the people of Massachusetts think,' . . . I'm going to say I'm interested in seeing this happen, but how will it take place?" says the Chamber's Staton. "You're going to have to come up with some pretty concrete evidence to back up what you've got to say, or no one is going to pay much attention to your campaign."

"But if you come in with the right information . . . ," Staton continues, "about how you're going to win this race, how you're going to take the resources, what you're going to do in fund raising, what's your campaign plan. . . . If you spell out what you're going to do, then you're going to impress a lot of people."

PAC managers say a candidate can build credibility by presenting poll results, a realistic budget, an assessment of an opponent's vulnerabilities, and names of prominent political and financial supporters back home.

Keep Those Cards and Letters Coming

A successful PAC pilgrimage seldom ends with a single visit. By supplying a steady barrage of updated poll results, press releases, and newspaper clippings, a candidate can keep the PAC community abreast of his progress and reinforce PAC interest in the campaign. PAC fund raising has become, as one consultant put it, "almost a constant public relations job."

Michigan Republican Representative Bill Schuette demonstrated his understanding of that law of PAC politics in his successful 1984 challenge to three-term Democrat Donald J. Albosta.

"The key thing is follow-up," Schuette reflects. "I would do a personal follow-up: letters, notes, newsletters, and press clips to let them know that you have something ongoing. In that respect, it's no different than when you're going after votes. I would go back to individuals time and time again, saying, 'I need your support.' Sometimes, approaching the PAC community is a similar process."

GOP consultant Cooper also sees similarities between the campaign a candidate undertakes for PAC money and the one he wages for votes back home. "You've got to keep hitting the PACs with material that establishes an identity. Nobody thinks of [the need to establish] name identification in the PAC community. But there is such a thing as name ID in the PAC community. You've really got to get it."

Great Expectations

Those who counsel candidates about PAC fund raising often urge them to temper their expectations about what their PAC pilgrimage will bring. Challengers and open-seat contenders who think a PAC visit pays big monetary dividends up front are in for a big shock.

"Candidates arrive here thinking that they're going to get $1 million just because they're wonderful, special, and running," says Nordlinger, who advises Democratic campaigns. "They are running to be 1/435th of one-half of one-third of the U.S. government. Yet somehow they think that they're a man of destiny at the moment of destiny and that the coffers will open and millions will roll into their war chest. . . . There's kind of a rude awakening."

Some candidates apparently are unaware of the pro-incumbent bias most PACs maintain; others misunderstand the limits governing the legal amount a PAC can contribute. Under the Federal Election Campaign Act, PACs can give $5,000 to a candidate in any primary, runoff, or general election.

Still others fail to make a distinction between the different kinds of aid offered a candidate by different kinds of political committees. Most corporate and labor PACs make financial contributions as well as so-called "in-kind" contributions—assistance of an organizational or technical nature.

For the ideological PACs, however, in-kind contributions usually are the rule. "We very rarely do any financial contributing," said Ellis of the conservative Free Congress PAC. "We might pay for a staff member on a candidate's staff to run the organization. . . . If they have a specific action, we might give cash for that. But the field man would make sure it goes for a specific project—manning phone banks, paying to install phones, that type of thing."

Jackson of the liberal NCEC buttresses that point. "NCEC doesn't just give cash," he says. "In fact, we'd rather not give money away. We do services better than we do money."

Heard It Through the Grapevine

If candidates often overestimate the amount of money they will receive from their Washington forays, they often underestimate how much their requests for money are influenced by communication within the PAC community. The conversation between one PAC director and another about a candidate may be crucial to that candidate's chances of receiving PAC support.

Pennsylvania Democrat Joe Hoeffel, who is seeking to avenge his 1984 loss to GOP Representative Lawrence Coughlin, has learned that the Washington PAC community acts as a network. "I was advised," Hoeffel says, "that the PACs in Washington are . . . somewhat inbred. They talk to themselves."

By landing a PAC's endorsement, a candidate assures himself access to that PAC grapevine. Through regular meetings, "meet-and-greet" sessions with candidates and other informal contact, members of the Washington PAC community share their lists of contenders who are strong and incumbents who are in trouble.

"These lists are the key to all of this," says Jackson. "Nobody gives away without looking at somebody's list."

Some PAC directors urge candidates to use their endorsement as a way of courting other PAC support. "We ask you to carry [our endorsement] with you as an entrée," says Staton of the Chamber of Commerce. "Because if people have confidence in us as an organization and feel that we've done good work in analyzing your race, then you won't have to work as hard to convince them to . . . help you."

Support for a candidate also can spread through the PAC community via the national parties, which have become an increasingly vital link between PACs and campaigns. PAC managers of all stripes say both national party organizations generally provide good intelligence about challengers and open-seat candidates—as well as coaching contenders about how to win support from PACs.

The national parties' attitude toward a challenger often helps PAC managers decide whether or not to recommend committing support.

"You need to get the NRCC [National Republican Congressional Committee] to run around saying, 'This is a great race; this is a targeted race; we need this race,'" said Calabrese. "PACs don't say, "OK, the NRCC has targeted this race, so we should support.' What they say is, 'That guy got the NRCC to target; therefore that guy convinced the NRCC of the same thing he convinced me of—that he's got his act together, that he's got a plan, that he's a viable contender.'"

Fund Raising in Reverse

Candidates who do not find themselves on PAC support lists should not abandon hope. An increasing number of contenders are taking advantage of a defensive strategy toward PACs.

Courting PACs that are unlikely to give to a challenger's campaign can prove profitable—if the challenger can convince the PAC to remain neutral or scale back support for the incumbent. Consultant Cooper calls this process "negative fund raising."

"In negative fund raising . . . you don't expect a nickel from anybody you send a communication to," says Cooper. "You're just trying to shut the opposition down."

"What you have to do is go out and be the salesman for the other side," Cooper continues. "Point out that, really, the incumbent is not a good bet—based on issues, winnability or otherwise."

GOP Representative Pat Swindall of Georgia, who won his suburban Atlanta House seat by ousting veteran Democrat Elliott H. Levitas in 1984, is quite familiar with negative fund raising.

"Much of my objective in coming to Washington," Swindall said of his 1984 PAC trips, "was not so much to raise money, but to minimize the contributions PACs gave to my opponent. If you can't get their PAC dollars, at least minimize their impact on your race."

"You'd certainly rather have the cash," echoed Missouri Republican Carrie Francke, who hopes to reverse the outcome of her unsuccessful 1984 challenge to Democratic Representative Harold L. Volkmer. "But If you can make a presentation to a PAC and influence them so they think it's questionable who will win—and so stay out of it—you've benefited your campaign."

Democrats also play the negative fund-raising game. "You've still got to go around to the Republican-oriented PACs, if for no other reason than to neutralize them or to keep their contributions lower," said Nordlinger, whose firm is advising Jontz's bid for the open 5th District in Indiana.

No Place Like Home?

While there is little argument that the Washington pilgrimage has become an institution in congressional campaigns, not everyone agrees that this is a positive development. A significant number of PAC directors feel that many candidates place too much emphasis on Washington—when they should be tending to PACs' local constituencies back home.

BIPAC's Budde is a prominent member of that camp. "I firmly believe that a good candidate with the right support from the local business community never has to leave the district in order to raise PAC money."

She places special emphasis on local support. Budde says that BIPAC's decision to back a challenger is influenced heavily by the level of support that candidate enjoys among members of his district's corporate community. The trip to Washington, she says, takes a back seat.

"They all have it backwards," Budde says. "They think that they come to Washington first . . . then they go back home and do all the rest of the stuff. But the real action is back home. . . . We're a lot more interested in how it plays in Peoria than how does it play in Washington."

Budde cites Connecticut's Rowland as one 1984 challenger who played the PAC game correctly. Following a rocky first trip to Washington in early spring of the election year, Rowland decided to steer clear of the PAC community and concentrate on cultivating elements closer to home.

"In essence . . . I didn't go back down to Washington," says Rowland. "I just realized that all I needed was some good people. I didn't need a bunch of fancy consultants and fancy polls. What I needed to do was go to super-markets and win votes."

Rowland's analysis may sound like wishful thinking to challengers facing the rigors of raising money against an entrenched incumbent. But his strategy of courting local business backing did help him attract BIPAC's attention.

Impressed with Rowland's support in the local business community, Budde says that BIPAC gave him a better-than-average campaign contribu-tion in 1984—even though she did not meet him until roughly a year after the election.

Not all of Budde's PAC colleagues share her militant attitude toward the Washington pilgrimage. But there is widespread agreement that by sowing seeds at home, a candidate vastly enhances his chances of reaping benefits from Washington PACs.

"You always have to struggle to convince candidates that they must raise . . . most of their money in their districts," said a political analyst working with a labor PAC. "They look at you like you're crazy. PACs are everything to them."

"I cannot envision a House race in which any of my clients—and they are all nonincumbents—is ever going to get more than 30 percent of his budget from PACs," said Cooper. "It would be folly for me to say, 'Focus on 30 percent and ignore the 70 percent.' "

THE MEDIA
AND POLITICAL
CONSULTANTS

Chapter

Three

The First Amendment's guarantee of freedom of the press both reflects and protects the political power of an institution that has always played an important role in the nation's politics. The publishers and pamphleteers of eighteenth-century America considered freedom of the press a natural liberty, and acted accordingly. Their criticisms of British and colonial authorities helped to plant the revolutionary seed in the minds of the colonists. Colonial governors were aware of the dangers of a free press and sought unsuccessfully to control it by requiring government licenses for printing. Moreover, the authorities did not hesitate to bring charges of seditious libel against journalists who criticized the government.

The freedom of the press that was won in the eighteenth century created an environment in which political journalists could and did flourish. Reporters could build successful careers by covering politics at state or national levels, although Washington inevitably became the mecca for the political press.

By the time of the New Deal, the Washington press had become a firmly entrenched establishment force in the nation's capital. Jonathan Daniels, an experienced Washington hand who had served as President Franklin D. Roosevelt's press secretary, commented, "It would be difficult to find a body of men who more clearly represent Washington than the gentlemen of the press who report it. There are notions, carefully cultivated, that they are in Washington but not of it, and that they stand in scrutiny but also in separation. Actually, of course, they are probably more representative of the good and the bad on the Capital scene than any other body of bureaucrats. As they stay in Washington, which most of them hope to do, they are at least as remote from the country as the administrators are."[1]

The media are a powerful political force at all levels of the government. A century before the advent of radio and television, Alexis de Tocqueville pointed out that the diversity and power of the press is a major characteristic of democracy, and particularly of a government such as that of the United States, which contains so many political subdivisions. "The extraordinary subdivision of administrator power," remarked Tocqueville, "has much more to do with the enormous number of American newspapers than the great political freedom of

---

[1]Jonathan Daniels, *Frontier on the Potomac* (New York: Macmillan, 1946), p. 159.

the country and the absolute liberty of the press."[2] Newspapers, concluded Tocqueville, can persuade large numbers of citizens to unite for a common cause. Moreover, "the more equal the conditions of men become and the less strong men individually are, the more easily they give way to the current of the multitude and the more difficult it is for them to adhere by themselves to an opinion which the multitude discard[s]. . . . The power of the newspaper press must therefore increase as the social conditions of men become more equal."[3]

The press has always attempted to create, in Tocqueville's terms, associations of citizens to back causes and candidates. The press attempts to be the king-maker for many of the ten thousand or more elected offices throughout the nation.

The growth of the electronic media, radio and television, added a new dimension to the traditional political role played by the press. While newspaper publishers and correspondents are free to express their political views, support-ing whatever candidates they choose, the electronic media are in an entirely different position. The airwaves used by the electronic media to communicate information are technically "owned" by the public. The government licenses broadcasting stations for a three-year period, after which it reviews the licen-see's conduct in relation to statutory and administrative standards to determine whether or not the license is to be renewed.[4] One of the regulatory standards governing broadcasting requires impartiality in the "equal time" for the presen-tation of opposing opinions. Broadcasters, unlike publishers, do not often en-dorse political candidates.

While broadcasting is supposed to be politically neutral, it is inevitably drawn into partisan politics. All news and public affairs programs have a slant, which indirectly shapes citizen attitudes on important issues. Statements about public policy are often made simply by the choice of subjects to be covered. The White House, which is so frequently the focus of media attention, complains constantly that it is not being treated fairly. Republicans attack the "Eastern liberal establish-ment" press, while Democrats always echo President Harry S Truman's lament: "I was sure that the American people would agree with me if they had all the facts. I knew, however, that the Republican-controlled press and radio would be against me, and my only remaining hope of communicating with the people was to get the message to the people in a personal way."[5]

However much politicians may criticize the media, they increasingly depend upon them to project their personalities and communicate their views to the

[2]Alexis de Tocqueville, *Democracy in America,* Vol. 2 (New York: Vintage Books 1954), p. 121. Tocqueville's volumes were first published in 1835.

[3]Ibid., p. 122.

[4]In fact, almost all license renewals are automatic, making the licensees virtually permanent owners of their stations.

[5]Harry S Truman, *Memoirs,* Vol. 2 (Garden City, N.Y.: Doubleday, 1956), p. 175.

electorate. Political consulting has become a major industry.[6] By 1952, 45 percent of households owned television sets, and not surprisingly, that year marked the advent of political television in a big way in presidential campaigns.[7] General Eisenhower, portrayed as the simple and sincere man from Abilene, easily won over the sometimes acerbic but always witty Adlai Stevenson of Illinois. The Stevenson campaign spent only $77,000 on television compared to Republican expenditure of $1.5 million on its media campaign. The use of media consultants and the expenditure of large sums of money for public relations has been considered *de rigueur* for almost all political campaigns, presidential, congressional, and at the state level, as television has become the principal political medium. Media consultants are the new political gurus.

[6]See Larry J. Sabato, *The Rise of Political Consultants* (New York: Basic Books, 1981).

[7]Ibid., p. 113.

S UCCESSFUL CAMPAIGNING RE-
quires a broad array of skills. Electoral politics has become a big
business because running for office is extraordinarily expensive, particularly at
the national level. Successful House candidates spend an average of approxi-
mately $250,000 to $300,000 to be
elected, while Senate races may cost as
much as $5 or $6 million.

Candidates not only have to raise large
amounts of money but also must deal
with an increasingly complex media
world. They must project a favorable
image—one of a dynamic, energetic, and
caring politician who takes the "right"
stand on major issues.

Candidates cannot begin to run a
successful campaign without political
consultants, whom they have come
to consider indispensable. Consultants
themselves have become an important
political force, shaping the electoral process and even influencing public policy
formation through their access to office
holders. As the following selection reveals, they are not simply hired guns, but
often carefully select their candidate-clients to fulfill their own political objectives
as candidates hire them to win elections.

13 Larry J. Sabato
HOW POLITICAL CONSULTANTS
CHOOSE CANDIDATES

There are several methods by which candidates are matched up with political
consultants. The first is consultant solicitation. When the principals in
Butcher-Forde Consulting, for instance, heard that there was no professional
management team supporting Howard Jarvis's 1978 proposition 13 tax-cut-
ting drive in California, they arranged a meeting with Jarvis, presented a plan
of action, and hustled the extremely lucrative account. While solicitation is
a common and necessary practice for lesser-known consultants, occasionally
the national firms also seek the account of a campaign that has either great
financial potential or a capacity to enhance their winning image and reputation. The D.M.I. polling firm systematically compiles a "druthers list" of the
most desirable campaigns and contacts them in an attempt to sign them up
(approaching political consultants working for the campaigns instead of the
candidates on occasion).

Rarely in past times did consultants actually recruit an individual to make
a race, but the practice is becoming disturbingly common due to the expansion of ideological political action committees. A professional manager like
Roy Day was once the exception in his role as Richard Nixon's original
sponsor. Day, though, was also chairman of the Republican Central Commit-

From *The Rise of Political Consultants: New Ways of Winning Elections,* by Larry J. Sabato.
Copyright 1981 by Larry J. Sabato. Reprinted by permission of Basic Books, Inc., Publishers,
New York.

tee of Los Angeles when he formed the Committee of One Hundred in 1946 to find an opponent for the Democratic incumbent U.S. congressman, Gerald Voorhis. Day placed advertisements on the front pages of twenty-six newspapers, and Nixon was one of the respondents. The future president was chosen to make his first race, launching his long political career. Today, however, consultants active in recruiting candidates have weak or nonexistent party credentials and sometimes are agents of party-rivaling political action committees, such as the Committee for the Survival of a Free Congress or the National Committee for an Effective Congress.

Most major consultants do not bother to recruit because ideologically they are not very choosy and they have far more business that walks in the door unsolicited than they can possibly handle. In the vast proportion of client-consultant matchings, the original contact is made by the future client, and the odds are great that prominent consultants will not be interested or able to take them. Richard Viguerie claims to turn away 98 percent of all the people who come to him. David Garth reports that, while he took only five campaigns in 1978, he was approached by statewide candidates in thirty-nine states, and in twelve of those states (or twenty-eight—he cited different figures in two separately published interviews) he was offered both sides of the race.

It is little wonder that a few consultants are so swamped with requests. Candidates and their staffs usually know little about the national professionals or their campaign technologies and are likely to seize upon one of the periodic glowing press accounts of one or another consultant's miracles, after which the candidate or campaign manager issues the order to secure consultant X at any cost. A bit of campaign shopping could do wonders for a campaign budget, but there is astoundingly little of that. When it occurs, it is worth noting. U.S. Senator Birch Bayh's well-organized 1974 reelection effort, for example, arranged interviews with eight political pollsters. The two finalists, Peter Hart and Patrick Caddell, were not well known at the time. (After final interviews of one and a half hours each, Caddell was chosen over Hart.)

Demand for consultant services has so increased since 1974 that it is doubtful that any such carefully staged selection is possible today. Most potential clients would simply not be worth the preliminary investment of so much of a consultant's time. Regrettably, the consultant crunch at the first level is forcing candidates to solicit help from much less experienced and sometimes less scrupulous second- and third-level professionals. Many of the unethical practices in the consulting business find their origin there.

One other method of matching candidates and consultants should be mentioned. Candidates are frequently referred to a particular consulting firm by a third party. Sometimes a firm's previous candidate-clients who were satisfied by the services rendered will pass along the experience while offering advice to new candidates. A consultant who is too busy to sign the candidate on will sometimes suggest the names of friendly associates or some young, struggling firm with which he is acquainted. Many PACs have semipermanent relationships with certain consultants and will suggest a linking of arms to a candidate being supported with PAC money. Finally, the candidate's state or national political party committee may work on a regular basis with consultants, and a recommendation may be forthcoming from party officials. In some midwestern states, particularly in the Republican camp, a few consultants have done all of a party's major candidates for a number of years and are hired almost by habit.

For the most part, one problem candidates do not have to worry about is locating ideologically compatible consultants. While the professionals are not without political belief, they rarely let it overrule their business sense. For most consultants ideology is a surprisingly minor criterion in the selection of clients. Party affiliation plays a larger role for some, but usually because serving candidates of both parties is impractical and hurts business. (A significant minority of the professionals, however, are actively hostile to the parties—even to the very notion of a political system.) Political reporter David Broder connected the consultants' party links and lack of pronounced ideology to the credibility and professionalism required for success in their business: "I think the nonideological style they adopt is not dissimilar to that of political reporters, mainly that they try to really separate their own feelings and emotions so that they don't get in the way of making a professional judgment."

But the full explanation has a major financial component, as political consultant Sanford L. Weiner, addressing his peers, frankly surmised:

> We would all like to think we have worked for candidates we believed in, and who represented our own individual political thinking. . . . Unfortunately, as with any profession, economics enter the picture. We have all, from time to time, represented clients whom we didn't particularly love, but who could help us pay the overhead.

The businessman's profit motive is admittedly powerful, and when combined with most political professionals' disinterest in issues and the stuff of government, a remarkable tolerance results. Robert Goodman can say without blush, "I call myself a Jacob Javits Republican, but I can stretch to the conservative ends without a problem." His standard of judgment for potential clients is heroic, not ideological: "We see politics as theater, living theater, and it is classic theater. There is a hero and there is a villain. Now we won't knowingly take on a villain. We like to feel that our candidate has the potential of being the hero." Fellow Republican consultant John Deardourff has a less charitable assessment of the "heroic standard": "Bob Goodman doesn't care who he works for. He'll build a big, noisy campaign, with a forty-seven-piece band, around anyone."

As its literature notes, Deardourff's firm makes its services "available to candidates we wish to see in public office." His partner, Doug Bailey, identified two areas (civil rights and women's issues) where "unless we generally shared the candidate's philosophy, we would feel so uncomfortable it would be a nonproductive and unpleasant relationship." Yet he admits to working for candidates who have opposed the Equal Rights Amendment and racial balancing of school systems through busing. In 1978 the Bailey-Deardourff firm also handled at least three candidates with solid antiabortion records. Chuck Winner of California's Winner-Wagner organization proclaims insistently and forthrightly his undying resistance to his state's often-used initiative and referendum process: "I oppose the idea of law by mob rule. I oppose the idea of doing away with representative democracy. I oppose the idea of losing basic protections for the minority." But almost all of his lucrative political work is referendum- and initiative-related. (Someone has to do it, of course.)

Generalist consultant Hank Parkinson (who claims to have worked for both the Democratic and Republican national committees) explains his lack of issue orientation by calling himself "a technician, not an ideologue. . . . I have turned down extremists on both ends of the spectrum, but mostly because they simply can't win." Some professionals are addicted to sports analogies to communicate their love of the game and disinterest in the philosophy behind the plays. Others report that their ideological attachments are fading over time as their exposure to politics lengthens, and that ideological rigidity is part of the problem in the political system they observe. Says Patrick Caddell:

> I'm basically liberal, but also basically convinced that most of those answers aren't working either. Rigid ideological structures are helping to screw up what's going on in terms of our ability to solve our real problems. I've said to people who say, "How do you work for McGovern and work for Carter?" It's very simple. In both cases, I happen to think that they were the best people running for president at the time.

These comments would be an anathema to a small but growing band of political consultants who are more rigid in their ideological prerequisites for candidate-clients. Conservative Richard Viguerie has never been accused of ignoring his direct-mail firm's business interests, yet he carefully considers the ideology of all his prospective clients and organizational subordinates. The right-wing political action committees, which Viguerie often helps to coordinate, sometimes have prospective candidates fill out written ideological examinations. Paul Weyrich, executive director of the Committee for the Survival of a Free Congress, gives a seventy-part questionnaire on issues and ideology to each candidate who approaches the group for assistance, and the answers are crucial to chances for funding.

Perhaps because the contemporary United States is in a conservative-dominated political era and a period of retrenchment for liberals, most tests of ideological purity are administered on the right. But in a recent time more attuned to left-wing philosophy, the 1960s, the same degree of selectiveness by liberal political professionals existed. Only days before President Johnson withdrew from the 1968 presidential race, one of his campaign assistants was forced to tell Johnson that his staff had great difficulty finding a New York advertising agency willing to take him on "because they are all [Vietnam] 'doves.' "

Ideology is also at least one of a number of considerations for some consultants not at the liberal or conservative extremes of the spectrum. The direct-mail firm of Craver, Mathews, Smith, and Co. has been known to reject issue groups because they were philosophically in conflict with the partners' views. David Garth has his staff carefully research the records of his petitioners (because he has learned not to trust their own accounting of their voting histories), and he pays careful attention to views on a number of social issues. Generalist Walter De Vries eventually switched from the Republican to the Democratic party to accommodate his progressivism, although business needs entered into the decision. As he wryly noted, "If you work only for progressive Republicans, your market is getting pretty small." Regional media consultant Marvin Chernoff insists on working for "the most progressive or liberal candidate in the race," yet this carefully worded criterion often allows signing on a moderate or conservative.

Even consultants who put ideology on the back burner (or off the stove entirely) have some rock-bottom standards and very general prohibitive criteria. Joseph Cerrell will not work for anybody that he would "have trouble voting for." Pollster William Hamilton, a moderate-liberal Democrat who has worked for conservatives, had the opportunity to take one of George Wallace's presidential campaigns but refused it. Bob Goodman also rejected Wallace and did not respond to preliminary soundings from a U.S. Senate candidate from Virginia (who was eventually successful in his electoral bid) because he was "a guy who would have taken the rent from poor little Nellie and thrown her on the streets." He continued: "We will not handle people we don't like as human beings. We will not handle people we think are dangerous at either extreme. We could not handle a John Bircher, a racist."

It is a delicious commentary on the American system that some of the least ideological professionals take their chosen political party dead seriously, and anyone who cares about the party system can be grateful that they do. A few are fierce partisans, having had their political baptism as party functionaries and occasionally having had years of direct party employment. One of these, Robert Odell, is inclined to take on just about any Republican in his direct-mail firm because, "Democrats do little or nothing that I respect and Republicans do nearly everything I respect." Striking a rare pose for a private consultant, Odell declares, "The most important goal for me is to make the

Republican party effective." Matt Reese holds the Democratic party in similar esteem, observing only half in jest that he is "a partisan without apology. I don't even like Republicans, except for Abraham Lincoln." And few professionals have shown as long and abiding a concern for a political party as Stuart Spencer and his partner, Bill Roberts, who both began their political careers as volunteers for the Republican party in California. Their consulting shop actually developed around the GOP and was encouraged by the party. Spencer explained that he and Roberts "wanted to be an extension of the party, a management tool that the party could use" and that they viewed each of their early consulting outings as "an opportunity for the Republican party." With the party's interests in mind, Spencer and Roberts gave Ronald Reagan an extended grilling when he approached them about his impending 1966 gubernatorial campaign in California. After a number of questions about his depth and experience, and whether he could win for the party or might instead become another Goldwater disaster, reportedly Reagan became exasperated and demanded: "Now, goddammit, I want to get some answers from you guys. Are you going to work for me or not?" The Spencer-Roberts agency finally did agree to handle him.

The greatest number of consultants, though, are simply not committed in any real sense to a political party. Michael Kaye, for instance, proclaims himself to be an Independent and the parties to be "bullshit." Revealingly, however, he still sensed that it was a mistake to work both sides of the street, comparing it to his practice while a product advertiser:

> People in political office, most of them are paranoid anyway. And I think it would make someone uncomfortable to think that I was working for a Republican at the same time I was working for a Democrat. That is why I work only for Democrats. I don't work for just Democrats because I think they are the only good pure people on this planet. It is the same reason that in the [product] advertising business I didn't work for two clients in the same business.

Yet for all of the danger supposedly involved in crossing party lines, consultants seem to yield frequently to the temptation. Democrat Peter Hart conducted Republican U.S. Senate nominee John Heinz's surveys in Pennsylvania in 1976 (and claimed he was told he could not take polls for Jimmy Carter as a consequence). David Garth has been "all over the lot," as one of his detractors termed his tendency to take moderate-to-liberal Democrats and Republicans indiscriminantly, and it was a surprise to no one in the profession when GOP Congressman John Anderson tapped Garth to help with his 1980 Independent presidential bid.

Another Democratic-leaning liberal firm, Craver, Mathews, Smith, and Co., took on Anderson's direct-mail program. The now-defunct firm of Baus and Ross in California secured the accounts of Richard Nixon, Barry Goldwater, and Edmund G. "Pat" Brown, Sr., within a few years of one another. The survey firm of D.M.I. not only once worked for both Democrats and Republicans, they actually polled both sides of the same congressional election district in 1966. Vincent Breglio, the D.M.I. vice president, took one side, and president Richard Wirthlin took the other. They ran the research independent of one another and provided consulting services to each side without crossing communications. Apparently the candidates were rather trusting souls who reportedly agreed to this outrageous arrangement (although it was quite a useful one for the firm's "win ratio"). D.M.I. converted permanently to Republicanism in 1967 when Michigan Governor George Romney asked the firm to join his presidential effort on the condition that they work only for the GOP. Convinced that the move was good for business, Wirthlin and Breglio made the switch over the objections of the Democratic members of the firm, who nevertheless stayed.

It is one thing to be apathetic about the party system and quite another to be hostile to it. The nonideological nature of American parties is the object of venomous rebuke by right-wing consultants such as Richard Viguerie and PAC leaders such as Paul Weyrich. Viguerie has flirted with a personal Independent candidacy and publicly expressed his hopes for a new conservative party to replace the GOP. Urging cross-party consulting for conservative candidates, Viguerie insisted that "conservatives must learn to disregard meaningless party labels." Weyrich's Committee for the Survival of a Free Congress practices Viguerie's preaching and has involved itself in party congressional primaries on both sides of the aisle, assisting the 1978 victories of the presidents of both the freshman Democratic and freshman Republican U.S. House classes. A "militant supporter" of Independent U.S. Senator Harry Byrd of Virginia, Weyrich believes that conservatives' "political victory will not come by the Republicans winning control but rather by a coalition of conservatives of both political parties getting together." The conservative Republican takeover of the U.S. Senate in 1980 may have given Weyrich second thoughts, but it hardly instilled in him any greater loyalty to the GOP. Barely had the votes been counted than Weyrich and other New Right leaders warned president-elect Ronald Reagan to hew closely to conservative ideology. Vice President-elect George Bush, suspected of moderate tendencies, was threatened in much stronger terms.

With the exception of the ideological PACs, party affiliation and ideology are by no means the only, or even the dominant, criteria for consultants in selecting their clients. The personal mesh between consultant and client seems to be of paramount importance, followed by the need for a balanced and economically rewarding program for the firm. There is a sort of ritualized mating dance when consultants and prospective clients meet, a mutual sizing-up and testing of one another that can sometimes be quite intense for all parties. Most consultants in preparing to meet with a candidate learn as much as possible about the individual ahead of time and request a full day of the candidate's time for the interview. They grill the candidate, peppering him with questions, many of them personal (in an attempt to ferret out scandal in advance). David Garth's interrogation is unusually issue-oriented: "How should the state or city be run? How should the money be distributed? What do you think about welfare?" Walter DeVries is particularly interested in the response to one query: " 'What makes you think you ought to be governor or United States senator?' And a lot of guys don't have very good answers. And if they haven't articulated in their own mind why they want to be governor, you can't do it for them." Matt Reese's mind is more directly on the prospects of winning when he confronts the candidate: "I ask how many people they've got and how much money. I know how to run a campaign with lots of people and little money. I know how to run a campaign with lots of money and few people. I love it when I've got lots of money and lots of people. I don't know what to do when I don't have any money and any people." In his interview sessions, Pat Caddell tries above all to test character to find the "real patriots in the sense of really caring about the country. If I were to apply one single criterion, it would be whether the individual really gives a good damn about what happens to the United States. Large numbers of politicians, frankly, could care less as long as they stay in office."

The personal interviews are enormously useful, and normally essential, for both the candidate and the professional. Sometimes serious potential problems are exposed and explored so that all parties can anticipate the campaign ahead. Frequently a consultant encounters a reluctant candidate and after a rewarding session actively encourages his candidacy. On the other hand, as one consultant reported, "Many times what you find out is that person really shouldn't be running for office. Either they have problems or when you really get down to it they are running because somebody else wants them to run . . . or because they see a lot of glamour in it."

The interviews are not always revealing, of course, and many consultants (at least the ones who have sufficient clientele to afford the luxury of leisurely choice) often require a number of interviews over several weeks or months before an agreement is concluded. But even with multiple meetings, decisions on taking clients are always gambles. Media consultant Tony Schwartz asks rhetorically, "How well can you really know a guy? You get to know your wife better after you get married and your secretary better after you've hired her." Still, most professionals believe they can sense whether the client understands and appreciates what they do and whether the personal relationship in the campaign is likely to be a pleasant, satisfying, and effective one.

While the personal evaluation and relationship is the most crucial nonpartisan element in the selection process, at least half a dozen other factors are taken into consideration. The revenue-producing potential of a campaign is almost always at the top of the list. A major race that will contribute substantially to a firm's economic objectives is a good bet to be selected, and campaigns are scrutinized to determine the likelihood they will meet their projected budgets. Consultants also consider the stress that a campaign will add to their personal schedules. Most have a fairly fixed limit on the number of campaigns they will take in any year, and they often try to cluster them geographically, which saves traveling wear and tear. No consultant forgets about the overall batting average, either; a reputation that has been so lovingly nurtured must be protected with a sufficient quota of expected victories and upset wins. And a spirit of cooperation and an appreciation of the consultant's role must be manifested not only by the candidate but also by the spouse and the key internal campaign staff aides.

Some consultants are reluctant to take on campaigns at certain levels (usually local or presidential, although some firms refuse gubernatorial clients). At least until John Anderson came along, David Garth refused to consider presidential clients, saying, "I don't really have any great desire to elect a president. . . . The kind of physical and emotional expenditure it takes doesn't make sense for the company." Garth also claims to use a form of collegial decision making absent in most firms, wherein his staffers and associates participate fully in the client selection process rather than accept his dictation of choices.

The direct-mail firms have a number of specialized criteria peculiar to their technology. Viguerie's organization insists that candidates prove they can raise significant funds on their own, partially because of the huge initial costs involved in a direct-mail program. And some firms, such as Craver, Mathews, Smith, and Co., refuse a significant percentage of the candidates and organizations that approach them because direct mail is not an appropriate device in many cases and will not turn a profit for the company or the clients.

Each consultant applies these criteria quite differently, giving more emphasis to some than others, and consequently he can judge particular candidates differently than his peers. The case of Bill Bradley's 1978 bid for the Democratic U.S. Senate nomination in New Jersey will serve to illustrate. Bradley's personal charm and flattering appeal to Michael Kaye's professional pride won the consultant over:

> Bill saw my work for the first time. Apparently, as he tells me, he instantly realized I was the guy without a doubt. . . . I liked the fact that he genuinely wanted me. I told him I would give him a decision after the weekend, because I was still wondering if I really wanted to fly back and forth to New Jersey all the time. I said, "Bill, don't bother me until next Monday." The next morning, he calls me. He said, "Mike, I know I've broken the rules, but I just have to tell you how much I want you to do this campaign. Maybe I didn't get that point across the other night, but I want you to know that we loved meeting you." That was very nice. Anyway, I did it and it was a marvelous year.

Kaye had not been Bradley's first choice, however; David Garth was. But Bradley's wooing of Garth had been much less successful, and Garth not only declined Bradley but signed on for Richard Leone, one of his opponents. Said Garth:

I didn't like Bradley. I interviewed him. It was awful. I asked him five or six questions. I asked him questions about energy, housing, the kind of things I think as a candidate for the U.S. Senate from the state of New Jersey he ought to know. He didn't know anything. I didn't ask him any questions like "Do you want to win?" or "Will you change your clothes?" I don't like that. Dick Leone was a personal friend of ours. We had worked with him in several campaigns. He probably would have been the best qualified guy in that race. He was also an Italian and I felt there was a shortage, quite frankly, of Italians in office, that we need more because it's a group that really feels unrepresented, the same as the blacks do.

Garth's comments make obvious the fact that political consultants have become preselectors in the nominating process, encouraging and dissuading candidacies often with the mere announcements of their choices of clients in a race. In this respect and in others—slate balancing, for example, as in Garth's determination that more Italians should be in office—modern political consultants have substituted for the party bosses of old and make decisions today that should more properly be the prerogative of party leaders. Peter Hart sounds like a more grammatical version of Tammany Hall's George Washington Plunkitt when he relates this anecdote:

I worked with [one candidate] in 1978 and came to the conclusion that he's a very, very bad human being and that I made a mistake. The person decided he'd seek office in 1980 and the guy made an appointment with me. I said, "I'm sorry to tell you, but I think you've got a character flaw. I'm sorry if nobody else has ever told you. I don't believe in you. I can't work to see that you get elected."

It is not that most political consultants look upon their preselector role cavalierly; some see it for what it is, a sobering responsibility. Sanford Weiner reminded his fellow consultants in a session of the American Association of Political Consultants that, in Watergate's wake, they had "a duty and a responsibility to screen would-be candidates more carefully than ever." But is it better for society to lodge this obligation with the political parties or with private individuals in the profit-making profession of consulting?

SOMETIMES POLITICAL CON-sultants become almost as famous as the candidates they represent. Pat Caddell is a case in point. He, like many consultants, will not work for a candidate who does not share his political beliefs and vision. Caddell is strongly identified with the Democratic party, where he works for liberal and middle-of-the-road candidates.

Caddell, like many of his colleagues, puts candidates through a screening process. He seeks "real patriots in the sense of really caring about the country." He has said, "If I were to apply one single criterion, it would be whether the individual really gives a good damn about what happens to the United States. Large numbers of politicians, frankly, could care less as long as they stay in office."[1]

Caddell believes that his polling and consulting services must be used to sup-port not only viable candidates but those who will make, in his opinion, an important contribution once elected. "Today there is a crisis of public confidence," he says, "not merely in specific office hold-ers, but in the functioning of government itself; not merely in bad policies, but the entire process of policy making. It is a crisis of confidence in the political pro-cess and the future of the nation."[2]

Caddell is once of many political con-sultants who have injected their own per-sonalities and values into the political process, helping to determine the kinds of candidates that run and even the poli-cies they work for once elected. Consul-tants are becoming an important political elite in their own right. The following se-lection portrays Pat Caddell and updates his political career, which has taken many twists and turns.

14 Lois Romano
PAT CADDELL: DOWN, BUT NEVER OUT

On one end of the line was Pat Caddell, pressing his case from a Washington pay phone. On the other end, in Wilmington, was the candidate's brother, telling Caddell he could not speak to Joe Biden right then.

"Jimmy, I want to talk to Joe," Caddell demanded into the phone. Jimmy Biden asked him what he wanted to say, offering to pass along Caddell's views. "Jimmy, I want to talk to Joe! You have Joe call me!" Caddell re-peated—adding that he had known Joe for 15 years and didn't need anyone to screen his calls.

It was the night before Biden ended his presidential campaign. Caddell's

[1]Larry J. Sabato, *The Rise of Political Consultants* (New York: Basic Books, 1981), p. 31.

[2]Ibid., p. 74.

From *Washington Post National Weekly Edition,* December 14, 1987. Copyright 1987 The *Washington Post.* Reprinted by permission.

man was done for, but the famed Democratic consultant wouldn't admit it—and now he couldn't even get him on the phone. "You people have formed a vigilante group to get my candidate out of the race," he told campaign spokesman Larry Rasky during one of his many calls that evening.

In 1972, at the tender age of 21, Caddell had been the pollster for Biden's first Senate race; now he desperately wanted his friend to be president. But in the week after the story broke that Biden had borrowed part of a speech from British Labor leader Neil Kinnock, according to members of Biden's staff, Caddell didn't take disappointment well. He yelled at a reporter, argued with colleagues, refused to work within the organization and looked for scapegoats.

Concede nothing, he urged. Attack the press.

He lashed out at his former partners, consultants Robert Shrum and David Doak, who are working on Missouri Rep. Richard A. Gephardt's campaign. Shrum and Doak, Caddell erroneously charged to Biden staffers, had produced the "attack video" that had been released to the media and used to highlight Biden's rhetorical borrowings. Later, he apologized to the Gephardt campaign.

From the senator's conference room, he screamed on the phone at the *New York Times* reporter who had written the original Kinnock story. Three senior campaign officials who witnessed the argument say he hurled profanities and pounded the receiver against a table during the call. Caddell says he didn't swear at the reporter, and he denies pounding the phone.

Caddell is large and intense, with a prominent nose and a dramatic white streak wandering down one side of his dark beard, and his demeanor has always been theatrical. Still, the scene the staffers describe was more than ordinarily disturbing. "I had to leave the room," says one. The others concur. Biden was horrified when he heard about the display, they say, and offered to phone the reporter with an apology.

Joe Biden had other reasons to be unhappy with his old friend. In a follow-up to the Kinnock story, he'd been accused of borrowing some of Robert Kennedy's language as well—language Caddell had inserted into a Biden speech but inadvertently not attributed to RFK. But beyond that, campaign staffers say, Caddell seemed to be putting his own interests above the candidate's.

So the man Biden once said was "like a little brother" to him wasn't even there when the candidate decided to give up his dream. One week after Biden withdrew from the race, he met with Caddell and told him his advice would not be welcomed in any future political endeavor. Later, although declining to be interviewed on the subject, Biden offered the following statement through a spokesman: "The senator wants it to be known that he has no animosity toward Pat Caddell, but that he has ended his relationship with him."

Caddell says that he "loves" Biden and that their friendship is still on. The statement, he assumes, means only that "we don't have a professional relationship anymore."

Meanwhile, Caddell stories took on a life of their own in political Washington. Campaign managers and aides for some of the remaining Democratic hopefuls jokingly assure each other that they have no plans to employ him. Says one: "[Democratic party Chairman] Paul Kirk's 11th commandment for party unity should be that no one hire Caddell for the general election."

"It's sad," says Gerald Rafshoon, a former Caddell roommate who worked closely with him during the Carter years, "but people are putting garlic in their windows."

Whoever thought it would come to this? That after 15 years of high voltage success working with George McGovern, Jimmy Carter, Gary Hart and Walter Mondale, not to mention Mario Cuomo, Bob Graham, Michael Dukakis, Paul Simon, Ted Kennedy and many others—15 years of being called "prodigy" and "genius" and "gifted" on the front pages—the boy wonder would be out of this campaign before the first vote was cast?

Sitting in his Georgetown office on a Saturday night, however, Caddell puts a very different face on the situation.

"I read," he says, "that 'Democratic insiders say Pat Caddell is dead as a consultant' and I'm [saying to myself], 'But I died already. I killed myself.'"

As proof, he produces a copy of his announcement, one year ago, that he was quitting elective politics. After considerable negotiation, he has agreed to an interview, which lasts three hours. He says he knows it's open season on him in some quarters, and even goes so far as to "apologize" to those he may have offended. But it is important to him that people understand one thing: The system is not rejecting him; he is rejecting it.

Caddell says people in Washington will believe anything about him. "There's a laugh-test standard here, a point where someone hears something ridiculous about somebody and they laugh and say, 'That's not true.' In my case, they just believe it."

He's right. Last spring, after the Donna Rice/Gary Hart fiasco, there was immediate speculation that Caddell had a part in bringing the story to light, and Caddell said in a recent *New York Times* interview that other political operatives had accused him of having a role. Caddell has ridiculed such talk, and no information has developed to support it, but it demonstrates the depth of anti-Caddell feeling.

He's become the butt of jokes such as: "He's like Jason in 'Friday the 13th'—you can't kill him, he just keeps coming back" (this from a former partner with a definite ax to grind). The "Bloom County" comic strip recently lumped him with Tammy Faye Bakker, Boy George and Ling-Ling among celebs whose careers could stand "a little shoring up." *U.S. News & World Report* declared him finished. The *Washington Monthly* slapped his name on the cover with those of four other Washington insiders. The message? "DON'T HIRE."

He's given all this a lot of thought, he says—but his friends maintain he still doesn't get the point.

"The tragedy of the Caddell story is that his personal actions have so corrupted his professional contribution that he may not be able to survive professionally," says Robert Beckel, who worked with Caddell during the Mondale campaign.

No one would use words like "tragedy" about Caddell, of course, if it weren't for the scope of that "professional contribution." And no smart politico would write him off when he's down—indeed, few would even talk about him on the record. Because at 37, Pat Caddell has the kind of skills that can bring him back from the grave again and again.

His polls—and more important, his reading of them—have been the core of highly regarded strategies for four presidential campaigns. He often seems to have an instinctive sense of where the electorate is, honing in particularly on what he likes to call the voter's "sense of alienation." Says Bill Schneider, senior fellow at the American Enterprise Institute: "His genius was to figure out how to first attract this alienated vote and then turn it into an antiestablishment campaign."

"His preparation of Mondale for his first debate with Reagan was nothing short of brilliant," says Tom Donilon, who worked with Caddell during the Mondale and Biden campaigns. "He had it right down to what Mondale's body language should be."

Says media consultant Robert Squier: "I made a last broadcast for Carter on election eve in 1976, and I couldn't have done it without Caddell. . . . He knew what doubts people had. . . . They wanted to see Carter stronger, so at Caddell's suggestion, I moved foreign policy high on the program. It was one of the times where you saw Caddell at his best."

No consultant can win them all, and Caddell has been associated with his share of nightmares. He helped draft Carter's ill-fated "malaise" speech in 1979, approved some negative ads in 1984 that seriously hurt Gary Hart in Illinois, and advised Coca-Cola while it was introducing New Coke (though his role in that ill-fated venture has been exaggerated).

Yet, ironically, a controversial Caddell memo to Carter—in which he wrote that "too many good people have been defeated because they tried to substitute substance for style"—could serve as a description of his own problems today: His substance has been appreciated. It's his style that has done him in.

Squier says that nine years after Pat Caddell saved that Carter broadcast, he recommended to then-Florida Gov. Bob Graham that he not rehire the pollster to handle his upcoming Senate race. "He had become difficult," Squier says. "I needed someone with his eye on the ball."

Now Squier likes to say: "I've been his friend and I've been his enemy and it takes less energy to be his enemy."

Caddell's may be the quintessential Washington tale of a young man who wanted to change the world, but rose too far too fast. As a result, former associates surmise, he soon stopped seeing himself as a mere pollster or adviser and began seeing himself as a maker of history, looming larger than his campaigns and his clients.

For all his political acumen, some say, he failed to grasp that he'd succeeded in what is essentially a very small arena. When his influence waned, so did people's tolerance, because he didn't play by that arena's established rules—rules like patience, hand-holding, sharing credit, massaging the media. With Caddell, it sometimes seemed that all successes were his successes; all failures belonged to someone else.

His temper became legendary. Stories are told, over and over, by veterans of past campaigns: of screaming fights ending with a standard refrain of "I'll ruin you!" or "You're finished!" Of intimidating calls, doors slamming shut, phones slamming down.

Not everyone sees him this way. Christie Hefner, Caddell's date for the 1977 inaugural, says he has always been a good friend. Former Kennedy speech writer Richard Goodwin says Caddell is brighter than most everybody else, but won't last long "in an environment where the ability to get along is prized over excellence and achievement." One friend, Mike McAdams, who worked with Caddell in the early '70s, emphasizes that "with Pat you have to know how to pick out the pearls. . . . "

Caddell himself offers three reasons for the animosity: his anti-establishment ideas, which he says people are threatened by; professional jealousy, because he has been "fairly successful"; and finally—yes, he admits, he has acted badly on occasion. "You can't be as controversial as I have gotten to be unless you have done a lot to stir the pot yourself," he says. ". . . I made some real mistakes."

But during the interview, he comes back to reasons one and two. He has been harsh sometimes, he says, because that has been his job. He has been a hired gun, paid to get things done. And you can't get things done by rolling over. "It is more than just my personality," he insists. "One thing logic dictates: People don't become obsessed the way they have become obsessed with me. People don't say the kind of things—it doesn't work itself into a frenzy if it's just my personality. There has to be something deeper. I'm not going to say I wish I had not acted the way I acted in some campaigns. . . . But I couldn't have had a career in this business if I couldn't work with people."

His senior year at Harvard was a heady time for Pat Caddell. With a $25,000 loan guaranteed by a friend, he was able to start a polling firm with two classmates. In the fall of 1971, a mutual acquaintance hooked him up with Gary Hart, then George McGovern's campaign manager. Hart paid Caddell's firm $500 to do a poll in New Hampshire; it showed that Edmund

Muskie's blue-collar support was thin. "So we sent McGovern into the factories," recalls McGovern aide Frank Mankiewicz. The Harvard whiz kid "applied a whole new dimension to surveys," Mankiewicz says. "If we wanted to know McGovern's following among divorced women with second homes who also collected rocks, Pat Caddell could tell us that." Coming off the McGovern campaign into the 1974 congressional races, he was one of the hottest pollsters in the business. A year later, Jimmy Carter signed him up—which was seen as a coup for the unknown Georgian. Caddell was 25 years old.

Carter fit perfectly into Caddell's theory that voters are sympathetic to an outsider. He didn't have to remake Carter into a populist farmer, from the South, with no Washington ties, but he helped define him for the voters. His polls tested specific levels of alienation in various segments of the electorate, as well as negative feelings toward other candidates.

The Georgian's victory brought Caddell to the height of his power. Never in history had a public-opinion analyst enjoyed such an intimate relationship with a president.

Fairly or unfairly, however, he is most remembered for his part in the crafting of Carter's "malaise" speech, in which the president told the nation it faced a kind of crisis of self-confidence—a message Americans clearly didn't want to hear. Walter Mondale, for one, had called the idea "crazy," but Caddell had reportedly taken his case to the first lady, who had brought it to Carter.

After Carter's loss in 1980, Caddell began candidate-shopping again. John Glenn turned him down and Mondale had hired Peter Hart, so he tried to create his own candidate—a "Mr. Smith" who could run on the outside track again. Biden was his first choice. Then Dale Bumpers of Arkansas, then Chris Dodd of Connecticut. They all said they didn't want to run.

Insiders started to snicker, saying Pat Caddell couldn't find a horse to ride. Finally, on New Year's Eve, Gary Hart summoned him to his Bethesda, Md., home. Caddell told Hart to focus on Iowa, which the campaign had considered bypassing. He also told the candidate—then invisible in the polls—that he must show passion and sharpen his message.

A few weeks after Hart stunned Mondale in the New Hampshire primary, stories were published detailing Caddell's contribution. Two of Hart's longtime staffers were annoyed at what they saw as his self-promotion.

In the fall of 1984, the Mondale campaign sent a message to Caddell that they would accept his help. The result was a memo so impressive that campaign chairman Jim Johnson asked Caddell to conduct major polling and develop a fall strategy.

Caddell is credited with advising Mondale not to go after Reagan personally in their first debate, but to use disarming kindness and assault his policies. It worked brilliantly, and for one of the few times in the campaign, it seemed as though Mondale might actually be gaining on the president. Shortly afterward, the *New York Times* reported that it had been Caddell's strategy that helped unsettle Reagan.

Some Mondale staffers were furious. Caddell had managed to get the glory once again.

Joe Biden was aware from the start that Caddell could be a problem, staffers say, but Biden genuinely liked and respected Caddell as well. Even with the press portraying Biden as a Caddell creation, the candidate remained committed to finding him a role. But the mere shadow of Caddell could cause problems, according to campaign aides.

Biden ultimately hired Tim Ridley, a veteran of Chuck Robb's and Frank Lautenberg's campaigns, who says he was leery of the Caddell connection. "Right from the beginning we wrestled with the fact that there were people out there who would want to shoot Joe Biden in hopes of wounding Caddell," says Ridley today.

Caddell sees the creation of a candidate's "message" as his strong suit. He contributed significantly to Biden's official announcement speech in early June, though the staff was concerned that his inserts seemed to criticize the electorate.

But on the morning after the speech, there was trouble. In his story on Biden's announcement, Paul Taylor of the *Washington Post* mentioned that Caddell had also worked on Carter's "malaise" speech. Caddell was furious, and accosted Taylor at a hotel in Des Moines. "I was on the elevator," Caddell recalls, "and when Paul walked on, I thought God had obviously set this up." He followed Taylor to the checkout counter, venting his anger with personal accusations Taylor characterizes as obscene.

"No, it wasn't helpful to the campaign," Caddell admits. "I told Joe about it. He gave me a chewing out."

Says Ridley: "This incident crystallized for Joe all the problems of Pat's involvement." Several weeks later, Biden and longtime aide Ted Kaufman told him it would be better if he didn't come to the first nationally televised debate in Houston.

At this point, according to campaign staffers, Biden couldn't figure out what to do with him, and Caddell himself was determined to define his role. He tried repeatedly to talk to Biden alone, they say. He flew to San Francisco to get Biden's ear. They had a long dinner, but there was no resolution to the question of his campaign role.

So Caddell turned to memo writing, producing at least two 100-page analyses of the campaign for Biden—one of which, two aides say, suggested a larger role for himself. But Biden did nothing in response.

In late August, Caddell came east to help prepare Biden, chairman of the Senate Judiciary Committee, prepare for the hearings on Judge Robert H. Bork's nomination to the Supreme Court. But he still hadn't reestablished his bond with the senator. He tried to get some time alone with Biden. Finally, he told one Biden aide: "I will not compete with these people to give Joe advice!"

During one August gathering in Biden's kitchen, according to Ridley, the candidate confided to his senior staff—his sister Valerie, Ridley, Kaufman and Donilon—that he simply didn't know what to do with Caddell. Then came the Kinnock story, and the question didn't matter anymore.

Opinion on Caddell's future role in the Democratic party is decidedly mixed. Like a troublesome slugger in a tight pennant race, he could still be picked up by another presidential team—but many influential Democrats say they can't buy that scenario at all.

For his part, Caddell continues to insist he can't be left out because he's already quit. He has no interest in campaigns, he says. What he does have an interest in is substance. He says he wants to contribute by speaking and writing. He's working on book proposals, he says, and jokes that even negative publicity helps generate interest. He says he's not going to "miss his wave."

He says that he's also working on some movie projects with his friend actor Warren Beatty, and that he loves teaching. "It changed my life," he says of the course he taught at the University of California at Santa Barbara. "Just to be able to give something to these kids." His students say he is a terrific teacher.

But does anyone believe he won't be back with a vengeance for at least one last campaign? Not a chance.

"Napoleon was exiled to the island of Elba, from which he returned for his great 100 days," says Christopher Matthews, a veteran observer of the Democratic wars. "Later, he was exiled to St. Helena, where he died. . . . The big question is whether this is Elba or St. Helena for him.

"I think there is a second coming of Pat Caddell."

TELEVISION ANCHORS NOT only make news but also may make political candidates. The ubiquitous media cover every aspect of presidential campaigns, focusing particularly on candidates' personalities and styles. Both electronic and print reporters seek newsworthy stories that will please their producers and editors sufficiently to run them on the nightly news or the front page. The following selection depicts the media's role in campaigning, illustrating how reporters have themselves become political insiders often fascinated more with the intriguing game of politics than with making sense of the issues.

15 Jonathan Alter
THE MEDIA AND CAMPAIGNING—'88 STYLE

Curtis Wilkie of the *Boston Globe* had dinner in New Hampshire recently with David Broder of the *Washington Post,* longtime dean of American political reporters. Wilkie is himself a veteran campaign correspondent, but he had just finished a three-year stint in the Middle East and felt out of touch with the 1988 campaign. Did Broder have a fix on what was happening? Broder didn't, and neither did anyone else Wilkie talked to. "Nobody knows what the hell's goin' on," says Wilkie. Pity the press corps. This year's dominant theme is shaping up as "uncertainty"—an idea that induces as much panic as excitement in the media. After all, political reporters are paid to sound as if they know what they're talking about.

Unfortunately, the press corps is held captive in Campaignland—the worst possible vantage point from which to make sense of anything. The extension cords that connect political coverage to the rest of the country have become hopelessly tangled. Stories that seem stale to reporters (e.g., candidate positions on education) are news to millions of people. And news that those millions might view as boring, trivial, or irrelevant (e.g., a staff resignation) is fresh, even explosive, to those inside the political echo chamber. The media seem as out of kilter as the presidential selection process itself, perhaps because they are now so much a part of that process.

Gary Hart, George Bush and Richard Gephardt have all scored points by attacking the press, which has become an issue this year as never before. But in doing so they have mostly succeeded in reinforcing the idea that the way the story is told is at least as important as they are. Reporters certainly think so. At the *Washington Post,* three political correspondents, Broder, Martin Schram (since departed) and now Paul Taylor, have written or are currently writing books not about presidential candidates as such, but about the way they are covered. After a while, dizziness sets in. Witness the now almost commonplace spectacle of an Iowa farmer being interviewed by a print reporter who is being shot by a still photographer who is being taped by a TV crew, all of which is the subject of a magazine's media story.

It will only get worse. Historically, the role of the media is greatest *after* the voting begins, when the totals are measured against expectations. Thus Eugene McCarthy in 1968 and George McGovern in 1972 "won" the New Hampshire primary without actually having done so. They simply did BTE (Better Than Expected). This year's conventional wisdom says that Sen. Paul Simon and Rep. Richard Gephardt need either first- or second-place showings in the Iowa caucuses and that Gov. Michael Dukakis must win in New Hampshire. The expectations have become so convoluted on the Republican side that it won't be enough for Sen. Bob Dole to beat a sitting vice president in Iowa—a stunning feat in any other year. Ludicrous as it sounds, Dole must win by a large margin to avoid a George Bush BTE victory. It's no wonder that the worst epithet that can be tossed at a candidate is "front runner."

But the expectations game is rapidly changing. This time reporters are more cautious about making flat-out predictions based on their gut feelings. That's because in the past almost everyone guessed wrong, which gave the candidates who were underestimated (e.g., Jimmy Carter in 1976) an enormous boost when they confounded expectations. "People like me who said it was really a two-man race between [Walter] Mondale and [John] Glenn in '84 are a little more cautious this time," says Jon Margolis of the *Chicago Tribune.* Oblivious to an 11th-hour surge by Gary Hart, *Newsweek* and the *New York Times,* among many others, reported with assurance on the eve of the 1984 New Hampshire primary that Mondale would win.

Such surprises are less likely this year. The reason is that the reporter with his political dowsing stick has been at least partly replaced by the "science" of "tracking" polls. These polls, used sparingly in 1984, are now a regular part of the survey research arsenal at many news organizations. Like a hospital EKG, tracking polls chart tiny blips in support just before an election, proving far more reliable than the nearly worthless polls published weeks or months before the voting. "The one real decision this time in the Fourth Estate was: 'You will not [surprise] us again'," says Jody Powell, Carter's former press secretary.

Small springboard: The new EKG approach spells trouble for candidates trying to beat the expectations game. Gephardt, for instance, seems to be surging in Iowa. But the time span required for identifying and digesting such information is now so short that a win for him will have been anticipated in the polls and thus somewhat devalued. The result is that whoever wins Iowa and New Hampshire may get less of a springboard effect than, well, expected.

Sneaking up on the process is also harder because there are now so many journalists covering it. Call it the pundit glut—too many reporters and analysts chasing too few angles in too fluid a news environment. The results are that genuine scoops are next to impossible and the status of the political correspondent within journalism is not what it once was. Reporters covering foreign affairs, national security or business have far more room for enterprise. The political beat is still coveted—after all, it's fun—but it doesn't have the stature of the days of Teddy White in the 1960s or the boys on the bus in the early '70s.

At the same time, the terms of success at political reporting are being redefined. Ronald Brownstein, who covers politics for the National Journal, views the change as generational: "[Jack] Germond and [Jules] Witcover will see a lot of union people and county chairmen, whereas the younger guys tend to talk more to pollsters and professors." The goal of the first approach is to find out who will win, though county chairmen and union leaders, as Germond and Witcover know better than anyone, don't have the clout they once did. The goal of the newer approach is to find out why certain candidates and themes are selling—a conceptual framework for understanding the election and the country. The weakness here is that the experts frequently know little more than the journalists themselves, since they are part of precisely the same culture. Often they are literally one and the same, which means that pundits (particularly on TV) are reduced to interviewing each other.

Despite the growth in the industry, national reporters and experts still compose a small universe of people—no more than 1,000—who handicap presidential politics. "It's like guys on a basketball team," says Mike Lavalle, owner of the City Grille, a popular hangout for the media crowd in Des Moines. "They come in and I almost expect them to high-five each other, saying, 'Great piece,' or something." Good local reporters can become superstars for a time in this universe, with network anchors hanging on their every word. David Yepsen of the *Des Moines Register* may have been interviewed more often than Alexander Haig. But he has a Cinderella problem. As Yepsen knows, the day after the Iowa caucuses he will turn into a pumpkin.

More substance: The familiar complaint heard from voters is that the press does not focus enough on the "issues." This is often true. On the Democratic side, for instance, there's an interesting debate about a national sales tax that receives scant attention amid the sound-bites featuring the most clever candidate put-downs of the day. But what's really missing, in terms of substance, is a more searching analysis of how each candidate would govern. Both Jimmy Carter and Ronald Reagan had records as governors that contained sharp lessons for their presidencies. Editors claim they ran stories detailing them. But when? The pieces appeared so early in the election year that hardly anyone was paying much attention. They were rarely repeated because the standards of the news business demand that reporting be "new." "After we've written story X or Y, we feel we've done it, even if practically no one's read it," says Bob Drogin of the *Los Angeles Times.* While this year's emphasis on character has been frivolous and excessive at times, at least it is an attempt to address the question of what a candidate would be like in office.

Do media judgments about competence and character affect the voters? This year's campaign offers one laboratory test of that question. One candidate, Bruce Babbitt, has received extremely favorable press coverage—he is depicted as the only contender with the courage to stand up for higher taxes. Another, Gary Hart, has been savaged by the media. His hope lies in tapping resentment toward the press and the maxim that it doesn't matter what they say as long as they show your face and spell your name right. Right now, anyway, polls put Babbitt behind and Hart ahead nationally, though Hart has slipped in Iowa.

The public may not believe it, but the media do not have much stake in individual candidates. The tone of coverage can change overnight, as an underdog candidate like Babbitt will learn if he wins some primaries. The media's real stake is institutional. On the nights of the Iowa caucuses and New Hampshire primary, watch for the battle between drama and truth. Having invested so heavily in the process, not to mention their own equipment and manpower, few news organizations will have the courage to pronounce either event a dud. Campaignland is now too self-important—and the media too big a player in it—to tolerate the idea that an event to which so much has been devoted could be anything less than a surpassing moment for American democracy.

FOR MANY POLITICAL CANDI-dates negative campaigning has become the tactic of choice. George Bush's 1988 presidential campaign depicted Massachusetts governor Michael Dukakis, for example, as a coddler of criminals in the "Willy Horton ads" that blamed the Democratic candidate for paroling a notorious criminal who committed a particularly heinous act after he was paroled. Negative campaigning does not always work, and may backfire against its perpetrator. (See Chapter 1, "The Lure of the Political Road.") The following selection gives students a rare glimpse behind the scenes of political campaigning as an experienced political consultant offers advice to candidates on how to defend against negative campaigning.

16 Joseph Napolitan
NEGATIVE CAMPAIGNING: WHAT IT IS, HOW TO USE IT, HOW TO DEFEND AGAINST IT

There is nothing new about negative campaigning. Examples exist of negative campaigning in presidential elections almost two centuries ago.

Picture this scenario: The candidate for president is a white male accused of keeping a black mistress and fathering several children by her. The opposition has attacked him openly as an atheist, a fanatic, a revolutionary, and someone likely to repudiate the national debt. And all of these charges are more or less true.

Imagine what Roger Ailes could do with that.

But the year was 1800 and the candidate was Thomas Jefferson, and, fortunately for America, he was elected anyway.

The virulence of modern campaigning and its unquestioned rate of success has developed as a result of a vastly more sophisticated delivery and distribution system for the negative messages. Television is the most important of these new delivery systems but certainly not the only one. In fact, in some cases it may not even be the best vehicle for negative attacks, although it certainly is one that gains the most attention. In fact, in some instances a virtually irrefutable last-minute tightly targeted direct-mail campaign may be far more damaging.

Let me make one point clear: I am not opposed to negative campaigning, per se. I use it in my campaigns; my opponents use it against my candidates.

And the immediate future, specifically the 1990 election cycle, seems certain to see an intensification of negative campaigning on the simple grounds that consultants and candidates believe it works and that they would not be able to win without it.

From *Campaign Industry News,* Vol. III, No. 3, 1989, pp. 18–21. Copyright 1989 Campaign Industry News, Inc. Reprinted by permission.

But I also believe there is a line that can be drawn between legitimate attacks on an opponent's record and insidious attacks skillfully designed to appeal to the voters' worst instincts in a highly emotional manner. These attacks, and how to handle them, form the primary focus of this article. But first let me describe what kind of negative charges I consider to be fair and appropriate. Basically, these center around what a candidate has said and done in his public career, and which are based on factual, documentable evidence.

The Legitimate Negative Ad

Here are some of the areas I consider perfectly legitimate grounds for criticizing a political opponent:

The candidate's public record: What the candidate has said, votes he has cast or missed, positions he has taken and promises he has not kept are suitable subjects for criticism.

Embarrassing statements or votes: Every incumbent, and probably other candidates as well, has said or done things he wishes at least some of his constituents had forgotten or never knew about. Some of these things are important, many undoubtedly are trivial. But if they are on the record they can be used.

Campaign promises impossible to fulfill: Promising to cut taxes and improve services, or proposing programs without providing a budget or cost analysis, are clearly impossible dreams.

Refusal to take a position: If a candidate ducks, dodges and hedges on controversial issues, he is fair game for criticism.

Refusal to make a financial disclosure statement or reveal the source of campaign funds: Lots of candidates have stumbled on this obstacle, usually because they think revealing certain information would do them more harm than trying to duck the issue.

Acceptance of funds from organizations which can benefit from the actions of his office: These attacks are especially effective if it can be proven that the candidate did use his office to help financial supporters.

Membership in restricted clubs: If it can be proven the opponent belongs to clubs that don't admit women, Jewish members, or other minorities, or belongs to organizations with extremist views, he or she can certainly be criticized.

Signing restrictive covenants: If the candidate has signed a restrictive covenant that forbids the sale of his home or property to minorities, he can be attacked for doing so.

Callous indifference to real problems: Such attacks work particularly well if it can be shown the candidate talks one game but plays another: e.g. calling for a crackdown on the spread of drugs but voting against funds to finance those efforts.

Positions on controversial issues: Any time a candidate takes a position on a controversial issue—abortion being the current hot topic—he alienates a segment of the electorate. (Still, in my opinion, it is better for a candidate to adopt a firm position than to try to hedge on controversial issues.)

Favoring a position most people oppose: This may be an act of courage, or stupidity, or religious belief. In New York one time, House Speaker Stanley Steingut tried to end Sunday shopping, which was very popular with a lot of people. Tony Schwartz produced a radio spot urging voters to call Steingut and express their opposition to his position and gave them Steingut's telephone number. Steingut not only changed his position, he also changed his phone number.

Catching an opponent in an outright lie: This is one of the most obvious areas of legitimate attack. If you catch your opponent telling a lie, you can attack his credibility by hammering away at the deception.

Also legitimate opportunities for criticism: Residency/Carpetbagging; Absenteeism; Refusal to debate; Arrogance; Criminal record; Dishonorable discharge from the military; Lack of qualifications for the office sought; Lack of competence; Lack of knowledge about everyday matters; Inconsistencies/Flip-flops; Broken promises in previous elections; Failure to vote.

Producer Bob Squier says he has his own standards for negative advertising: "It should be honest," he says, "and it should be fair. It is possible to be honest without being fair. I won't use a spot unless I consider it both honest and fair.

Insidious Negative Imagery

Now let's move to the shadowy area I call insidious negative advertising. Three of the definitions of "insidious" in Webster's Dictionary are: "Harmful but enticing," "Having a gradual and cumulative effect," and "deceitful." Two of the synonyms suggested are "treacherous" and "seductive." I think all of these apply to certain kinds of negative advertising.

Negative advertising isn't always beneficial to the candidate or to the cause making the charge. Often it backfires, and usually with a little help from the opposition.

After reviewing and analyzing many negative television spots from recent campaigns, I have come to these conclusions about what I term insidious spots.

They seldom are on a substantive issue: The subject is peripheral and/or irrelevant to the main thrust of the campaign. The attacks call for a purely negative response. In the broad sense, they usually are not true—but often contain a germ of truth; that germ of truth is magnified and blown all out of proportion. More often than not, charges are made by implication.

Insidious attacks often use symbolism in patriotic and moralistic terms: Thus the charges by George Bush against Michael Dukakis in 1988 on the Pledge of Allegiance. Invariably these spots take a small incident and blow it out of all proportion; they exaggerate and magnify insignificant incidents.

They make it appear the subject of the attack has control over a situation when he actually does not: Again, Dukakis had no control over the recitation of the Pledge of Allegiance in Massachusetts schools. Insidious spots frequently use hoary technique of guilt by association. They capitalize on words or phrases that have come to have a negative connotation among some groups; examples—"ultra-liberal," "Kennedy-Democrat," "soft on crime," "socialist theory," "left wing."

Insidious attacks are seldom made directly by the candidate or his campaign: More often the charges are made by some third-party entity, allegedly without the campaign's consent. Often responsibility for especially vicious attacks is vigorously denied by the candidate and his campaign advisers; then after all the damage had been done, somebody's head may roll, usually belonging to some minor functionary well down in the chain of command.

The facts are usually distorted in insidious spots: Yet if the spot works, it will stay on the air even if refuted unless pressure is exerted to remove it. And if the facts are not refuted, the spot will run forever; if the subject of the attack chooses to ignore it, for whatever reason, the spot will stay on the air until the candidate airing the spot decides it has done its job.

Finally, the insidious ad tries to capitalize on the theory "Where there's smoke there's fire": Too many voters are all too ready to believe the worst. Some of the most vicious insidious spots—such as accusing a candidate of being a homosexual in a district where this is sure to hurt him—are based on this theory. The seed is planted; the weed grows in its own environment.

Two additional points to remember about insidious campaigning:

Direct mail at the very end can have a powerful impact: Letters or mailgrams carrying a false message and targeted to hit at the very last moment, the day before the election or election day itself, can have a powerful last-minute influence in swaying the vote.

Even the so-called legitimate news media make insidious attacks on candidates they oppose: Sometimes these can be even more damaging than direct attacks by a candidate because they come under cloak of new objectivity.

Beating the Mudslingers: What Do You Do?

The question now becomes: What does your candidate do when he or she is targeted as the victim of insidious advertising? These are my recommendations:

Reaction must be strong and immediate: Counterattack swiftly; Hold the opposition candidate personally responsible for the attacks; Many times the candidate himself must personally respond: Get credible individuals or institutions to respond as surrogates for the candidate.

If spots really are libelous, bring legal action: Accuse the opposition of dirty campaigning and mudslinging; Impute the integrity of the attacker; Never settle for letting some low-level worker be the fall guy. If your attacker has a consultant who is a member of the American Association of Political Consultants or the International Association of Political Consultants, move to have him or her expelled.

Be combative: Never let an insidious attack go unchallenged unless you have an insurmountable lead—and maybe not even then. React but don't overreact. Use good humor when it works.

Always conduct negative research on your own candidate as well as your opponent: Try to preempt charges you know will be made; Make sure your candidate really knows how to answer the charge; Don't deny the truth; Don't lie about your opponent; Don't lie about yourself. Make sure as a consultant you know what skeletons are hanging in your candidate's closet.

Try to take a known negative and turn it into an asset: If there is something in your candidate's background that at first glance seems like a negative but which can be presented in a positive manner, consider doing so.

Be prepared: Suppose there is some legitimate area of concern in your candidate's background that the opposition may or may not know about. Prepare some materials in advance, ready to go on at a moment's notice if the issue arises. If it doesn't, forget about it.

It's unlikely any candidate will need to employ all of these possible responses to reactions, but he should be aware of the options available if it becomes necessary to use them.

"Doing a Dukakis"

According to Howard Kurtz of the *Washington Post,* the spate of negative advertising in the 1988 campaign created a new term, "to do a Dukakis," which, Kurtz says, means to "passively ignore an opponent's attack."

It sure didn't work for Dukakis and it is unlikely to work for anyone else as the intensity of negative campaigning increases. Under present conditions, no consultant in his right mind is going to advise any client to "do a Dukakis" in the forthcoming elections.

SUCCESSFUL POLITICAL CANDI-dates learn to deal with the media from the day they run for office until they retire. The grist of the reporter's mill is information, and sometimes misinformation. Reporters follow political candidates like hawks stalking their prey, hoping that in one fell swoop they will be able to capture information that will command a front-page headline or a spot on the nightly television news. At least that is the view of the press held by many politicians.

The focus of the most intense press attention is, understandably, presidential politics, both running and governing.

Before Richard Nixon boarded over the indoor White House pool to make a press-briefing room, presidential aides going to their offices in the West Wing walked through a press lounge. There, one White House aide told the author, the "piranha" eagerly waited to devour White House staffers. In the paranoiac atmosphere that so frequently pervades politics, the press is always the enemy unless it is controlled. Every president in the modern era, from Franklin D. Roosevelt to Ronald Reagan, has attempted to manage the news. William Safire defines managed news as "information generated and distributed by the government in such a way as to give government interest priority over candor."[1]

The media are, to use the phrase of Douglass Cater, the fourth branch of the government.[2] The press, which now includes the electronic as well as the print media, has appointed itself guardian of the public interest. Although many members of the press have a cozy relationship with public officials, upon whom they depend for valuable information, the theory of the press that is taught in journalism schools requires reporters to distance themselves personally from the subjects of their stories. The adversary relationship between investigative reporters and the government enables a reporter to ferret out the facts no matter how unpleasant they may be.

Although the Washington press includes reporters like Bob Woodward and Carl Bernstein, whose investigations of the Nixon White House's coverup of the break-in at the Democratic National Headquarters in the Watergate office complex led to impeachment proceedings against the president and to his resignation, these reporters are exceptions and not the rule. Understandably, the seductive Washington environment, in which power and status mean everything, has co-opted many. The press has become part of the Washington establishment because it has learned to play the game of power politics itself. The Gridiron Club, an old and exclusive organization of newspaper people, symbolizes the press elite. Annually it invites members of the political establishment to join it in a fun-filled session of humor and satire. The spirit of camaraderie that prevails at such a gathering can be appreciated by those on the inside. President and Mrs. Reagan were the highlights of the club's meeting in 1982, as the first lady skillfully performed a skit that satirized the prevailing press view of her activities.

The Gridiron Club may roast politicians, but its members recognize that the

[1]William Safire, *Safire's Political Dictionary* (New York: Random House, 1978), p. 397.

[2]Douglass Cater, *The Fourth Branch of the Government* (Boston: Houghton Mifflin, 1959).

press and the politicians are in the same broader club of the politically powerful. Washington reporters recognize that to be at the top of the newspaper profession they must have access to the top of the political world. The linkage between success and power often softens the adversary stance of the press.

Washington's political centers of power recognize that the press is an important fourth branch of the government. Presidents, members of Congress, and even Supreme Court justices know that managing the news will buttress their power and may even be a key to survival. Presidents, especially during their first few years in office, feel besieged by a press that they consider hostile and unfair. Even before he became president, John F. Kennedy went out of his way to

warn an aide about the press, "Always remember that their interests and ours ultimately conflict."[3]

Kennedy cultivated political reporters, and his good press relations not only helped him to win the presidential election in 1960 but also buttressed his presidency. Richard Nixon blamed his 1960 defeat on an unfair press, an attitude that was intensified after he lost his race for the California governorship in 1963. Nixon understandably put managing the news at the top of his agenda when he became president.

All presidents would like to manage the news, which, in the view of Jimmy Carter's press secretary Jody Powell in the following selection, gives the White House the right to lie when national security is at stake.

17   Jody Powell
THE RIGHT TO LIE

Since the day the first reporter asked the first tough question of a government official, there has been an ongoing debate about whether government has the right to lie.

The debate took on its present form one day in 1963, when then Pentagon spokesman Arthur Sylvester, for reasons known only to himself, responded to the question officially and honestly. "Yes," he said, "under certain circumstances I think government does have the right to lie."

The resulting furor has made every sitting press secretary and senior government official leery of the question from that day since. Like all my predecessors, I was always careful not to give a direct response. It was one of those questions for which you prepare and keep on file a standard evasion. But Sylvester, of course, was right. In certain circumstances, government has not

[3]William Safire, *Safire's Political Dictionary,* p. 397.

From *The Other Side of the Story* by Jody Powell. Copyright 1984 by Jody Powell. Reprinted by permission of William Morrow & Company, Inc.

only the right but a positive obligation to lie. For me, that right-obligation flows directly from two other principles:

First, that government has a legitimate right to secrecy in certain matters because the welfare of the nation requires it. In other cases, individuals, even public figures, have a certain right to privacy because common decency demands it.

Secondly, the press has a right to print what it knows within very broad limits, without prior restraint, because the survival of democratic government depends on it.

Those two principles are often in conflict. Fortunately, the confrontation is not usually irreconcilable. Questions can be evaded. Answers can be devised that may mislead, but do not directly misrepresent. A "no comment" can sometimes be used without its being taken as a confirmation. Or the reporter can be sworn to secrecy himself and told why it is that certain information would be terribly damaging if published.

That is usually the case, but not always. Occasionally, the conflict is so sharp and the matter involved so important that there is no way to slide off the point. There is simply no answer that is both true and responsible. In such cases, the only decent thing to do is to lie and, I would argue, to make it the most convincing lie you can devise.

In my four years in the White House, I was only faced with that type of situation twice. The first involved a question from a so-called reporter who was noted for trading in gossip and personal scandal, and who worked for a publication that had an even worse reputation in that regard.

The question involved the personal life of a colleague and that of his family. To have responded with what I believed to be the truth would have resulted in great pain and embarrassment for a number of perfectly innocent people. Beyond that, I could see no reason why the matter should be of public interest.

I had little doubt that an evasion or "no comment" would be taken as more than adequate confirmation by this particular writer, and no doubt whatsoever that there was no hope of successfully appealing to a sense of compassion and fair play. So I lied.

I did not just deny the allegation, but went to some trouble to construct a convincing argument as to what I suspected to be the case. Apparently, it worked, probably because others who were asked responded in much the same way I did. In any case, the story never appeared in print anywhere that I know of.

I have absolutely no regrets for what I did, and can say without hesitation that I would do the same thing again if similar circumstances arose. Quite simply, it seems to me that to the extent journalism insists upon the right to probe into matters that can destroy families and ruin careers, but which in no way involve a breach of public trust, it must also grant the right to those who become targets to defend themselves by the only means available.

Moreover, there will inevitably be a disputed area between journalists and public figures over what is, and what is not, a legitimate matter of public interest. In some cases, the answer may not be clear, even to the most unbiased observer, except in retrospect. And it hardly needs to be said that a *post hoc* decision that a personal matter should have remained private is of absolutely no benefit to those who have been hurt by its publication.

The other situation in which I believed, and still believe, that I had an obligation to lie occurred in April of 1980.

Following the collapse of the first of two attempts to negotiate an agreement with the Iranian government to secure the release of our hostages, because those nominally in positions of authority either could not or would not live up to their promises, the president began to look more seriously at a military rescue operation.

He had given orders for work to begin on such an option as soon as the hostages were seized. At that time, there seemed to be no feasible way to go about it with a decent chance of success. In the intervening months, as the Pentagon studied, planned, and trained, and as we learned more about the situation in the embassy compound through intelligence operations and the news media, the chances for a successful attempt began to increase.

Although I knew the work was being done, I knew nothing about its specifics, and indeed did not want to know, until March 22, 1980. In a meeting at Camp David to review our options following the disintegration of the first agreement, Secretary of Defense Brown and Joint Chiefs of Staff Chairman General David Jones presented a full briefing on their plans for a rescue operation.

It was impressive, both because of the work that had gone into it and the intelligence that we had managed to gather, and because the detailed consideration of such an option inevitably has a powerfully sobering effect on anyone with a say in whether or not it will be implemented.

Still, no one seemed to feel that this was the correct choice at the time. There were some questions raised about whether some aspects of what was necessarily a complex plan could not be simplified. More important in the decision not to go ahead then was the willingness, although reluctant, to give diplomacy one last chance. No one doubted that there would be American casualties, even in a successful operation. One Israeli soldier and three hostages had been killed at Entebbe, and the problems that faced our planners, and would face the strike force, were many times more difficult than anything the Israelis had confronted. There had also been messages from our intermediaries, and indirectly from Iranian officials, almost begging for a chance to put the negotiated agreement back on track.

Even though no one argued that day that we should choose the rescue option, I left the meeting feeling that we were heading down a road that would soon bring us to that choice unless the Iranians suddenly came to their senses. Despite my agreement with the decision to try the diplomatic approach again, I had to admit to myself that the odds seemed to be against the Iranians' implementing the agreement they had already reneged on once.

On the morning of April 11, shortly after that second diplomatic effort had indeed collapsed, the president called me into his office a few minutes before the regular Friday morning foreign-policy breakfast was to begin. During most of the administration, I had not attended these breakfasts on a regular basis. When the president felt that the agenda required my presence, he would let me know. Occasionally, I would ask to be included if I had a point I wanted to raise, or if I felt the need to listen to the discussion on a particular topic.

Once the hostage crisis began, however, I asked to attend on a regular basis, so that I could keep abreast of the latest thinking by the decision makers, as well as the often fast-breaking events. The president readily agreed. So I was somewhat surprised that morning when he said that he wanted to talk to me about whether I should attend the breakfast.

Then he explained that one of the topics, not included on the written agenda, was the rescue mission. I could tell, or thought I could, by his tone of voice and expression that this had now become a serious option for him.

Was this something I would rather not know about? the president asked. Would it make my job easier if down the road I could honestly claim to have had no knowledge of this option?

I replied that I had given some thought to the matter since the Camp David session. It seemed to me that if he decided to go ahead with the rescue option, we would need an aggressive effort to protect its secrecy. That might involve purposely misleading or even lying to the press. If it did, I was the person to do it. And if I did it, I wanted to have the information necessary to make my effort successful. Since I was also being asked about the Iran crisis almost every day, I said, there was the chance that I might inadvertently compromise the mission unless I knew exactly what activities were the most sensitive.

The president said he had expected that would be my response, and he agreed with it, but he had wanted to hear it from me.

Then he added with a hint of a smile, "If you have to lie to the press, I may have to fire you when this is all over, you know. I'm not sure I can have a press secretary who won't tell the truth to the press."

"That," I said, "would be doing me a real favor."

"And an even bigger one for the country," said the president with what I hoped was a smile, as he turned to walk to the Cabinet room, where his foreign policy team was waiting.

The briefing, on which I took no notes, was much the same as the earlier session at Camp David. Maps and charts were positioned on an easel and occasionally spread on the table for closer examination. The questions and suggestions from three weeks earlier had been taken into account, and the military planners had come up with a few new wrinkles on their own.

By the time it was over, I sensed that the men around the table, including the president, were leaning strongly toward ordering the plan to be implemented. The comments that followed confirmed my hunch. I added my endorsement, and emphasized again my feeling that we would need to give some thought to cover stories and an aggressive effort to protect the secrecy of the mission if the president decided to go ahead.

The only partial demurral came from Deputy Secretary of State Warren Christopher. Although he was inclined to recommend that the president order the mission, as he made clear later, he did not know how Secretary of State Vance (who was taking a brief and well-earned vacation) would react and did not feel that he should express a personal opinion.

The president said he was tentatively inclined to proceed with the mission, but would defer a final decision until he had discussed it with Vance.

As we got up to leave the room, I found myself standing next to Harold Brown. "Mr. Secretary," I said, "the president is going to go with this thing, I can sense it. If we can bring our people out of there, it will do more good for this country than anything that has happened in twenty years."

"Yes," said Brown, "and if we fail, that will be the end of the Carter presidency."

"But we really don't have much choice, do we?"

The Secretary shook his head no as we walked out the door.

A moment later, Helen Thomas, of UPI, walked around the corner from the press room on the way to my office.

"Big meeting, huh?" she called down the short corridor. "You guys decide to nuke 'em?"

Brown and I both nodded yes, and I offered to let Helen and her colleagues know in plenty of time to be on the scene when the warheads struck.

If she only knew, I thought.

In fact, one of the problems we faced, once the president made his final decision four days later, was the number of press people in Teheran. As part of his objections, Cyrus Vance had warned that the Iranians might seize some of the several hundred Americans still in Teheran, thus leaving us with more hostages to worry about, even if the mission was a success. A fair number of this group were journalists.

I told the president that I saw no way for us to make the reporters come home, short of telling the news organizations what was about to happen, and that was clearly out of the question. Still, he felt an obligation to try. The president's first inclination was to order them home. I argued against this. There was no way to enforce the order, and I suspected that the attempt would so enrage the news executives that they would insist on keeping people there who might have been planning to come back anyway.

"Some of them are so ornery that they might just send an extra correspondent over to prove they can do it," I said.

In the end, we decided to use the increasingly volatile situation in Iran as an excuse to try to get journalists and other Americans to come home.

At a news conference on April 17, the president announced that he was prohibiting all financial transactions between Iranians and Americans and barring all imports from Iran. Then he stated that "to protect American citizens," he was banning all travel to Iran.

These steps, he said, would "not *now* be used to interfere with the right of the press to gather news."

"However," he continued, speaking slowly and precisely, "it is my responsibility and my obligation, given the situation in Iran, to call on American journalists and newsgathering organizations to minimize, as severely as possible, their presence and their activities in Iran."

As we had feared, the only effect was to provoke angry calls, particularly from the networks. After listening to Washington bureau chiefs and presidents of news divisions berate us for trying to repeal the First Amendment and stifle news coverage for political ends, I finally lost my temper with Sandy Socolow of CBS.

"Look Sandy," I said, "the president told you what he thinks you ought to do, and I have nothing to add to it. I warned him that you people would get on a high horse, but he wanted to do it anyway. I personally don't give a good goddamn what you people do. If I had my way, I'd ask the fucking Ayatollah to keep fifty reporters and give us our diplomats back. Then you people who have all the answers could figure out how to get them out."

As soon as I hung up the phone, I regretted having lost my temper. Not because I feared that I had hurt Socolow's feelings—he is not an overly sensitive fellow—but because I was worried that my angry response might have implied that something dramatic was about to happen. I had come that close to saying that he would have to accept the consequences for what happened if he ignored the president's warning, but had caught myself in time. I vowed to keep my temper in check, at least until this operation was complete.

The president's statement of April 17, in addition to being a futile attempt to get Americans out of Teheran, also fit into our cover story. By announcing additional sanctions, he implied that there would be a period of time during which we would wait and see if they would work before any other actions were taken. I, and others who knew what was actually afoot, strengthened this impression with background briefings.

We also suggested that if we were forced to consider any sort of military option, it would be something like a blockade or mining of harbors. This was the cover story we had devised for the military movements necessary to prepare for the rescue mission. On several occasions I speculated with reporters off the record about the relative merits of a blockade as opposed to mining.

We had, in fact, ruled out both of these options. They were unlikely to force the Iranians to yield, and once attempted would have to be followed up by an escalation of military force if no response was forthcoming. We would thus be starting down a road the end of which no one could see. We also believed that once any sort of military move was made, the Iranians as part of any general reaction might tighten security around the embassy, which we knew to be extremely lax, or disperse the hostages, thus denying us the rescue option.

The problems associated with the blockade were much the same as those associated with bombing power stations or other valuable targets in Iran—ideas that were being advanced by several columnists and commentators. I had suggested to the president earlier that what he ought to do was "bomb the hell out of every dam and power station in Iran. Let the Ayatollah shoot two hostages and call on the Russians for help, then turn the whole thing over to Agronsky and Company to handle."

His response is not printable.

By the week of April 20 it was becoming clear that our cover story was working too well. All the talk about mining and blockades was making some people nervous and everyone curious. That presented a problem. We did not want anyone, even on the White House staff, snooping around in an effort to find out what was going on. They just might stumble on something. In addition, once the staff begins to talk a great deal about anything, it is only a short time before the press gets interested, too.

But this also presented us with an opportunity to reinforce our cover story. On Tuesday, April 22, little more than forty-eight hours before the Delta Team would enter Iranian air space, Hamilton called a staff meeting to address the concerns that were buzzing about the staff. He assured them all that we had no plans, at the moment, for mining or blockading. When asked about a rescue mission, he lied.

As soon as I heard what had taken place, I began to prepare for a press call. It came less than ninety minutes after the meeting ended. Jack Nelson, bureau chief of the *Los Angeles Times,* wanted to talk to me about something he had heard from a "pretty interesting staff meeting you people had this morning." I said I had not been there but would check with Hamilton.

I then called Hamilton to tell him what I was about to do. I hated to do it to Nelson, who was one of the more decent journalists that I had gotten to know since coming to Washington, and one who would become a good friend once the administration was over. But I did not feel that I had any choice. I knew what he wanted to talk about. It was an opportunity to reinforce the web of deception we had constructed to protect the rescue mission.

When I called Nelson back, he said he had heard that some staffers had expressed concern that we were about to take some action that might "involve us in a war." I confirmed this report and repeated Hamilton's assurances that we were planning no military action whatsoever, and certainly nothing like a rescue mission.

Later that day, Nelson came by my office to continue our discussion. Toward the end of that conversation, he asked, "You people really aren't thinking about doing anything drastic like launching a rescue mission, are you?"

This was the moment of truth, or, more accurately, of deception. Up to this point, I had only repeated false statements made by others, an admittedly fine distinction, but a distinction nevertheless. Now I was faced with a direct question. With a swallow that I hoped was not noticeable, I began to recite all the reasons why a rescue operation would not make any sense. They were familiar because they were exactly the ones that it had taken four months to figure out how to overcome.

"If and when we are forced to move militarily, I suspect it will be something like a blockade," I said, "but that decision is a step or two down the road."

I made a mental note to be sure to call Jack and apologize once the operation was completed, hoping he would understand.

The result was a story in the *Los Angeles Times* reporting Hamilton's assurances to the staff that no military action was in the offing, and that a rescue operation was still considered to be impractical.

When I read it the next day, I remember hoping that some Iranian student at Berkeley had enough loyalty to the Ayatollah to phone it in to Teheran.

Two days later the hostage rescue attempt ended in disaster. Nelson, to his credit, seemed to understand what I had done, even though he could not explicitly condone it. Most other reporters reacted in similar fashion when the story of my deception came out. A few even stopped by to say privately that they would have done the same thing in my position. A few others were quoted, anonymously, as saying that I had destroyed my credibility and ought to resign.

The issue quickly faded as we dealt with the spectacle of Iranian leaders boasting over the bodies of American servicemen, the tortured but eventually successful efforts to secure their return, and the ceremonies honoring their courage and dedication to duty.

There were a few attempts to exploit the situation for political purposes: Stories were planted with reporters that the mission had been discovered by the Soviets and a call from Brezhnev had brought about the cancellation, and that the military commanders had wanted to go ahead after the loss of three helicopters but the president had lost his nerve and ordered them to turn back. These attempts at disinformation were largely unsuccessful. Later, as we shall see, those responsible for these efforts were able to find journalists whose indifference or incompetence made them useful political tools.

In October of 1983, . . . controversy flared again between the White House and the press over the relative rights and responsibilities of the two institutions. The occasion was the American invasion of Grenada, and there were several reasonably separate issues involved.

The first was the same one that I had dealt with three and a half years prior: the right of government to lie. On the afternoon before American forces landed in Grenada, CBS White House correspondent Bill Plante learned from a reliable source that an invasion would take place at sunrise the next morning. He checked with the White House Press Office and got a flat denial. "Preposterous," said spokesman Larry Speakes. Other reporters got the same response from other government officials.

The decision by the Reagan administration to deceive journalists rather than risk the possibility that the invasion plans would be disclosed seemed to me to be eminently defensible.

When I asked Plante later what he would have done if the White House had confirmed the invasion plans, his response was "I don't know; we would have tried to find some way to use what we knew without endangering the operation."

That in itself would seem to confirm the wisdom of the White House judgment. You cannot expect government to leave such questions in the hands of the fourth estate. The consequences of an error are too severe.

Moreover, given the extent of eavesdropping capabilities in Washington, it would be an unacceptable risk to have Mr. Plante and others at CBS chatting at some length over open telephone lines about how they would use the information. By the time their decision was made it most likely would be moot.

Some journalists were willing to agree privately that this situation was one of those in which there was no other choice but to lie. Most, however, were unwilling to endorse publicly the idea that lying could be condoned under any circumstances, feeling that government does enough lying as it is without any encouragement from them.

They make the very valid point that once you step away from the categorical, there is no easily discernible place to draw the line.

Still the essential dilemma remains. What about those situations where an evasion simply will not work, where a "no comment" is almost certain to be taken as a confirmation? If, at the same time, the information to be protected is of sufficient importance, if lives are at stake for example, a lie becomes in my estimation the lesser evil of the choices available. It is ludicrous to argue that soldiers may be sent off to fight and die, but a spokesman may not, under any circumstances, be asked to lie to make sure that the casualties are fewer and not in vain.

Churchill made the point with his usual flair in 1943. "In wartime," he said, "truth is so precious that she should be attended by a bodyguard of lies."

Unfortunately, once one steps onto the slippery slope of relativism, firm footing cannot be established, even on the basis of "wartime" or "lives at stake." There are other dilemmas that can and do arise, where calculated deception might be appropriate.

Although I never faced it personally, the protection of an important intelligence source or method, even in peacetime, might be one.

And what about the protection of an important diplomatic initiative? I almost faced such a situation at Camp David when reports of bad blood between Sadat and Begin arose and when there were leaks about Sadat's threat to break off the talks. . . . I was able to deal with those problems without telling a bald-faced lie, but that was mostly a matter of luck.

In the midst of the Grenada controversy, a columnist revealed that the premature publication by Jack Anderson of a story about Henry Kissinger's secret diplomatic initiatives had damaged, although not fatally, the movement toward normalization of relations with China. That initiative became arguably the most significant strategic event since the Second World War. Would lying have been appropriate in an effort to keep it on track?

In the early months of the Carter administration the *Washington Post* published accounts of secret payments through the CIA to King Hussein of Jordan. The story appeared on the day that Secretary of State Vance arrived in Aman to discuss a Middle East peace initiative with Hussein. Needless to say, the result was a less than positive environment for the talks.

In that case, we had chosen to be candid with the *Post* and appeal to their sense of responsibility. From our point of view the effort was a failure. Although we had not asked them not to publish the story, feeling that such a request would be futile, we had requested a delay. When it came out at the most unfortunate of all possible times, we felt the *Post* was guilty of bad faith. The *Post* maintained that the timing was a result of a misunderstanding.

In any case, the question remains. In our judgment the *Post* had enough information to go with the story whatever we said. But what if we had concluded that it was possible to kill the story with a lie, would we have been justified in doing so?

To take another step down the slope, what degree of deception would be acceptable from a Justice Department official trying to protect the rights of an innocent person whose name had cropped up in an investigation?

Or what about a spokesman at Treasury attempting to avoid the premature disclosure of information on a financial decision that could lead to severe damage to innocent parties and great profits for those in a position to take advantage of the leak?

The problem becomes, as noted above, where precisely to draw the line. There is no convenient place. About the best one can do is to argue that it must be drawn very tightly, for practical as well as moral considerations. Distinctions may be difficult at the margins, but we can all tell the difference between mountains and molehills. If government does have the right to lie in certain situations, that right is as precious as the truth it attends. It must not be squandered on matters of less than overriding importance.

Which brings us to another issue in the Grenada controversy. Many correspondents said that the exchange between Speakes and CBS was not the cause but the catalyst for their outrage. They charged that the administration had repeatedly lied to them on matters that were in no way vital to national security or the protection of lives. They listed examples that ranged from the dates of resignations to travel plans to attempts to square the facts with some off-the-cuff presidential remark.

They also pointed to a history of efforts to curtail the flow of information from the screening of calls to White House officials from reporters by the communications and press offices to proposals for the review of anything written by thousands of government officials after they leave office. (At this writing, Congress has wisely blocked this last absurdity, but the administration has vowed not to give up.)

That attitude was not unanimous, but it was clearly shared by a large number of White House correspondents. And that is a dangerous set of circumstances for the administration and potentially for the nation. The danger for the administration is that it will find itself lacking credibility across the board, that no explanation will be accepted at face value and every action will be subject to the most unflattering interpretation.

For the nation, the danger lies in the fact that an administration that is generally believed to be dishonest will not command the respect necessary to protect legitimate secrets. There are many cases in which truths less vital than the timing and objective of military operations are protected by successful appeals to reporters not to publish. The full and exact reasons for such requests cannot always be disclosed, because they too may be quite sensitive. Needless to say, such appeals—which amount to a request to "trust me"—can only be effective in a climate of mutual trust.

To the extent that this climate was placed in jeopardy following the Grenada controversy, the problem was not primarily a conflict over government's right to lie about issues of ultimate importance, but a perceived pattern of deception solely for the sake of convenience—of lies designed to protect and promote nothing more precious than someone's political backside.

Even during the Grenada operation, there were lies from the government that were difficult to justify by any reasonable standard. Claims that coverage was curtailed, after the invasion had begun, because of concern for the safety of reporters were poppycock. Even experienced spokesmen had a hard time making that argument with a straight face.

Similarly, attempts to blame the decision to restrict coverage on "military commanders" were deceptive and cowardly and dangerous. There is no doubt that many uniformed military officers hold the press in less than great esteem or that the restricted coverage was completely in line with their preferences. But that is not the point. Such decisions are always subject to White House review. And they were repeatedly brought to the attention of White House officials. If the preferences of the military commanders were honored, it was because the president and his men agreed with them.

This refusal to accept responsibility for one's own actions was dangerous in this case because it served to exacerbate tensions between the military and the fourth estate, to heighten mutual distrust on both sides. These tensions are already high enough and that problem is going to be with us for the indefinite future. Already it works against responsible and accurate reporting of national security issues. It also promotes an unreasoning distrust of all things military in our society. There is, in my view, no excuse for an administration's hiding behind the armed forces simply to avoid facing ticklish questions.

A related issue has to do with how much the White House press secretary should be told in situations such as this. It very quickly became clear in this particular case that the press secretary and the press office had been kept in the dark until the invasion was under way. Mr. Speakes and his people were not intentionally lying themselves when they denied the reports from Plante and other newsmen; they were merely passing on what they had been told by members of the National Security Council staff.

This quickly became a bone of contention within the White House. Mr. Speakes and his people were none too happy about the way they had been treated. One deputy resigned as a result. However, more senior White House officials declared themselves well pleased with the procedure and stated that they would handle things the same way if similar situations arose in the future.

Mr. Speakes made it clear that if a lie was required and he was to be sent out to tell it, he wanted to know what was at stake. And he was exactly right. Keeping the press secretary in the dark can create serious problems.

First, it inevitably erodes the press secretary's effectiveness. It costs him in prestige and status, factors that may mean more than they should in Washington, but still cannot be ignored. The press secretary's job is tough enough as it is; he deserves every break his colleagues can give him. Putting the guy whose business is information in a position that makes him appear to be uninformed, out of touch, and not trusted makes no sense over the long haul.

Beyond that, if a secret is worth lying about to protect, it makes sense to come up with the most effective lie possible. Most sensitive operations are accompanied by a cover story, designed to provide an innocent explanation for bits and pieces that might leak out. Since the first group of people that such a story must convince is the press, having the press secretary involved in designing the story is not a bad idea. He more than anyone else is likely to know what will be convincing and what will not.

Furthermore, the use of the story, if it ever becomes necessary, is likely to be more effective if the person who puts it out knows exactly what he is trying to do. Dealing with the press, particularly in ticklish situations, is very much an art. You cannot treat the press secretary like a robot and then expect him to perform like an artist.

Another danger in keeping the press secretary uninformed comes from the way in which a press office operates. When a new question arises or an issue looks like it is going to get hot, the press office begins to function very much like a news organization. Deputy and assistant and deputy assistant press secretaries immediately get to work calling all over the government to try to find out what is really going on and where it may lead.

As information is gathered, it is often passed on to the reporter who has made the query in bits and pieces as part of a continuing exchange of information and ideas. Needless to say, if there is something highly sensitive that has to be protected, the press secretary needs to know about it. Otherwise, this process could stumble into and lead to the uncovering of information that should be kept secret.

In matters large and small, keeping the press secretary in the dark is risky business. If he cannot be trusted with sensitive information, he should be replaced. Failing that, he ought to be given the information he needs to do his job effectively.

Having said all that, however, I suspect that the most important lesson from this episode is to be found in the fact that the press was a clear loser in its fight with the administration over Grenada. It lost in the court in which such matters will eventually be decided—the court of public opinion. In the immediate aftermath of Grenada it was sometimes difficult to tell which the American people enjoyed more, seeing the president kick hell out of the Cubans or the press.

And the reasons the fourth estate lost were to a large extent its own fault.

The strength of the public reaction in favor of the administration's policy of denying access to the press was a shock to many Washington journalists. The more thoughtful were concerned as well as surprised.

It is true that the press is particularly vulnerable among our major institutions because it is so often the bearer of sad tidings, the forum for criticism of ideas, individuals, and institutions that Americans hold dear. It is also true, as journalists are fond of pointing out, that their job is not to win popularity contests. But the vocal and sometimes vicious public reaction against the press in the wake of Grenada was more than just some sort of "shoot the messenger" syndrome.

In part it sprang from the way the fourth estate handled the terrorist bombing of our marine headquarters in Beirut, which occurred just prior to the Grenada operation. The behavior of some news organizations was not the sort that would inspire public confidence in their judgment or self-restraint.

There was, for example, the repugnant spectacle of CBS camped ghoulishly at the home of parents awaiting word on the fate of their marine son in Beirut. And they hit the jackpot. The boy was dead. So they got to film the arrival of the casualty officer and the chaplain bringing the tragic news to the parents.

The tragic scene, for which every standard of good taste and decency demanded privacy, was then offered up to satisfy the voyeurism of the worst segments of the American television audience and the demands for the higher ratings that are believed, with some justification, to come with sensationalism.

Nor was this sort of gross insensitivity confined to television. A few days after the Beirut bombing, readers of the *Washington Post* were treated to the incredibly insensitive comments of a *Newsweek* executive describing at some length what a wonderful thing the tragedy was for his magazine:

"We are exhilarated by this. It's the sort of thing *Newsweek* does best—react to a big story in a big way. We'll be pulling out all the stops. . . . one hell of a story . . . pursuing a variety of angles . . . expect lot of competition, it's the biggest story of the year."

If the tasteless coverage of the Beirut tragedy was a factor in the public's reaction to Grenada, it was by no means the whole of it. The attitudes reflected did not develop over a few days or weeks.

If the government has in this and other instances been guilty of excess in the exercise of what I believe to be its legitimate right to mislead and even deceive on matters of vital import, the fourth estate has also been guilty of excess in its cavalier insistence on the right to do as it pleases with little regard for good judgment, good taste, or the consequences of its actions—and the American people know it.

One consequence of the information explosion has been that more and more Americans have had the opportunity to see news coverage of incidents they knew something about. And they have come away disillusioned, and sometimes angry, because of the wide gap that too often existed between what they knew to be the case and what was reported.

And if they were foolish enough to try to set the record straight by appealing for a correction, they also ran head on into that determination never to admit a mistake, much less do anything about it.

The public's reaction to Grenada ought to be a danger signal for journalism. The question . . . is how the fourth estate will react. The greatest danger is that the reaction will be defensive, a renewed determination to pretend that nothing is wrong except the shortsightedness and lack of sophistication of the American public.

THE
PRESIDENCY

Chapter
Four

The administrations of Lyndon B. Johnson and Richard M. Nixon changed the perspective of many Americans about the presidency. In spite of the bitter partisanship that always precedes presidential elections, the office of the presidency before Lyndon B. Johnson had always been treated with great reverence, which often extended to the person who occupied the White House. This is not to suggest by any means that presidents had always been extolled for their virtues and placed on a kingly throne, for anyone familiar with American history knows that there have always been bitter personal attacks on presidents by a wide assortment of critics. And these presidential critics were not above calling their prey "mentally unbalanced." Nevertheless, most presidential biographies concentrated on the heroic and not the neurotic qualities of their subjects. An eloquent illustration of this is Carl Sandburg's biographical volumes on Abraham Lincoln as well as more recent books on presidents by such authors as James David Barber or Doris Kearns, not to mention Bob Woodward and Carl Bernstein, whose work reveals the major differences between past and present approaches to assessing presidents.[1]

Although the administration of Lyndon B. Johnson seemed rational to his supporters, other persons, particularly critics of the Vietnam War, believed the president to have relentlessly, single-mindedly, and more importantly *irrationally* embarked on a highly destructive policy. David Halberstam began an extensive study of the history of the war to determine how the United States became involved. His best-selling book *The Best and the Brightest,* published in 1972, emphasized the role of personalities, not so much of the president himself as of his top-level advisers, in making the critical decisions committing the country to the war.[2] In the same year, political scientist James David Barber published his ground-breaking book *The Presidential Character,* in which he made personality profiles of a variety of presidents to assess the effect of presidential character on performance. With the publication of Barber's book, psychopolitcs came of age.

James Barber attempted a complex classification of different character types

---

[1]See James David Barber, *The Presidential Character* (Englewood Cliffs, N.J.: Prentice-Hall, 1972); Doris Kearns, *Lyndon Johnson and the American Dream* (News York: Harper & Row, 1976); Bob Woodward and Carl Bernstein, *The Final Days* (New York: Simon & Schuster, 1976).

[2]David Halberstam, *The Best and the Brightest* (New York: Random House, 1972).

and came to the conclusion that the best presidents were what he termed "active-positive." The active-positive president is achievement-oriented and productive and has well-defined goals. He is rational, "using his brain to move his feet." Above all, he is flexible; he can change his goals and methods as he perceives reasons for altering his course of action. He has a sense of humor about the world and, more importantly, about himself. John F. Kennedy was, according to Barber, an ideal active-positive president.

Perhaps even more significant than the active-positive presidents are the "active-negative" presidents. These are the presidents that may do irreparable damage, according to Barber. They have a compulsive need to work because of personal problems and a misguided "Puritan ethic." They are ambitious and power-hungry but lack goals beyond that of rising to power. They tend to be politically amoral, as was Richard Nixon, but may take on false and misleading goals, such as making the world safe for democracy, as did Woodrow Wilson. The great energy of the active-negative type is frequently directed in irrational ways, and once set in a course of action the active-negative president tends to become very rigid, especially in face of opposition and criticisms from the outside. Because of personal insecurity, the active-negative president surrounds himself with yes-men in order to fortify him in confrontation with the hostile world outside. Barber's portraits of various active-negative presidents, including Richard Nixon, when taken in conjunction with the portrait of President Nixon in Bob Woodward and Carl Bernstein's *Final Days,* is truly frightening. Because of the enormous power that presidents possess, it is especially important to examine their characters and styles, which set the tone of presidential administrations.

The selections in this chapter illustrate various dimensions of presidential personality and, what is frequently overlooked, the way in which the personalities and styles of the president's staff can influence the political process.

I N THE FOLLOWING SELECTION political scientist James David Barber presents the thesis that it is the total character of the person who occupies the White House that is the determinant of presidential performance. "The presidency," he states. "is much more than an institution." It is not only the focus of the emotional involvement of most people in politics but also is occupied by a person whose emotions inevitably affect his or her conduct. How presidents are able to come to grips with their feelings and emotions often shapes their orientation toward issues and the way in which they make decisions. Particularly important is the way in which presidents cope with their staffs in an era when the presidency is more institutional than personal. The president's character and style remain the most important influence upon operations in the White House.

18 James David Barber
PRESIDENTIAL CHARACTER, STYLE, AND PERFORMANCE

When a citizen votes for a presidential candidate he makes, in effect, a prediction. He chooses from among the contenders the one he thinks (or feels, or guesses) would be the best president. He operates in a situation of immense uncertainty. If he has a long voting history, he can recall time and time again when he guessed wrong. He listens to the commentators, the politicians, and his friends, then adds it all up in some rough way to produce his prediction and his vote. Earlier in the game, his anticipations have been taken into account, either directly in the polls and primaries or indirectly in the minds of politicians who want to nominate someone he will like. But he must choose in the midst of a cloud of confusion, a rain of phony advertising, a storm of sermons, a hail of complex issues, a fog of charisma and boredom, and a thunder of accusation and defense. In the face of this chaos, a great many citizens fall back on the past, vote their old allegiances, and let it go at that. Nevertheless, the citizen's vote says that on balance he [or she] expects Mr. X would outshine Mr. Y in the presidency.

This [book] is meant to help citizens and those who advise them cut through the confusion and get at some clear criteria for choosing presidents. To understand what actual presidents do and what potential presidents might do, the first need is to see the man whole—not as some abstract embodiment of civic virtue, some scorecard of issue stands, or some reflection of a faction, but as a human being like the rest of us, a person trying to cope with a difficult environment. To that task he brings his own character, his own view of the world, his own political style. None of that is new for him. If we can see the pattern he has set for his political life we can, I contend, estimate much better his pattern as he confronts the stresses and chances of the presidency.

The presidency is a peculiar office. The founding fathers left it extraordinarily loose in definition, partly because they trusted George Washington to invent a tradition as he went along. It is an institution made a piece at a time by successive men in the White House. Jefferson reached out to Congress to put together the beginnings of political parties; Jackson's dramatic force extended electoral partisanship to its mass base; Lincoln vastly expanded the administrative reach of the office; Wilson and the Roosevelts showed its rhetorical possibilities—in fact every president's mind and demeanor has left its mark on a heritage still in lively development.

But the presidency is much more than an institution. It is a focus of feelings. In general, popular feelings about politics are low-key, shallow, casual. For example, the vast majority of Americans knows virtually nothing of what Congress is doing and cares less. The presidency is different. The presidency is the focus for the most intense and persistent emotions in the American polity. The president is a symbolic leader, the one figure who draws together the people's hopes and fears for the political future. On top of all his routine duties, he has to carry that off—or fail.

Our emotional attachment to presidents shows up when one dies in office. People were not just disappointed or worried when President Kennedy was killed; people wept at the loss of a man most had never even met. Kennedy was young and charismatic—but history shows that whenever a president dies in office, heroic Lincoln or debased Harding, McKinley or Garfield, the same wave of deep emotion sweeps across the country. On the other hand, the death of an ex-president brings forth no such intense emotional reaction.

The president is the first political figure children are aware of (later they add Congress, the Court, and others, as "helpers" of the president). With some exceptions among children in deprived circumstances, the president is seen as a "benevolent leader," one who nurtures, sustains, and inspires the citizenry. Presidents regularly show up among "most admired" contemporaries and forebears, and the president is the "best known" (in the sense of sheer name recognition) person in the country. At inauguration time, even presidents elected by close margins are supported by much larger majorities than the election returns show, for people rally round as he actually assumes office. There is a similar reaction when the people see their president threatened by crisis: if he takes action, there is a favorable spurt in the Gallup poll whether he succeeds or fails.

Obviously the president gets more attention in schoolbooks, press, and television than any other politician. He is one of very few who can make news by doing good things. His emotional state is a matter of continual public commentary, as is the manner in which his personal and official families conduct themselves. The media bring across the president not as some neutral administrator or corporate executive to be assessed by his production, but as a special being with mysterious dimensions.

We have no king. The sentiments English children—and adults—direct to the Queen have no place to go in our system but to the president. Whatever his talents—Coolidge-type or Roosevelt-type—the president is the only available object for such national-religious-monarchical sentiments as Americans possess.

The president helps people make sense of politics. Congress is a tangle of committees, the bureaucracy is a maze of agencies. The president is one man trying to do a job—a picture much more understandable to the mass of people who find themselves in the same boat. Furthermore, he is the top man. He ought to know what is going on and set it right. So when the economy goes sour, or war drags on, or domestic violence erupts, the president is available to take the blame. Then when things go right, it seems the president must have had a hand in it. Indeed, the flow of political life is marked off by presidents: the "Eisenhower Era," the "Kennedy Years."

What all this means is that the president's *main* responsibilities reach far beyond administering the executive branch or commanding the armed forces. The White House is first and foremost a place of public leadership. That inevitably brings to bear on the president intense moral, sentimental, and quasi-religious pressures which can, if he lets them, distort his own thinking and feeling. If there is such a thing as extraordinary sanity, it is needed nowhere so much as in the White House.

Who the president is at a given time can make a profound difference in the whole thrust and direction of national politics. Since we have only one president at a time, we can never prove this by comparison, but even the most superficial speculation confirms the commonsense view that the man himself weighs heavily among other historical factors. A Wilson reelected in 1920, a Hoover in 1932, a John F. Kennedy in 1964 would, it seems very likely, have guided the body politic along rather different paths from those their actual successors chose. Or try to imagine a Theodore Roosevelt ensconced behind today's "bully pulpit" of a presidency, or Lyndon Johnson as president in the age of McKinley. Only someone mesmerized by the lures of historical inevitability can suppose that it would have made little or no difference to government policy had Alf Landon replaced FDR in 1936, had Dewey beaten Truman in 1948, or Adlai Stevenson reigned through the 1950s. Not only would these alternative presidents have advocated different policies—they would have approached the office from very different psychological angles. It stretches credibility to think that Eugene McCarthy would have run the institution the way Lyndon Johnson did.

The burden of this book is that the crucial differences can be anticipated by an understanding of a potential president's character, his world view, and his style. This kind of prediction is not easy; well-informed observers often have guessed wrong as they watched a man step toward the White House. One thinks of Woodrow Wilson, the scholar who would bring reason to politics; of Herbert Hoover, the Great Engineer who would organize chaos into progress; of Franklin D. Roosevelt, that champion of the balanced budget; of Harry Truman, whom the office would surely overwhelm; of Dwight D. Eisenhower, militant crusader; of John F. Kennedy, who would lead beyond moralisms to achievements; of Lyndon B. Johnson, the southern conservative; and of Richard M. Nixon, conciliator. Spotting the errors is easy. Predicting with even approximate accuracy is going to require some sharp tools and close attention in their use. But the experiment is worth it because the question is critical and because it lends itself to correction by evidence.

My argument comes in layers.

First, a president's personality is an important shaper of his presidential behavior on nontrivial matters.

Second, presidential personality is patterned. His character, world view, and style fit together in a dynamic package understandable in psychological terms.

Third, a president's personality interacts with the power situation he faces and the national "climate of expectations" dominant at the time he serves. The tuning, the resonance—or lack of it—between these external factors and his personality sets in motion the dynamics of his presidency.

Fourth, the best way to predict a president's character, world view, and style is to see how they were put together in the first place. That happened in his early life, culminating in his first independent political success.

But the core of the argument . . . is that presidential character—the basic stance a man takes toward his presidential experience—comes in four varieties. The most important thing to know about a president or candidate is where he fits among these types, defined according to (a) how active he is and (b) whether or not he gives the impression he enjoys his political life.

Let me spell out these concepts briefly before getting down to cases.

Personality Shapes Performance

I am not about to argue that once you know a president's personality you know everything. But as the cases will demonstrate, the degree and quality of a president's emotional involvement in an issue are powerful influences on how he defines the issue itself, how much attention he pays to it, which facts and persons he sees as relevant to its resolution, and, finally, what principles and purposes he associates with the issue. Every story of presidential decision making is really two stories: an outer one in which a rational man calculates and an inner one in which an emotional man feels. The two are forever connected. Any real president is one whole man and his deeds reflect his wholeness.

As for personality, it is a matter of tendencies. It is not that one president "has" some basic characteristic that another president does not "have." That old way of treating a trait as a possession, like a rock in a basket, ignores the universality of aggressiveness, compliancy, detachment, and other human drives. We all have all of them, but in different amounts and in different combinations.

The Pattern of Character, World View, and Style

The most visible part of the pattern is style. *Style is the president's habitual way of performing his three political roles: rhetoric, personal relations, and homework.* Not to be confused with "stylishness," charisma, or appearance, style is how the president goes about doing what the office requires him to do—to speak, directly or through media, to large audiences; to deal face to face with other politicians, individually and in small, relatively private groups; and to read, write, and calculate by himself in order to manage the endless flow of details that stream onto his desk. No president can escape doing at least some of each. But there are marked differences in stylistic emphasis from president to president. The *balance* among the three style elements varies; one president may put most of himself into rhetoric, another may stress close, informal dealing, while still another may devote his energies mainly to study and cogitation. Beyond the balance, we want to see each president's peculiar habits of style, his mode of coping with and adapting to these presidential demands. For example, I think both Calvin Coolidge and John F. Kennedy were primarily rhetoricians, but they went about it in contrasting ways.

A president's *world view consists of his primary, politically relevant beliefs, particularly his conceptions of social causality, human nature, and the central moral conflicts of the time.* This is how he sees the world and his lasting opinions about what he sees. Style is his way of acting; world view is his way of seeing. Like the rest of us, a president develops over a lifetime certain conceptions of reality—how things work in politics, what people are like, what the main purposes are. These assumptions or conceptions help him make sense of his world, give some semblance of order to the chaos of existence. Perhaps most important: a man's world view affects what he pays attention to, and a great deal of politics is about paying attention. The name of the game for many politicians is not so much "Do this, do that" as it is "Look here!"

"Character" comes from the Greek word for engraving; in one sense it is what life has marked into a man's being. As used here, *character is the way the president orients himself toward life*—not for the moment, but enduringly. Character is the person's stance as he confronts experience. And at the core of character, a man confronts himself. The president's fundamental self-esteem is his prime personal resource; to defend and advance that, he will sacrifice much else he values. Down there in the privacy of his heart, does he find himself superb, or ordinary, or debased, or in some intermediate range? No president has been utterly paralyzed by self-doubt and none has been utterly free of midnight self-mockery. In between, the real presidents move out on life from positions of relative strength or weakness. Equally important are the criteria by which they judge themselves. A president who rates himself by the standard of achievement, for instance, may be little affected by losses of affection.

Character, world view, and style are abstractions from the reality of the whole individual. In every case they form an integrated pattern: the man develops a combination which makes psychological sense for him, a dynamic arrangement of motives, beliefs, and habits in the service of his need for self-esteem.

The Power Situation and "Climate of Expectations"

Presidential character resonates with the political situation the president faces. It adapts him as he tries to adapt it. The support he has from the public and interest groups, the party balance in Congress, the thrust of Supreme Court opinion together set the basic power situation he must deal with. An activist president may run smack into a brick wall of resistance, then pull back and wait for a better moment. On the other hand, a president who sees himself as a quiet caretaker may not try to exploit even the most favorable power situation. So it is the relationship between president and the political configuration that makes the system tick.

Even before public opinion polls, the president's real or supposed popularity was a large factor in his performance. Besides the power mix in Washington, the president has to deal with a national climate of expectations, the predominant needs thrust up to him by the people. There are at least three recurrent themes around which these needs are focused.

People look to the president for *reassurance,* a feeling that things will be all right, that the president will take care of his people. The psychological request is for a surcease of anxiety. Obviously, modern life in America involves considerable doses of fear, tension, anxiety, worry; from time to time, the public mood calls for a rest, a time of peace, a breathing space, a "return to normalcy."

Another theme is the demand for *a sense of progress and action.* The president ought to do something to direct the nation's course—or at least be in there pitching for the people. The president is looked to as a take-charge man, a doer, a turner of the wheels, a producer of progress—even if that means some sacrifice of serenity.

A third type of climate of expectations is the public need for a sense of *legitimacy* from, and in, the presidency. The president should be a master politician who is above politics. He should have a right to his place and a rightful way of acting in it. The respectability—even religiosity—of the office has to be protected by a man who presents himself as defender of the faith. There is more to this than dignity, more than propriety. The president is expected to personify our betterness in an inspiring way, to express in what he does and is (not just in what he says) a moral idealism which, in much of the public mind, is the very opposite of "politics."

Over time the climate of expectations shifts and changes. Wars, depressions, and other national events contribute to that change, but there also is a rough cycle, from an emphasis on action (which begins to look too "political") to an emphasis on legitimacy (the moral uplift of which creates its own strains) to an emphasis on reassurance and rest (which comes to seem like drift) and back to action again. One need not be astrological about it. The point is that the climate of expectations at any given time is the political air the president has to breathe. Relating to this climate is a large part of his task.

Predicting Presidents

The best way to predict a president's character, world view, and style is to see how he constructed them in the first place. Especially in the early stages, life is experimental; consciously or not, a person tries out various ways of defining and maintaining and rising self-esteem. He looks to his environment for clues as to who he is and how well he is doing. These lessons of life slowly sink in: certain self-images and evaluations, certain ways of looking at the world, certain styles of action get confirmed by his experience and he gradually adopts them as his own. If we can see that process of development, we can understand the product. The features to note are those bearing on presidential performance.

Experimental development continues all the way to death; we will not blind ourselves to midlife changes, particularly in the full-scale prediction case, that of Richard Nixon. But it is often much easier to see the basic patterns in early life histories. Later on a whole host of distractions—especially the image-making all politicians learn to practice—clouds the picture.

In general, character has its *main* development in childhood, world view in adolescence, style in early adulthood. The stance toward life I call character grows out of the child's experiments in relating to parents, brothers and sisters, and peers at play and in school, as well as to his own body and the objects around it. Slowly the child defines an orientation toward experience; once established, that tends to last despite much subsequent contradiction. By adolescence, the child has been hearing and seeing how people make their worlds meaningful, and now he is moved to relate himself—his own meanings—to those around him. His focus of attention shifts toward the future; he senses that decisions about his fate are coming and he looks into the premises for those decisions. Thoughts about the way the world works and how one might work in it, about what people are like and how one might be like them or not, and about the values people share and how one might share in them too—these are typical concerns for the post-child, pre-adult mind of the adolescent.

These themes come together strongly in early adulthood, when the person moves from contemplation to responsible action and adopts a style. In most biographical accounts this period stands out in stark clarity—the time of emergence, the time the young man found himself. I call it his first independent political success. It was then he moved beyond the detailed guidance of his family; then his self-esteem was dramatically boosted; then he came forth as a person to be reckoned with by other people. The *way* he did that is profoundly important to him. Typically he grasps that style and hangs onto it. Much later, coming into the presidency, something in him remembers this earlier victory and reemphasizes the style that made it happen.

Character provides the main thrust and broad direction—but it does not *determine,* in any fixed sense, world view and style. The story of development does not end with the end of childhood. Thereafter, the culture one grows in and the ways that culture is translated by parents and peers shape the meanings one makes of his character. The going world view gets learned and that learning helps channel character forces. Thus it will not necessarily be true that compulsive characters have reactionary beliefs, or that compliant characters believe in compromise. Similarly for style: historical accidents play a large part in furnishing special opportunities for action—and in blocking off alternatives. For example, however much anger a young man may feel, that anger will not be expressed in rhetoric unless and until his life situation provides a platform and an audience. Style thus has a stature and independence of its own. Those who would reduce all explanation to character neglect these highly significant later channelings. For beyond the root is the branch, above the foundation the superstructure, and starts do not prescribe finishes.

Four Types of Presidential Character

The five concepts—character, world view, style, power situation, and climate of expectations—run through the accounts of presidents in [later chapters of Barber's book], which cluster the presidents since Theodore Roosevelt into four types. This is the fundamental scheme of the study. It offers a way to move past the complexities to the main contrasts and comparisons.

The first baseline in defining presidential types is *activity-passivity.* How much energy does the man invest in his presidency? Lyndon Johnson went at his day like a human cyclone, coming to rest long after the sun went down. Calvin Coolidge often slept eleven hours a night and still needed a nap in the middle of the day. In between the presidents array themselves on the high or low side of the activity line.

The second baseline is *positive-negative affect* toward one's activity—that is, how he feels about what he does. Relatively speaking, does he seem to experience his political life as happy or sad, enjoyable or discouraging, positive or negative in its main effect. The feeling I am after here is not grim satisfaction in a job well done, not some philosophical conclusion. The idea is this: is he someone who, on the surfaces we can see, gives forth the feeling that he has *fun* in political life? Franklin Roosevelt's Secretary of War, Henry L. Stimson, wrote that the Roosevelts "not only understood the *use* of power, they knew the *enjoyment* of power, too. . . . Whether a man is burdened by power or enjoys power; whether he is trapped by responsibility or made free by it; whether he is moved by other people and outer forces or moves them— that is the essence of leadership."

The positive-negative baseline, then, is a general symptom of the fit between the man and his experience, a kind of register of *felt* satisfaction.

Why might we expect these two simple dimensions to outline the main character types? Because they stand for two central features of anyone's orientation toward life. In nearly every study of personality, some form of the active-passive contrast is critical; the general tendency to act or be acted upon is evident in such concepts as dominance-submission, extraversion-introversion, aggression-timidity, attack-defense, fight-flight, engagement-withdrawal, approach-avoidance. In everyday life we sense quickly the general energy output of the people we deal with. Similarly we catch on fairly quickly to the affect dimension—whether the person seems to be optimistic or pessimistic, hopeful or skeptical, happy or sad. The two baselines are clear and they are also independent of one another: all of us know people who are very active but seem discouraged, others who are quite passive but seem happy, and so forth. The activity baseline refers to what one does, the affect baseline to how one feels about what one does.

Both are crude clues to character. They are leads into four basic character patterns long familiar in psychological research. In summary form, these are the main configurations:

Active-positive: There is a congruence, a consistency, between much activity and the enjoyment of it, indicating relatively high self-esteem and relative success in relating to the environment. The man shows an orientation toward productiveness as a value and an ability to use his styles flexibly, adaptively, suiting the dance to the music. He sees himself as developing over time toward relatively well-defined personal goals—growing toward his image of himself as he might yet be. There is an emphasis on rational mastery, on using the brain to move the feet. This may get him into trouble; he may fail to take account of the irrational in politics. Not everyone he deals with sees things his way and he may find it hard to understand why.

Active-negative: The contradiction here is between relatively intense effort and relatively low emotional reward for that effort. The activity has a compulsive quality, as if the man were trying to make up for something or to escape from anxiety into hard work. He seems ambitious, striving upward, power-seeking. His stance toward the environment is aggressive and he has a persistent problem in managing his aggressive feelings. His self-image is vague and discontinuous. Life is a hard struggle to achieve and hold power, hampered by the condemnations of a perfectionistic conscience. Active-negative types pour energy into the political system, but it is an energy distorted from within.

Passive-positive: This is the receptive, compliant, other-directed character whose life is a search for affection as a reward for being agreeable and cooperative rather than personally assertive. The contradiction is between low self-esteem (on grounds of being unlovable, unattractive) and a superficial optimism. A hopeful attitude helps dispel doubt and elicits encouragement from others. Passive-positive types help soften the harsh edges of politics. But their dependence and the fragility of their hopes and enjoyments make disappointment in politics likely.

Passive-negative: The factors are consistent—but how are we to account for the man's *political* role-taking? Why is someone who does little in politics and enjoys it less there at all? The answer lies in the passive-negative's character-rooted orientation toward doing dutiful service; this compensates for low self-esteem based on a sense of uselessness. Passive-negative types are in politics because they think they ought to be. They may be well adapted to certain nonpolitical roles, but they lack the experience and flexibility to perform effectively as political leaders. Their tendency is to withdraw, to escape from the conflict and uncertainty of politics by emphasizing vague principles (especially prohibitions) and procedural arrangements. They become guardians of the right and proper way, above the sordid politicking of lesser men.

Active-positive presidents want most to achieve results. Active-negatives aim to get and keep power. Passive-positives are after love. Passive-negatives emphasize their civic virtue. The relation of activity to enjoyment in a president thus tends to outline a cluster of characteristics, to set apart the adapted from the compulsive, compliant, and withdrawn types.

The first four presidents of the United States, conveniently, ran through this gamut of character types. (Remember, we are talking about tendencies, broad directions; no individual man exactly fits a category.) George Washington—clearly the most important president in the pantheon—established the fundamental legitimacy of an American government at a time when this was a matter in considerable question. Washington's dignity, judiciousness, his aloof air of reserve and dedication to duty fit the passive-negative or withdrawing type best. Washington did not seek innovation, he sought stability. He longed to retire to Mount Vernon but fortunately was persuaded to stay on through a second term, in which, by rising above the political conflict between Hamilton and Jefferson and inspiring confidence in his own integrity, he gave the nation time to develop the organized means for peaceful change.

John Adams followed, a dour New England Puritan, much given to work and worry, an impatient and irascible man—an active-negative president, a compulsive type. Adams was far more partisan than Washington; the survival of the system through his presidency demonstrated that the nation could tolerate, for a time, domination by one of its nascent political parties. As president, an angry Adams brought the United States to the brink of war with France and presided over the new nation's first experiment in political repression: the Alien and Sedition Acts, forbidding, among other things, unlawful combinations "with intent to oppose any measure or measures of the government of the United States," or "any false, scandalous, and malicious writing or writings against the United States, or the president of the United States, with intent to defame . . . or to bring them or either of them, into contempt or disrepute."

Then came Jefferson. He too had his troubles and failures—in the design of national defense, for example. As for his presidential character (only one element in success or failure), Jefferson was clearly active-positive. A child of the Enlightenment, he applied his reason to organizing connections with Congress aimed at strengthening the more popular forces. A man of catholic interests and delightful humor, Jefferson combined a clear and open vision of what the country could be with a profound political sense, expressed in his famous phrase, "Every difference of opinion is not a difference of principle."

The fourth president was James Madison, "Little Jemmy," the constitutional philosopher thrown into the White House at a time of great international turmoil. Madison comes closest to the passive-positive, or compliant, type; he suffered from irresolution, tried to compromise his way out, and gave in too readily to the "warhawks" urging combat with Britain. The nation drifted into war, and Madison wound up ineptly commanding his collection of amateur generals in the streets of Washington. General Jackson's victory at New Orleans saved the Madison administration's historical reputation; but he left the presidency with the United States close to bankruptcy and secession.

These four presidents—like all presidents—were persons trying to cope with the roles they had won by using the equipment they had built over a lifetime. The president is not some shapeless organism in a flood of novelties, but a man with a memory in a system with a history. Like all of us, he draws on his past to shape his future. The pathetic hope that the White House will turn a Caligula into a Marcus Aurelius is as naive as the fear that ultimate power inevitably corrupts. The problem is to understand—and to state understandably—what in the personal past foreshadows the presidential future. . . .

A FTER HIS FIRST YEAR IN OF-
fice President George Bush's
popularity surpassed that of all
but three prior presidents after they had
been in office for a year. Only Harry S
Truman, John F. Kennedy, and Lyndon B.
Johnson had higher approval scores than
Bush after the ninth month of their presidencies. Their respective 77, 75, and 74

percent approval ratings only slightly exceeded Bush's 68 percent rating. Bush's
popularity continued in his second year,
a time when the public acceptance of
most presidents is on the decline. Bush's
nonconfrontational style, described in
the following selection, undoubtedly accounted for much of his success with the
public, the media, and Congress.

19 Fred Barnes
FEARLESS LEADER:
BUSH IN THE WHITE HOUSE

In the Cabinet Room in October, President Bush and Republicans from
Capitol Hill talked war. The road, so smooth for Bush's first nine months in
the White House, had gotten bumpy. He blinked when a coup threatened to
topple Manuel Noriega in Panama, suffered embarrassing losses to Democrats
in Congress on child care and abortion, then backed off temporarily from his
full-court press for a tax cut on capital gains. Newt Gingrich, the House GOP
Whip, goaded the President by saying his Democratic foes are "unbelievably
partisan." Pete Domenici, a senior Republican Senator, argues that Senate
Majority Leader George Mitchell was scoring zingers aimed at Bush. "You've
got to fight back," Domenici said.

Sorry, Senator, but Bush does not wish to lead an offensive. "I'm willing
to be tough," he said. But he's not willing to sound tough. When Domenici
urged Bush to attack Congressional Democrats, John Sununu, the White
House chief of staff, interjected: "Why don't you guys attack?" Domenici's
response was that no one pays attention when they do. He's right, but Bush
was unpersuaded. He and his advisers have latched onto a style that allows
Bush to take aggressively conservative positions—on abortion and spending
cuts, for instance. It doesn't allow him to appear to be combative, shrill, or
sharply partisan. That's for other, and just Republican bomb throwers like
Gingrich. If Sununu, Press Secretary Marlin Fitzwater, and White House
aides want to get belligerent, fine, but not Bush.

At his anniversary press conference on November 7 (one year after his
election), Bush performed according to plan. He talked up bipartisanship and
voiced only faint criticism of Democrats. "I'm going to continue to extend my

hand to Congress," he said in scripted remarks. In answering a question, Bush insisted the White House is doggedly "trying to cooperate in a bipartisan fashion." The problem is that Congress won't "move quickly" to enact Bush's proposals. The President also called Congress "insensitive." You can't get much milder than that. As for Mitchell, the Democrat who derailed Bush's capital gains cut, Bush was not about to question motives. "Maybe with George Mitchell," he said, "there's an honest difference on capital gains." This was not the kind of retort Domenici and other Republicans had in mind.

The Bush approach got positive reinforcement from a national survey conducted in mid-October by Bob Teeter, the President's personal pollster and political adviser. The poll made such a strong impression on Bush that he cited it twice during his press conference. Teeter found that even after the Panama fiasco, Bush is viewed positively by three-fourths of the American people. Asked specifically if Bush's performance was just right, too bold, or too cautious, three-fourths said just right. Asked who's to blame for the deficit and inaction on the budget, 65 percent pointed the finger at Congress, only 16 percent at Bush. As for whom people consider the leader of the Democratic Party, Jesse Jackson finished first, Mario Cuomo second. Mitchell and House Speaker Tom Foley barely registered. "They're invisible," says Teeter.

So why go eyeball-to-eyeball with them? "Right now there's no one in Congress who's viable as an opponent of the President," said a senior White House aide. By attacking them, "The President might just build them up." Besides, Democrats "haven't won very much, if anything. In terms of rhetoric, they've had temporary offensive in the press and it seems to have fallen flat." The strategy "is to stick to our guns and be kind of moderately quiet— that's not a good term—or quietly tough. How can you be bothered when you're at 75 percent and winning all your programs?" The aide says that if Mitchell blocks a capital-gains cut this year, it will pass in 1990. Then there are all the summits, from the session on December 2 and 3 in the Mediterranean with Mikhail Gorbachev to another economic summit next summer, an arms control summit, a NATO summit, and so forth. The point is that summits are usually popularity builders.

One example of the White House style occurred right after the October 24 meeting with GOP Congressional leaders. Bush kept his cool, but Fitzwater stormed back to the press room ready to attack. "We believe we have the votes to get passage of capital gains in the Senate, just as we had the votes in the House," he said. "And we find it very difficult to understand that the [Democratic] leadership would be willing to hold the entire United States budget in this fashion just to make a political point on capital gains." Domenici also delivered a strong attack, "but nobody else jumped in," says Fitzwater. Mitchell fired back at both Fitzwater and Domenici. The back-and-forth faded out after a day. Fitzwater concluded that he, like Bush, gained nothing by attacking. "It doesn't look like that's the best strategy," he says.

A better example involves Bush's veto of a spending bill that included federal money for abortions in the case of rape or incest. The veto prompted Democrats to vow to attach the same provision to other bills. Pro-life Republicans told the White House they might be able to draft compromise language that would get Bush off the hook. Bush waited and waited before deciding on November 2 that no compromise was workable. Sununu called Representative Chris Smith, who was holding an antiabortion strategy session in his office at the time. Sununu says he was actually returning a call from Smith, but never mind. What's important is that Sununu said Bush would veto any bill that included federal funding for abortion. Sununu was asked if this would apply to a continuing resolution, the veto of which might force the federal government to shut down. "Absolutely," said Sununu.

There's irony in this. Bush has changed positions on abortion and is uncomfortable dealing with the issue. Yet there's no issue during his Presidency on which he's taken a more airtight conservative position. Of course, that's not the way he sounds. At his press conference, he downplayed abortion. "Is it the most important issue for me? Absolutely not," he said. And it isn't to most people either, he said. To prove this he trotted out the Teeter poll. "That issue ranks about ninth to fourteenth," he said. Actually, in response to the question of what's the biggest national problem, it came in eleventh, with 4 percent. (Fifty-seven percent said drugs, 18 percent said homelessness.) Bush also expressed tolerance of pro-choice Republicans. "I don't fault people who come down differently on this," he said. "There's plenty of room for difference."

A third example of Bush's style occurred on the sequester of $16 billion in federal funds for 1990 under Gramm-Rudman. In his statement, Bush was firm but apologetic. "I deeply regret the tone of partisanship that has entered the economic policy debate," he said. "I would very much have preferred a fair and balanced debate—and vote—on merits. But the Congressional process has bogged down. Now the stalemate must be broken." At his press conference, he asked reporters to join him in pressing Congress to send budget legislation to him so the sequester can be lifted. "Join me in this noble crusade," he said.

In truth, a lot of White House aides will be unhappy if Congress approves spending cuts that are acceptable to Bush. They jumped at the chance to impose the sequester. Sununu, Budget Director Richard Darman, and Vice President Dan Quayle see it as an opportunity to make deep, permanent cuts with no gimmicks. Bush went along readily. "He likes Gramm-Rudman," an aide said. Even Teeter and Fitzwater, who aren't right-wing ideologues, are enthusiastic about the sequester. "We ought to take the sequester for the whole year," Fitzwater says. "It's real budget reduction. We can say to the Democrats, 'you keep whining about budget reduction, but we're doing it.'"

The sequester requires across-the-board cuts in all programs. Though the Pentagon takes the biggest hit, the loudest complaints didn't come from

Defense Secretary Dick Cheney. They came from Transportation Secretary Sam Skinner and Jack Kemp, the Secretary of Housing and Urban Development. Still, Bush didn't flinch. He's concluded, correctly, that with the sequester he'll have a far better shot at reaching the 1991 deficit target of $64 billion without raising taxes. Moreover, a Bush adviser said, "we think it's a good position to fight the Democrats on."

Of course, Bush would never say that. Nor was he the one who chastised Senate Republican leader Bob Dole for suggesting the White House has given up on getting a capital-gains cut this year. (The White House did give up on tacking the cut on the budget or debt limit.) Sununu got the job of talking to Dole and to Walt Riker, Dole's press secretary. Riker had been quoted in a wire report as saying Bush had "thrown in the towel" on capital gains. "That's dead wrong," Sununu told Riker. He said Riker ought to correct anything he'd said to the contrary. "That was the end of the conversation," said Sununu.

THE WORLD OF THE WHITE House staffer is unique. In the rarefied atmosphere of the West Wing of the White House the president's press secretary, national security adviser, top personal assistants and troubleshooters, and other staffers who are particularly close to the president work near the Oval Office. Occupying physical space that is near the president is of enormous symbolic significance, being generally taken to reflect a close relationship with the president himself. Not all of the White House staff works in the West Wing; many occupy offices in the old and new executive office buildings, which are respectively adjacent to and directly across Pennsylvania Avenue from the White House. The formal executive office building overlooks the West Wing. President Carter moved Vice President Walter Mondale into an office in the West Wing to symbolize a close presidential–vice presidential relationship (the former vice president's office is occasionally used for ceremonial functions and stands ready to receive vice presidents in the future).

The White House staff is a relatively new institution; President Roosevelt created it in 1939 as part of his reorganization plan establishing the executive office of the president. The White House staff, however, did not come into its own as an independent force until much later. Although it always included powerful and influential persons, its original purpose was best expressed by Harry Truman: "The presidency is so tremendous that it is necessary for a president to delegate authority. To be able to do so safely, however, he must have around him people who can be trusted not to arrogate authority to themselves."[1] Truman continued, "Eventually I succeeded in surrounding myself with associates who would not overstep the bounds of that delegated authority, and they were people I could trust. This is policy on the highest level: it is the operation of the government by the Chief Executive under laws. That is what it amounts to, and when that ceases to be, chaos exists."[2]

President John F. Kennedy put together a dynamic and forceful staff that was later inherited by Lyndon B. Johnson and described as "the best and the brightest" by journalist David Halberstam.[3] Halberstam argued persuasively that major White House decisions escalating the Vietnam war during the Johnson administration could be traced directly to powerful White House staffers such as Walt Rostow, McGeorge Bundy, and Robert McNamara (who later changed from hawk to dove and resigned his position as secretary of defense to become president of the World Bank).

It was during the Nixon years that the White House staff, controlled by H. R. (Bob) Haldeman and John Ehrlichman, arrogantly wielded power around Washington in the name of the president. The White House staff was dubbed the "Palace Guard," because of its reputation for preventing direct access to the president by cabinet officers and other top officials. Like Truman, Nixon recognized the need to delegate power, but unlike Truman, he

[1]Harry S Truman, *Memoirs: Volume 1, Year of Decisions* (Garden City, N.Y.: Doubleday, 1955), p. 228.

[2]Ibid.

[3]David Halberstam, *The Best and the Brightest* (New York: Random House, 1972).

did not recognize the critical importance of retaining absolute control over his own staff. Many of the acute embarrassments to the White House that occurred during the Nixon administration, including possibly the Watergate break-in itself, might have been avoided had the president been less optimistic about the system of broad delegation of powers that he established in the White House.

Regardless of who is president, the tendency of those on the White House staff is to aggrandize their personal power. White House staffers continually seek to be in the good graces of the president, which not only may involve backroom intrigue among different individuals and groups of staffers, but also tends to mute honest criticism of the president if he embarks on what an ambitious staffer feels to be the wrong course of action. In the following selection George Reedy, a longtime associate of Lyndon B. Johnson, both on Capitol Hill and in the White House, provides a succinct personal account of the way in which the institution of the presidency affects staffers. Reedy was Lyndon Johnson's press secretary in 1964–1965, after which he returned to private life, only to be summoned back to the White House in 1968 as a special adviser to the president on domestic matters. When Johnson was in the Senate, Reedy served him at various times, both as a staffer on the committees Johnson chaired and as a member of the senator's personal staff. Reedy's thesis is that the atmosphere of the White House tends to breed "blind ambition," to borrow John Dean's phrase, on the part of staffers, even though their personalities might not have revealed this trait before they entered the White House.

20 George E. Reedy
THE WHITE HOUSE STAFF: A PERSONAL ACCOUNT

The most frequently asked question of any former presidential assistant is whether he misses the White House. My answer is a heartfelt no!

It is an institution which can be regarded with a far higher degree of approbation from the outside—where reverence softens the harsh lines of reality—than from the inside. Like any impressionistic painting, it improves with distance. . . . The factor that I have missed in most of the works on the presidency I have read is the impact of the institution on individuals. The literature on the subject seems to assume that the White House somehow molds the man and his assistants into finer forms and that the major problem of government is to assure channels through which these forms will have full expression. It is virtually taken for granted that the proper objective of a study of our chief executive is to identify those inhibiting factors which frustrate his efforts to resolve national problems and to devise mechanisms which will remove those frustrations. This is a type of study which should be continued on a priority basis. The frustrations are many and could be catastrophic.

But the analysis is inadequate. It ignores the fundamental reality of society, which is that institutions are manned by individual human beings and that government—regardless of the managerial flow charts produced by the behavioral scientists—is still a question of decisions that are made by people. The basic question is not whether we have devised structures with inadequate authority for the decision-making process. The question is whether the structures have created an environment in which men cannot function in any kind of a decent and humane relationship to the people whom they are supposed to lead. I am afraid—and on this point I am a pessimist—that we have devised that kind of a system.

To explain this, I must start with a highly personal reaction. The trouble with the White House—for anyone who is a part of it—is that when he picks up a telephone and tells people to do something, they usually do it. They may sabotage the project, after they have hung up the phone. They may stall, hoping that "the old son of a bitch" will forget about it. They may respond with an avalanche of statistics and briefing papers in which the original purpose will be lost and life will continue as before. But the heel click at the other end of the wire will be audible and the response—however invalid—will be prompt. There will be no delay in assurance, however protracted may be performance.

This is an unhealthy environment for men and women whose essential business is to deal with people in large numbers. It is soothing to the ego, but it fosters illusions about humanity. It comforts the weary assistant who may have gone round the clock in his search for a solution to an insoluble problem, but it paves the way for massive disillusionment. And for the very young, the process is demoralizing. It creates a picture of the world which is ill adapted to that which they will face once the days of glory come to an end. There should be a flat rule that no one be permitted to enter the gates of the White House until he is at least forty and has suffered major disappointments in life.

My own heart is back in the Senate, where I spent so many years of my adult life either as a newspaperman or a staff assistant. This is not because the people at the other end of Pennsylvania Avenue are any better in terms of character, wisdom, or goals. It is simply that their egos must face daily clashes with similarly strong egos who stand on a par and who do not feel any sense of subordination. In the Senate, no course stands the remotest chance of adoption unless a minimum of fifty-one egotistical men are persuaded of its wisdom, and in some cases the minimum is sixty-seven. These are preconditions under which even the most neurotic of personalities must make some obeisance to reality.

The inner life of the White House is essentially the life of the barnyard, as set forth so graphically in the study of the pecking order among chickens which every freshman sociology student must read. It is a question of who has the right to peck whom and who must submit to being pecked. There are only two important differences. The first is that the pecking order is determined by the individual strength and forcefulness of each chicken, whereas in the White House it depends upon the relationship to the barnyard keeper. The second is that no one outside the barnyard glorifies the chickens and expects them to order the affairs of mankind. They are destined for the frying pan and that is that.

The White House does not provide an atmosphere in which idealism and devotion can flourish. Below the president is a mass of intrigue, posturing, strutting, cringing, and pious "commitment" to irrelevant windbaggery. It is designed as the perfect setting for the conspiracy of mediocrity—that all too frequently successful collection of the untalented, the unpassionate, and the insincere seeking to convince the public that it is brilliant, compassionate, and dedicated.

There are, of course, men who seethe inwardly over this affront to human dignity—most of whom either go smash or leave quietly, their muscles set rigidly to contain an indescribable agony. There are, of course, the warm and relaxed permanent White House staff members, secure in their mastery of the essential housekeeping machinery of the mansion and watching with wry amusement and some sympathy the frenetic efforts to shine forth boldly of those who have only four years out of all eternity to grab the brass ring. But the men of outrage are few and for some reason avoid each other after they slip out the side door. There are experiences which should not be shared. A reunion would lead only to a collective shriek.

It is not that the people who compose the menage are any worse than any other collection of human beings. It is rather that the White House is an ideal cloak for intrigue, pomposity, and ambition. No nation of free men should ever permit itself to be governed from a hallowed shrine where the meanest lust for power can be sanctified and the dullest wit greeted with reverential awe. Government should be vulgar, sweaty, plebeian, operating in an environment where a fool can be called a fool and the motivations of ideological pimpery duly observed and noted. In a democracy, meanness, dullness, and corruption are entitled to representation because they are part of the human spirit; they are not entitled to protection from the harsh and rude challenges that such qualities must face in the real world.

It is not enough to say that the White House need not be like this if it is occupied by another set of personalities. It is not enough to point out that I may subconsciously be exaggerating the conditions which I describe in overreacting to the reverence that has characterized most studies of the presidency. The fact remains that the institution provides camouflage for all that is petty and nasty in human beings, and enables a clown or a knave to pose as Galahad and be treated with deference.

Is my reaction purely personal disappointment or shaped by service in a specific White House in a specific administration? Obviously, no man can be truly objective about an experience so central to his life and so vital to all his goals and his aspirations. All I can say is that I am fully aware of the treacherous nature of one's sensory mechanisms in surveying the immediately surrounding universe. I have taken this factor into account and tried to allow for it in every possible way. . . . I believe that what I am saying is more than the conclusion of one man in a unique set of circumstances.

The thirty years I have spent in Washington have been punctuated with a number of telltale incidents. I have observed, for example, that former White House assistants are reticent about their experiences. When pressed for a description they invariably resort to words like "richly rewarding" and "fulfilling"—the clichés that men always use when they wish to conceal, rather than to convey, thought. And their congratulations to newly appointed assistants begin always with perfunctory "best wishes" and then shift to heartfelt friendly tips on how to survive. Only once have I felt a genuine flash of fire. It came from one of the top "assistants with a passion for anonymity" of the Roosevelt days. I described to him White House life as I saw it and his response—which was passionate—was: "Don't worry! That's the way it has always been and that's the way it will always be!"

I have a feeling that Camelot was not a very happy place. Even the gentle language of Malory does not fully cloak hints of intrigue, corruption, and distrust—reaching as high as Guinevere. And the "Table Round" seems better adapted to boozing in a vain effort to drown disappointment than to knightly discourse on chivalrous deeds and weighty matters of state.

In fact, Malory makes virtually no effort to describe Camelot as a seat of government. King Arthur was presumably beloved by his subjects because he was wise and valiant. But how did he handle road building, public charity, or the administration of justice? Such questions had to wait several hundred years for the advent of Mark Twain, whose entirely fictitious (and wholly irreverent) account was probably much closer to the reality than that produced by the original sources.

It is this aspect that gives cause for concern. The psychological ease of those who reside in Camelot does not matter except to the individuals themselves. But the type of government that Camelot produces affects every individual and, ultimately, can determine the character of the society in which we all must live.

It is my highly pessimistic view that Camelot will no longer suffice—however effective it may have been in the past. As a rallying point for men who would beat off dragons and ogres, it was superb. As a device to lead us through the stresses of modern life, it is wholly inadequate. And one of the few historical principles in which I still retain faith is that an inadequate government will either fall or resort to repression.

There is no reason to believe that the United States is exempt from the forces of history. We have no special writ from the Almighty which will substitute for normal human wisdom. There is no evidence that such wisdom is being applied effectively to the overwhelming problems that beset us nor is there any light on the horizon. And while it may seem premature at this point, we may well be witnessing the first lengthening of the shadows that will become the twilight of the presidency.

W HEN U.S. PRESIDENT-ELECT George Bush chose New Hampshire governor John H. Sununu to be his White House Chief of Staff, he both paid off a political debt and made a like-minded conservative the head of his political team. As governor of the Granite State Sununu had been instrumental in assuring Bush's victory over Kansas Senator Robert Dole in the crucial 1988 New Hampshire presidential primary. In announcing the appointment, Bush told reporters that Sununu would bring a "refreshing new perspective" to the White House, gained from serving three terms as New Hampshire governor and from his experiences as an educator and engineer. Sununu, born in Havana, Cuba, on July 2, 1939, earned Bachelor's Master's, and PhD degrees, all in mechanical engineering, from the Massachusetts Institute of Technology in Boston. He then taught at Tufts University for 17 years and served as its Associate Dean of the College of Engineering. He was elected governor of New Hampshire in 1982 and was reelected in 1984 and 1986. Becoming White House Chief of Staff, Sununu has lived up to his reputation for being a strong-willed and take-charge person, as the following account of his White House leadership style reveals.

21 David Hoffman and Ann Devroy
THE WHITE HOUSE
TOUGH GUY

In contrast to the kinder, gentler image cultivated by his boss in his first year in office, White House Chief of Staff John H. Sununu has emerged as a bare-knuckles, partisan slugger with a volcanic temper and an aversion to conciliation and compromise.

In the name of the president, he has unleashed a fiery anger at senators and House members, often given misleading information to reporters, and chewed out political appointees and staff aides, according to several dozen officials in government and politics.

Republican Senator John McCain of Arizona says Sununu "reminds me of a successful military officer. The commanding officer is the good guy and the exec is the disciplinarian. It's almost a perfect match."

Republican Sen. Warren B. Rudman of New Hampshire says of Sununu and President Bush: "I think there's a gulf of difference in their personalities. I don't think George Bush enjoys tough personal confrontation. He just doesn't enjoy it. John doesn't have a problem in doing it. If John Sununu would take a true-or-false test, 'Is it true you would rather take the flak?' he'd mark it true with a big X."

From *The Washington Post National Weekly Edition,* February 5–11, 1990. Copyright 1990 by the *Washington Post.* Reprinted by permission.

Rep. Mickey Edwards of Oklahoma, chairman of the House Republican Policy Committee, says Sununu "has extremely strong opinions and is not terribly receptive to others even when he doesn't know what he is talking about."

Sununu acknowledges his reputation and his role.

"I know it means I'm going to be perceived as the guy who has to say no, and the president as the guy who . . . might say yes. There hasn't been any planning in the roles; it's just something I understood when I took the job— that end of the stick would be mine."

Wielding the stick with enthusiasm, Sununu has left his mark on the first year of Bush's presidency. Working for a president who is not strongly ideological, Sununu has been an activist for conservatives, quietly helping to block or kill some appointments and helping to influence Bush on such issues as abortion. In part because of his background in engineering and science, he has been an influential adviser to Bush on scientific and technological issues, such as the FSX fighter-plane deal with Japan and the controversy over global warming.

Even while he works to influence policy, Sununu often tries to mask his direct involvement, refusing to acknowledge his participation in meetings or his behind-the-scenes role in killing a nomination or altering a policy. Officials say Sununu is reluctant to acknowledge his role out of concern that he be viewed as an honest broker who is not taking sides.

Sununu has sought to enforce loyalty to a president who demands it from his subordinates. For example, he has encouraged other White House aides to turn in their colleagues if they are suspected of being the source of leaks to the news media.

Many officials and politicians interviewed for this article say that Sununu, while aggressive and intelligent, has provided little overall political strategy for the president on domestic-policy issues and that Bush needs more effective and focused direction, particularly in plotting and carrying out his legislative goals.

These officials say Bush has enjoyed an unusually high public approval rating in his first year, and Sununu's associates point to this as evidence of the chief of staff's effectiveness. But critics suggest Bush has not used his public standing to accomplish much on his domestic agenda.

Every president sets his own pace and methods of operating, and the role of his chief of staff can be a critical factor in his success or failure. For example, President Ronald Reagan focused on the big picture and let his chiefs of staff handle details. With the exception of Donald T. Regan, Reagan had chiefs of staff who were skilled negotiators and conciliators with Congress and the news media—James A. Baker III, Howard H. Baker, Jr., and Kenneth M. Duberstein.

But Bush likes to handle the details himself, and rather than a smooth ambassador to Congress, the news media, and special interests, he wanted a hard-nosed operator as chief of staff, according to associates of the president.

Bush signaled this desire long before he picked Sununu. These sources say Bush's early preference was to give the job to businessman and former Nixon administration official Frederic V. Malek, who also had a reputation as a tough operator.

Says one Republican familiar with the workings of both the Reagan and Bush administrations: "In the end, George Bush is always his own chief of staff. At the end of the day, he is on the phone calling everyone on everything. He's the one deciding who's going to come to the stag dinner at the White House that night, or what's going to happen on whatever."

By the accounts of others, Sununu manages much the way Bush does, making decisions case by case as issues are presented.

At the beginning of each day, Sununu meets with Bush with a binder filled with decisions for Bush generated by the staff, the Cabinet and himself. At the end of each day, Sununu returns for another meeting to review the day.

Some of those who work closely with Sununu report that he is overburdened but does not share enough of his job.

"He needs to delegate more," says one associate who sees Sununu daily.

Andrew Card, Jr., deputy to Sununu, calls his boss "the throat of the funnel" to Bush. "He is not a gatekeeper as much as he is the funnel into which everything is poured."

Card says Sununu has "an open-door policy with a lot of unstructured time and no rigid meeting schedules. He does not like regimented meetings, either by time slot or title, so you have legislative strategy meetings all the time when you need them, but you don't have a legislative strategy group that meets every Tuesday."

Another White House official says: "It's very ad hoc. A lot of stuff that's done is done on the fly—it's faster that way." Many of Sununu's meetings are open to anyone who walks in the door, according to associates.

Sununu says he and Bush privately have talked about long-term strategy, but these discussions are "a relatively close hold."

Others say the White House has devoted little attention to the kind of focused strategy that was instrumental in Reagan's early legislative accomplishments. What strategies that do exist are often cooked up by others such as Budget Director Richard Darman, whose hopes for a "grand compromise" on the deficit were not realized last year.

Sununu acknowledges that he and Bush have little interest in the kind of concentrated thematic management of the presidency that proved effective for Reagan. "We just don't operate that way," he says. "We don't have an education week and then a drug week and then a foreign policy week."

A Republican with direct personal ties to the president says: "This is a White House consumed with day-to-day tactics, much like the president is. At the morning staff meetings, all you heard is what's up, what's going on, what do we have to react to today. It's not how do we want to approach the next week, the next several weeks."

The lack of an overall strategy was most evident in the way fiscal and tax issues were handled last year, critics say. Bush came into office seeking a bipartisan solution to the budget deficit problem, and promised to hammer one out through negotiation with Congress. An early deal was put together in April, at which time the president and his advisers, including Darman, expressed hope for a more significant bipartisan negotiation in the fall that would slice the deficit for several years.

But this "grand compromise" slipped away from them largely because the capital gains tax-break issue blew up into an intensely partisan contest with the new Democratic leadership in Congress, spoiling the climate for any deficit negotiations.

Senate Majority Leader George J. Mitchell of Maine made a maximum effort to block a capital gains tax break, setting up a fight with Bush.

The decision to push for the tax break regardless of the consequences came from the White House, not from congressional Republicans, should capital gains be the number one priority, they would say "no," says a conservative Republican senator.

In the end, Bush got neither the capital gains tax cut nor the grand compromise on spending and taxation. Instead he got "sequestration," the automatic budget cuts that take effect when Congress and the president fail to reach agreement by the start of the fiscal year, and a subsequent one-year deal on the deficit.

The confrontation in the autumn months has left some in Congress angry about the treatment they received from Sununu, a former New Hampshire governor who was known for his acerbic attacks on state legislators there.

On the strength of his aggressive personality, Sununu enjoyed wide influence in his small state. In Washington, however, he has left many lawmakers with a sense that he is looking down his nose at them.

"We have to keep telling the governor from time to time it's not quite like dealing with the legislature, because the president doesn't have line-item veto and some other things like that," said House Minority Leader Robert H. Michels of Illinois when the capital gains tax break was set aside last year.

Edwards, the policy committee chairman, got into such a heated discussion with Sununu over presidential prerogatives in a foreign policy bill that the chief of staff hung up on him three times. The congressman says Sununu "didn't understand what was in the bill, he didn't know what he was talking about" and when Edwards tried to tell him, Sununu "slammed down the phone . . . At least I think he did—I found myself talking to a dial tone."

Democratic Sen. Timothy E. Wirth of Colorado says Sununu is disliked by many Democrats because of what he calls a "condescending" attitude toward many on Capitol Hill. Sununu, he says, "comes out of a state where the legislators are part time and not enmeshed in broad domestic and foreign policy issues," a state where Sununu "could impress everyone with the strength of his intellect," dominating the news media and politics.

Sununu "doesn't understand or doesn't want to understand" that Congress is different, he says. "He has no respect for the intellectual capacity of any of us. He comes up here with that kind of attitude, and our attitude is, who elected you? He in no way acknowledges that there are smart people in Congress too."

A senior White House official says Sununu "does have some problems on the Hill. He is so loyal to George Bush, or so committed to defending the Bush position, that he leaps instantly to the defense at all times, even when there is recognizable merit in suggestions that this or that could be handled better or that an issue should be reexamined."

Ed Rogers, Sununu's executive assistant, says the chief of staff does not suffer gladly those he considers inadequately prepared or intellectually inferior. "What provokes Sununu is not being prepared. He is smarter than most of us," Rogers says.

Sununu has collided with influential members in both parties, and some of them say they have concluded that Bush, who recently called himself a "healer," simply does not want to get his hands dirty—leaving it to Sununu instead.

For example, when Senate Democrats, led by Judiciary Committee Chairman Joseph R. Biden, Jr., of Delaware, were seeking to expand Bush's antidrug proposals, Sununu told a group of GOP lawmakers that Biden's ideas were "mostly plagiarism" from the president—a reference to charges in the 1988 presidential campaign that Biden had copied speeches from a British politician.

"You can't aim a lower blow," says a Republican senator, who notes how this technique let Bush stick to the high road. Sununu "fulfills this role of the hatchet man to the nth degree," the senator says.

Sununu, asked about the remark, claims he had made it in total privacy with the lawmakers and never expected it to become public. In fact, Sununu's remark was telephoned to reporters by his aide, Rogers, who encouraged them to use it.

In another example, Sununu collided with Republican Sen. Pete Wilson of California over Wilson's vote against the White House on the FSX fighter plane deal with Japan. The senator, who is running for governor, had what an informed Republican Party official calls "an altercation on the phone" with Sununu. A source close to the senator confirms this and says, "Wilson shot straight, and Sununu didn't like it."

Republican National Committee Chairman Lee Atwater has labeled Wilson's race for governor the party's top priority for 1990, but as a result of the clash with Sununu, the senator was unsuccessful in repeated efforts to get

Bush to speak at a California fund-raiser for him in 1989. One is planned for this month.

Sununu asserts that Bush had no time in California last fall to campaign for Wilson, who had helped Bush in the 1988 presidential race.

"If Pete Wilson is concerned that perhaps he should have supported the president on FSX, we're pleased to hear that he recognizes that we do pay attention to who supports the president," Sununu says.

Sununu's volcanic temper often does not respect protocol. Walt Riker, press secretary to Senate Minority Leader Robert J. Dole of Kansas, told reporters, accurately, that Bush had agreed not to try to attach the capital gains measure to other bills most likely to get through in the session—in effect, delaying action until this year.

When Sununu saw Riker's comments in a wire service story, he immediately telephoned him directly, rather than complain to Dole. In a voice that could be heard in nearby offices, Sununu screamed at Riker that Bush had not given up on capital gains and that Riker had better put out a "[expletive] correction."

At the same time, Sununu has won praise from members of Congress for giving them extensive direct access to the president, which many felt had been denied during the Reagan administration. Rudman recalls Sununu setting up a long luncheon for the senator to brief Bush on a recent visit to China; another time he and Sununu walked in on Bush for an impromptu meeting. "I was flabbergasted," Rudman says. "I served here under Reagan and that never happened."

Although he attempts to mask the extent of his role, Sununu is deeply involved in domestic policymaking. Cabinet members and White House officials say he and Darman are the most influential of Bush's advisers on domestic issues.

Sununu "really does dominate the decision-making process at the White House totally," says conservative Rep. Vin Weber of Minnesota. "You would often find in the Reagan administration, you'd ask, 'how do I influence the decision on this issue?' and it would be 'you need Jim Baker,' and on issue X, it would be 'see if you can get his friend Ed Meese to talk to the president,' or on something else, it would be 'enlist Cap Weinberger.' When you ask how to influence decision making in the Bush White House, it's always the same answer: Sununu."

A White House official who is well informed about domestic policy decisions says Sununu "has very strong views on some issues" and makes them heard. For example, Sununu has been at the forefront of those who question the scientific data on which environmentalists have based warnings of the "greenhouse effect," a global warming of Earth's atmosphere caused by industrial gases.

Sununu also is opposed to abortion and was deeply involved in negotiations over spending bills at the time Bush was threatening vetoes because of language that would have permitted more abortions. Some participants in the negotiations praised Sununu for helping the antiabortion forces.

Sununu says, "I never, never argued the case to the president one way or the other."

"Conservatives owe a huge debt to John Sununu," says the White House official familiar with domestic policy. I think some of us didn't sufficiently appreciate how conservative he is. It is a tribute to John Sununu's cleverness that he has managed not to be so associated with the conservative position that he becomes a lightning rod because of that."

P
RESIDENT THEODORE ROOSE-
velt called the presidency a "bully
pulpit." Referring to Teddy
Roosevelt's metaphor, William Safire
writes: "The image of the White House as
a pulpit with the whole nation as congregation—linked with the zesty adjective
'bully' meaning first-rate, or admirable—
has been frequently used ever since."[1]
Clearly presidents strive to exert moral
leadership from their White House pulpit.
How effective they are depends not only
on their deeds but their words, and the
president's speechwriters often determine the content and eloquence of presidential "sermons."

White House speechwriters have
rarely elaborated upon their role, however, and the literature of the presidency
contains scant reference to them. In his
well-known book *Decision-making in
the White House,*[2] Special Counsel to
the President Theodore Sorensen does
not make a single reference to his role as
President John F. Kennedy's speechwriter. Referring to the Kennedy and
Johnson administrations, George E.
Reedy writes, "In the last two administrations, the Special Counsels have been primarily speechwriters (Theodore Sorensen and Harry McPherson), and while
both were men of high legal competence
their opinions on points of law were
rarely sought or offered. It was open
knowledge, not only in the White House
but to the Washington community at
large, that their ability to put on paper
sentences that would parse grammati-
cally was the key to their position in the
heirarchy."[3]

Sorensen and McPherson were part of
presidential speechwriter teams, reflecting the practice of modern presidencies
to employ a variety of speechwriters,
some of whom become well known
while others remain anonymous. Many
write books about their experiences, including the author of the following selection, who, while taking us behind the
scenes of the Reagan White House, gives
us a rare account of what is like to be a
president's speechwriter.

[1]William Safire, *Safire's Political Dictionary* (New York: Random House, 1978), p. 83.

[2]Theodore Sorensen, *Decision-making in the White House* (New York: Columbia University Press, 1963).

[3]George E. Reedy, *The Twilight of the Presidency* (New York: The World Publishing Company, 1970), p. 86.

22 Peggy Noonan
CONFESSIONS OF A WHITE HOUSE SPEECHWRITER

I first saw him as a foot, a highly polished brown cordovan wagging merrily on a hassock. I spied it through the door. It was a beautiful foot, sleek, perfectly shaped. Such casual elegance and clean lines! But not a big foot, not formidable, maybe even a little . . . frail. I imagined cradling it in my arms, protecting it from unsmooth roads.

I was yanked from my reverie by the movement of an aide, who bent past the foot and murmured, "You're in luck, Mr. President. The meeting with the speechwriters is canceled." The foot stopped, then wagged more merrily still. Talk and light laughter. Someone closed the door.

I was supposed to have met the boss, after two months writing speeches for him. Along with a few of the speechwriters, I had waited in a room outside the Oval Office and everything was fine until an official from the National Security Council [NSC] walked in and saw a speechwriter with whom he didn't get along. "I'm not going to a meeting where I'm on an equal footing with him," I heard him say as he huffed down the hall. The meeting was canceled. Dick Darman, to whom the speechwriting department reported, said, "Sorry, but that's the way it goes."

Anyway, I'd seen his foot. At least I'd have a story for my friends.

I had joined the White House early in 1984, after three years writing Dan Rather's radio commentaries. CBS News isn't exactly a garden where they grow Reagan speechwriters, but that didn't work against me. When conservatives came through the newsroom for interviews, a technician or editor would always bring them by to meet me, as if to say, "See, we have one too."

That's how I met an editor of William Buckley's National Review and told him of my longing to write for the President, whose views I shared. He passed my name along to Ben Elliott, head of the White House speechwriting department, who, long ago and far away, had himself worked at CBS. He asked me to come in and talk. In February, on the day of the New Hampshire primary, he offered me a job.

Joining the Reagan White House as a speechwriter was like joining CBS in radio. Right church, wrong pew; right company, wrong division. There was an odd and general feeling about the speechwriters, one that was expressed in a slight snicker. Perhaps it was the snicker the guys in the plant reserve for the public relations types who float through now and then, a snicker that says: You're part of the wind machine while we do the real work on the assembly line!

At first I decided that part of the problem was the speechwriters' comportment, because they tended to be sadsacks and complain, and resentment isn't a magnetic personal style, but in time I came to a different conclusion. The snickers were a kind of protective reaction. In a White House so dependent on rhetoric, the people around the President—and their secretaries and the secretaries' friends down the hall—came to see it as an act of loyalty to the President to dismiss the people who wrote the script.

What I remember from my first days at work was walking the high marble hallways and tall cool stairs of the Old Executive Office Building [E.O.B.]. An aide told me, "When they're new they walk right down the middle; when they've been here awhile they hug the walls." He was right.

The E.O.B. is part of the White House complex within the gate but separated from the West Wing by a short street called West Executive Avenue. Most of the White House offices were in the E.O.B., and people who worked here called it there—the White House.

I was introduced to the staff. "Peggy is from CBS, where she worked with Dan Rather, and their show was nominated for many awards—"

"The Lenin Prize!" said a bearded speechwriter.

"Now, Dana," said Ben.

"Ben, when are we going to see the President again?" he said. "It would really help us to meet with him and hear what he's thinking about."

"I know, Dana," Ben said.

"How long is it since you met with him?" I asked.

"More than a year."

"It's more than a year since you saw the President?"

"Well, since we met. We see him all the time. We wave to him."

They gave me a little office that faced a courtyard that never got the sun. I could look out and see the exhaust system of the E.O.B. An old radiator hissed forlornly, carrying into my office metallic rumblings from the deepest insides of the old Victorian building. It was dank and clanked; it smelled like history.

I loved that funny office. I used to sit there in the late afternoon in a red velveteen chair and read the papers of the Presidency in the glow of an old lamp. In the White House they keep big, thick volumes of the Presidents' speeches, utterances and meetings with the press. I'd take a few volumes from the library upstairs and read them at random. Soon I realized what I was looking for: the grammar of the Presidency, the sound and tone and tense of it. And then I knew exactly where to go: to the modern President who had sounded most like a president, the one who set the standard for how the rest should sound. I went to FDR.

I had read about Roosevelt over the years and knew he liked the poem "Invictus"—*'I am the master of my fate/I am the captain of my soul'*—and saw now that he had absorbed its victorious rhythm so that it had become his own triumphant cadence, a sound that echoed not only in his speeches but even in his recorded conversation.

I'd think: This is how Reagan should sound.

It was hard for me to make friends. Not that people weren't nice—they were—but we led different lives. The men and women my age (I was in my early 30's) were not like New York people. They were married and had two little children; they had such settled lives! And I was shy, and when I am shy I look impassive and when I look impassive I look formidable, and some people were shy with me.

It was a daily challenge for me to walk into the mess by myself. Young men would look up, impassive, and look down and continue to chew. Women would look up, nod pertly and look down and chew. But mostly there were men, men in suits, and when they gestured the light caught their Presidential cufflinks. In time I forced myself to go, unaccompanied, to the big, round staff table where those without lunch partners sat.

I would listen, thinking, "This is like a tutorial, a movable tutorial that never stops. These people are like the bright intense people in college who couldn't stop talking about Hawthorne and Tennyson and the Lake Poets." Only the topic was public policy, and there was a freshness to it.

It was the authentic sound of the Reagan revolution, buzzing around me.

"Peg, hi, Mike Horowitz, O.M.B. [Office of Management and Budget]! Heard all about ya, welcome!" He turns back to the men, throws his arm over a chair. "Now the thing we have to keep in mind in welfare reform is the 14-year-old kid in the inner city who has been unwittingly encouraged by this great lumbering government of ours to take steps in her life that are ultimately harmful to her. She's had a baby she's not equipped to care for, she's just made her mother a grandmother at the age of 30, she's stuck now without an education, without options, with no particular promise. She has been used and abused by the very system created to help her! And who will speak for her? No one, because precious few in this debate care about anything but the biases and demands of their own constituencies. Thus: stasis. Pass the ketchup!"

"Yes," says Doug Holladay of Office of Public Liaison [O.P.L.], "you're right, but that gets us back at least in part to values and the role they play. And that brings up the delicate question of how to bring back and encourage the values that all of us, black and white, lived by in this country for generations, for centuries."

"But without being labeled irrelevant to the debate or sentimental about a past that never was," says Judi Buckalew, also of O.P.L.

"Let me fill you in on what's happening in our sincere if admittedly at this point inadequate attempts to overhaul and improve our farm program and see if you can't draw some surprising parallels," offers Fred Khedouri of O.M.B.

"Wait here's Lenczowski," says Horowitz, motioning toward an N.S.C. staffer. "John, that statement of yours that a lot of the people pushing right now for an arms agreement must just love signing ceremonies because without a serious commitment to verification it's all a charade was just . . . super! Fred, go ahead."

It was music to my ears. All these intelligent, well-motivated people talking about important things and trying to understand America.

Little by little I settled in. There were times when I thought that I was viewed as . . . a little different. Not quite an oddball, not quite a strange one, not quite a walking occasion of sin, but those phrases came into my mind. A secretary told me, "You dress different." I was at that time partial to long black skirts and soft black boots. "That's not so bad," she said, "but everybody here at your particular level wears suits with a sort of man-tailored blouse and a scarf or a tie. But what's really different is your hair. You have this long, free-flowing hair. Most of us have shorter, neater hair."

Another young woman took me aside and said, "I heard you had wine in the mess."

"Yeah."

"And smoked cigarettes."

"Oh, yeah. It was my friend's birthday and we were celebrating and I guess we stayed too long. Was it . . . sort of noticed?"

"I heard about it."

"Was it disapproved?"

"Well . . . it wasn't considered average."

What was considered average?

I went to lunch with a man I met at a brunch, a lobbyist for a big insurance consortium. "The Carter folks used to hang out at a bar on Pennsylvania Avenue called Sarsfield's," he told me. "It was wild, it was a zoo. Sunday was the big night. All the bartenders and waitresses from around town would go there to drink and the Carter people would show and there'd be fights in this corner and heavy drinking over there. It was wild those days."

"Is there a Reagan hangout?"

"Nope."

"I didn't think so. You know, no one has ever said to me after work, Let's go for a beer or a cup of coffee. At CBS, people were always going out. Here there's nothing. I think they go home and they fall asleep at 11:03 and get up at 5:45 and go jogging and then they eat cereal with the kids and correct their homework at the table and come in at 7:15 with their briefcases and say, 'Good morning, what can we do to advance traditional values today!'"

My first speech was what former speechwriters have called Rose Garden Rubbish, though I never heard that phrase in my years at the White House. It was a Rose Garden appearance in which the President was to announce and praise the teacher of the year. You would think this would be easy: praise teaching, announce the winner, praise her, and that's it, neat and nice, five minutes. But it was my first speech, so I included a defense of the West and an analysis of Bloomsbury's contribution to Keynesian notions of expediency as illustrated in the famous saying "In the long run we're all dead." It ran a little long.

I got my information on who the teacher was and what we should say from a researcher who got it from the advance office. I got my advice on the tone from Ben—don't go too long, because it's hot in the Rose Garden and he's standing in the sun and reading from cards and that's not his best read. It's an annual speech—ask research for copies of what he's said in the past. "And remember, it always has to be positive with him. Never 'I'll never forget,' always 'I'll always remember.' "

I listened, I tried, I froze. The President would be saying these words! They were history! (They would go in the books!)

Ben had said: If you get in a bind call Bill Bennett at the National Endowment for the Humanities, he's brilliant and he really cares about teaching.

I called his office. He called me back from an airport. "I'm a new speechwriter for the President," I said, "and I need some help. The subject is teachers. He's announcing the teacher of the year. I hate to bother you, but—"

"When do you need it?"

"Now."

"Oh, nice to have time. O.K.: 'A Man for All Seasons,' Sir Thomas More's speech to Richard Rich. Rich is a bright young man not sure of his future. More tells him, 'Be a teacher.' Rich says, 'And if I'm a great teacher, who will know it?' More says, 'You, your students, God. Not a bad audience that.' Or words to that effect. Beautiful speech, and true. Look it up, gotta go, bye."

I used it. The President, to my pride and disappointment, did not change a word. The day of the ceremony I went to the Rose Garden. It was a warm, humid day in April, and the sun was strong. The press was gathered in front, looking around, scoping the joint. Their eyes never stop: Who's that talking to Deaver, who's with Baker? I stood in the back behind a row of chairs.

The President bounded out of the Oval Office into the sunlight and stood at a lectern on the grass. He cleared his throat. "Thank you, ladies and gentlemen."

It was him. I began to pace back and forth. In a jerky way. I began to swallow, and wet my lips. It was so exciting to finally see him saying my words written on my typewriter with my hands. I looked up at the roof and saw the little window where Caroline Kennedy looked out when her father honored the astronauts. I looked at the Colonnade. I looked at the grass, my shoes. I looked at—the Secret Servicemen, who were looking back. They stared at me, blank-faced and ready. One of them was walking toward me.

"Would you like to sit, miss?"

"Oh, no, not really. I'm not a guest, I mean, I'm not supposed to be in the audience, I'm not supposed to be here, I'm . . ."

"Who are you, please?"

"Oh, I'm the new speechwriter. I wrote this and I'm nervous, that's why I'm pacing, I'm sorry, would you like me to leave?"

"No," he said, nodding, his tongue pressing against his cheek. "It's all right. As you were. Proceed."

First Big Stupid Thing I Did

One day, I got a call I didn't want. Jim Rosebush, the first lady's chief of staff, wanted me to come over to the East Wing to work on a speech for Mrs. Reagan.

I went to Ben. "I mean no offense, but we settled this before I came. If I were a man I could write for her, but as a woman they'll say I'm the First Lady's speechwriter who now and then does a speech for the President."

Ben sighed. "I knew this would happen. I told them you're not here for that."

"Can we do anything?"

"She's upset because she doesn't like her speeches. She doesn't think Peter's stuff is muscular enough."

"Well, I'm a girl and I'm not muscular enough, either. Girls are sissies and don't use verbs."

"Nice try. Look, do it this once and if he asks again I'll take care of it."

I wrote a nice bad speech, so sugary you had to lick your fingers afterward. "My life didn't begin until I met Ronnie." "I can tell you as a mother that nothing, nothing is as important as the welfare of a child." The kid didn't miss a cliché. Peter, the speechwriter she'd rejected, offered hopefully, "When she talks about drugs she likes to say things like 'The things I've seen would make the strongest heart break.'"

I figured if Peter wrote that and she didn't like his work, I should write it too.

I sent it in. Rosebush called. "Congratulations," he said, "she loved it!"

A week later he asked that I "polish up" another speech. I went to Ben. "There's nothing wrong with helping out a little," he said. A week later Rosebush called.

"I want you to write another speech."

I said I'd have to check that out. He said, "I'm sure there's no problem, the President's speechwriters write for the First Lady. She *is* the First Lady of the country, you know." I said, "But I came down here to write for the President and—"

"Well, if you think you're too good—"

"No, no, but I just want to write for the President."

"Well, we'll see."

A moment later Ben called. "Go."

I called Rosebush's office and offered to come over. He asked exactly when I'd be there. "Ten minutes," I said. "No, make it 20," he said. "O.K., 20."

"Twenty on the dot," he said.

He offered me a seat and proceeded to talk about the weather and politics and how did I like it here. Odd, I thought, this busy man killing time.

Mike Deaver walked in.

"What's all this about?" he said with a scowl as he threw his briefcase onto a chair.

"This is Peggy Noonan," said Rosebush, "who is refusing to write speeches for the First Lady."

"Urrgh," I said, choking.

"We need her help, but she doesn't want to help us."

Deaver looked at me.

"Mr. Deaver," I said, "I don't want to be unhelpful but I joined up here a few weeks ago to write for the President. I'm sure the First Lady is going to be very important to the campaign and I'm sure she'll have a lot of speaking engagements and—and I think she'll need a lot of help. But I can't do it because that's not why I came here."

Deaver looked at me. "Well, I don't think we're going to settle this here," he said. "We'll work this out later. Jim, since I'm here, let's finish our talk about—"

I gathered my papers and ran. "I have to get a speech to the President," I said over my shoulder at Rosebush, who was making little pyramids with his hands and tapping them together.

I made a decision. I was not going to become the First Lady's speechwriter and I was not going to keep worrying about it. I called Darman. This is important, I said. He chuckled and told me to come by.

I told him what had happened. "I'm going to have to leave here and go back to New York and my nice job writing for CBS News unless we settle this and I must tell you I can't settle it by agreeing to write the First Lady's speeches. I asked Ben before I came here and he promised I wouldn't have to do it, I was worried about it from the beginning because I'm a woman and—"

"You're not going to write the First Lady's speeches. It will be taken care of. Any other problems?"

I was taken aback, and a little disappointed. Here I was all wound up. I wanted to have to insist.

"No."

"Are we enjoying our job?"

"We are coming to terms with the facts of our employment."

"I'm pleased. Do come again."

"Thank you, it's been a pleasure."

"Me too."

A few days later I passed Rosebush and a few of his assistants as I walked along looking at the portraits of the First Ladies in the part of the White

House known as the residence. "Will you be coming by soon?" he asked brightly.

"No!" I said brightly. "I will not! Talk to Dick Darman! Thank you! Thank you! Goodbye!" I kept walking.

What I should have done, of course, was act very friendly and explain with some pain that I'm just unable to do it, Jim, but if there's ever anything else I can do for you. . . . Or I should have said I was eager to help but Dick and Ben wouldn't free me up, the election, I'm working so hard. Instead I did a very un-Washington thing: I showed joy in my victory. Rosebush scowled. His assistant scowled. I had made enemies. I didn't care.

I have asked myself since: If I knew then that the first lady was the major and decisive force she was in that White House would I still have rejected the call to write for her? And the answer, I think, is yes.

A few weeks later I was walking through the East Wing when I saw the First Lady and her entourage coming my way. I'd never met her and didn't know if I was supposed to look at her and make eye contact and say hello or leave her to her privacy, of which she'd not had much these many years. I decided to look to see if I could see anything interesting in her eyes. She looked at me in a way that seemed to have no meaning. Then she looked down at what I was wearing, which was, unfortunately, a wrinkled khaki skirt and a blue work shirt and heavy walking shoes with white woolen socks. Not exactly White House issue, but I was going walking. She looked me up and down and I swear her mouth curled. She looked away and said something to an aide. The next time I saw her coming I hid behind a pillar.

Second Big Stupid Thing I Did

I was invited to the mess to have lunch with Maureen Reagan. I think Nancy Risque in the Congressional Affairs office arranged it. I got there late. Maureen was already there, with two assistants. Her face was like the face of Bette Davis in *Elizabeth the Queen* when Errol Flynn did something impertinent. I couldn't think of any good conversation. She did not appear to be attempting to think of any. At one point someone mentioned the board game "Trivial Pursuit" and I piped up that I'd heard the Canadian version was better. There was silence as I remembered what I'd read about the Canadian version in yesterday's paper. Unlike the American version, it contained the question "How many months after their marriage was Ronald and Nancy Reagan's daughter Patty born?"

The phone rang. Saved by the bell. A steward plugged in a phone and murmured to Miss Reagan. "Mr. Baker's office," he said. She picked it up, listened, glowered, slammed down the phone. "Goddammit!" she spat. "Let's go." She left in a huff. I lingered over coffee and thought: you just made a bad impression on a powerful person with a volatile temperament. Congratulations, you're doing really well.

Third Big Stupid Thing I Did

I was writing the president's remarks for a meeting of a Republican women's group. Maureen Reagan was involved with the group. I knew how to recoup my mistake with her: I called the East Wing and told them that I would soon be finished with the speech and would like her to look at it. They called back: Miss Reagan wants the speech immediately upon its completion.

I wrote a good speech, a fine speech, a dazzling speech. It connected things that had never been connected, it asserted itself, it was—intellectually substantial and yet marked by a kind of sunny, big-chested *bonhomie.* I sent it over and waited for the raves. The next morning, Maureen called me personally.

"Page two," she said.

"Yes," I smiled.

"Kill it."

"What?"

"Kill it. And three. Page four, second graph, kill."

"Gee, Maureen. I don't know. Don't you think this is pretty good? Where I mention the rise of the conservative columnists and Safire and all the percolation of ideas from our side—"

"Are you refusing?"

"Well, I don't know. I'm saying, though, that—"

Click.

I had the distinct impression my rehabilitation program was not achieving the desired effect. I sat in silence. I had done it again, but it wasn't my fault, I was really trying, I meant well. But—is the President's daughter really supposed to control what he says? That's really dumb, that's really—

The phone rang.

"Peggy? This is Dick Darman. I see you're already making an impression. I have spent the past 20 minutes saving your job. Miss Maureen Reagan was just over here telling some very important people that you should be fired."

"Oh no."

"Did you say no to her?"

"No, I just, I didn't say no but she wanted me to do some things that I thought were wrong."

"All right, listen to me. Are you listening?"

"Yes."

"This is what you say when Maureen Reagan tells you to do something. You say, 'Yes Maureen, you bet Maureen, right away Maureen.' Do you have that?"

"Yes."

"Good. What are you going to say when Maureen Reagan calls?"

"Yes Maureen you bet Maureen how high Maureen."

"Even better. And when you're done you call me and tell me what stupid thing you said yes to and I'll take care of it."

I had a Maureen Plan after that. I was going to apologize and whatever she told me I was going to do and I was going to be very eager about it. But she never called again. A few years later I sat across from her at a big dinner. She made believe she didn't see me.

I hoped to meet the President. I continued writing speeches. They were not the most important speeches, but each had a weight of its own and I strived to make each special. I thought about the audience. I would think how happy they were to be near the president and how each deserved something special, something personal. I experimented with special jokes and witticisms in parentheses at the top of the page; I did not endear myself to the researchers when I asked them to go back again and again to find out who the leader of such and such an organization was and what his nickname was and has he ever met the president? And in the town where he's speaking, what are the people talking about, is there a local problem like a garbage scow nobody wants, does the local school have a winning team, what's the big local department store and are they hiring? Anything to make it seem as if someone had thought about his speech and these people. I would write them and send them in; the president would read them and never complain.

I will always remember—actually I will never forget—the first time I got a response. I received a speech back from the president and in the upper right-hand corner where he put his initials to show he'd read it there was the usual RR, but beneath that I saw his faint script. "Very Good," it said.

I stared at it. Then I took a pair of scissors and cut it off and taped it to my blouse, like a second-grader with a star. All day, people noticed it and looked at me; I would beam back in a quietly idiotic manner. They would look away. In the mess, one of the president's lawyers, Peter Rusthoven, nodded hello, saw the paper, read it, put his head in his hands and screamed softly. That was my favorite reaction.

I met him face to face my fourth month there. I had been lobbying, of course. "I can't write well without hearing the person I'm writing for talk in conversation," I would tell Ben. "I have to hear where they breathe in a sentence and what humor is for them." "If you think he sounds stale, maybe it's because the speechwriters haven't met with him in more than a year," I'd tell Darman.

Finally, after the President returned from Europe, where he had attended the 40th anniversary celebrations of D-Day and given the address at Pointe du Hoc, I was to meet him. With Darman and the entire top staff. That was one of the odd things about the Reagan White House—wherever the President was, his top staff was. They'd sit there in a row in his office like frogs on a log, staring at the President. I used to wonder: don't they have work to do?

We waited outside the President's office. An aide inside opened the door— the doors in the West Wing never make a sound, you feel the air and that's how you know they're swinging—and motioned us in.

There he was, behind his desk turning toward me: a big, tall, radiant man, impeccably tailored, his skin soft, pink, and smooth. He twinkled at me. I was the new one, and the only woman. He walked to me and took my hand. It is the oddest thing and true, even though everyone says it: it is impossible to be nervous in his presence. He acts as if he's lucky to be with you. "Well," he said, "it's so wonderful to meet you. Please, please sit down. Well, so!"

We sat, I in the spot on the couch immediately to his right. I don't really remember what we talked about. There was no reason for the meeting beyond "The new speechwriter's unhappy and let's let her meet him or she may leave." The President sat up straight in his chair, a piece of beige plastic in his ear. I was surprised how big his hearing aid is, or rather how aware of it you are when you're with him. There was a quizzical look on his face as he listened to what was going on around him, and I realized: he doesn't really hear very much, and his appearance of constant good humor is connected to his deafness. He misses much of what is not said straight to him, and because of that he keeps a pleasant look on his face as people chat around him.

The meeting lasted half an hour. Conversation ambled. The President looked around sometimes as if to say: "What are we doing here, folks?" I felt guilty at taking his time.

The night before, Mario Cuomo had given his speech to the Democratic Convention. Everyone around me agreed it had not been a great speech, but I thought it had been a speech of great power. Nevertheless, it had clearly got under the President's skin. He resented its implicit accusation of heartlessness and ignorance of the true condition of his country.

The President looked at me. "Larry Speakes says all the reporters have been asking questions about it. I asked him to draw up a list of what they're saying at the briefing. I just got it and sat down and wrote my answers for the news conference. Would you mind if I read them to you?"

Would I mind? Hey, buddy, I don't have time to sit around listening to the private musings of the leader of the free world as he speculates on how to answer his most eloquent critic. "Oh, please, yes," I said.

He retrieved the list from his desk and read off some answers, some of which were snappy. I smiled at them. They were all facts and figures about the economy. "Seven million new jobs created, 600,000 new businesses incorporated. If that's depression, let's have more of it!"

As we left, he took my hand. "You know, a while ago I wanted to call you about something, but . . ." He shook his head. He couldn't remember.

"Peggy wrote the Pointe du Hoc speech, Mr. President," said Ben.

Reagan lit up. "That's it. That was wonderful. It was like 'Flanders Fields.' I read it upstairs and when I read something I like to look up at the corner to see the name and I saw Noonan. I meant to call you and never—"

"Oh, that's O.K."

"But it was wonderful. Were you there? Well, after the speech the original Pointe du Hoc fellows came up and told me how much they liked it and there were tears in their eyes. And you know, I talked with this fellow—the day before, when the Rangers recreated the climb up those cliffs, this fellow went up with them just as he had 40 years ago and he made it to the top with those kids. Boy, that was something."

"Boy, that was something." That's how he talks, like a happy working-class American boy from the '30s.

I had been in the White House less than five months at that point. I had seen how the White House worked and how speechwriting works. What I was learning was what Dick Darman later said at Ben's goodbye party two years later, that speechwriting in the Reagan White House was where the philosophical, ideological and political tensions of the administration got worked out.

Speechwriting was where the Administration got invented every day. And so speechwriting was, for some, the center of gravity in that Administration, the one point where ideas and principles still counted; and for others—at the State Department, for instance—speechwriting was a natural and unhappy force of nature, a black hole from which no sophisticated thought could escape.

What an apprenticeship I had! It would serve me well over the next two and a half years, as I worked for the President who remained for me an object of awe and mystery. And it stood me in good stead after I left the White House and worked for George Bush during his Presidential campaign and in the days just before he took office.

Ultimately, I decided to leave speechwriting after a postelection challenge from a friend who paraphrased George Orwell: " 'You should do anything for your side but write for it.' If you stay where you are, you will let politics decide what you do and do not write, do and do not see. Or you can take whatever talent you have and be a writer. You have to decide."

Which I did, and after five years in Washington, I left the world of speechwriting.

THE CONGRESS

Chapter Five

Congress is a fascinating amalgam of individual characters, personalities, and styles, which help to shape the institution. Personality is particularly important, as it affects congressional leadership, both of party leaders and of committee chairpersons. Different personality types in positions of power within Congress develop contrasting styles that influence the way Congress operates. For example, the Senate under the majority leadership of Lyndon B. Johnson operated very differently than it did under Mike Mansfield. Johnson's active-negative character was evident in the Senate as in the White House. His personality compelled him to seek control over the Senate, which he managed through knowledge of the strengths, weaknesses, and needs of his colleagues; skill in manipulation of institutional procedures; and an extraordinary ability to persuade others. Each senator became a challenge to Johnson, who sought personal loyalty above all else. The aggressive and dominating style of Lyndon Johnson as majority leader of the Senate was similar to but much more flamboyant than that of his mentor, House Speaker Sam Rayburn, and it stemmed from different personal needs.

In sharp contrast to Johnson's style was that of Mike Mansfield, who was elected majority leader in January 1961 and served until his retirement at the end of the ninety-fourth Congress in 1976. Mansfield's style was, to say the least, more muted than Johnson's. He treated each senator with great respect and as an equal. No attempt at a personal cult of leadership was evident during Mansfield's tenure. Johnson was highly effective as a personal leader, whereas Mansfield's effectiveness was as a team player. The contrasting personalities of Johnson and Mansfield go a long way toward explaining differences in Senate operation during their periods of leadership. Under Mansfield, senators were far freer to pursue their own legislative interests without fear of retaliation if they happened to disagree with the majority leader. Mansfield's style became the model for his successor, Robert Byrd. Howard Baker, too, led by consensus, not by command, in a Senate that would no longer tolerate Johnson's system of unilateral control.

Personality is as important in the House as in the Senate in determining who runs for positions of party leadership, and what their styles of leadership will be. Sam Rayburn, Speaker of the House for seventeen years, enforced discipline. Like Lyndon Johnson in the Senate, Sam Rayburn knew every member of the House, their constituencies, and their needs and aspirations. He was able to use

213

this information to consolidate his power as Speaker. Again like Johnson, Rayburn operated on a highly personal basis. The House was his constituency, as the Senate was Johnson's, and he did not hesitate to involve Republicans as well as Democrats in his decisions. The election of John McCormack as Speaker of the House in 1962 brought profound changes, primarily because of the contrasting personalities of Rayburn and McCormack. Robert L. Peabody says:

> Peaceful succession brings on more incremental change, but the impact of such *different personalities* as Rayburn and McCormack on the Office of the Speaker was considerable. McCormack's style was both more institutional and partisan than Rayburn's. He called more meetings to discuss legislative strategy and involved the Majority Leader and Whip to a much greater extent than Rayburn did. . . .
>
> The telephone was one of McCormack's most effective weapons—"I'd call the devil if I thought it would do any good." In contrast, Rayburn operated on a more independent and personal basis. He preferred the intimacy and informality of after-the-session gatherings of the "Board of Education." The Whip organization was used less frequently and Rayburn almost never called a party caucus beyond the opening meeting.[1]

Both Rayburn and McCormack, although differing in their personalities and styles, provided effective leadership to the House. In contrast, Carl Albert of Oklahoma, who became Speaker in 1971, displayed a personality and style critics denounced as weak and ineffective. Peabody points out that "one reason he easily advanced to the speakership was summed up in a widely affirmed statement—'Nobody's mad at Carl.' "[2] Being a "nice guy" is usually a reflection of the inability to make hard decisions that inevitably antagonize others.

After an extensive analysis of congressional leadership, Peabody concluded:

> Of the twenty variables highlighted in this analysis, the most pervasive and continuing influence upon leadership's selection for party office has been exerted by the personality and skill of the candidate and, especially, of the incumbent. Every leader in Congress, as in other organizations, brings to office a unique set of characteristics: age, ambition, education, health, personal skills, prior political and professional experience—in sum, a personality. Not only does this personality affect the opportunities he may have to obtain a leadership position, they also, in part, influence the extent to which he can maintain office and perhaps even alter the scope and potential of a given party position. A leader's personality, his strengths and liabilities, also is the single most important variable that affects his ability to withstand or succumb to a challenge.[3]

[1]Robert L. Peabody, *Leadership in Congress* (Boston: Little, Brown, 1976), p. 309. Italics added.

[2]Ibid., p. 155.

[3]Ibid., p. 498.

Personality is also a factor in the selection of committees and in the functioning of committee chairmen. The Senate Government Operations Committee (renamed the Governmental Affairs Committee in 1977), under the chairmanship of Senator Joseph McCarthy from 1953 until 1955, operated very differently than it has at any other time because of the senator's distinctive personality and style. Likewise, the Senate Foreign Relations Committee under the chairmanship of Senator J. William Fulbright from 1959 until his defeat in 1974 underwent notable changes under the subsequent chairmanship of Senator John Sparkman of Alabama.

South Carolina Republican Strom Thurmond from 1984 to 1986 ran the Senate Judiciary Committee in an entirely different way than did both his predecessor, Massachusetts Senator Edward Kennedy, and his successor, Delaware Senator Joe Biden, who took charge in 1987.

Weak chairmen, strong chairmen, chairmen who seek the limelight, and those who use chairmanships for "grand-standing," all have contrasting personalities and styles. The committee system is an important institution of Congress, and the way it functions largely depends on the personalities of committee members. Committees are used to advance the goals of their heads and key members, who are attempting to gain power and status within and without Congress. Thus the legislative work of committees is often undertaken as much to serve personal ambition as to respond to constituents' needs; legislators use the committee hearing and investigation process for personal aggrandizement as well as for legislation.

Beyond Capitol Hill personality is also a key factor in determining the way in which representatives and senators relate to their constituents. Personal choice and preferences determine the amount and kinds of electoral responsibilities that will be delegated to staff, how much time a candidate will spend in his or her district, the nature of constituent contacts—whether in large or small groups, or one-on-one—and what type of media will be emphasized. Political campaigning always reflects the character and style of the candidate.

P OLITICAL SCIENTIST RICHARD F. Fenno, Jr., lists three incentives that guide to varying degrees the behavior of members of Congress: (1) re-election; (2) power and influence *within* Congress; (3) good public policy.[1]

Member goals are not mutually exclusive, but members usually do pursue one more than the others. Junior House members, for example, who have not yet secured their electoral bases, devote more time, energy, and resources to winning reelection than to climbing the congressional ladder of power. But once members of Congress can count on electoral support, which House members usually do after they have served several terms, they can devote more time to their Washington careers. A House member in his second term observed, 'I haven't been a congressman yet. The first two years, I spent all of my time getting myself reelected. So I won't be a congressman until next year.'[2] Being a congressman means to most members being free to pursue internal power and influence without having to worry about constituency pressures.

Members of the House and the Senate as well can take either the *committee* or *party and leadership* routes to power. The first involves seeking the most prestigious committees, such as the House Ways and Means, Appropriations, and Rules committees, or the Senate Foreign Relations, Judiciary, Finance, and Appropriations committees. It is difficult and sometimes impossible for junior congresspersons and senators to obtain seats on these committees. They often have to wait years before they can get on the panels of their choice.

Moreover, junior members may prefer what are called *reelection committees,* such as Agriculture, Interior, and Insular Affairs, which have jurisdiction over matters of more direct and special concern to their districts. Of course, members of Congress can and have used their positions on the more prestigious committees, particularly Appropriations, Finance, and Ways and Means, to boost their reelection prospects by tending to constituency interests and claiming credit for benefits flowing to their districts. But these and other influential committees represent and serve the broader memberships of the House and the Senate, diminishing the capacity of any single committee member to give priority in committee deliberations to interests of his or her district.

Although most members seeking internal power take the committee route, a select and, in some cases, a chosen few rise to the top through service to their congressional parties. In this arena House members who set their sights particularly high aim to become Speaker, which is one of the most powerful positions not only in Congress but in the entire government. It is a long journey to the speakership. The majority party determines who will fill the position but chooses only someone who has performed effectively in lower-party leadership posts. The House majority leader often succeeds to the speakership, having been elected by the party to the next highest position. The party caucus chairman and the chief

---

[1] See Richard F. Fenno, Jr., *Congressmen in Committees* (Boston: Little, Brown, 1973) and *Homestyle* (Boston: Little, Brown 1978).

[2] Fenno, *Homestyle,* p. 215.

whip then may compete to become majority leader. The chairman of the Rules Committee, who occupies what is essentially a party leadership position, may also join the fray if he or she is particularly ambitious. Of course no one is excluded from running for party posts, although generally the party leadership track is confined to those who have chosen it over the committee route to power.

The following selection portrays one of the most powerful members of the House of Representatives, who took the committee route to power and influence.

Woodrow Wilson, in his famous book entitled *Congressional Government* (1885), called committee chairmen the "futile barons" of Congress, who wield absolute power over their committee fiefdoms. More than one hundred years later Hedrick Smith, one of the most astute observers of the Washington political scene, labeled committee chairmen the "prime ministers" of our government.[3] There is little doubt that the subject of the following study, Michigan Congressman John Dingell, is one of the prime ministers of Capitol Hill.

23   David Rogers
MAN OF CAPITOL

Most members of Congress tax, spend and borrow. John Dingell muscles, questions and regulates.

As the chairman of the Energy and Commerce Committee, Mr. Dingell can be both advocate and arbiter in disputes between the Baby Bells and American Telephone & Telegraph, hospitals insurers, stockbrokers and banks. Because of its historic role in creating agencies such as the Securities and Exchange Commission [SEC], the panel that he heads reaches into executive-branch decision-making in a fashion matched by few others. That authority, bolstered by the fact that Mr. Dingell also personally leads the committee's Investigations and Oversight Panel, gives him a hunting license to probe much of corporate America—oil, rails, securities, communications, science—and he is the legislative switchman on the freightlines of commerce.

"Talk to me," invites the burly Michigan Democrat, but before the words are out, his arm settles on his target's shoulder with the weight of a 4x4 post—pressure treated. "We have a very good friendship," says Rep. Edward Madigan, an Illinois Republican and senior member of Energy and Commerce. "I think I'm high on his list—after General Motors, Ford, Chrysler and Detroit Edison."

[3]Hedrick Smith, *The Power Game: How Washington Works* (New York: Random House, 1988).

Behind his restless, bullying energy, the 63-year-old Mr. Dingell is a study in power—and a study in Congress itself as the institution seeks to regain direction in a new decade. For more than a half century, the Dingell family has held a seat in the House, and few lawmakers are more identified with the entrenched legislative government that endures as presidents come and go.

Growing Up in Congress

"Let's go back home," Mr. Dingell tells an aide upon leaving the White House for the Capitol. As a boy, he walked the stone-tiled halls with his father. As a chairman, his love of procedure and iron hand emulate Sam Rayburn, who ran the Commerce Committee early in the New Deal before becoming Speaker.

"You have given me no reason to undo what my father and Sam Rayburn did," Mr. Dingell once told an executive seeking to weaken a 1930s public-utility holding-company law.

Like a modern Judge Roy Bean, Mr. Dingell uses his dominating personality to pressure witnesses—and force action—even without any specific legislation.

He snorts at the "whole helluva mess of bonuses" paid before Drexel Burnham Lambert Inc.'s demise—and letters go out to the SEC demanding an accounting. (SEC Chairman Richard Breeden said . . . that the SEC is looking into Drexel's payment of $260 million of bonuses in cash and stock to its employees.)

In full-page newspaper ads, Bolar Pharmaceutical Co. blasted him last fall for creating a "climate of fear" in the generic-drug industry. Months later, the New York company was embarrassed when its outside counsel acknowledged that the company had submitted false documents to the Food and Drug Administration.

No Man to Con

"You don't try to con John Dingell," says Sen. Ted Stevens, an Alaska Republican whose own legislative style also tends to the Sam Peckinpah school. "I don't think at the moment he has a peer as chairman of an oversight committee," Speaker Thomas Foley says.

"I am first among equals; I am not the boss," Mr. Dingell says with a laugh, explaining himself to Polish Solidarity leaders here to learn about committee procedure. His voice quavers as he—the great-grandson of a Polish immigrant—becomes a teacher for the new parliament. "They are a model of strength and endurance and courage and dedication," he says later. "I'd rather see a lot more of that kind of thing around me."

Mr. Dingell longs for a more activist federal government even as he senses that his own democratic institution—Congress— may be faltering. In the past year, scandal has swept away old leadership allies, and he himself has come to symbolize the parochialism that often characterizes Congress and his party.

Mr. Dingell's alliance with the auto industry—and reluctant pursuit of a new clean-air law—strains the patience of liberal friends. He provoked a bitter fight by insisting on acting on a business-backed product-liability bill before the 1988 elections. His aggressive investigative style brought embarrassment last year when an aide—since dismissed—was found to have authorized secret tapings of phone conversations in a securities-industry probe.

"I'm not big power; I *hold* big power," Mr. Dingell says. But power draws him into a Washington establishment far removed from his political heritage. Before becoming a congressman, Mr. Dingell's father was a jack-of-all-trades, pipeline supervisor, beef dealer and news printer—the consummate little guy who overcame poor health to fight for medical care for others. Describing the capital's lobbyists in 1936, he said, "There are altogether too many cheap lawyers here whose practice is about on a par with petit larceny, who would starve to death anywhere but in Washington."

Today, Mr. Dingell hunts with and befriends the same lobbying corps. Although organized labor remains his largest single source of political funds, corporate political action committees [PACs] gave the lion's share of more than $1 million received by the chairman's organization over the past three election campaigns. The issues that Energy and Commerce deals with tend less to pit unions against business than to pit industry against industry—making the committee the leading magnet for special-interest money in the House.

PACs have contributed an estimated $25 million or more to current committee members in the past three election campaigns, and special-interest money has become a form of patronage within the panel. In the last Congress, for example, Mr. Dingell overrode caucus rules and pushed through a change in how members are assigned to subcommittees. That single stroke cut the power of rival subcommittee chairmen and helped his younger allies win lucrative assignments to panels with jurisdiction over cash-rich industries able to give large amounts.

His Many Roles

In the bloody fight over his product-liability measure—a crucial issue to Michigan powers Ford Motor and Upjohn—Mr. Dingell was unsparing in his anger over opposition from trial lawyers. In other cases, as in a fight between television networks and producers over whether the networks can share program-syndication rights, Mr. Dingell can seem to dance with both sides. At one point, he supported the networks on a critical procedural motion, then gave the producers a bill barring the Federal Communications Commission from acting in favor of the networks.

Mr. Dingell's aggressive expansion of his jurisdiction is near-legendary, but the reaction of his fellow chairmen is more complex than it first appears. Former House Banking Committee Chairman Fernand St. Germain once yielded jurisdiction to Mr. Dingell, knowing that Energy and Commerce would slow down a bill Mr. St. Germain feared was moving too fast in his own panel. Similarly, Mr. Dingell, in a celebrated jurisdictional battle with the House Public Works Committee in 1987, had strong support among his fellow chairmen but lost largely because of GOP opposition to his increased power.

"Power is a tool . . . like a hammer or a saw or a wrench," Mr. Dingell says. Standing 6 foot 3 inches, this blacksmith's grandson prefers the hammer. He pounds witnesses with rapid-fire questions, often accompanied by abrasive commentary that puts his target at a disadvantage. "One of the things I have found with rascals is they generally tend to try to retreat into a state of blissful ignorance," said Mr. Dingell in an aside aimed at Safeway executive Walter Schoendorf in a 1987 hearing. "He just dominates," says Mr. Schoendorf, laughing about the experience today. "There's not much give-and-take."

Rooted in New Deal

Others find it harder to laugh, and after 35 years in Congress, Mr. Dingell can seem less a lawmaker than a law unto himself. His roots remain in New Deal liberalism, but he mostly divides his world between friends and enemies. Scientists complain that his aggressive investigations of alleged research fraud cast a chilling effect over future inquiry.

Environmentalists are baffled at what they see as changes in a man once perceived at the forefront of their movement. With a few exceptions, Mr. Dingell says environmental leaders are "fishy friends: They tend to be very, very ungrateful." Reviewing Mr. Dingell's environmental voting score, the Audubon Society's Brock Evans calculates "50 out of 100. That's not bad if he was from Alabama."

As chairman today, Mr. Dingell speaks of respect for authority, but in the past he himself has been quick to challenge the leadership. In 1985, he almost single-handedly frustrated an effort by now-Speaker Foley to better organize House Rules. He regularly harassed the first Commerce Committee chairman he served under, Oren Harris of Arkansas, and helped weaken the last one, West Virginia's Harley Staggers, before gaining the job himself. In frustration, former House Speaker Thomas O'Neill once considered sending a bill to Mr. Dingell's committee for only 36 hours.

But beneath this hard-boiled image is a complex, even romantic man. When Mr. Dingell's first marriage collapsed in the 1970s, he raised the four children—one as young as two—himself. When beleaguered then-Speaker James Wright broke into tears at a heated news conference last year, Mr.

Dingell gave his friend time to regain his composure before the TV cameras by setting off a round of applause.

Mr. Dingell was slow to embrace the Equal Rights Amendment for women but, in 1964, risked his career by actively supporting in floor debate the Civil Rights Act during a tough Democratic primary. In recent years, when a black staffer ran for the Harvard board of overseers on an anti-apartheid divestment platform, Mr. Dingell made telephone calls—without notice—on her behalf.

Strong Desire to Win

What is most consistent is Mr. Dingell's desire to win and dominate. He has no use for what he sees as the unelected elites who intrude on his party—his turf. "I used to say I support the platform. I haven't said that for years," he says. He denounces Ralph Nader as an "unmitigated scoundrel." (The consumer activist has said worse about Mr. Dingell.)

In fact, Mr. Dingell's oversight subcommittee amounts to his own Dingell's Raiders, and, despite his scorn for many environmentalists, he is a naturalist who has sketched wildlife and spells accurately the Latin name—oreamnos—of the mountain sheep in a painting on his wall.

Above all, Mr. Dingell is a government man. For him, regulation has enduring value, and the sweep of Energy and Commerce's jurisdiction—from steel leghold animal traps to heart valves to golden parachutes—suits his purposes. Asked to name two failures of Congress, he cites Vietnam and the swine flu liability debacle of the late 1970s.

To get the answers he needs, Mr. Dingell brings the government to bear. Energy and Commerce's annual budget of more than $5.1 million for investigations and studies surpasses any in the House. Recent records of the General Accounting Office, Congress's investigative arm, show that it commits more personnel and spends more travel money in support of Mr. Dingell's panel than it does for the Armed Services and Ways and Means Committees combined.

"It would be fair to say I love Congress," says Mr. Dingell, and, as with the Capitol itself, there is about him a sense of constancy amid the changing seasons and sessions of lawmaking. In 1964, during the civil-rights fight, he remembers early press reports saying he would lose his primary. Today, a young woman who worked in his Washington office then and was the niece of his campaign manager is the wife of Speaker Foley. A seven-year-old son, Christopher Dingell, is now a tall Michigan state senator and potential successor, but the father isn't yet ready to yield.

"I am not drunk on power, I am not getting rich in this goddamn place, I can assure you of that," John Dingell says. "I do view this as a place where I serve."

THE "INCUMBENCY EFFECT" makes it virtually impossible for outside challengers to win congressional elections. Typically over 90 percent of House incumbents who choose to run win with victory margins ranging from 58 to 80 percent of the vote. Incumbent senators, who are more likely to be challenged because of the high visibility of their offices and the much sought-after political prize of their seats, typically win more than 80 percent of their reelection contests. Nevertheless, campaigns against incumbents, although usually quixotic, are always fun for candidates and staffers who enjoy the political game. And, as the following account of such a campaign illustrates, challengers never give up the hope, however slight, that they can win.

24 Mark G. Michaelsen
MY LIFE AS A CONGRESSIONAL CANDIDATE

It was quite late and I was in bed, just drifting off to sleep, when the telephone rang. The caller identified herself as working for the *New Republic.*

I snapped to attention. The *New Republic!* As the Republican candidate for Congress in Wisconsin's Seventh District in 1984, I was accustomed to late-night calls from journalists, usually wire-service reporters racing to meet a deadline. But never had I received a call from such an important publication.

I told her what a fine magazine I thought the *New Republic* was and how much I had enjoyed a recent article on Sandinista human rights abuses. At the same time, my mind raced ahead: How did I come to their attention? Was it my stand on family issues or defense? The quixotic campaign of a 26-year-old neophyte against an entrenched seven-term liberal incumbent Democrat? My skillful exploitation of the resentment of northern Wisconsin sportsmen toward an agreement to let American Indians ignore fish and game laws?

What would the article say, I wondered. Would it be favorable or unfavorable? It didn't really matter. Regardless of tone, a *New Republic* article mentioning my candidacy would surely unlock a torrent of political action committee contributions, instantly transforming my campaign from amateur shoestring effort to formidable, well-financed juggernaut. Big Mo was just around the corner; I could taste it.

What could I do for the caller, I asked.

"We've noticed we haven't received your subscription renewal," she said. "If this is just an oversight, we'll be happy to continue sending you the *New Republic* until we receive your check."

From *The American Spectator,* November 1989. Reprinted by permission.

My dreams popped like a big soap bubble. This wasn't a reporter, it was a telephone solicitor!

On election night, 1984, I was blown out by incumbent David R. Obey, who received 61 percent of the vote. That same night, President Ronald Reagan trounced Walter Mondale in one of history's great landslides. In Wisconsin's Seventh Congressional District, Reagan beat Mondale 53 percent to 46 percent. So much for coattails.

The obvious question is *why*. Why would a 26-year-old kid with no name identification challenge the formidable 49-year-old chairman of the Joint Economic Committee, who had served in Congress since 1969, when former Rep. Melvin R. Laird vacated the seat to become Nixon's defense secretary?

The answer: almost by accident. I didn't mean to be the candidate. A native of central Wisconsin, I was working at Hillsdale College in Michigan in early 1984, when I learned that Wisconsin state senator Walter John Chilsen was mulling a run against Obey. Obey had edged the former senate majority leader in the 1969 special election to fill Laird's seat. There had been no rematch. I let Chilsen know that I was interested in helping him oust Obey. He put me in touch with his Washington consultant, who suggested I become campaign finance director.

I pored over district vote totals and read whatever I could find about district demographics, funding-raising, issues, Obey's voting record, and public speaking. It would be tough, but with a strong coattail effect from Reagan's re-election, a ton of money spent on advertising and mail, and a little bit of luck, Chilsen could win in November. I was excited by the possibilities.

When Chilsen opted not to vacate a safe seat in the state senate to challenge Obey, I was disappointed. Election after election, Seventh District Republicans had fielded token challengers with little financial support— retired vacuum cleaner salesmen, bankrupt mobile-home moguls, a fellow named Burger who campaigned wearing a chef's hat and a white apron, and so on. None had received more than 38 percent of the vote.

I stepped forward. I had the energy, the knowledge of national issues, the speaking skills, and the fund-raising prowess to be the candidate. I had a deep love for, and knowledge of, the towns and cities, forests and dairy farms of the Wisconsin Seventh District, which sprawls across all or part of eighteen of the state's central and northwest counties. I cared deeply about America's future and was a dedicated conservative. I had some connections in the conservative movement in Washington. Those were my strengths.

But I had weaknesses, too. Almost no one outside my hometown had ever heard of me. I didn't hold public office. I wasn't rich. I hadn't lived in Wisconsin for four years. And my name was really hard to pronounce, an alliterative tongue-twister which confounded broadcasters, statesmen, and voters.

I figured these weaknesses could be overcome with an advertising campaign which started with a spot where people mispronounced my name, perhaps ending with a tag line such as "It doesn't matter how you say it. Mark Michaelsen for Congress." With name identification established, spots clobbering the incumbent on issues would follow. The media campaign would end with warm, sentimental spots about shared values and dreams for a better future, loaded up with pretty Wisconsin pictures: "It's morning again in north-central Wisconsin."

With pride and gratitude, I accepted the unanimous endorsement of Seventh District Republicans. On the advice of Chilsen's consultant, I procured a promise from district Republican leaders to raise a hefty amount of start-up cash. That money would be necessary to hire a talented campaign manager and finance director, and to get started raising big money and enlisting an army of volunteers for what would be the strongest challenge ever to Obey. I packed my belongings in a U-Haul trailer to head home for Wisconsin.

The months flew by, an endless stream of parades, speeches, fundraisers, and county fairs. Cows were admired, good deeds were praised, and hands were shaken.

"I'm Mark Michaelsen," I said, dratting the troublesome moniker, and offering a handshake. "I want to work for you in Washington."

"You've got an uphill road ahead of you," nodded the object of my greeting.

"I'm Mark Michaelsen," I said, extending my hand. "I want to be your congressman."

"Ah, you've got a tough row to hoe," observed my new acquaintance.

Maybe it was the Ogema Christmas Tree Festival. Or the Spooner Rodeo. Or the Central Wisconsin State Fair.

"I'm Mark Michaelsen," I said, smiling and proffering my calloused mitt. "I'm running against Dave Obey."

"You've got a tough, uphill road to hoe," said the voter.

Exactly! This unintentional mixed metaphor perfectly described my plight. Imagine a man using a garden implement to try to dislodge asphalt from a road running almost straight uphill, like one of Hercules's mythological labors. That was me.

The money trickled, not poured in. The promised Republican cash never materialized. The PACs, seeing no "viability" (their word for a snowball's chance in hell) in my election, weren't about to invest in my race. I faced the American campaign Catch 22: I couldn't raise money until I showed momentum, I couldn't show momentum until I raised money.

Top consultants were hired, then fired. My campaign manager quit; he said he was homesick for Chicago. And, worst of all, my opponent ignored me—ignored my stinging press releases, critical of his votes on school prayer, national security, and federal spending; ignored my call for debates throughout the district; ignored my very existence as a candidate.

At least I had the van.

A small group of hometown supporters had purchased an aging Ford Econoline, painted it red, white, and blue, and outfitted it with a bed and desk. But most impressive was the public address system, which allowed me to blare Sousa marches at deafening volumes while I greeted voters along parade routes.

One day I was late for an interview at a television station in one of the District's remote cities and I couldn't find a place to park. Desperate, I left the van in a parking ramp near the studio. After the interview, I was leaving the ramp when I noticed how low the ceiling was getting. Suddenly I heard a sickening crunch. My roof loudspeakers crashed to the ground.

I retrieved them and continued my progress toward the exit. Headroom continued to shrink. Twenty feet from the exit the van's roof began to scrape on the concrete ceiling. I had to let nearly all the air out of the tires to finally escape. Behind me, a dozen cars were lined up, their egress blocked by my embarrassing plight.

What kind of idiot was causing their delay, I could feel them wondering. "Michaelsen for Congress," answered my van in eight-inch letters.

As the grand finale to a candidate training school sponsored by the National Republican Congressional Committee, would-be GOP congressmen were herded into Gold Room of the White House to be photographed with the President and Vice President.

I was somewhat nervous and tongue-tied when I met the Leader of the Free World. I should have said, "Mr. President, dairy farmers of northern Wisconsin are concerned about your agriculture policy" or implored him to come campaign on my behalf. Instead, I mumbled something about having worked for Hillsdale, which he had visited and praised. President Reagan grinned genially, and we sat. He hadn't heard a word; I'd spoken in his bad ear.

As we sat in the ornate chairs by the fireplace, cameras whirring, he cocked his head and said, "Wisconsin. That's just north of my old stomping ground in Illinois." He leaned forward and put his hand on the arm of my chair. He was a nice man.

We shook hands and I left, to be replaced by another candidate. I was already kicking myself for being such a boob with President Reagan. I fared better with the Vice President.

I'd met George Bush twice before, during the 1980 Wisconsin presidential primary. I inquired about one of his sons whom I'd also met in 1980. He became quite animated. His son and daughter-in-law were expecting their first child any day.

Newcomers to my current office see my pictures with Ronald Reagan and George Bush and assume the photographs are clever forgeries purchased from an arcade.

Election night found me in a local watering hole, appropriately named The End of the Line, watching returns and swilling something strong with a few of my friends. As the returns came in it was clear I had lost, and lost big. For most of my acquaintances from campaign school, the night would end similarly. That night only thirteen GOP candidates would unseat Democratic opponents despite the avalanche of support for President Reagan at the top of the ticket.

For me, it could have been even worse. Although Obey outspent me nearly five to one, my 92,507 votes were both the highest total and highest percentage of votes cast against Dave Obey since he was elected in 1969. I won one northern county and lost another by only five votes. I won my hometown by a landslide, but lost my home county. My campaign treasury finished with a slight surplus; I owed no creditors. The worst possible result would have been to amass a huge debt, come very close, and lose; that might have tempted me to run again in 1986. At least now I would never have to wonder what I could have done differently to put me over the top.

L YNDON B. JOHNSON, A MEM-ber of the Senate freshman class of 1948, was majority leader from 1955 until 1960, when he was elected vice president. His experience in Washington predated his Senate career; he had been a congressional staff member in 1931 and at the age of 28 had defeated seven other candidates in a special election to fill the seat of the tenth Texas congressional district left vacant by the death of the incumbent representative.

Johnson was a consummate politician from the very beginning of his stay in Washington. He embraced the New Deal and became a favorite of President Franklin D. Roosevelt; he even supported the president's ill-fated courtpacking plan, which was opposed by many of Roosevelt's Washington supporters.[1]

While still a congressman, Johnson ran and was defeated in a special election for a Senate post vacated by the death of incumbent Senator Morris Sheppard in 1941. Johnson continued to serve in the House (with a brief leave in 1942 to serve as a naval reserve officer) until, with John Connally as his campaign manager, he defeated arch-conservative Governor Coke Stevenson in the Democratic primary in 1948 by eighty-seven votes out of almost a million cast. As there was essentially no Republican opposition in Texas at that time, the election in the Democratic primary was tantamount to victory in the general election held in November.

When Johnson became majority leader, the "Johnson era" began in the Senate. The "Johnson system" of power reflected his personality and style: He unhesitatingly rewarded his friends, from whom he demanded loyalty, and punished his enemies. His formal powers as majority leader were minimal. His chairmanship of the Democratic Steering Committee, for example, did not automatically guarantee him personal control over Democratic committee assignments. But he developed an informal network of power, and a dazzling style that came to be known as "The Treatment."

[1]In 1937 Roosevelt recommended legislation to Congress under which he would be given authority to appoint one new Supreme Court justice for each justice over seventy years old. At the time there were six septuagenarian justices, so that Roosevelt could easily have "packed" the court with his own appointments.

25

Rowland Evans and Robert Novak
THE JOHNSON SYSTEM *1)*

To build his Network, Johnson stretched the meager power resources of the majority leader to the outer limit. The mightiest of these was his influence over committee assignments. Still, it was not comparable to the absolute power enjoyed by Nelson Aldrich a half century before. As chairman of the Democratic Steering Committee, Johnson steadily widened the breach in rigid seniority rules, working delicately with a surgical scalpel, not a stick of dynamite.

In January 1955, his ally and adviser, Clinton Anderson, pressed his claim for an overdue assignment on either Foreign Relations or Finance. Each committee had one vacancy. But former Vice President Alben Barkley, who had just returned to the Senate as a "freshman" from Kentucky in the 1954 elections, asked for the Finance Committee—a request that could scarcely be denied. A further complication was the still unresolved problem of Wayne Morse, the Oregon maverick who had bolted the Republican party in the 1952 campaign and, after two years in the political wilderness as an "Independent," now joined the Democratic caucus in 1955. Morse's decision was vital to Johnson. It provided him with the narrow one-vote margin he needed to cross the bridge, incalculably important in terms of power, from Minority Leader to Majority Leader. Thus, it was incumbent upon Johnson to give Morse a good committee assignment, and Morse wanted Foreign Relations.

Johnson duly explained these facts of life to Anderson, who agreed not to insist (as he well could have) on either Finance or Foreign Relations. But Johnson remembered his old friend's personal loyalty and, on a 1956 speaking engagement in New Mexico, he publicly—and unexpectedly—promised that Clint Anderson would become the next chairman of the Joint Atomic Energy Committee. That post, because of New Mexico's Los Alamos atomic installation, would solidly enhance Anderson's prestige. To make good his promise, Johnson was required to jump Anderson over none other than Richard Russell, who outranked Anderson on the joint committee.

The Foreign Relations maneuvers temporarily drew the sharp-tongued Morse to Johnson, in sharp contrast to a year earlier. In January 1954, Morse had told an ADA Roosevelt Day Dinner in Texas: "Johnson has the most reactionary record in the Senate. Look at his voting record. If he should ever

From *Lyndon B. Johnson: The Exercise of Power* by Rowland Evans and Robert Novak. Copyright 1966 by Rowland Evans and Robert Novak. Reprinted by arrangement with New American Library, New York, New York.

have a liberal idea, he would have a brain hemorrhage . . . ."[1] But a little more than a year later, ensconced on the Foreign Relations Committee, Morse gently confided to the Senate: "During the past year, I have been the beneficiary of one kindness after another from Lyndon Johnson. I consider him not only a great statesman but a good man."

And as chairman of the Joint Atomic Energy Committee, Anderson was even more pleased than he would have been on Foreign Relations. The only grumbling over Johnson's ingenious shuffling came from Russell, who had not agreed in advance to step aside for Anderson. But the grumbling was private and soft, not public and bitter. Lyndon Johnson could count on Dick Russell not to make a public fuss about such matters.

Two years later, Anderson was the center of far more devious committee maneuvers by Johnson. After the presidential election of 1956, Estes Kefauver of Tennessee and John F. Kennedy of Massachusetts, who had competed on the national convention floor at Chicago for the vice-presidential nomination the previous summer, were competing again—this time for a single vacancy on Foreign Relations. Johnson, who had backed Kennedy against Kefauver at Chicago, was not trying to bring Kennedy closer to his orbit. He was determined to have the vacancy go to Kennedy over Johnson's old foe, Kefauver. But how to get around Kefauver's four-year seniority bulge over Kennedy? In December 1956, long before Congress convened, Johnson telephoned Anderson with a most curious question: "How are you getting along with your campaign for the Foreign Relations Committee?"

Anderson was puzzled. Could Johnson have forgotten that his "campaign" had ended two years earlier? But Johnson persisted.

"This may be your chance," he said.

Before Anderson could reply that he had his hands full as chairman of Atomic Energy, Johnson rushed on.

"You have seniority now over Jack Kennedy," Johnson explained. "But if you don't claim it, Estes Kefauver may get there first."

Johnson's ploy suddenly came through to Anderson. Both Anderson and Kefauver were members of the Class of '48 and therefore had equal seniority. If they both applied for the one vacancy on the Foreign Relations Committee, Johnson could throw up his hands in the Steering Committee, declare a standoff—and give the vacancy to Kennedy. Anderson went along with this neat strategy, and Kennedy was given the seat, just as Johnson wanted.

Johnson's use of power to influence committee assignments cut both ways. "Good" liberals, such as Humphrey, could be prematurely boosted into the

---

[1] Johnson retaliated in kind: "Texas doesn't need any outsiders to come in and tell them [sic] how to vote. I don't think Texas will pay any more attention to him than the Senate does." In those early days of his leadership, Johnson was far more ready to engage fellow senators in a war of words than he would be later.

Foreign Relations Committee, and a "bad" liberal, such as Kefauver, could be made to cool his heels for years. A "bad" liberal such as Paul Douglas could be barred from the Finance Committee for eight long years, while five fellow members of the Class of '48 (Kerr, Long, Frear, Anderson, and Johnson himself) and one from the Class of '50 (Smathers) were finding places there.[2] Senators who dared to function too far outside the Johnson Network waited long to get inside the prestige committees.

In these clandestine committee maneuvers, Johnson seldom exposed his hand. But in the routine committee shifts, he enjoyed wringing out the last drop of credit. One evening in early January 1955, shortly after the committee assignments for the Eighty-fifth Congress had been settled and announced, Johnson invited a couple of friends into his majority leader's office in the corner of the Capitol for a political bull session over Scotch and sodas. Nothing relaxed him more than these feet-up, hair-down chats. They invariably lasted well into the night and they invariably ended in long, often hilarious LBJ monologues, full of ribald yarns and racy mimicry.

Suddenly, he interrupted himself. "My God," he said, "I forgot to call Senator Stennis and congratulate him." Stennis had been valuable to Johnson a month earlier in the McCarthy censure fight, and now had just landed a coveted seat on the Appropriations Committee—thanks to Lyndon Johnson. Johnson reached over, cradled the phone between his shoulder and chin, and dialed.

Mrs. Stennis answered the phone, and the conversation commenced. "Ma'm, this is Lyndon Johnson, is your husband there? . . . He isn't? . . . Well, I must tell you, Ma'm, how proud I am of your husband and how proud the Senate is, and you tell him that when he gets home. The Senate paid him a great honor today. The Senate elected your husband to the Appropriations Committee. That's one of the most powerful committees in the Senate and a great honor for your husband. I'm so proud of John. He's a great American. And I know you're proud of him, too. He's one of my finest Senators. . . ." Accompanying this monologue were nods and winks in the direction of Johnson's fascinated audience.

Johnson went on to tell Mrs. Stennis how the Steering Committee had selected her husband unanimously for the Appropriations spot and how the full Senate had unanimously concurred, but implicitly he was belaboring the obvious—that it wasn't the Steering Committee or the full Senate that really was responsible. It was LBJ.

Johnson quietly commandeered other bits and pieces of Senate patronage that previous majority leaders ignored. To cement his budding alliance with

---

[2]This extraordinary treatment of Douglas also reflected Johnson's desire to keep the Finance Committee free of Northern liberals opposing special tax advantages for the oil and gas industry. But if Douglas had been a "good" liberal in the Humphrey mold, Johnson could have shaved a point, since the Finance Committee was already so stacked in favor of the oil and gas industry.

Senator Margaret Chase Smith, for instance, he arranged for a special staff member of the Senate Armed Services Committee to be appointed by her and to be responsible to her alone, even though she was a Republican on the Democratic-controlled committee, and only a fourth-ranking Republican at that.

Although in the past, office space for senators, a source of sometimes intense competition, had been distributed by strict seniority as a routine housekeeping chore of the Senate's sergeant-at-arms, Johnson quickly perceived its value as a weapon of influence and fitted it into his growing system of rewards and punishments. When Paul Douglas lost that top-floor Capitol office to Johnson in 1955, the Senate took notice. It was a dramatic sign of the consequences of a lack of rapport with the majority leader. Johnson skillfully exploited the gleaming New Senate Office Building in 1958, with its spanking new suites, as an inducement for help on the floor. Senator Mike Monroney of Oklahoma, sometimes troublesome for Johnson, was brought into line on one bill with the award of a handsome corner suite that Johnson knew Monroney coveted.

Johnson also kept his ears open to discover which senator—or senator's wife—was really anxious to go on which senatorial junket abroad. At a cocktail party early in 1957, Johnson was chatting with the wife of Frank Church, the young, newly elected liberal Democrat from Idaho. Mrs. Church innocently revealed that she had always wanted to see South America. Knowing that Frank Church might become a valuable addition to the Johnson Network, the majority leader saw to it that he was named to the very next delegation of senators to visit South America.

Even before that, however, Frank Church had reason to be grateful to Lyndon Johnson. Bitterly opposed by the Idaho Power Company and other private-power interests because of his public-power stand, Church was hard-pressed for funds in his 1956 campaign for the Senate. He sent an S.O.S. to the Senate Democratic Campaign Committee in Washington. Senator Smathers, chairman of the campaign committee, was dubious about pouring money into what seemed a hopeless cause in a small mountain state. But Johnson and Bobby Baker argued Church's cause, and their wishes prevailed.

De facto control of the campaign committee's funds was one of Johnson's least obvious but most effective tools in building his Network. He controlled the distribution of committee funds through both its chairman—first Earle Clements and later George Smathers—and through its secretary, Bobby Baker. More often than not, the requests for campaign funds were routinely made to Baker, and the money was physically distributed by him. Johnson further tightened his control when Clements was named the committee's executive director after his Senate defeat in 1956. Johnson got the most out of the committee's limited funds (at the time a mere four hundred thousand dollars) by shrewdly distributing them where they would do the most work. In the small mountain states like Idaho, a ten-thousand-dollar contribution could change the course of an election. But in New York or Pennsylvania, ten thousand dollars was the merest drop in the bucket. Johnson and Baker tried to reduce contributions to Democrats in the industrial Northeast to the minimum. Since senators seldom bite the hand that finances them, these westerners were naturally drawn into the Johnson Network, while the Eastern liberals tended to remain outside.

But this ingenious stretching of the majority leader's limited stock of patronage could not by itself explain the brilliant success of the Johnson Network. The extra, indeed the dominant, ingredient was Johnson's overwhelming personality, reflected in what came to be known as "The Treatment."

The Treatment could last ten minutes or four hours. It came, enveloping its target, at the LBJ Ranch swimming pool, in one of LBJ's offices, in the Senate cloakroom, on the floor of the Senate itself—wherever Johnson might find a fellow senator within his reach. Its tone could be supplication, accusation, cajolery, exuberance, scorn, tears, complaint, the hint of threat. It was all of these together. It ran the gamut of human emotions. Its velocity was breathtaking, and it was all in one direction. Interjections from the target were rare. Johnson anticipated them before they could be spoken. He moved in close, his face a scant millimeter from his target, his eyes widening and narrowing, his eyebrows rising and falling. From his pockets poured clippings, memos, statistics. Mimicry, humor, and the genius of analogy made The Treatment an almost hypnotic experience and rendered the target stunned and helpless.

In 1957, when Johnson was courting the non-Senate Eastern liberal establishment, he summoned historian and liberal theoretician Arthur Schlesinger, Jr., down from his classroom at Harvard. Wary at the prospect of his first prolonged meeting with Johnson (whom he suspected of disdaining the liberal cause), Schlesinger had in his mind a long list of questions to ask Johnson. Never known for shyness, Schlesinger was nevertheless on his guard when he entered Johnson's Capitol office and sat in front of the great man's desk.

The Treatment began immediately: a brilliant, capsule characterization of every Democratic senator: his strengths and failings, where he fit into the political spectrum; how far he could be pushed, how far pulled; his hates, his loves. And who (he asked Schlesinger) must oversee all these prima donnas, put them to work, knit them together, know when to tickle this one's vanity, inquire of that one's health, remember this one's five o'clock nip of Scotch, that one's nagging wife? Who must find the hidden legislative path between the South and the North, the public power men and the private power men, the farmers' men and the unions' men, the bomber boys and the peace lovers, the eggheads and the fatheads? Nobody but Lyndon Johnson.

Imagine a football team (Johnson hurried on) and I'm the coach, and I'm also the quarterback, I have to call the signals, and I have to center the ball, run the ball, pass the ball. I'm the blocker (he rose out of his chair and threw an imaginary block). I'm the tackler (he crouched and tackled). I'm the passer (he heaved a mighty pass). I have to catch the pass (he reached and caught the pass).

Schlesinger was sitting on the edge of his chair, both fascinated and amused. Here was a view of the Senate he had never seen before.

Johnson next ticked off all the bills he had passed that year, how he'd gotten Dick Russell on this one, Bob Kerr on that one, Hubert Humphrey on another. He reached into his desk drawer and out came the voting record of New Jersey's Clifford Case, a liberal Republican. You liberals, he told Schlesinger, are always talking about my record. You wouldn't question Cliff Case's record, would you? And he ran down the list and compared it to his voting record. Whatever Johnson had on those two lists, he came out with a record more liberal than Case's.

Johnson had anticipated and answered all of Schlesinger's questions. The leader rolled on, reiterating a theme common to The Treatment of that time. He'd had his heart attack, he said, and he knew he'd never be president. He wasn't made for the presidency. If only the good Lord would just give him enough time to do a few more things in the Senate. Then he'd go back to Texas. That's where he belonged.

Breathless now, ninety minutes later, Schlesinger said good-bye and groped his way out of Johnson's office. Eight years later, he was to record his impressions. Johnson had been "a good deal more attractive, more subtle, and more formidable than I expected." And, he might have added, vastly more entertaining.

The Treatment was designed for a single target or, at most, an audience of three or four. In large groups, what was witty sounded crude, what was expansive became arrogant. It was inevitable, then, that when Johnson allowed The Treatment to dominate his "press conferences" a sour note entered his relations with the press. Reporters en masse didn't like being on the receiving end of The Treatment. Johnson's failure to understand that annoyed the press, which in turn made Johnson increasingly wary and suspicious. Unable to tame the press as he tamed so many senators, he foolishly took offense at routine questions, and was quick to find a double meaning in the most innocent point raised by a reporter. Although Senate reporters and Washington's top columnists were captivated in their *private* sessions with Johnson in his office or at the LBJ Ranch, his press conferences were fiascoes. They simply could not be harnessed to The Treatment. . . .

EDWARD M. KENNEDY AND Robert C. Byrd have fundamentally different personalities, which have shaped their respective Senate careers. Each, like most of his colleagues, has sought power and status on Capitol Hill. But the route to power each has selected reflects a different background, character, and style. Kennedy is a star and has embraced an individualistic style; through the astute use of the committees he chairs he has sought to put the Kennedy imprint upon legislation, investigations, and committee reports. Kennedy's style represents the "new Senate," in which individual senators are more independent of their colleagues. They seek power not so much through the traditional emphasis upon collegial cooperation but by gaining personal recognition among colleagues for hard work on committees, specialized knowledge, and legislative accomplishments. There remains an important collegial aspect to these efforts, but in the modern Senate an increasing number of members tend to focus on the separate worlds of their committees more than upon the collective demands of the institution.

Robert Byrd, in contrast to Kennedy, adopted a collegial style of operation; he sought positions of leadership in the Senate body rather than emphasize his individual power through committees. Because of his service to fellow senators, Byrd was elected majority whip and majority leader. His personality was more muted than that of Kennedy, his style less flamboyant and aggressive. As the following selection makes clear, each has made an important contribution to the Senate.

26 Laurence Leamer
ROBERT BYRD AND EDWARD KENNEDY: TWO STORIES OF THE SENATE

The Capitol is the greatest public building in America. Visitors can sit in the House and Senate galleries, climb the broad staircases, roam the marble halls, and ride the elevators. They can go almost anywhere they choose. Yet hidden within the Capitol are offices and nooks and gathering places that are private. On the House side of the Capitol, down a back staircase from the House floor, stands an unmarked door. Behind the door is a dark room shrouded in drapes, with an old desk and a few chairs casually arranged. Here Speaker Sam Rayburn's "Board of Education" used to meet each afternoon over bourbon and water to talk politics. Fifteen years after Rayburn's death the star of Texas is still there, painted in ornate style on the far wall.

On the Senate side of the Capitol there are fifty-four private rooms used

Excerpts from *Playing for Keeps in Washington* by Laurence Leamer. Copyright 1977 by Laurence Leamer. Reprinted by permission of Doubleday, a division of Bantam Doubleday Dell Publishing Group, Inc.

by senators. Some are no more than rude accumulations of government-issue desks, chairs, and paintings. Others are exquisitely decorated with antiques, political memorabilia, ornate telephones. The largest office is a three-room suite that can be reached by going down a narrow staircase just off the main corridor. These are the offices out of which Bobby Baker, the assistant to Senate majority leader Lyndon Johnson, operated. Baker had worked there until he was convicted of abusing his position and sent to prison.

These are the rooms that Edward "Ted" Kennedy of Massachusetts claimed as his own in 1969 when he was elected Democratic whip, the number-two position in the Democratic leadership. Then the offices had all the sweaty urgency of a political boiler room. The suite was full of Kennedy people. The phones rang constantly. Journalists hurried in and out. Now and again Kennedy came bursting in for a few minutes before rushing off somewhere else. There was always something happening. There had never been anything quite like it in the Senate.

In 1971 Robert C. Byrd of West Virginia defeated Kennedy and took over the suite. From all appearances, Byrd did not think the suite a grand prize but more a gift kept for occasional use. The doors might stay locked for days. Byrd decorated the rooms with just enough pictures and artifacts so that the suite became indisputably his. On the wall he put mounted whips that Senator Joseph Montoya of New Mexico had given him and a copy of a *Parade* magazine story about himself ("Senate Whip Bob Byrd: From Poverty to Power").

On the wall of the outer office hung pictures of the fourteen men who had served as Democratic whip. From Jay Hamilton to Hubert Humphrey, from Morris Sheppard to Russell Long, from Lister Hill to Lyndon Johnson, the first twelve faces looked forth with the fleshy, canny confidence of the professional politician. But Kennedy and Byrd were different. Kennedy's picture had the perfect looks of a Hollywood publicity glossy. Byrd, for his part, looked half-embarrassed, as if in the act of allowing himself to be photographed he was giving away something that he did not want to give away.

As much as Kennedy and Byrd were different in appearance from the twelve men who preceded them, so were they different from each other. They were two of the most powerful men in Washington. They did not like each other. They did not like each other's politics. In their distinct ways they symbolized what power had become in the modern Senate.

Senator Robert Byrd walked down the main corridor of the Capitol, down a narrow staircase, and unlocked the door to the whip's office. Many senators travel with a flotilla of aides, but Byrd almost always walks alone. He is a little man with a chalk-white face and black-and-white streaked hair swept back in a high pompadour. He looks like a wary sparrow, with a face that could be found up most any hollow in Appalachia, the face of a man who had missed some basic nutrient. It belonged to the man who was on the verge of becoming the Senate majority leader—the most powerful and prestigious position in Congress.

Byrd is a man of religious intensity, both public and private, the personification of the self-made man, a man of deep, unfathomable ambition, beyond perhaps anyone else's in the Senate. He sought power, wooed power, lived with and for power. . . .

The Senate that Byrd was sworn into in January 1959 was still dominated by Southerners like Lyndon Johnson of Texas and Richard Russell of Georgia. A conservative might believe that a certain lassitude and the petty corruption of privilege were merely the exhaust fumes given off by the Senate as it made its stately way through history. Senator Thomas Dodd of Connecticut, for instance, had an elderly retainer known as the "judge" who slept blissfully at a desk outside the senator's office.

The Senate had not yet spread out into the nearly completed New Senate Office Building. Donald R. Matthews, an academician, was finishing work on a book on the Senate, *U.S. Senators and Their World.* He broke Senate offices down into two general types: the bureaucratic and the individualistic. In the bureaucratic offices, "the senator has delegated considerable nonroutine responsibilities to his staff, established a fairly clear-cut division of labor and chain of command." The individualistic offices were "vest pocket operations in which the senator has delegated only routine tasks and in which the staff has little influence and less authority."

Byrd was arriving in the Senate as it was going through a profound evolution. The old Senate, the Senate of "individualistic" offices, had just been portrayed in *Citadel: The Story of the United States Senate,* a book by William S. White. White wrote of the U.S. Senate as "an institution that lives in an unending yesterday where the past is never gone, the present never quite decisive, and the future rarely quite visible. It has its good moments and its bad moments, but to the United States it symbolizes, if nothing else at all, the integrity of continuity and wholeness." This Senate was an institution where, when a man was sworn in, he assumed a mantle of dignity and honor. It was honor enough for any man to be in this body.

When the *Citadel* came out, Senator J. William Fulbright noticed that for a few days some of his colleagues attempted to play senator, walking the halls of Congress as if they were wearing togas. On January 15, 1957, Lyndon B. Johnson had a luncheon for the six new Democratic senators. He gave the six freshmen autographed copies of *Citadel* and he told them that they should think of the book as a kind of McGuffey's *Reader.*

Johnson knew that White's Senate was not his, but he may have found a certain comfort in that mythical body. To White, the Senate was a great conservative body, the naysayer and watchman of democracy. But what gave the Senate its greatness were individual senators with individual ideas. They worked in the body of Congress to transform their ideas into legislation that would affect the nation. When Johnson had come to Washington, George Norris of Nebraska was still in the Senate. For years Norris had studied how to protect the land and the people. He had prepared his bill for the Tennessee Valley Authority, and he had defended it as if it were a part of his very being, which in a sense it was. Robert Wagner of New York was in the Senate too. For years he worked on the great legislation of the New Deal, including the labor bill that bears his name. Bob La Follette and Robert Taft were also in the Senate in those years. What these senators had in common was an organic relationship between what they believed, the people they served, and what they did and said to achieve their ends.

When Robert Byrd entered the Senate, he accepted the life of the Senate as the central reality of his being. "Over the years he has cloaked himself in what he perceives to be senatorial dignity and aura," said one of Byrd's former aides, "but even when he arrived, there really was very little dignity left and the aura was gone."

Byrd allied himself with Lyndon Johnson of Texas and more closely yet with Richard Russell of Georgia. Those who watched Byrd often thought him great only in petty things. But to a man who revered the Senate as much as Byrd, there were no petty duties. In 1960, during an all-night civil rights filibuster, Byrd talked for a record twenty-one hours. Five years later in another filibuster, he talked for fifteen hours. Byrd was always ready to volunteer for the KP duty of legislative life. The Senate was based on rules and precedents. And Robert Byrd, alone of his generation, was willing to learn the rules and the precedents. He studied them until he knew them as did no one else and then he studied them some more.

Byrd performed duties, great and small, for senators of every persuasion, North and South, Democrat and Republican. He helped colleagues whenever he could. When he had helped, he sent them notes saying that he had been glad to be of service. These he filed away. In 1967 he was elected Secretary of the Democratic Conference, the number-three position in the Senate Democratic leadership. Four years later he defeated Ted Kennedy and became Senate whip, the number-two position in the Senate Democratic leadership.

As a Senate leader, Byrd worked even harder. He knew the Bible, the book of Senate rules and the book of precedents, and these were just about the only books he figured he would ever have to know. He had read the 900-page collection of precedents cover to cover, two times, and late at night at home he was reading it for the third. When the Senate was planning to go into closed session on matters of national security, he would go over Rule 35 once again. When there was going to be a vote on cloture, he would read the rule on cloture. Byrd knew the rules and he knew the precedents and could make them turn upside down and dance on their heads. It was *his* Senate now, and he left the floor rarely.

The Washington Monument splits the window of his vast inner office in the Capitol. Senator Byrd speaks quietly, the twang of the hills in his voice: "The Senate is a forest. There are ninety-nine animals. They're all lions. There's a waterhole in the forest. I'm the waterhole. They all have to come to the waterhole. I don't have power but I have knowledge of the rules. I have knowledge of the precedents. I have knowledge of the schedule. So I'm in a position to do things for others.

"Now the majority leader is the dispatcher, the engineer, the fellow at the head of the engine who's looking out from the dark night at the headlight down the railway, pulling on the throttle a little harder, pushing on the throttle a little, or leveling off a little, moving it along. Or he determines to move over on this sidetrack or that sidetrack. This legislative organism, with its power, has to have direction. It has to have a leader, but he doesn't have the power. He's the umpire, the referee. He doesn't have any more of that raw power than any other senator has.

"The president, he has power. He's the chief executive of this country. The presidency of the United States should in reality seek the man. Someone said that. That's the way it ought to be. People ought not to be persuaded by a person's pretty teeth, by his smile, or by the way he cuts his hair—by his charisma. That's misleading. That's not to say that a person with pretty teeth and a pretty smile and a handsome build and charisma may not have the ability. But they don't necessarily go together either."

Talking about pretty teeth and a pretty smile and the cut of a man's hair, Robert Byrd could have been sketching a caricature of Edward Kennedy. Byrd and Kennedy were the two Janus faces of the Senate, Byrd often looking backward to a past that had never been, Kennedy looking forward to a future that might never arrive. They approached their work as differently as two men in the same profession possibly could. They also had different conceptions of power and how to use it.

Edward Moore Kennedy walked down the center aisle of the Senate to be sworn in as the junior senator from Massachusetts on January 9, 1963. He had the accent and bearing of the Kennedys, but was a big, brawny fellow with a rousing, friendly manner that suggested an Irish politician of a half century past. He was the scion of a family that seemed destined to dominate American political life in the last decades of the twentieth century as had the Adams family in the first decades of the nation's history. . . .

Kennedy fit unobtrusively into the traditional role of the freshman senator. One morning he went around to see Senator James Eastland of Mississippi, chairman of the Judiciary Committee and champion of the old Senate. He drank bourbon with the senior senator and Eastland discovered that the Kennedys were not all alike. He went around to see Senator Richard Russell of Georgia, Robert Byrd's patron, and he went to the Senate prayer breakfast, too—once at least—and led his colleagues in prayer.

While Kennedy might act out such old-fashioned rituals of the Senate, he was still the most modern of freshmen. A decade later, James Macgregor Burns, a biographer of Kennedy, would call him a "presidential senator." Kennedy was a presidential senator not only in the sense that he had become the sole bearer of the Kennedy legacy and heir apparent to the White House. He was presidential in the way he went about being a senator. He launched a frenetic, permanent presidential-like campaign within the very Senate.

In the favored analogy of his staff, Senator Kennedy stood at the center of a circle of aides who flowed in and around him. The Kennedys had always had a special talent for acquiring and using people whose talents met the needs of the moment. They attracted members of that natural aristocracy of the able and the ambitious. These aides were perhaps no more talented than those around other contenders for the ultimate prize in American politics. But in the livery of the Kennedys, they seemed to serve with extraordinary energy and devotion, and in the end they were, in one way or another, rewarded in kind.

One of those who was there when Kennedy entered the Senate was Milton Gwirtzman, now a Washington lawyer.

"From the beginning Kennedy knew how to use his staff," Gwirtzman observed. "Even in his first term he had that lineup outside his office. There were perhaps six professionals then and Kennedy used them as a multiplier." To a Borah or Taft or Wagner, the idea of a senatorial multiplier would have been absurd. It would, indeed, have been impossible, for until the Legislative Reorganization Act of 1946, most senators had only a clerk and a secretary.

Kennedy was one of the first senators to employ his staff so systematically that he helped create a new definition of "senator." Kennedy not only used the half dozen or so aides who were his natural due, but he subsidized two others. Gwirtzman, for one, left the staff in 1964 but for the next six years was paid $18,000 a year by the Park Agency, a Kennedy family conduit, for speeches and advice. Kennedy, moreover, had a press secretary. That itself was a relatively new position on the Hill: a media-savvy specialist who measured success in newsprint and television time, not merely in a product called legislation.

Kennedy understood how to develop his staff so that they would serve him. He did not want any one Super Aide around him who might become for him what Ted Sorensen had been for Jack. He did not want an alter ego. What he did want was a group of people who could work on their own, self-motivated young men ambitious for themselves and for him, men whose competitiveness with one another might sometimes spill over into jealousies, but whose energies and ideals could be channeled into furthering Senator Ted Kennedy and his career.

In those first years in office, Kennedy did not draw on his name. He did not use his power in ways that were memorable or important. He had a quotation from Machiavelli as his maxim: "power not used is power saved."

Machiavelli, however, was writing about power that had once been used. Kennedy was hoarding a commodity whose worth he could not know until he used it. He was acting as if even he accepted the common definition of himself as the last and the least of the Kennedys—the kid brother.

During the day Kennedy abided by all the rituals of egalitarianism: bantering with aides, employing the ersatz intimacy of first names. However, if an aide stepped over a certain line, visible only to Kennedy, that aide learned to regret it. By day they might be members of a team but not in the evening. It was simply understood that if you worked for Ted Kennedy you did not go to social gatherings that he attended. You learned to treat his family in a special way. An aide had taken a phone call from Rose Kennedy in Hyannisport one day. "Your mother called," the aide said when Kennedy returned to the office. "You mean *you* talked to *my* mother?" Kennedy said. If politics was one world, and social life another, then the family was yet a third and the most exalted of Kennedy's worlds. Here the subordinates were not allowed to trespass, even for a moment.

On that November afternoon in 1963 when President John F. Kennedy was assassinated in Dallas, Ted Kennedy was performing that most thankless of tasks foisted on the freshman: presiding over a nearly empty Senate. When he learned of the shooting and he finally reached his brother on the telephone, Robert Kennedy told him, "You'd better call your mother and your sisters." In their division of the duties of mourning, it fell to Ted Kennedy to comfort the family.

By that next June, Kennedy had prepared his public face. His party back in Massachusetts was preparing to nominate him for his first full term in office. Kennedy, however, was still on the floor of the Senate waiting to vote on the civil rights bill. It was so typical of his life to have a dozen people, a dozen decisions, a dozen proposals backed up waiting for him.

Kennedy finally left Washington for Massachusetts by private plane, accompanied by Senator Birch Bayh of Indiana and his wife Marvella, and aide Ed Moss. It was no kind of weather to be flying in a private plane, but Kennedy lived in a world of days that were scheduled too tight, cars that were driven too fast, planes that were flown when they shouldn't have been. On the approach to the airport outside Springfield, the plane crashed. The Bayhs were injured, the pilot was dead, Moss would die soon afterward, and Kennedy had cracked ribs, a punctured lung, and three damaged vertebrae.

Kennedy spent the next six months in bed. . . .

While still in the hospital, Kennedy won reelection in Massachusetts with 74.4 percent of the votes. In New York, his brother Bob defeated Kenneth Keating for a Senate seat by a much closer margin. Afterward his brother had come up to visit in the hospital. The two Kennedys had posed for the photographers. "Step back a little, you're casting a shadow on Ted," one of the photographers said to Bob Kennedy.

"It'll be the same in Washington," Ted Kennedy said laughing.

During the nearly four years that the two Kennedys served together in the Senate, Ted Kennedy largely deferred to his brother and to his leadership. In 1965 he took over the chairmanship of the Subcommittee on Refugees and Escapees. This was his first chairmanship, the natural legacy of the seniority system. It was a moribund subcommittee concerned largely with refugees who had fled Communist Europe. But it represented more staff and an area that he could now legitimately make his own.

Ted took the subcommittee and expanded its mandate to the refugees of Southeast Asia. He used it as his ticket of admission to the issue of Vietnam. He went to Vietnam and the papers were full of the poignant testimony of human suffering. . . .

It was not until after the murder of his brother Bob in 1968 that Ted Kennedy, the senator, began to fully emerge. In his time of mourning he had gone sailing for days on end, and drinking, and carousing. Then in August in Worcester he had given a speech important enough to be televised nationally. He told his audience that he had been at sea. But he said, "There is no safety in hiding. Not for me, not for any of us here today . . . like my brothers before me, I pick up a fallen standard." He went on to talk about the Vietnam war and all it had cost in money and blood. He proposed that the United States unconditionally end the bombing and negotiate a peace. . . .

The next office Kennedy did seek was one that his brothers would never have considered. In January he defeated Russell Long, that son of Louisiana, and son of oil, to become majority whip. The whip had a series of thankless bureaucratic duties such as rounding up senators and arranging schedules. He was, nonetheless, the number-two leader in the Senate. Kennedy set out to make the whip more than that. He brought in some of his own academic and other expert advisors to forge a cohesive policy for the Democrats. Senators, however, are a jealous and self-protective group. A hundred different policies were better than one, if the one came stamped with the mark of a particular senator. Worse yet, Kennedy simply did not perform the mundane, pesky tasks of the whip as they were supposed to be. Bored by them, he foisted such chores as he could onto his staff.

Kennedy was drinking heavily. At times his face had the florid look that showed him a full-blooded member of the race of Irish drinkers. Then in July on vacation he had gone over to Chappaquiddick Island to attend a party for some of Bobby Kennedy's "boiler-room girls." He had left with one of them, Mary Jo Kopechne, and the next morning the police had found her body in Kennedy's overturned Oldsmobile off a bridge on a dirt road on Chappaquiddick Island.

Kennedy, according to his own statement, had dived down to try to get her out and then he had left and gone back to his friends to get help. He had not contacted the police until the next morning. The Kennedys, whatever else one said about them, had always showed the grace under pressure that Hemingway had called the mark of courage, the mark of a man. The private Kennedy had failed that night, as those around him failed. "It was in part a failure of staffing," one of his aides said. "He had no one with him to tell him he was crazy."

Within hours Kennedy had left the island. He retreated into that flimsy story; he made a televised public statement prepared by Ted Sorensen, Gwirtzman, Richard Goodwin, and Burke Marshall and then backed into legal refuges, the power of wealth and position, and the sympathy that people of Massachusetts had for him and for his family. . . .

Until that night at Chappaquiddick, Kennedy had appeared an inevitable choice for the 1972 presidential nomination. But that was all over. When Kennedy returned to the Senate, Mike Mansfield, the majority leader, as goodhearted a man as was to be found in that body, noticed Kennedy pausing for a moment in the cloakroom. "Come here," Mansfield said encouragingly. "Come here, right back where you belong." To the last of the Kennedys, it was a phrase not without its ironies. . . .

R ARELY DOES A POWERFUL congressional party leader give up his post to become a committee chairman. However, when the committee is one of the most powerful in the body, such as the Senate Appropriations Committee, an effective chair cannot only serve constituents better than a party leader but also can continue to be a powerful force in the body. The following selection reveals how former Senate Majority Leader Robert Byrd (D-W. Va.) maintained and perhaps enhanced his power on Capitol Hill when he stepped down as party chief to head the Appropriations Committee.

Jackie Calmes

27 FROM MAJORITY LEADER TO COMMITTEE CHAIRMAN: HOW ROBERT BYRD WIELDS POWER IN THE SENATE

Some of those close to the Senate Appropriations Committee like to quip that Robert C. Byrd would be the strongest chairman in years if only because he came to the coveted job before age had sapped his health and senses. Even Byrd is in on the macabre joke. He quotes South Carolina's Democratic senator: "Fritz Hollings one day said, 'We have a real, live chairman now!' "

But the verdict on Byrd goes well beyond simple vitality: After one year on the job, the West Virginia Democrat is emerging as the most powerful Appropriations chief in a generation. It's sweet praise for the proud man who gave up the Senate's top spot, the majority leadership, after years of sniping about his style.

"I would say that he is the strongest leader in that role of chairman that I have served under," says Oregon's Mark O. Hatfield, the committee's senior Republican and the only other recent chairman (1981–87) not enfeebled by age.

At 72, after spending 22 of his 31 Senate years in its leadership circle, Byrd says his new post is the one he always wanted. Some observers say it is the one for which he is best suited.

Byrd was often criticized during his tenure as Democratic leader for being too stilted and old-fashioned to represent his party in the TV age. But in the insiders' world of Appropriations, he is succeeding in the model of the 1950s-era committee chairmen, the benevolent dictators he watched as a new senator. "He embraces power," says Sen. Thad Cochran, R-Miss. "He doesn't shirk from it."

As majority leader, Byrd at best was first among equals on the Senate floor,

From *Congressional Quarterly Weekly Report,* December 9, 1989, pp. 3354–3359. Copyright 1989 by Congressional Quarterly, Inc. Reprinted by permission.

subject by its wide-open rules to the whims of the most junior members, and beholden for his job to his demanding fellow Democrats. But in the ornate Capitol committee room, he gavels away with the security of one who leads by right of seniority, without fear of the filibusters and non-germane amendments that stymie floor action for a majority leader.

No longer under party pressure to be a media-smart political visionary, Byrd now is judged and respected for his devotion to institutional and legislative detail. He is compared to a technically competent plant manager, a conductor who runs the trains on time.

"He's done a good job, a very good job," says Sen. Pete V. Domenici, R-N.M. "As difficult as things are, given the budget constraints, he's led."

When the full committee met, it approved the allocation of funds in record time. Some past sessions had taken days and multiple roll-call votes.

Similarly, Byrd unveiled his September counter proposal to President Bush's call for higher anti-drug funding only after consulting with the subcommittee heads and Hatfield. His proposal, which became the basis of a compromise after much wrangling with Republicans and the administration, provided a bigger increase, allocated more money to treatment efforts to balance Bush's emphasis on prisons, and made small, across-the-board cuts in the 1990 appropriations bills to offset the extra funding.

Awaiting His Turn

Byrd tried to lead in his former role, and often did. The 100th Congress, his last term as majority leader, was among the most productive in years.

But his dozen years as Democratic chief were filled with enough disappointments that by early 1988 Byrd announced he would not seek the job again. Half of those years were spent as minority leader—"a purgatory if not worse"—and in that time he was challenged twice from within his own ranks, reflecting Democrats' longing for a telegenic foil to Ronald Reagan.

Byrd's fallback was an enviable one. In 1989, he inherited both the Appropriations chairmanship and the post of president pro tempore, a ceremonial job for the Senate's senior majority member that satisfies Byrd's love of parliamentary ritual.

"If I had had the opportunity to be Appropriations chairman before this year, I would have taken it. It is the position I always wanted since I went on the committee 31 years ago," Byrd says. "But I had to take my turn."

Seven men—six Democrats and Hatfield—held the job in that period. The Democrats included some of the Senate's major postwar figures—Carl T. Hayden of Arizona, Richard B. Russell of Georgia, Allen J. Ellender of Louisiana, John L. McClellan of Arkansas and Warren G. Magnuson of Washington—but most were aged and near the end of their careers by the time they assumed the chair.

Five of the six Democrats were ailing, and three died in office. Byrd succeeds John C. Stennis of Mississippi, a revered 41-year Senate veteran who retired at age 87 in ill health after a single term at Appropriations.

At the House Appropriations Committee, where senators in general and Byrd in particular have never been popular, a top aide said recently that any grumbling about Byrd "just reflects the thinking of people who aren't used to having a leader as Senate Appropriations chairman."

A Style Suited to the Job

By all accounts, it is the job rather than the man that has changed. In fact, some of the praise reflects a measure of relief that he is no longer majority leader.

"He transferred the same style of leadership to the committee . . . a very sober-type, serious, no-monkey-business, all-business type of leadership, with a knowledge of exactly how he wanted to get from point A to point B," Hatfield says.

But Hatfield and others agree that Byrd's style has worked better in the committee than it did on the floor. The panel's membership is smaller (29), its rules tighter and partisanship rare as members swap support to steer federal dollars to their home states.

Looking back over his first year as chairman, Byrd said, "I used the same approach that I always used as majority leader and minority leader. My approach was to counsel others, and work individually with senators . . . to develop a consensus. I think as time went on, I developed a pretty good level of unity in my party, and I've done the same at Appropriations."

Byrd says his consultation with the subcommittee chairmen "makes them feel that they're part of the team." Members do credit Byrd for consulting them, though there is some feeling that he actually is informing the senators about decisions that he and his staff already have worked out.

Also, by meeting with senators one-on-one, Byrd's own power is enhanced. He can pick off members' support individually until he has the votes to assure the outcome he wants. The approach suits Byrd not only politically, but personally. An intensely private, insular man, he has never been comfortable in clubby situations.

As majority leader, a former aide recalls, "Byrd was not particularly fond of large group settings, particularly when a great deal of power was collected in one room. [In a small group] he felt he was more in control, [that there was] less possibility of a spontaneous revolution."

A Man Apart

For a man who loves the Senate as his home, Byrd has never been close to other members of the family. As he said in an extraordinary, angry moment on the Senate floor in 1987, "I understand that I am not very well-liked around here."

He spends off-hours not socializing or relaxing but educating himself—reading histories, Shakespeare, the Bible, even the dictionary, and writing his own Senate history series—in a drive for self-improvement that has consumed him since his days as an orphan in West Virginia's coal fields. A box in his office reads, "Secret of Success," and opens to say, "Work."

Sen. Wyche Fowler Jr., D-Ga., recalls that when Sen. Frank R. Lautenberg, D-N.J., asked Byrd how he'd spent the August recess, Byrd said he'd reread a multivolume history of England. After Lautenberg quipped that he hoped Byrd had his kings straight, Byrd recited each one in order.

At Appropriations, it is said privately that members follow Byrd not because they like him, but because they fear him.

"I've heard that very frequently," Hatfield says. "I suppose it's one of those situations where there's a careful line drawn between respect and affection—a lot of respect but not a great deal of affection. And I think that's too bad."

Amid their general praise for Byrd's stewardship, members and staff do complain about the bang of his gavel—the symbol of his obsession with quick and orderly action. "The gavel probably could be struck a little less loudly and still command respect," Cochran says.

He has embarrassed his equally proud colleagues by admonishing them in public sessions, or summarily gaveling their requests out of order. "I am a grown man, and this is not a grade school," one senator said.

But while Byrd clearly runs the show at Appropriations, he defers to the subcommittee heads in matters under their jurisdiction. Byrd himself remains chairman of one subcommittee, with broad responsibility for the Interior Department, national parks, mines, Indian affairs and the arts.

"The committee is run with a firm hand, but the subcommittee chairmen still have quite a bit of autonomy," says Warren B. Rudman, N.H., senior Republican on the subcommittee for the Commerce, Justice and State departments and the judiciary. "I haven't seen a lot of interference at all. He just likes to keep the trains running on time."

One feud that did break into the open involved Rudman's Democratic counterpart, Commerce Subcommittee Chairman Ernest F. Hollings.

The September morning after Byrd unveiled his anti-drug funding proposal at a Capitol press conference, Hollings led his panel to approve what he and Rudman called a better alternative. It provided a smaller increase, all for the law enforcement programs covered in Hollings' subcommittee bill, and a smaller offsetting cut in other programs.

Just as Hollings finished describing the plan, Byrd entered, huddled with him for a brief and audibly testy exchange, then abruptly left. Until the matter was resolved, Byrd refused to schedule full committee action on Hollings' subcommittee bill.

Committee members dismiss the incident as a misunderstanding between two proud senators with a history of strained relations. In the last decade, when Byrd was Democratic whip and heir apparent to retiring Majority Leader Mike Mansfield, Hollings had considered challenging the West Virginian.

Wielding Power . . .

The same drug-funding issue also soured Byrd's relations with the Bush White House, and particularly with budget director Richard G. Darman.

Those relations "went very, very well up to the drug package," Hatfield says. "Then there was a time when he just did not respond to their telephone calls, to their offers to meet with him. He felt they had invaded and overplayed their indirect role in the legislative process, and therefore challenged the role of the House and Senate. He told me, 'You're the [Republican] spokesman, and I take your word and your position for these things as representing the administration.' "

By contrast, during the spring Byrd had successfully joined with the administration to oppose a major $822 million drug-funding boost that the House included in the 1989 supplement appropriations bill. That angered many congressional Democrats, who wanted to make a party stand against drugs, but Byrd was intent on avoiding the threatened veto of his first bill as chairman.

"I felt there ought to be more [anti-drug] money, but there was a time to get that money and we were two or three months ahead of that point," he recalls. "It was the wrong time, and I had a supplemental appropriations bill that I felt would be lost entirely if we took on an additional issue."

Some Appropriations sources suggest that Byrd's stance would have been different as majority leader, the party point man. Byrd himself notes the change in his role: As Appropriations chairman, his responsibility is to his committee's work, he says, while "the party leader has to protect the party's program . . . One is apt to be cast into controversial roles."

But would he have acted differently on the supplemental bill had he still been majority leader? "I can't say," Byrd replies after a pause.

His later fight for higher drug funding in September, during action on the 1990 appropriations, combined the roles of both committee and party leader. As Appropriations chairman, Byrd was delivering on his spring promise that more money would be provided in regular appropriations for 1990, and devising a way to pay for the increase that would be least painful to other programs. As a senior Democrat, he was trying to put a party stamp on a matter of widespread voter concern. In the House, which jealously guards its prerogatives as the originator of the annual appropriations bills, Byrd's take-charge operation of the Senate committee has required some getting used to.

"Previously we'd deal with our own Senate [subcommittee] counterparts one-on-one. Now there's the overriding presence of Bob Byrd," says Rep.

William Lehman, D-Fla., chairman of the House Appropriations Committee's Transportation Subcommittee.

At year's end, for example, Byrd stepped in to break an impasse between House and Senate subcommittees negotiating the agriculture bill. Sen. Dale Bumpers, D-Ark., was holding out against Jamie L. Whitten, D-Miss., Chairman of both House Appropriations and its Agriculture Subcommittee, to get a $1.1 million grant for a home-state firm providing chemicals information to farmers.

Byrd offered to find money elsewhere, in the Interior appropriations. That did not please Byrd's opposite number at the House's Interior panel, Chairman Sidney R. Yates, D-Ill.

Inevitably there has been institutional rivalry—notably during the supplemental bill debate. On a personal level, many House members have long considered Byrd cold and stubborn, the epitome of the pompous senator. In years past, they occasionally would block West Virginia projects out of spite.

That makes the latest praise all the more surprising: House appropriators have been impressed by Byrd's command of his panel and his ability to move bills through the Senate. In September, spending bills were moving from subcommittee to full committee and floor passage in as few as two or three days.

"He's done an outstanding job," says Rep. John Murtha, D-Pa., chairman of House Appropriations' Defense Subcommittee.

Outside his committee, Byrd has assiduously guarded its turf against others in Congress and the White House, reclaiming some of the panel's prestige that eroded under the budget changes of recent years. Always a stickler for parliamentary rules and procedure, he now channels that zeal to protect Appropriations' right to determine spending levels.

The turf fights inevitably have aggravated lawmakers off the committee, just as Byrd's quick gavel and occasional disciplinarian-like lectures have irritated those who are on it.

In a powerplay this fall, he revived a long-dormant rule and successfully battled the Senate Foreign Relations Committee's practice of mandating minimum amounts of funding for certain foreign aid programs.

In Congress' final hours last month, a $100 million provision for social service block grants to the states was stripped from a major deficit-reduction package and passed separately—after Byrd objected that non-appropriations bills were not the place for spending proposals.

Also at his behest, Senate negotiators on a bill (HR 3611) authorizing drug-fighting aid to South American nations forced the House to drop a number of provisions specifying how money would be spent. Though Byrd was not on the conference committee, its statement on the final compromise pointedly noted that the House earmarks were dropped "at the insistence of the chairman of the Senate Appropriations Committee."

Byrd's protectiveness of his turf extends outside Congress. Enraged by a lobbying firm's efforts to steer federal money to its clients, Byrd used his Interior Appropriations bill to shepherd into law new disclosure requirements. They require recipients of federal funds to report the names and pay of lobbyists hired to obtain those funds, and bar the use of federal money for lobbying costs.

. . . And Delivering

Byrd's anti-lobbying campaign began when he learned that the firm was taking credit for securing an $18 million research center for West Virginia University. That struck at Byrd's pride in his own renowned ability to get the pork for his state.

Because of his reputation, few took Byrd seriously in 1988 when he said he was forgoing another bid for majority leader because he could do more for West Virginia at Appropriations.

But he moved immediately to live up to his vow. The 1989 supplemental spending bill included $75 million to rebuild a radio telescope at the National Radio Astronomy Observatory in Green Bank, W.Va., and $6.6 million for rural-airport subsidies on which his state depends. The subsidies got another $30.7 million in the 1990 transportation bill this fall—less than the Senate provided but much more than the urban-oriented House wanted.

Byrd's own list shows that he secured more than $400 million for West Virginia projects in the 1990 appropriations bills. That sum does not include millions of dollars more for the state's share of programs for which Byrd is a leading proponent, including Economic Development Administration funds, rural-airport subsidies, coal-research efforts and unspecified, flood-control projects.

The Interior measure was predictably generous to West Virginia. As Byrd notes, just the $11.7 billion for fisheries and wildlife projects is more than the president requested for the entire country. The Bureau of Mines got $34 million more than Bush sought, mostly for health and safety programs important to Byrd's state.

According to a House aide, Whitten joked last spring that the supplemental conference was delayed "because Byrd discovered there was one West Virginia county he had not taken care of." But, the aide added, "Byrd's no more parochial than anyone else, particularly anyone in his high position."

"Where I Want to Be"

Byrd's transition to that position seemed smooth from the start this year, though few doubted that it was difficult for him to forfeit the majority leadership.

"I think that having the dual role of president pro tem of the Senate and the chairmanship of the committee has probably helped," Hatfield says. "As president pro tem, he is still able to occupy a very important role in Senate proceedings."

The job entitles Byrd to preside over his cherished Senate whenever he chooses, and he has done so more than any predecessor in memory. "I'm a very active president pro tem," Byrd says. "I put more work into it."

He also has put more money into it. The office received $296,000 for 1990, nearly double the 1989 appropriations. Byrd says funding had not kept pace with inflation or the office's responsibilities to oversee Senate organizations. The staff also helps on Byrd's history project.

That labor of love has eased his transition, too. Now at work on the second book, Byrd recently checked out 44 volumes of the *Congressional Record* from the Senate Library for one weekend's research.

"I think the man's just been keeping so busy that probably in some way he's relieved of not having the nitty-gritty, everyday activity leadership to worry about," Hatfield says.

Whether staring down from the Senate presiding officer's chair, or managing his Appropriations Committee's legislation, Byrd takes pride that he has not interfered with his successor, Majority Leader George J. Mitchell, D-Me.

"Extraordinary kudos go to Byrd," says Fowler, a member of Mitchell's circle. "He has not second-guessed Mitchell, except when Mitchell asks. He walked away and held his peace."

"I severed my ties with that responsibility," Byrd says simply. "I had it many years, I walked away from it, I don't want it again. I am where I want to be and doing what I want to do."

WEST VIRGINIA SENATOR Robert Byrd's junior colleague John D. Rockefeller IV seems to have taken a leaf from Byrd's book on how to achieve power in the Senate, as he too has gained prestige in the body by paying careful attention to its norms and customs. Unlike Byrd, the native son of a coal miner, Rockefeller, the scion of a dynasty, moved to West Virginia in 1964 to work in a poverty program. He stayed and was elected to the state legislature in 1966, where he served one term. Then in 1968 he successfully ran for the state-wide office of West Virginia Secretary of State. After a brief stint as a college president in the 1970s, he became governor of West Virginia in 1977 and was reelected in 1980, serving the two terms allowed by the state constitution. Although Rockefeller has presidential ambitions, he has achieved Senate power not by grandstanding and seeking high visibility but in the "old-fashioned" way—by hard work, respect for colleagues, and developing a reputation for policy expertise—as the following account of his Senate career illustrates.

28 Julie Rovner
ROCKEFELLER'S PATH
TO SENATE POWER

In an era of new-age, sound-bite, press-release politics, John D. Rockefeller IV has chosen a decidedly old-fashioned path to power in the Senate.

Rockefeller, D-W.Va., whose very name commands attention, spent his first years in the Senate firmly on the back benches, learning the chamber's folkways, attending to committee work and familiarizing himself with the issues.

That was a marked contrast to some other members of the Class of 1984, such as Senators Al Gore, D-Tenn., Phil Gramm, R-Tex., and Tom Harkin, D-Iowa, who sought and won high visibility. And it surprised pundits who had been touting Rockefeller as presidential timber from the day he entered politics.

But Rockefeller's slow, steady course is paying off. Through labor and luck, he is heading into his first re-election campaign as an emerging Senate power. He commands the respect of Senate leaders and is wielding influence in his committees. As the spotlight he has shunned seeks him more often, talk of presidential possibilities could resurface.

Rockefeller has made his mark most clearly in health policy. Last year, his first as chairman of the Finance Subcommittee on Medicare and Long-Term

From *Congressional Quarterly Weekly Report,* January 27, 1990, pp. 236–239. Copyright 1990 by Congressional Quarterly, Inc. Reprinted by permission.

Care, he was credited with pushing to fruition a far-reaching overhaul of the way Medicare pays doctors.

Now, as chairman of the Pepper Commission, a bipartisan, bicameral group of health policy makers, he is facing a tougher challenge—one that could either polish his reputation as a political heavyweight or tarnish it before it gains much luster.

The commission is to make recommendations by March 1 on how to pay for long-term care for the elderly and how to ensure access to health services for the estimated 31 million Americans who lack health insurance. Both questions have defied piecemeal attempts to address them, and both divide policy makers and health-industry experts.

Rockefeller, a relative novice at health policy, has his hands full in seeking a consensus among 15 strongwilled commission members, nearly all of whom have more expertise.

Because it includes virtually all of the health experts in Congress, the commission will have a head start on legislative action for its recommendations—assuming it can agree on some. But unless Rockefeller, as chairman, can sell the commission's product to a wider audience, he will glean little political benefit from it. And that is an area where he remains untested.

Physician-Payment Reform

In a world where professional talkers abound, Rockefeller has made a specialty of listening.

"You know what he did the first year or so? All he did was listen," says Dave Durenberger, R-Minn., a Finance colleague and one of four Pepper Commission vice chairmen. "And he still does; that's his style."

Rockefeller's most striking achievement to date was his unexpected success in winning enactment last fall of an overhaul of Medicare's physician-payment system.

As part of budget-reconciliation legislation (HR 3299), both chambers passed legislation to shift Medicare to a new fee schedule that pays doctors based on the relative work, training and expenses required to provide a given treatment of service. The bills differed in several important ways, including their provisions to gain control over the volume of services that doctors provide.

Rockefeller and Durenberger, the subcommittee's ranking Republican, set out to forge a compromise.

Rockefeller and his staff "got everybody together—they consulted early and often with both House subcommittee chairmen and interest groups," says one lobbyist who was involved in the process. "They went the extra mile to involve everybody in the takeoff so they would all be there at the landing. . . . It was a textbook case of the right way to do it."

Despite their efforts, however, the plan nearly died. By Nov. 17, House and

Senate negotiators had agreed on most health-related elements of the recon-
ciliation package—but not on physician-payment reform.

At that point, Rockefeller says, "I was told it was dead and lay off it"—an
order from Finance Chairman Lloyd Bentsen, D-Tex., that he chose to defy.
"I wasn't going to stand for it. It was stupid" to let something so important
die so close to the finish line.

Instead, Rockefeller set up a meeting for the following day—a Saturday—
which he practically begged leading conferees to attend.

Henry A. Waxman, D-Calif., author of one of the competing House plans,
was at synagogue that morning. But when he got home, he says, "there were
half a dozen messages on my answering machine from Jay asking me to come
to the meeting." He went.

"He's not an easy man to say 'no' to," says Rep. Bill Gradison, Ohio,
ranking Republican on the Ways and Means Subcommittee on Health.

Durenberger says, "There's a genuineness in his interest in your opinion
that makes it difficult when he says, 'Yes, but. . . .' It's pretty hard when he's
been nice to you not to be nice to him."

After hours of hard bargaining, then and on subsequent days, a compromise was reached, with Rockefeller pushing the whole way. Gradison says,
"The last rites were being administered when he came along. . . . Clearly, he
deserves credit for saving it."

Bentsen, too, praises Rockefeller's accomplishment: "He never gave up. He
was very tenacious."

Tougher Going Ahead

Although Rockefeller bucked his elders on the question of when to quit,
he has been slower to venture his views on points of policy.

Because he has considerably less expertise in health matters than most of
those he works with, Rockefeller sees himself primarily as a mediator. "I
come at everything with the idea of, 'Is there a way of solving this, and can
we do it together?' I'm bipartisan by my nature and I think that helps and
I think Republicans respond to that."

Some say Rockefeller can be too accommodating. "Jay doesn't want to
offend anybody," says Rep. Pete Stark, D-Calif., chairman of the Ways and
Means Health Subcommittee and a Pepper Commission vice chairman. "But
at some point you've got to decide where the winners and losers are."

That time may be at hand with the Pepper Commission, where things so
far are not running very smoothly. Two days of closed meetings in Annapolis,
Md., this month failed to produce a consensus. Although the group is scheduled to meet again Feb. 5, Rockefeller has already moved back the deadline
for decision making.

There also have been complaints about the secrecy surrounding the proceedings. Rockefeller refused to release his own working proposal, and in

some cases, commission members have been given documents at meetings only to have them taken back at meetings' end.

"There's been no other choice," says Rockefeller. "The secret to the Pepper Commission is that I have caused people to come out with what they really think . . . And you can't do that in public. You can't embarrass or put on the spot senior people like that."

Minding P's and Q's

Rockefeller's deference to "senior people" is part and parcel of his old-fashioned approach to building a Senate power base.

Instead of going for the headlines, he chose, when he first arrived, what he calls "the Bradley model," after fellow Finance Committee Democrat Bill Bradley, N.J., another nose-to-the-grindstone senator who figures prominently in presidential speculation.

"I used to talk about it with Bill Bradley," Rockefeller says. "Don't say much, work hard, learn stuff, and when you have, then go get it."

Indeed, Rockefeller remembers being invited to join "a classic early 'let's get on TV [junket]' with a group of nameless senators . . . who went roaring down to Central America within seven minutes of getting sworn in. And instinctively, I knew the answer was no."

His low-key approach also "reflects somewhat my way of doing things," says Rockefeller, who "can't wait to open up and start reading" briefing books for hearings, and who color-codes his highlighting. "There's a certain element of personality in there."

Democrat Robert C. Byrd, his senior West Virginia colleague and chairman of the Appropriations Committee, has encouraged Rockefeller.

"The way to become influential in this body is to know your subject well, and the other people will start to listen to you. . . . Senator Rockefeller is doing that," Byrd says. "He doesn't want to get ahead on his name. He wants to be judged on his merit."

Seizing Opportunities

Of course, being in the right place at the right time hasn't hurt.

"If Claude Pepper hadn't died, he wouldn't be chairman of this commission," says Waxman, chairman of the Energy and Commerce Subcommittee on Health and the Environment.

Rockefeller agrees, noting that but for George J. Mitchell's ascent to majority leader, he also would not be chairman of a Finance subcommittee.

But he has not been shy about taking advantage of opportunities when they arise. "He begged me to let him be chairman when Claude died. He loves this stuff," Stark says. "This is not something he didn't go after. He was not a blushing, bashful virgin bride dragged to the altar by his hair."

Still, Rockefeller seems considerably less drawn to the limelight than some of his colleagues.

"That old line about workhorses and show horses is really true," Majority Leader Mitchell, D-Maine, said in an interview. "The senators know who does that work."

Mitchell and Bentsen have given Rockefeller more than mere accolades.

Bentsen wrote 1987 legislation creating the National Commission on Children, a 36-member group assigned to develop policies to promote the health and well-being of children. He saw to it that Rockefeller was appointed to the commission and supported his selection as chairman. The commission, whose members include comedian Bill Cosby and pediatrician T. Berry Brazleton, is scheduled to complete deliberations in 1991.

Bentsen also split the former Health Subcommittee, headed by Mitchell in the 100th Congress, into two panels so that Rockefeller could be a subcommittee chairman.

"I thought he would be effective," Bentsen says. "He's fulfilled my expectations."

Mitchell, whom Rockefeller supported for majority leader in 1988, appointed Rockefeller to replace him on the high-visibility Pepper Commission. Rockefeller became chairman last June, after the death of the man for whom the commission was named, Rep. Claude Pepper, D-Fla.

Now, even though he originally intended to specialize in trade on the Finance Committee, Rockefeller has become captivated with health policy, much as Mitchell was before him.

"It's sort of replaced defense at center stage," Rockefeller says, "except defense only ruined the national budget. Health ruins the family, corporate and national budgets and destroys people right and left and leaves out people right and left."

Rockefeller says he plans to keep his primary focus on health.

"I can't think of anything more useful that I could be doing in the Senate than working on that. For my state, for the country and for my own sense of satisfaction.

The Future Is Now?

If Rockefeller's emergence into the Senate spotlight thrusts him into the presidential sweepstakes speculation, it won't be the first time.

In 1968, *The Wall Street Journal*—in a story headlined "Will Rockefeller Be President in 1976?"—touted the 30-year-old's bright political future on the strength of no more than his primary-election nomination to be West Virginia's secretary of state.

Two years later, when Secretary of State Rockefeller helped engineer the primary-election defeat of several sitting state senators, *The New York Times* took up the chorus. "In a party that is searching desperately for younger national leaders, Mr. Rockefeller is often mentioned as a future presidential or vice presidential possibility," wrote *Times* political correspondent R. W. Apple Jr.

Rockefeller's 1972 loss to Republican Arch A. Moore Jr. in his first race for governor dimmed his star somewhat. But he came back to win the governorship in 1976, and in 1983, as he was finishing his second term as chief executive, the presidential talk was raised again, this time by *People* magazine, which called him "one heir apparent" in the "early line on the 1988 presidential race."

So is he tired of being asked when he will run for president?

"Politicians don't get tired of that," he says, smiling, then quickly denying that anything is imminent. "I'm not without ambition, but there's no sense of pressure within me to respond to that ambition now because I'm so thoroughly happy with what I'm doing."

And he insists that people shouldn't read anything into the fact that in 1989 he made his first "road" speech as senator outside West Virginia in the ever-important presidential primary state of New Hampshire.

He used the opportunity to chide his audience about the acid-rain problem from the perspective of a coal-state politician. "I got no applause during the speech, but boy, did they listen," he says.

Country Roads

The incident was typical. Although known for his self-deprecating humor, Rockefeller is serious about his adopted state.

"My eyes are squarely on West Virginia," he says, noting that he keeps a third of his staff at home working on more than 14,000 constituent cases. "I really work hard on the state."

Rockefeller's road to West Virginia began in Washington nearly 30 years ago. R. Sargent Shriver, President John F. Kennedy's brother-in-law and first director of the Peace Corps, enlisted him as his assistant in 1961. Although Rockefeller had voted for Kennedy, he was a registered Republican at the time.

"I grew up in a Republican family," he says, noting that his uncle Nelson had sought the 1960 GOP presidential nomination.

But Jay Rockefeller, like countless others his age, was swept up in the Kennedy allure.

"It was a time in Washington that was just indescribable," he says. "It was so idealistic, and government was terrific and public service was the best thing to be in."

His becoming a Democrat, he says, "just clearly had to be. . . . And what's odd is that literally 80 percent of my generation" in the Rockefeller family "are Democrats. And serious Democrats; participating, activist, liberals."

Besides becoming a Democrat, Rockefeller abandoned his early specialty in the Far East, and in 1964 joined the Peace Corps' new domestic counterpart, VISTA, as a volunteer.

"I didn't go to West Virginia to do politics. I went to West Virginia to do VISTA," he says. He decided to stay "because it was so direct. It was direct action. It wasn't sitting there writing books about Japan. . . . And that led to politics."

Characteristically, he started at the bottom and worked his way up.

First came two years in the West Virginia House of Delegates, followed by a term as secretary of state, then the failed run for governor, after which he briefly served as president of West Virginia Wesleyan College.

In 1976 Rockefeller won the governorship, and in 1980 he was re-elected, defeating 1972 victor Moore, who was seeking to make a comeback.

The $12 million in personal funds Rockefeller spent on the 1980 race, which included buying television time in the Washington, D.C., and Pittsburgh markets to reach West Virginia voters, gave rise to the ubiquitous "Make Him Spend It All, Arch!" bumper stickers.

Unable to serve more than two consecutive terms, Rockefeller, to no one's surprise, ran for the Senate in 1984, when Jennings Randolph (1958–85) retired.

But during his second term as governor, the state "really got bombed by the recession," as Rockefeller put it. As governor, he took much of the blame. "Presiding over 21 percent unemployment is not exactly exhilarating," he says.

Indeed, it took another $12 million campaign to beat political neophyte John Raese, and even then, Rockefeller won with only 52 percent of the votes. Polls also showed he had a disturbingly high 40 percent negative rating.

"When he went to Washington, the political advice he got to cut down on that negative rating was just to stay quiet," says Dick Grimes, political editor of the *Charleston Daily Mail.*

Rockefeller concedes that was part of the reason for his early low profile. "I wanted to be sure that my own people in West Virginia didn't think I was coming up here to showboat or run for the presidency; that I really cared about the job, which I do."

But that was not the only reason. "I think that what counts around here is that you have a collegial relationship with your colleagues; that you're known to be serious; that you're known to work hard," Rockefeller says.

The Name

Rockefeller is not eager to embarrass himself, either. He is acutely conscious of the benefits and the responsibilities that go with his name.

"It is not exactly a heavy burden," Rockefeller says. "If you can think of five minuses, I can think of 100 pluses. I'm very proud to be that and very happy to be that, and it's allowed me to do a lot of things in my life that I otherwise probably could not or would not have done."

Not that others don't tease him about it. During Senate consideration Nov. 7 of legislation to increase the federal debt ceiling, Rockefeller wanted to offer an amendment to ensure continued funding of health benefits for retired coal miners.

Gramm quipped, "I am tempted to say to my dear colleague from West Virginia that if he wants to offer that amendment so bad, maybe he could float the national debt for a few days."

Rockefeller rejects suggestions from some critics that he could have put his name and fortune to better use faster.

For example, when Sen. Robert F. Kennedy, D-N.Y., was assassinated in 1968, Nelson Rockefeller, then governor of New York, wanted to appoint Jay to replace him.

The younger Rockefeller refused. "That would have been one of the worst exercises of judgment, both moral and political, that I could think of. . . . I turned it down because I was in West Virginia; I was committed to West Virginia and running for secretary of state in West Virginia."

Among other things, he says, "I was not ready to be in the Senate" in 1968. By taking his time, he says, "I really know West Virginia intimately. In 20 years in state politics, it's hard to explain in Washington, D.C., but it gives me a grounding, some practical sense."

Now, he says, "There's a lot of things I know that a lot of other folks here don't. Those of us who have been governors, who have come up through state politics, have dealt with people intimately."

THE
COURTS

Chapter
Six

Character, personality, and style help to shape the judiciary at all levels. A true picture of the judicial process would not be complete without a personality profile of the actors that are involved, including judges, prosecuting attorneys, lawyers for the defense, plaintiffs and defendants, and, in some cases, jurors. At the trial level the drama of the courtroom is shaped by all of the personalities who take part. The full-fledged and celebrated criminal trial is, however, a rarity, and personality usually affects the judicial process outside the public view.

The character of judges inevitably has a profound effect on the judicial process. At the trial court level their personalities determine the way in which they run their courts. At the appellate level, and particularly on the Supreme Court, their personalities and styles determine the effect they will have on colleagues. The character of judges has been molded long before they reach the bench. Certainly it would be profitable to apply James Barber's character classification of presidents to judges. An active-positive judge would deal with cases quite differently than would an active-negative judge. The value system of the former would be better developed and more likely to affect opinions without at the same time being rigid. An active-negative judge would be opportunistic on the bench and, particularly below the Supreme Court, would always be keeping an eye out for the possibility of higher judicial or political office. The character of some judges will cause them to seek the emulation of colleagues, and other will exhibit a strongly independent and iconoclastic streak. Some judges will attempt to control everything that goes on in their courts and will seek rights of defendants who they feel deserve a break. The character of every courtroom will reflect the personality and style of the presiding judge.

The Supreme Court is unique, not only because its decisions are far-reaching, but also because it is affected more by group dynamics among the justices than other courts are. Coalitions are formed, and pressures are used to change minds. The effectiveness of the chief justice and the influence of other justices largely depend on their personalities. A strong and persuasive personality can often change colleagues' minds. Potentially an important leader, the chief justice presides over the weekly, secret conferences of the justices, gives his or her opinion first, and votes last. Voting with the majority determines which majority justice will write the opinion. A forceful chief justice can bring unity to a divided Court and in some cases bring about unanimity on politically crucial decisions,

259

such as the desegregation decision in *Brown v. Board of Education,* decided in October 1953. After the Brown case had been taken up by the Court, Earl Warren used his considerable powers of persuasion and his highly personal leadership style to bring unanimity to a highly divided Court.[1]

Judicial decision making, at both Supreme Court and lower levels, is a far more fluid process than is commonly known. In commenting on Supreme Court decisions in the decade that ended with the Brown decision, one scholar concluded on the basis of the private papers of Supreme Court justices that "hardly any major decision in this decade was free of significant alteration of vote and language before announcement to the public."[2] Justices often change their minds regardless of their seeming ideological commitment. Group pressure has its effects on Supreme Court justices as on ordinary human beings. The "freshman effect" causes instability in voting patterns among new justices to the Supreme Court.[3] Freshman justices may follow rather than lead their colleagues during their initial period of assimilation into the Court, although this certainly was not true of Chief Justice Earl Warren, who was a pivotal justice from the time he was appointed in 1953.

Most Supreme Court justices have had little or no prior judicial experience before joining the Court, and almost without exception those justices ranked as great or near-great have been more "political" than "judicial" in their styles.[4] Many of the most effective justices from John Marshall to Earl Warren held elected or appointed political offices and often were highly partisan politicians. This political experience helped to shape their style of operation once on the Court. The Court was viewed as a political arena, in which pressure and persuasion could be used to change the minds of colleagues on cases that had far-reaching ramifications.

Although the Supreme Court is somewhat more cloistered than the other branches of the government, the justices do not remain in isolation from each other or from Congress, the president, and administrative officials. Conflicts between the Court and other branches are often smoothed through personal contacts. While the New Deal Court was turning down much of Roosevelt's New Deal legislation, Justice Harlan F. Stone, at an informal party, gave Frances Perkins, FDR's secretary of labor, the idea to use the taxing and spending

---

[1]See S. Sidney Ulmer, "Earl Warren and the Brown Decision," *Journal of Politics* 33 (1971): 689–702.

[2]J. Woodford Howard, Jr., "On the Fluidity of Judicial Choice," *The American Political Science Review* 52 (March 1968): 43–56, at p. 44.

[3]Ibid., p. 45.

[4]An interesting rating of Supreme Court justices by law school deans and professors of law, history, and political science, undertaken in 1970, may be found in Henry J. Abraham, *Justices and Presidents* (New York: Oxford University Press, 1974), pp. 289–290. Holmes and Cardozo were notable exceptions to usual lack of prior judicial experience among justices ranked as great.

authority of Article 1 to support the Social Security Act.[5] The Court is not supposed to give advisory opinions, but nothing prevents a justice from informally communicating his ideas to the president or member of the administration. Justice Felix Frankfurter remained a close personal friend of Franklin Roosevelt after he was appointed to the Court, and Abe Fortas was a constant political adviser to President Lyndon B. Johnson. Hugo Black, who wrote the majority opinion in the 1952 *Steel Seizure* case, which held that President Truman did not have independent constitutional authority to seize the steel mills, invited President Truman to dinner to help keep the president and the Court on good terms with each other. Justice William O. Douglas, who was present, described the incident in his autobiography as follows:

> Hugo loved company and long conversations. His spacious garden in his exquisite Alexandria home was ideal for that purpose during spring and summer. He loved to entertain there; and when, during the Korean War, the Court held on June 2, 1952, that Truman's seizure of the steel mills was unconstitutional, Hugo asked me what I thought of his idea of inviting Truman to his home for an evening after the decision came down. I thought it a capital idea. So in two weeks Hugo extended the invitation and Truman accepted. It was stag dinner, and only Truman and members of the Court were present. Truman was gracious though a bit testy at the beginning of the evening. But after the bourbon and canapes were passed, he turned to Hugo and said, "Hugo, I don't much care for your law, but, by golly, this bourbon is good." The evening was great step forward in human relations, and to Hugo Black, good human relations were the secret of successful government.[6]

As this anecdote shows, the personalities and styles of the justices affect external as well as internal relationships.

---

[5]Frances Perkins, *The Roosevelt I Knew* (New York: Viking, 1946), p. 286.

[6]William O. Douglas, *Go East Young Man* (New York: Random House, 1974), p. 450.

NOWHERE IN GOVERNMENT IS the impact of character and personality more important than on the Supreme Court. Each week while the Court is in session, the justices meet secretly in conference to deliberate their decisions on cases involving some of the important issues that confront our government, such as discrimination, freedom of speech and press, the death penalty, the busing of schoolchildren, executive privilege, the separation of church and state, and abortion. The decisions of the Court take precedence over those of the president, the Congress, and the state legislatures, and the actions of the Court are unreviewable.

The scales of justice are supposed to be balanced through a rational, deliberative process that carefully and objectively ascertains the facts of individual cases and applies the law. However, the law is not readily defined objectively but requires interpretation to give it meaning. The process of judicial interpretation necessarily involves a high subjective element. It is the subjectivity of the law that permits and even encourages judges to apply their own values and prejudices in making decisions. And, on the Supreme Court, where the justices must work in close contact with their colleagues, interpersonal relationships among "the Brethren" may influence the outcome of a case as much as the ideological orientation of the justices.

The private world of the Supreme Court, like that of the other branches of the government, is characterized by maneuvering among the justices to gain internal power and status. The highly personal and political dimension of Supreme Court decision making has generally been overlooked in the study of constitutional law. The following selection gives a behind-the-scenes view of the role of personalities in the historic Supreme Court decision that held that women have a constitutional right to obtain abortions.

29 Bob Woodward and Scott Armstrong
THE BRETHREN AND
THE ABORTION DECISION

Douglas had long wanted the Court to face the abortion issue head on. The laws in effect in most states, prohibiting or severely restricting the availability of abortions, were infringements of a woman's personal liberty. The broad constitutional guarantee of "liberty," he felt, included the right of a woman to control her body.

Douglas realized, however, that a majority of his colleagues were not likely to give such a sweeping reading to the Constitution on this increasingly volatile issue. He knew also that the two cases now before the Court— challenging restrictive abortion laws in Georgia and Texas (*Doe v. Bolton* and

From *The Brethren* by Bob Woodward and Scott Armstrong. Copyright 1979 by Bob Woodward and Scott Armstrong. Reprinted by permission of Simon & Schuster, Inc.

Roe v. Wade)—did not signal any sudden willingness on the part of the Court to grapple with the broad question of abortions. They had been taken only to determine whether to expand a series of recent rulings limiting the intervention of federal courts in state court proceedings. Could women and doctors who felt that state prosecutions for abortions violated their constitutional rights go into federal courts to stop the state? And could they go directly into federal courts even before going through all possible appeals in the state court system? Douglas knew the Chief wanted to say no to both these jurisdiction questions. He knew the Chief hoped to use these two cases to reduce the number of federal court cases brought by activist attorneys. The two abortion cases were not to be argued primarily about abortion rights, but about jurisdiction. Douglas was doubly discouraged, believing that his side was also going to lose on the jurisdiction issue.

These are difficult cases, the Chief said. No one could really tell how they would come out until the final drafting was done. . . .

Brennan and Marshall counted the vote five to two—Douglas, Brennan, Marshall, Stewart, and Blackmun for striking the laws; the Chief and White dissenting.

Douglas, however, thought there were only four votes to strike the laws. Blackmun's vote was far from certain. He could not be counted on to split with the Chief on such an important issue.

For his part, Blackmun was for some kind of limited ruling against portions of the laws, but he had not decided what to do. . . .

. . . The puzzle was Blackmun.

The Chief's assignment sheet circulated the following afternoon. Each case was listed on the left side in order of the oral argument, the name of the justice assigned to write each decision on the right.

It took Douglas several moments to grasp the pattern of the assignments, and then he was flabbergasted. [Flouting Court procedure,] the Chief had assigned four cases in which Douglas was sure the Chief was not a member of the majority. These included the two abortion cases, which the Chief had assigned to Blackmun. He could barely control his rage as he ran down the list. Was there some mistake? He asked a clerk to check his notes from the conference. Douglas kept a docket book in which he recorded his tabulation of the votes. It was as he suspected. . . .

Never, in Douglas's thirty-three years on the court, had any chief justice tried to assign from the minority in such fashion. For two terms now there had been incidents when the Chief had pleaded ignorance, had claimed he hadn't voted, had changed his vote. Until now they had been isolated instances.

On Saturday, December 18, Douglas drafted a scathing memo to Burger, with copies to the other justices. He, not the Chief, should have assigned the opinions in four of the cases. And, Douglas added, he would assign the opinions as he saw fit.

The Chief's response was back in a day. He conceded error in two of the

cases, but insisted that the voting in the two abortion cases was too complicated. "There were . . . literally not enough columns to mark up an accurate
reflection of the voting," Burger wrote. "I therefore marked down no votes
and said this was a case that would have to stand or fall on the writing, when
it was done.

"This is still my view of how to handle these two sensitive cases, which,
I might add, are quite probable candidates for reargument."

Douglas ascribed to Burger the most blatant political motives. Nixon favored restrictive abortion laws. Faced with the possibility that the Court
might strike abortion laws down in a presidential-election year, the Chief
wanted to stall the opinion, Douglas concluded.

Blackmun was by far the slowest writer on the Court. The year was nearly
half over and he had yet to produce a first circulation in a simple business
case that had been argued the first week. . . . It was the kind of case in which
Douglas produced drafts within one week of conference. But in the abortion
cases, Douglas had a deeper worry. The Chief was trying to manipulate the
outcome.

Blackmun might circulate a draft striking portions of the restrictive abortion laws. But as a judicial craftsman, his work was crude. A poor draft would
be likely to scare off Stewart, who was already queasy, and leave only four
votes. Or if Blackmun himself were to desert the position—a distinct possibility—precious time would be lost. Either defection would leave only a four-
man majority. It would be difficult to argue that such a major decision should
be handed down on a four-to-three vote. There would be increasing pressure
to put the cases over for the sort of case that Nixon had in mind when he
chose Powell and Rehnquist.

Blackmun was both pleased and frightened by the assignment. It was a
no-win proposition. No matter what he wrote, the opinion would be controversial. Abortion was too emotional, the split in society too great. Either way,
he would be hated and vilified.

But from Blackmun's point of view, the Chief had little choice but to select
him. Burger could not afford to take on such a controversial case himself,
particularly from the minority. Douglas was the Court's mischievous liberal,
the rebel, and couldn't be the author. Any abortion opinion Douglas wrote
would be widely questioned outside the Court, and his extreme views might
split rather than unify the existing majority. Lastly, Blackmun had noticed
a deterioration in the quality of Douglas's opinions; they had become increasingly superficial.

Brennan was certainly as firm a vote for striking down the state abortion
laws as there was on the Court. But Brennan was the Court's only Catholic.
As such, Blackmun reasoned, he could not be expected to be willing to take
the heat from Catholic antiabortion groups. Marshall could not be the author
for similar reasons: an opinion by the Court's only black could be unfairly

perceived as specifically designed for blacks. That left only Stewart. Black- mun believed that Stewart could certainly relish the assignment, but he clearly had trouble going very far.

Blackmun was convinced that he alone had the medical background and sufficient patience to sift through the voluminous record for the scientific data on which to base a decision. He was deeply disturbed by Douglas's assump- tion that the Chief had some malicious intent in assigning the abortion cases to him. He was *not* a Minnesota Twin.

True, Blackmun had known the Chief since they were small children and had gone to Sunday school together. They had lived four or five blocks apart in the blue-collar Daytons Bluff section of St. Paul. Neither family had much money during the Depression. The two boys had kept in touch until Black- mun went to a technical high school.

Blackmun's seven years at Harvard, however, put the two men worlds apart. Burger had finished local college and night law school in six years and was already practicing law when Blackmun came back to clerk for a judge on the court of Appeals. Blackmun was best man at Burger's wedding, but the two drifted apart again as they established very different law practices.

Blackmun tried to tell his story every chance he got. His hands in his pockets, jingling change uncomfortably, he would explain how he had prac- ticed in Minneapolis, where large law firms concentrated on serving major American corporations. Burger had practiced in St. Paul, across the river, in the political, wheeler-dealer atmosphere of a state capital.

"A Minneapolis firm," Blackmun would say, "will never practice in St. Paul or vice versa." Left unsaid was the disdain so obvious in the Minneapolis legal community for St. Paul lawyers.

But Blackmun was a hesitant and reserved storyteller, and he was never sure that the others got the message. Douglas, however, should have realized by now that Harry Blackmun was no Warren Burger twin.

Blackmun had long thought Burger an uncontrollable, blustery braggart. Now, once again in close contact with him, he was at once put off and amused by the Chief's exaggerated pomposity, his callous disregard for the feelings of his colleagues, his self-aggrandizing style. "He's been doing that since he was four," he once told Stewart.

Blackmun was just as aware as Douglas was of the Chief's attempts to use his position to manipulate the Court. Douglas was correct to despise that sort of thing. But this time, Blackmun felt, Douglas was wrong. When he arrived at Court, Blackmun had assumed the Chief's job as scrivener for the confer- ence. Burger had finally given up trying to keep track of all the votes and positions taken in conference, and had asked Blackmun to keep notes and stay behind to brief the Clerk of the Court. Even then the Chief sometimes misstated the results. Blackmun would deftly field the Chief's hesitations, filling in when he faltered. When Burger misinformed the Clerk of the Court, Blackmun's cough would cue him.

"Do you recall what happened there, Harry?" the Chief would then say. "My notes seem to be a bit sporadic."

Blackmun would fill in the correct information as if Burger had initiated the request.

Part of the problem was that the Chief spread himself too thin. He accepted too many social, speaking, and ceremonial engagements, and exhibited too little affection for the monastic, scholarly side of the Court's life. As a result, Burger was often unprepared for orals or conference. Too often, he had to wait and listen in order to figure out which issues were crucial to the outcome. His grasp of the cases came from the summaries, usually a page or less, of the certified memos his clerks prepared. The Chief rarely read the briefs or the record before oral argument.

The problem was compounded by Burger's willingness to change his position in conference, or his unwillingness to commit himself before he had figured out which side had a majority. Then, joining the majority, he could control the assignment. Burger had strained his relationship with everyone at the table to the breaking point. It was as offensive to Blackmun as it was to the others. But one had to understand the Chief. For all his faults, here was a self-made man who had come up the ladder rung by rung. Blackmun did not begrudge him his attempts at leadership.

The abortion assignment really amounted to nothing more than a request that Blackmun take first crack at organizing the issues. It was one of those times when the conference had floundered, when the briefs and oral arguments had been inadequate, when the seemingly decisive issue in the case, jurisdiction, had evaporated. The Court had been left holding the bull by the tail.

Blackmun was not so naive as to think that the Chief had given him the abortion cases with the intention of having him find a broad constitutional right to abortion. But he was distressed by Douglas's implicit suggestion that he was unfit for the assignment or was somehow involved in a deception.

Blackmun also knew that he, after all, had a unique appreciation of the problems and strengths of the medical profession. At Mayo, he had watched as Doctors Edward C. Kendall and Philip S. Hench won the Nobel prize for research in arthritis. He rejoiced with other doctors after their first successful heart-bypass operation, then suffered with them after they lost their next four patients. He sat up late nights with the surgical staff to review hospital deaths in biweekly meetings, and recalled them in detail. He grew to respect what dedicated physicians could accomplish. These had been terribly exciting years for Blackmun. He called them the best ten years of his life.

If a state licensed a physician to practice medicine, it was entrusting him with the right to make medical decisions. State laws restricting abortions interfered with those medical judgments. Physicians were always somewhat unsure about the possible legal ramifications of their judgments. To completely restrict an operation like abortion, normally no more dangerous than minor surgery, or to permit it only with the approval of a hospital committee or the concurrence of other doctors, was a needless infringement of the discretion of the medical profession.

Blackmun would do anything he could to reduce the anxiety of his colleagues except to spurn the assignment. The case was not so much a legal task as an opportunity for the Court to ratify the best possible medical opinion. He would take the first crack at the abortion case. At the least, he could prepare a memo to clarify the issues.

As was his custom, Douglas rushed through a first draft on the cases five days after conference. He decided not to circulate it, but to sit back and wait for Blackmun. He was still bitter toward Burger, whom he had taken to calling "this Chief," reserving "The Chief" as an accolade fitting only for retired Chief Justice Earl Warren. But Douglas broke his usual rule against lobbying and paid a visit to Blackmun. Though he would have much preferred that Brennan write the draft, he told Blackmun, "Harry, I would have assigned the opinion to you anyway."

Reassured, Blackmun withdrew to his regular hideaway, the justices' second-floor library, where he worked through the winter and spring, initially without even a law clerk to help with research.

Brennan, too, had little choice but to wait for Blackmun's draft. But in the interval, he spotted a case that he felt might help Blackmun develop a constitutional grounding for a right to abortion. Brennan was writing a majority opinion overturning birth-control activist Bill Baird's conviction for distributing birth-control devices without a license *(Eisenstadt v. Baird)*. He wanted to use the case to extend to individuals the right to privacy that was given to married couples by the 1965 Connecticut birth-control case.

Brennan was aware that he was unlikely to get agreement on such a sweeping extension. He circulated his opinion with a carefully worded paragraph at the end. "If the right to privacy means anything, it is the right of the individual, married or single, to be free from unwarranted governmental intrusion into matters so fundamentally affecting a person as the decision whether to bear or beget a child."

That case dealt only with contraception—the decision to "beget" a child. He included the reference to the decision to "bear" a child with the abortion case in mind. Brennan hoped the language would help establish a constitutional basis, under the right to privacy, for a woman's right to abortion.

Since the last paragraph was not the basis for the decision, Stewart could join it without renouncing his dissent in the 1956 case. Brennan got Stewart's vote.

But Blackmun was holding back. The Chief was lobbying Blackmun not to join Brennan's draft. Brennan's clerks urged their boss to lobby Blackmun.

Brennan refused. Blackmun reminded him, he said, of former justice Charles E. Whittaker, who had been paralyzed by indecisiveness. Whittaker's indecision had ended in a nervous breakdown and his resignation. Former Justice Felix Frankfurter had misunderstood Whittaker's indecision and had spent hours lobbying him. Instead of influencing him, Frankfurter had drawn Whittaker's resentment. No, Brennan said, he would not lobby Blackmun.

Blackmun finally decided not to join Brennan's opinion, but simply to concur in the result. That worried Brennan. Without adopting some logic similar to that provided in the contraception case, Blackmun would have difficulty establishing a right to abortion on grounds of privacy.

With the official arrival of Powell and Rehnquist, the Chief scheduled a January conference to discuss which cases should be put over for reargument before the new nine-man Court. Burger suggested that cases with a four-to-three vote should be reargued. His list included the abortion cases, . . .

Blackmun spent his time—apart from oral argument, conferences, and a bare minimum of office routine—in the justices' library. Awesome quantities of medical, as well as legal, books were regularly carried in. But all indications pointed toward no circulation of a first draft until much later in the spring. . . .

Blackmun began each day by breakfasting with his clerks in the Court's public cafeteria, and clerks from the other chambers had a standing invitation to join them. Blackmun would often spot a clerk from another chamber eating alone and invite him over. He seemed, at first, the most open, unassuming, and gracious of the justices.

Breakfast-table conversation generally began with sports, usually baseball, and then moved on to the morning's headlines. There was an unspoken rule that any discussion of cases was off limits. Where other justices might openly debate cases with the clerks, Blackmun awkwardly side-stepped each attempt. The law in general was similarly out of bounds. Blackmun turned the most philosophical of discussions about law around to his own experience, or to the clerk's family, or the performance of a younger sibling in school.

The clerks in his own chambers saw a different side of Blackmun which betrayed more of the pressure that he felt. The stories were petty. An office window left open all night might set him off on a tirade. It was not the security that worried Blackmun, but the broken social contract—all clerks were supposed to close all windows each night. Number-two pencils, needle-sharp, neatly displayed in the pencil holder, need include only one number three or a cracked point to elicit a harsh word. If Blackmun wanted a document photocopied, and somehow the wrong one came back, he might simply fling it aside. An interruption, even for some important question, might be repulsed testily.

The mystery of the Blackmun personality deepened. His outbursts varied in intensity and usually passed quickly. "Impatient moods," his secretary called them. But they made life more difficult; they added an extra tension.

Yet none of his Court family—clerks, secretaries, or his messenger—judged Blackmun harshly. They all knew well enough the extraordinary pressures, real and imagined, that he worked under.

From his first day at the Court, Blackmun had felt unworthy, unqualified, unable to perform up to standard. He felt he could equal the Chief and Marshall, but not the others. He became increasingly withdrawn and professorial. He did not enjoy charting new paths for the law. He was still learning. The issues were too grave, the information too sparse. Each new question was barely answered, even tentatively, when two more questions appeared on the horizon. Blackmun knew that his colleagues were concerned about what they perceived as his indecisiveness. But what others saw as an inability to make decisions, he felt to be a deliberate withholding of final judgment until all the facts were in, all the arguments marshaled, analyzed, documented.

It was a horribly lonely task. Blackmun worked by himself, beginning with a long memo from one of his clerks, reading each of the major briefs, carefully digesting each of the major opinions that circulated, laboriously drafting his own opinions, checking each citation himself, refining his work through a dozen drafts to take into account each justice's observations. He was unwilling, moreover, to debate the basic issues in a case, even in chambers with his own clerks. He preferred that they write him memos.

Wearing a gray or blue cardigan sweater, Blackmun hid away in the recesses of the justices' library, and his office had instructions not to disturb him there. The phone did not ring there, and not even the Chief violated his solitude. Working at a long mahogany table lined on the opposite edge with a double row of books, Blackmun took meticulous notes. He spent most of his time sorting facts and fitting them to the law in a desperate attempt to discover inevitable conclusions. He tried to reduce his risks by mastering every detail, as if the case were some huge math problem. Blackmun felt that if all the steps were taken, there could be only one answer.

These abortion cases were his greatest challenge since he came to the Court. Beyond the normal desire to produce an opinion that would win the respect of his peers in the legal community, Blackmun also wanted an opinion that the medical community would accept, one that would free physicians to exercise their professional judgment.

As general counsel at the Mayo Clinic, Blackmun had advised the staff on the legality of abortions the hospital had performed. Many of them would not have qualified under the Texas and Georgia laws now in question.

Blackmun plowed through both common law and the history of English and American law on the subject. He was surprised to find that abortion had been commonly accepted for thousands of years, and that only in the nineteenth century had it become a crime in the United States. At that time, abortion had been a very risky operation, often fatal. The criminal laws had been enacted largely to protect pregnant women.

The use of antiseptics and the availability of antibiotics now made abortion relatively safe, particularly in the first few months of pregnancy. The mortality rates of women undergoing early abortions were presently lower than the mortality rates for women with normal childbirths. That medical reality was central for Blackmun. It was itself a strong medical justification for permitting early abortions.

A decision to abort was one that Blackmun hoped he would never face in his own family. He presumed that his three daughters felt that early abortions should be allowed. He claimed to be unsure of his wife Dottie's position. But she told one of his clerks, who favored lifting the restrictions, that she was doing everything she could to encourage her husband in that direction. "You and I are working on the same thing," she said. "Me at home and you at work."

By mid-May, after five months of work, Blackmun was still laboring over his memorandum. Finally, he let one of his clerks look over a draft. As usual, he made it clear that he did not want any editing. The clerk was astonished. It was crudely written and poorly organized. It did not settle on any analytical framework, nor did it explain on what basis Blackmun had arrived at the apparent conclusion that women had a right to privacy, and thus a right to abortion. Blackmun had avoided extending the right of privacy, or stating that the right to abortion stemmed from that right. He seemed to be saying that a woman could get an abortion in the early period of pregnancy. The reason, however, was lost in a convoluted discussion of the "viability of the fetus," the point at which the fetus could live outside the womb. Blackmun had added the general notion that as the length of the pregnancy increased, the states' interest in regulating and prohibiting abortions also increased. But there was no real guidance from which conclusions could be drawn. Blackmun had simply asserted that the Texas law was vague and thus unconstitutional.

The clerk realized that the opinion could not settle any constitutional question. It did not assert, or even imply, that abortion restrictions in the early months of pregnancy were unconstitutional. The result of this opinion would be that restrictive laws, if properly defined by the states, could be constitutional.

The draft seemed to fly in the face of Blackmun's statements to his clerks. "We want to definitely solve this," he had told them. But he seemed to be avoiding a solution.

In the Georgia case, he had found that the law infringed on a doctor's professional judgment, his right to give advice to his patients. Blackmun proceeded from the doctor's point of view; a woman's right to seek and receive medical advice did not seem an issue.

Blackmun's clerk, who favored an opinion that would establish a woman's constitutional right to abortion, began the laborious task of trying to rehabilitate the draft. But Blackmun resisted any modification of his basic reasoning or his conclusions. He circulated the memo to all chambers with few changes.

Stewart was disturbed by the draft. Aside from its inelegant construction and language, it seemed to create a *new* affirmative constitutional right to abortion that was not rooted in any part of the Constitution. Stewart had been expecting a majority opinion. Blackmun's memo did not even have the tone of an opinion, merely of a tentative discussion.

Stewart decided to write his own concurrence, specifying that family-planning decisions, including early abortions, were among the rights encompassed by the Ninth Amendment, which says that all rights not specifically given to the federal or state governments are left to the people. Rather than identify the rights that women or doctors have, Stewart preferred to say that states could not properly interfere in individuals' decisions to have early abortions. He circulated his memo two weeks after Blackmun's but immediately joined Blackmun's original.

Douglas saw no shortage of problems with the Blackmun draft, but Blackmun had come a long way. At least it was a step in the right direction. Though Douglas was still holding on to his concurrence, he did not circulate it. Instead, he joined Blackmun.

At the time, the Court was considering an antitrust case against a utility company, the Otter Tail Power Company, which operated in Minnesota. Douglas saw an opportunity to flatter Blackmun. "Harry, you're not a Minnesota Twin with the Chief," he told him. "I am the real Minnesota Twin, . . . We were both born in Minnesota and you were not."

Blackmun appreciated the point.

"Furthermore, Harry, I belong to the Otter Tail County regulars. You can't belong, because you weren't born there."

Douglas regaled Blackmun with stories of his father's life as an itinerant preacher in Otter Tail County, and he praised Blackmun's abortion draft. It was one of the finest presentations of an issue he had ever seen, he said. Blackmun was ecstatic. Douglas, the greatest living jurist, had freed him of the stigma of being Burger's double. Soon, Blackmun had five votes—his own and those of Douglas, Brennan, Marshall, and Stewart. It was one more than he needed; it would have been a majority even if Powell and Rehnquist had participated.

For White the term had its ups and downs like any other year at the Court. He had been a fierce competitor all his life. He loved to take control of a case, pick out the weaknesses in the other justices' positions, and then watch them react to his own twists and turns as he pushed his own point of view. When he could not, which was often, he took his frustrations to the third-floor gym to play in the clerks' regular full-court basketball game.

Muscling out men thirty years his junior under the boards, White delighted in playing a more competitive game than they did. He dominated the games by alternating savage and effective drives to the basket with accurate two-hand push shots from twenty feet. White consistently pushed off the clerk trying to cover him, calling every conceivable foul against the hapless clerk, while bitching about every foul called against himself. He regularly took the impermissible third step before shooting. The game was serious business for White. Each man was on his own. Teamwork was valuable in order to win, not for its own sake.

One Friday afternoon White was out of position for a rebound, but he went up throwing a hip. A clerk pulled in the ball and White came crashing down off balance and injured his ankle.

The justice came to the office on crutches the next Monday: He would be off the basketball court for the rest of the season. He asked the clerks to keep the reason for his injury secret. The clerks bought him a Fussball game, a modern version of the ancient game of skittles. It was competition, so White enjoyed it, but it lacked for him the thrill of a contact sport like basketball—or law.

On Friday, May 26, Byron White read a draft dissent to Blackmun's abortion decision that one of his clerks had prepared. He then remolded it to his liking. The structure of Blackmun's opinion was juvenile; striking the Texas law for vagueness was simply stupid. The law might have several defects, but vagueness was not among them. The law could not be more specific in delineating the circumstance when abortion was available—it was only to protect the life of the mother.

Blackmun was disturbed by White's attack, but whether it made sense or not, it showed him that he had more work to do. The more he studied and agonized over his own memo, the less pleased he was. He needed more information, more facts, more insight. What was the history of the proscription in the Hippocratic oath which forbade doctors from performing abortions? What was the medical state of the art of sustaining a fetus outside the womb? When did life really begin? When was a fetus fully viable? What were the positions of the American Medical Association, the American Psychiatric Association, the American Public Health Association?

These and dozens of other questions plagued Blackmun. His opinion needed to be stronger. It needed more votes, which could mean wider public acceptance. A nine-man court was essential to bring down such a controversial opinion. "I think we can get Powell," he told his clerks.

One Saturday toward the end of May, the Chief paid Blackmun a visit, leaving his armed chauffeur-bodyguard in the outer office. Blackmun's clerks waited anxiously for hours to find out what case the Chief was lobbying. The Chief finally left, but Blackmun also departed without a word to his clerks. The next week, the Chief shifted sides to provide the crucial fifth vote for Blackmun's majority in an antitrust case against professional baseball (*Flood v. Kuhn*).

The following Saturday, June 3, Blackmun drafted a memorandum withdrawing his abortion opinion. It was already late in the term, he wrote. Such a sensitive case required more research, more consideration. It would take him some time both to accommodate the suggestions of those in the majority, and to respond to the dissenters. Perhaps it would be best if the cases were reargued in the fall. He asked that all copies of his draft memo be returned.

Douglas was once again enraged. The end of the year always involved a crunch. Of course, there was tremendous pressure to put out major opinions without the time to fully refine them. That was the nature of their work. The pressure affected them all. It was typical that Blackmun could not make up his mind and let his opinion go. Douglas had heard that the Chief had been lobbying Blackmun. This time, Burger had gone too far. The opinion had five firm votes. It ought to come down. It was not like cases with only four votes that might change when Powell's and Rehnquist's votes were added. Douglas also did not want to give the Chief the summer to sway Blackmun.

Burger was taking the position that there were now five votes to put the case over to the next term—Blackmun, White, Powell, Rehnquist, and himself. Douglas couldn't believe it. Burger and White were in the minority; they should have no say in what the majority did. And Powell and Rehnquist had not taken part; obviously they could not vote on whether the case should be put over.

The looming confrontation worried Blackmun. There were no written rules on such questions, and Douglas's apparent willingness to push to a showdown would further inflame the issue. Finally, Blackmun turned to Brennan, who was sympathetic. Obviously the opinion could not come down if its author did not want it to come down. But Brennan also wanted it out as soon as possible.

Blackmun said he understood that Douglas did not trust him, but insisted that he was firm for striking down the abortion laws. The vote would go the same way the next year. They might even pick up Powell. That would make the result more acceptable to the public. He would be able to draft a better opinion over the summer.

Brennan was not so certain of Blackmun's firmness. At the same time, he did not want to alienate him. He agreed to tell Douglas that he, too, was going to vote to put the case over for reargument. He was fairly certain Marshall and Stewart would join. That would leave Douglas protesting alone.

Douglas was not pleased by the news of Brennan's defection. But the battle was not yet over. He dashed off a memo, rushed it to the secretaries for typing and to the printers for a first draft. This time, Douglas threatened to play his ace. If the conference insisted on putting the cases over for reargument, he would dissent from such an order, and he would publish the full text of his dissent. Douglas reiterated the protest he had made in December about the Chief's assigning the case to Blackmun, Burger's response and his subsequent intransigence. The senior member of the majority should have assigned the case, Douglas said, . . .

Douglas knew a fifth Nixon appointment was a real possibility on a Court with a seventy-four-year-old man with a pacemaker; with Marshall, who was chronically ill; and with Brennan, who occasionally threatened to quit. . . .

Borrowing a line from a speech he had given in September in Portland, Douglas then made it clear that, despite what he had said earlier, he did in fact view the Chief and Blackmun as Nixon's Minnesota Twins. "Russia once gave its Chief Justice two votes; but that was too strong even for the Russians. . . ."

"I dissent with the deepest regret that we are allowing the consensus of the Court to be frustrated."

Douglas refined his draft three times, circulated it, and left for Goose Prairie.

The Court erupted in debate over whether Douglas was bluffing or was really willing to publish the document. Though sympathetic to his views, Brennan, Marshall, and Stewart could not believe that Douglas would go through with it. No one in the history of the Court had published such a dissent. The Chief might be a scoundrel, but making public the Court's inner machinations was a form of treason. And the reference to the Russian Chief Justice with two votes was particularly rough. They pleaded with Douglas to reconsider. His dissent would undermine the Court's credibility, the principal source of its power. Its strength derived from the public belief that the Court was trustworthy, a nonpolitical deliberative body. Did he intend to undermine all that?

Douglas insisted. He would publish what he felt like publishing. And he would publish this if the request to put over the abortion decision was not withdrawn.

But, the others argued, what good would it do to drag their internal problems into public view?

It would have a sobering influence on Blackmun, Douglas retorted. It would make it harder for him to change his mind over the summer.

Brennan's impatience with Douglas turned to anger. Douglas had become an intellectually lazy, petulant, prodigal child. He was not providing leadership. Douglas was never around when he was needed. His departure for Goose Prairie was typical. He was not even, for that matter, pulling his share of the load, though he certainly contributed more than his share to the tension. The ultimate source of conflict was the Chief. But Douglas too was at fault.

Finally, Brennan gave up arguing.

Blackmun then took it up, pleading with Douglas to reconsider. He insisted that he was committed to his opinion. He would bring it down the same way the next term; more research would perhaps pick up another vote.

Douglas was unconvinced. He needed time to think it over. His clerks would remain instructed to publish the opinion if the cases were put over for reargument.

But Blackmun had made his point. Douglas finally decided that he couldn't publish. It would endanger next term's vote on the abortion cases.

No longer speaking to his own clerks, whom he blamed for slow mail delivery to Goose Prairie, Douglas called Brennan and told him to have his dissent held. A memo came around to the Justices from Douglas's chamber asking for all the copies back.

The conference agreed to put over the abortion cases, but they would not announce their decision until the final day of the term. . . .

Harry Blackmun returned to Rochester, Minnesota, for the summer of 1972, and immersed himself in research at the huge Mayo Clinic medical library. Rochester and the clinic were home to Blackmun, a safe harbor after a stormy term. He worked in a corner of the assistant librarian's office for two weeks without saying a word to anyone on the Mayo staff about the nature of his inquiry.

In his summer office in a Rochester highrise, Blackmun began to organize the research that would bolster his abortion opinion. He talked by phone nearly every day with one of his clerks who had agreed to stay in Washington for the summer. . . .

The clerk who was working on the opinion began to worry that one of the other clerks, strongly opposed to abortions, might try to change their boss's mind. He took no chances. Each night he carefully locked up the work he had been doing for Blackmun. At the end of the summer, he carefully sealed the latest draft in an envelope, put his initials across the tape, and had it locked in Blackmun's desk. Only Blackmun's personal secretary knew where it was.

Powell also made abortion his summer research project. As a young lawyer in Richmond in the 1930s, Powell had heard tales of girls who would "go away" to Switzerland and New York, where safe abortions were available. If someone were willing to pay for it, it was possible to have an abortion.

Powell understood how doctors viewed abortion. His father-in-law had been a leading obstetrician in Richmond, and his two brothers-in-law were obstetricians. Powell had heard all the horrifying stories of unsanitary butchers and coat-hanger abortions.

Nevertheless, Powell came quickly to the conclusion that the Constitution did not provide meaningful guidance. The right to privacy was tenuous; at best it was implied. If there was no way to find an answer in the Constitution, Powell felt he would just have to vote his "gut." He had been critical of justices for doing exactly that; but in abortion, there seemed no choice.

When he returned to Washington, he took one of his law clerks to lunch at the Monocle Restaurant on Capitol Hill. The abortion laws, Powell confided, were "atrocious." His would be a strong and unshakable vote to strike them. He needed only a rationale for his vote.

In a recent lower court case, a federal judge had struck down the Connecticut abortion law. This opinion impressed Powell. The judge had said that moral positions on abortion "about which each side was so sure must remain a personal judgment, one that people may follow in their personal lives and seek to persuade others to follow, but a judgment they may not impose upon others by force of law." That was all the rationale Powell needed.

Brennan and Douglas worried that votes might have shifted since the previous spring. Blackmun remained a question mark, Stewart might defect, and they were not sure what Powell would do.

At conference on October 12, Blackmun made a long, eloquent, and strongly emotional case for striking down the laws. Stewart too seemed ready to join. But the big surprise was Powell. He made it six to three.

Immediately after conference, Douglas called Blackmun to tell him that his presentation had been the finest he had heard at conference in more than thirty years. He hoped the call would sustain Blackmun for the duration.

Before the end of October, Blackmun's new draft in the abortion case was circulated to the various chambers. . . .

The clerks in most chambers were surprised to see the justices, particularly Blackmun, so openly brokering their decision like a group of legislators. There was a certain reasonableness to the draft, some of them thought, but it derived more from medical and social policy than from constitutional law. There was something embarrassing and dishonest about this whole process. It left the Court claiming that the Constitution drew certain lines at trimesters and viability. The Court was going to make a medical policy and force it on the states. As a practical matter, it was not a bad solution. As a constitutional matter, it was absurd. The draft was referred to by some clerks as "Harry's abortion."

By early December, Blackmun's final draft had circulated. Stewart's and Douglas's concurrences were finished, and White's and Rehnquist's dissents were ready. There was still nothing from Burger. . . .

Stewart and Brennan thought he was stalling. The Chief was scheduled to swear in Richard Nixon for his second term as president on January 20. It would undoubtedly be embarrassing for Burger to stand there, swearing in the man who had appointed him, having just supported a sweeping and politically volatile opinion that repudiated that man's views.

At the Friday, January 19, conference, the Chief said that his schedule had been busy, and he still had not gotten to the abortion decision. Stewart figured that, having manipulated a delay until after the inaugural, Burger would acquiesce. The others wanted a Monday, January 22, announcement, three days later, and Burger said that he would have something.

Over the weekend, he wrote a three-paragraph concurrence. Ignoring the sweep of the opinion he was joining, Burger said that one law (Texas) was being struck because it did not permit abortions in instances of rape or incest, and he implied that the other law was being struck because of the "complex" steps that required hospital board certification of an abortion. He did not believe that the opinion would have the "consequences" predicted by dissenters White and Rehnquist, and he was sure that states could still control abortions. "Plainly," he concluded, "the Court today rejects any claim that the Constitution requires abortion on demand."

The day of the scheduled abortion decision the Chief sat in his chambers reading the latest edition of *Time* magazine. "Last week *Time* learned that the Supreme Court has decided to strike down nearly every antiabortion law in the land," an article said. The abortion decision had been leaked.

Burger drafted an "Eyes Only" letter to the other justices. He wanted each justice to question his law clerks. The responsible person must be found and fired. Burger intended to call in the FBI to administer lie-detector tests if necessary.

Dutifully, Rehnquist brought up the matter with his clerks. It was harmless in this case, he said. But in a business case, a leak could affect the stock market and allow someone to make millions of dollars. None of Rehnquist's clerks knew anything about the leak, but they asked him if it were true that the Chief was thinking of lie-detector tests. "It is still up in the air," Rehnquist said. "But yes, the Chief is insisting."

Rehnquist's clerks were concerned. Such a witch hunt would be met with resistance. Certainly, some clerks would refuse to take such a test and would probably have to resign. The Chief is mercurial, Rehnquist explained. "The rest of us will prevail on him."

Brennan summoned his clerks and read them the Chief's letter. It was another example, he said, of the Chief usurping the authority each justice had over his own clerks. "No one will question my law clerks but me," Brennan said. Then in a softer voice, he added, "And I have no questions." The real outrage for Brennan was not the leak but the delay. If the Chief had not been intent on saving himself and Nixon some embarrassment on Inauguration Day, there probably would have been no damaging leak.

Marshall asked what his clerks knew about the incident. When he was assured that they knew nothing, he told them to forget it.

Douglas treated the letter as he had treated a request from the Chief the previous term that all clerks be instructed to wear coats in the hallways. He ignored it.

Powell was out of town, so one of his clerks opened the Chief's letter. The clerk had talked to the *Time* reporter, David Beckwith, trying to give him some guidance so he could write an intelligent story when the decision came down. But the delay in announcing the decision had apparently left *Time* with a scoop, if only for half a day.

The clerk called Powell and told him about the Chief's letter and his own terrible mistake in talking with Beckwith. He volunteered to resign.

That would not be necessary, Powell said. But a personal explanation would have to be given to the Chief.

Powell called Burger and explained that one of his clerks, a brilliant and talented young lawyer, was responsible. The clerk realized his mistake and had learned his lesson. The clerk went to see the Chief.

Burger was sympathetic. Reporters were dishonest and played tricks, he said. It was a lesson everyone had to learn.

Apparently never expecting to learn so much about the little deceptions of both reporters and sources, Burger pressed for all the details. It took nearly forty-five minutes to satisfy his curiosity.

The clerk concluded that Burger understood, that he was being a saint about the matter. Burger wanted a memo detailing exactly what happened. The clerk would not have to resign.

Later, the Chief met with top editors of *Time* in an off-the-record session. He labeled Beckwith's efforts to get inside information at the Court improper, the moral equivalent of wiretapping.

Blackmun suggested to his wife, Dottie, that she come to Court to hear case announcements on Monday, January 22. He did not tell her why. As Blackmun announced the decisions, Powell sent a note of encouragement to Blackmun's wife. Powell suspected they were about to witness a public outcry, the magnitude of which he and Blackmun had not seen in their short time on the Court.

"I'm very proud of the decision you made," Dottie later told her husband.

After the abortion decision was announced, Blackmun took congratulatory calls through most of the afternoon. But former President Lyndon Johnson died that same day, and the news of his death dominated the next morning's newspapers.

Blackmun was unhappy that the abortion decision did not get more attention. Many women, especially the poor and black, would not learn of their new rights. But the outcry quickly began, led by the Catholic Church. "How many millions of children prior to their birth will never live to see the light of day because of the shocking action of the majority of the United States Supreme Court today?" demanded New York's Terrence Cardinal Cooke.

John Joseph Cardinal Krol, of Philadelphia, the president of the National Conference of Catholic Bishops, said, "It is hard to think of any decision in the two hundred years of our history which has had more disastrous implications for our stability as a civilized society."

Thousands of letters poured into the Court. The guards had to set up a special sorting area in the basement with a huge box for each justice.

The most mail came to Blackmun, the decision's author, and to Brennan, the Court's only Catholic. Some letters compared the justices to the butchers of Dachau, child killers, immoral beasts, and Communists. A special ring of hell would be reserved for the justices. Whole classes from Catholic schools wrote to denounce the justices as murderers. "I really don't want to write this letter but my teacher made me," one child said.

Minnesota Lutherans zeroed in on Blackmun. New Jersey Catholics called for Brennan's excommunication. Southern Baptists and other groups sent over a thousand bitter letters to Hugo Black, who had died sixteen months earlier. Some letters and calls were death threats.

Blackmun went through the mail piece by piece. The sisters of Saint Mary's hospital, the backbone of the Mayo Clinic, wrote outraged letters week after week. He was tormented. The medical community and even his friends at Mayo were divided. Blackmun encountered picketing for the first time in his life when he gave a speech in Iowa. He understood the position of the antiabortion advocates, but he was deeply hurt by the personal attacks. He felt compelled to point out that there had been six other votes for the decision, besides his, that the justices had tried to enunciate a constitutional principle, not a moral one. Law and morality overlapped but were not congruent, he insisted. Moral training should come not from the court but from the church, the family, the schools.

The letters continued to pour in. Every time a clergyman mentioned the decision in his sermon, the letters trickled in for a month from members of the congregation. The attack gradually wore Blackmun down. At breakfast with his clerks, when the discussion turned to the decision, Blackmun picked up his water glass reflectively, turning it slightly on edge and staring into it in silence.

The criticism also drew Blackmun and Brennan closer. Blackmun wrote Brennan a warm thank you note: "I know it is tough for you, and I thank you for the manner in which you made your suggestions."

Brennan tried to cheer up Blackmun. Doing the right thing was not often easy, he said. The one thing in the world Brennan did not want known was his role in molding the opinion.[1]

Blackmun did not cheer up easily. The hysteria on each side of the issue convinced him that any decision would have been unpopular. However, the deepest cut came when the state of Texas filed a petition for rehearing that compared Blackmun's conclusion, which held that a fetus was not a person, to the Court's infamous 1857 decision that said that Dred Scott, a slave, was not a citizen or person under the Constitution. Blackmun thought that comparing his opinion with the Court's darkest day of racism was terribly unfair. And, after all, it had been Stewart who had insisted on that part of the opinion.

Months later, Blackmun gave a speech at Emory Law School in Atlanta.

---

[1]When the clerks later put together bound volumes of the opinions Brennan had written that term, they included the abortion opinions, and on page 156 they wrote, "These cases are included with Justice Brennan's opinions for the October term 1972 because the opinions for the Court were substantially revised in response to suggestions made by Justice Brennan."

He was chatting with students and faculty when a petite young woman with black curly hair ran up the steps to the stage. She squeezed through the group, threw her arms around Blackmun and burst into tears. "I'll never be able to thank you for what you have done. I'll say no more. Thank you."

The woman turned and ran from the room.

Blackmun was shaken. He suspected that the woman was probably someone who had been able to obtain an abortion after the Court's decision. He did not know that "Mary Doe," the woman who had filed one of the original suits in Texas under a pseudonym, had just embraced him.

E VEN HIS STRONGEST OPPO-
nents concede that former Justice
William J. Brennan, Jr.'s opinions
are worth examination because of his
"preeminence in forming our constitutional law for a third of a century."[1] His
flexible approach to constitutional interpretation and his liberal views are well
known. But the man behind the opinions,
who exerted such strong leadership and
who shaped much of modern constitutional law, was, like most constitutional
justices, hidden from public view. The
following selection sheds light on the
character, personality, and style of one of
the twentieth century's leading Supreme
Court justices, whose resignation in 1990
left a liberal void that is unlikely to be
filled for years to come.

30 Lynn Rosellini
JUSTICE WILLIAM BRENNAN, JR.: THE MOST POWERFUL LIBERAL IN AMERICA

Sometimes, when the buzzer summons Justices to the robing room in the old
marble building, William J. Brennan, Jr., steps from his chambers and pauses.
For just a moment, Brennan watches the figure emerging from the office next
door and is startled into reminiscing. William O. Douglas? Tom Clark? But
no, the man approaching is Justice Antonin Scalia, a jurist far more conservative than the liberal Brennan. Douglas and Clark are dead, as are almost all
of Brennan's former Supreme Court colleagues. This is 1990, and everything
has changed.

In the old days, Brennan and Earl Warren and Hugo Black and others
would adjourn for lunch upstairs in the Court dining room, or Milton Kronheim's famed salon for liberals in Northeast Washington, for ardent debate.
The Warren Court, with Brennan as chief lieutenant, was busy extending the
rights of the poor and minorities in those electric times. In 1967, a typically
tumultuous year for that era, Brennan didn't file a single dissent.

But nowadays, Bill Brennan lunches alone at his desk. He rarely writes a
majority opinion in controversial cases, and last term he wrote 15 dissents.

"You had your day," says his wife Mary, when she senses his discourage-
ment. "Now let them have theirs." But Brennan doesn't like the arrangement
one bit. "Yes," he tells her, "but I'm right!"

The Resounding Impact

He is a tiny, cherubic figure in a brown fedora, shuffling down the Court
corridors. Always a smile. Always a nice word for Paul, an elevator operator,

[1]Robert H. Bork, *The Tempting of America* (New York: The Free Press, 1990), p. 220.

From *U.S. News & World Report,* January 8, 1990. Copyright 1990 *U.S. News & World Report.* Reprinted by permission.

or Wanda, a security guard. "Did Waldo get in any trouble today?" he will ask about her dog. Or, "How is your love life these days?"

It is hard to imagine that this unimposing figure may have had more influence on the lives of Americans over the past three decades than any jurist in the nation, and that even in controversies to come, his views will have unusual weight. It was Brennan, more than almost anyone else on or off the bench, who helped guarantee that blacks could gain admission to public schools and colleges, that women would have access to the same jobs as men and that indigent defendants would have the right to lawyers. Last June, Brennan wrote the controversial opinion upholding the right of protesters to burn the U.S. flag. And he is expected to play a role in closely decided current cases involving issues such as the right to die. Liberals, like Harvard Law Professor Laurence H. Tribe, call him one of the grand guardians of civil liberties in the 20th century. Conservatives denounce him for expanding the rights of criminals and drawing a rigid line between church and state. Dwight D. Eisenhower, who appointed Brennan in 1956, called him "the second biggest mistake I ever made." (The first was his appointment of Earl Warren.)

Sense of Mission

Yet for all Brennan's influence, he remains a mystery. Most Americans can't even identify him, and the few who can tend to think of him as just another doddering liberal jurist. They don't see his sense of mission, the passion to rescue the underdog that percolates incessantly through his 83-year-old frame. For Brennan's determination to be "right" is often obscured by his own cerebral bent, his courtly manners, his tolerant nature and the inherent secrecy of the Court itself.

He is nothing if not disarming. Women who meet him want to squeeze his cheeks because, as one Court security guard observed, "he's so cute." Men are baffled by his lack of guile. Once, after former Reagan administration official William Bradford Reynolds made headlines by calling Brennan's opinions "perhaps the major threat to individual liberty" in the U.S., the Justice greeted Reynolds at a Court reception with a smile and a "Hi, Brad." Reynolds hesitated. "I guess you've seen the newspaper headlines," he said. Brennan nodded and gripped his hand warmly. "I read it," he said, "and I didn't see anything at all inappropriate." Now, Reynolds marvels at Brennan, calling him "the *most* delightful, congenial man that you could ever care to meet."

For some public officials, such bigheartedness may be a pose, but for Brennan, it seems to be a natural outgrowth of his absorption in the "big picture." He constantly forgets details: His blood-pressure medicine, his schedule, his phone calls. Yet he can tell you exactly what Chief Justice John Marshall wrote in *Barron v. Baltimore* in 1833, and precisely what provision of the U.S. labor laws was in question in *Jencks v. U.S.* in 1956.

Brennan wouldn't consider using his influence to get a dinner reservation at a fashionable restaurant or a deal on a $36,000 Toyota Lexus his wife has her eye on. But he will pace his apartment at 3 A.M., pondering how to get a majority to join him in championing the rights of the underprivileged. (He rewrote his opinion in *Baker v. Farr,* the 1962 case that helped establish one-man-one-vote, 10 times.)

He won't worry a second about 10,000 demonstrators poised on the Court steps. "It's such a sad waste of time," he says. "Those demonstrations don't affect a single vote." Yet the possibility that he might inadvertently be thoughtless or rude can trigger a fit of anxiety. One recent morning, waiting to board an airplane for Newport, R.I., where he was to attend a judicial conference, Brennan clapped his hand to his mouth in horror.

"I forgot to call the Chief," he said, referring to Chief Justice William Rehnquist, whom Brennan had neglected to inform before leaving town.

"Well, go call him now," said Mary.

"I bet I've missed him," said Brennan, fishing in his pocket for change. "He's probably on the bench." Brennan hurried to a pay phone, as his wife, who worked as his secretary for 26 years before marrying him in 1983, shook her head in bemusement. "If he doesn't get him," she said, "he'll worry all day."

Brennan's sense of mission originated with his father, an Irish immigrant who shoveled coal at the Ballantine Brewery in Newark, N.J. Brennan, Sr., worried about workers who were crippled by burns from the huge boilers, exhausted from 12-hour workdays and often unable to feed their families.

At night, the elder Brennan, who fled poverty in his homeland in the late 19th century, sat at dinner with his wife and eight children, railing against what he'd seen during the day. "Something must be done," he would say repeatedly. "These people have no one to stand up for them."

The father went on to organize a labor union and run for Newark city commissioner, a post he held for 13 years. The son earned a scholarship to Harvard Law School and in time landed a seat on the New Jersey State Supreme Court. But he never forgot his father's message. "However lowly the station," he now says, "every individual must have the same protection as the rich of every provision of the Bill of Rights."

To this day, Brennan, a lifelong Democrat, has no idea why Ike appointed him to the bench, though historians say it was to curry favor with Democrats and Catholics. But for the next 13 years, Brennan and Chief Justice Earl Warren met every Thursday afternoon to discuss the strategy that would produce sweeping liberal changes in the nation's laws. The two men were an unlikely pair: Warren, 6-foot-1-inch California pol, and Brennan, the wizened little Newark judge who supplied the legal mastery the Chief himself lacked. In time, Brennan emerged as the master tactician of the Warren Court, a consensus builder who repeatedly managed to get five votes for liberal positions on civil rights and individual liberties.

In part, Brennan's success lay in his careful crafting of opinions, always leaving room for competing perspectives. Colleagues who at first voiced doubts would in the end often find themselves joining Brennan (as several did in a landmark 1964 libel ruling that gave sweeping rights to the press). He also had a knack for planting little-noticed ideas that would later bloom as precedents. In a 1972 case involving an unmarried woman, Brennan inserted a phrase guaranteeing that in childbearing, individuals have the right to be "free from unwarranted government intrusion." The following year, that phrase helped undergird the right to abortion established in *Roe v. Wade*.

Changing Times

Brennan's energy was formidable, too. In the mornings, he was at his desk long before his clerks. "He's trying to kill himself," Mary Fowler (then his secretary) recalls her mother saying, "Don't let him kill you." At night, he plowed through stacks of briefs at a rickety card table in his Georgetown living room. Only on weekends did he relax, as Justices John Harlan and Bill Douglas and other pals gathered to debate social policy and sample Marjorie Brennan's osso bucco.

But by the 1970s, the makeup of the Court—and the texture of Brennan's private life—had begun to shift. When Warren E. Burger became Chief Justice in 1969, Brennan's victories became fewer, although he won decisions affirming the separation of church and state and defending affirmative action. His critics renewed their claims that Brennan was legislating from the bench. To make matters worse, his health was failing, and Marjorie, his wife of half a century, was dying of cancer.

Tragedy's Impact

Ever since they eloped in 1928 (Brennan's father had wanted him to finish law school first), Marjorie had been the linchpin of Brennan's existence. Every day after the cancer struck, he left for the hospital at 6 A.M., staying at her bedside until shortly before the Court convened at 10. "He was devoted," recalls former Justice Lewis F. Powell, Jr. "He would leave the Court as soon as he came off the bench and go to the hospital and do his work late at night." When Marjorie died in 1982, Brennan says, he came close to crumbling. "There are some people who are not able to live alone," says his daughter, Nancy. "My father is one of them."

Mary Fowler, then 68, noticed the change. "He was lonely, depressed," she recalls. At night, he'd go home to his empty apartment, often forgetting to eat. Finally, one evening after work, Brennan invited Fowler out to dinner. Before long, she was joining him for lunch at Kronheim's and evening movies.

A few months later, Fowler, who had always called Brennan "Justice," typed out a message from Brennan to his colleagues: "Mary Fowler and I were married yesterday and we have gone to Bermuda."

Now she calls him "darlin." He calls her "honey." They stroll the halls of the Court hand in hand and tease each other relentlessly. Mary Brennan disagrees with some of her husband's liberal views, particularly his long-standing opposition to the death penalty, and Brennan loves to kid her. "Just remember," he says, "I've got the vote."

The rejuvenated Brennan stopped talking about retirement seven years ago. Instead, he arrives at the Court every morning about 7:30, slipping his key into the old oaken door and flipping on the lights in his empty chambers. He still works with a yellow legal pad and pencil, still gropes through cluttered drawers for one of his half-dozen worn copies of the Constitution. And when he goes to bed at night, he still falls asleep instantly, then wakes a few hours later, as he has for 33 years, worrying about pending cases. Often, he jots a note on a bedside notepad or slips out of bed and stares out at the office and apartments next door, until answers come. "He agonizes till he gets his five votes," says Mary. Adds Brennan: "The flag-burning case—I got excited about that one."

Unlikely Allies

With the addition of President Reagan's third appointment to the Court, Justice Anthony Kennedy, the Rehnquist conservatives for the first time dominated Brennan's liberals last term. And in a way, that's what made Brennan's 5–4 flag-burning opinion, his most controversial ruling of 1989, an important example of his enduring influence. Brennan's senior status gives him the power to assign the writing of majority opinions when the Chief Justice is in the minority, and so Brennan assigned the flag-burning ruling to himself. It was classic Brennan opinion, defending First Amendment rights without celebrating flag burners, thereby enabling unlikely allies Scalia and Kennedy to join. At the time, George Bush implicitly denounced the ruling, disputing Brennan's claim that state statutes that prohibit flag burning limit free speech. Other Republicans, angered by Brennan's last outrage, salivated even more at the prospect of replacing the aging and often ailing Justice.

But Brennan vows he will stay on. "We still have a great many people who aren't enjoying this country's blessings," he says. "Many because of race, many because of religion, many because they're handicapped. The spread between the well-to-do and not so well off seems to be growing. I just think we're not living up to our potential as we should."

Of course, Brennan is also reluctant to depart because he distrusts the conservative majority on the Rehnquist Court. It has already begun to restrict the very measures that Brennan fought so hard to establish, including women's access to abortion and the rights of criminal suspects, and Brennan worries about affirmative action. "If the Court doesn't flatly cut back affirmative action, it will narrow it further," he predicts. "I will dissent as strenuously as I can."

Out of Sync

It is tempting to conclude that this 83-year-old jurist, plagued by a stroke, a cancerous throat tumor and the loss of his gallbladder, is out of touch with post-Reagan America. Certainly, in the hushed and protected chambers of the Court, where the outside world seldom intrudes, even the curious can lose touch. Mary Brennan likes to tell the story of how Brennan took his granddaughter to the movies one day and was appalled that tickets cost $6. When the girls asked for a Coke, Brennan gave her 50 cents. "He was so surprised," says Mary, pointing out that movie Cokes now cost at least $1.25. "That's how out of sync he is with outside life."

And yet, in a more fundamental sense, he's not out of sync at all. Indeed, what is most unusual about Brennan may be the degree to which he threads his philosophical commitment to civil liberties and democracy through the fabric of his everyday life. On an airplane, this Supreme Court Justice sits scrunched up, uncomplaining, in the middle seat in tourist class. In the car, he insists on riding up front so he can talk to the driver. "He deals with everybody the same way, the maintenance man and the President," says his son, Hugh.

One day last summer, when Brennan's flag-burning opinion was released, a neighbor across the hall in his apartment complex hung a flag from his door in protest. Mary Brennan was horrified, but the Justice just chuckled.

"Forget it, honey," he said. "They have a First Amendment right to express themselves too."

Bill Brennan may still care about being right. He may still support liberal positions that many citizens loathe. But long ago, he gave up keeping score or discouraging disagreement. And in an era when Americans have come to expect pettiness and deceit from their leaders, Brennan's career is a reminder that the ingenuous can still both serve and flourish.

A SUPERIOR INTELLECT, SELF-confidence, and strong but not inflexible views on constitutional interpretation are important leadership qualities on the Supreme Court. Justice William J. Brennan, Jr.'s strong and consistent liberal views were an important ingredient of his leadership. The following portrayal of the Court's most dynamic conservative illustrates how a forceful personality combined with strong views on the Constitution are important leadership qualities.

31 Joan Biskupic
JUSTICE ANTONIN SCALIA: DYNAMO ON THE COURT

Antonin Scalia was neither the first of Ronald Reagan's appointments to the Supreme Court nor the one who tipped the court's ideological balance. But he may leave the most vivid imprint on American jurisprudence of the three Reagan justices.

"His influence will be greater than his tenure," predicts Rep. Mike Synar, D-Okla. "He's articulate as hell."

Adds Rep. Don Edwards, D-Calif., a committed liberal, "His aggressive leadership is formidable."

Decidedly conservative, Scalia is to the right of most of his colleagues on the court. But he has the kind of personality that may end up pulling the majority more in his direction.

On a bench weighted with older men, Scalia stands out. At 54, he almost bursts with energy—both intellectual and physical.

He is argumentative and articulate. Though his words are often sharp, their bite is usually tempered by wit and by Scalia's congenial manner.

When attorneys come before the court for oral arguments, Scalia is an aggressive questioner and a master of the hypothetical. He has a spirited, sometimes playful way with language that makes his arguments from the bench and his written opinions highly engaging.

In the 1988 *Bendix Autolite Corp. v. Midwesco Enterprises Inc.*, for example, he rejected as inapt a balancing test the majority was using: "It is more like judging whether a particular line is longer than a particular rock is heavy."

In the 1988 *Frisby v. Schultz,* an attorney for a Wisconsin town was trying to defend the town's picketing ban and asked the court to reconsider the cliche that all streets are quintessentially public forums.

Scalia rejoined, "One man's cliche is another man's fundamental principle."

From *Congressional Quarterly Weekly Report,* March 24, 1990, p. 916. Copyright 1990 by Congressional Quarterly, Inc. Reprinted by permission.

Born in Trenton, N.J., on March 11, 1936, Scalia grew up in Queens, N.Y. He graduated from Georgetown University in 1957 and Harvard Law School in 1960.

After beginning his legal career in private practice in Cleveland, Scalia taught law at the University of Virginia in the late 1960s.

He served in the Nixon and Ford administrations, first as general counsel in the White House Office of Telecommunications Policy, 1971–72; then as chairman of the Administrative Conference of the United States, 1972–74. He was an assistant attorney general in the Justice Department's Office of Legal Counsel, 1974–77.

After he left Justice, Scalia taught at the University of Chicago Law School. Reagan named him to the U.S. Court of Appeals for the District of Columbia in 1982 and to the Supreme Court in 1986. He drew considerably less scrutiny than either Sandra Day O'Connor, Reagan's first high court nominee, or Anthony M. Kennedy, his final appointment. The Senate confirmed Scalia 98–0.

Some observers believe Scalia's government service colors his judicial view of the regulatory process, causing him to favor the executive branch.

His narrow approach to reading federal statutes, sometimes called textualism, is beginning to draw the attention of members of Congress. They fear that Scalia's philosophy may lead to court decisions that are contrary to what Congress intended in a particular statute.

Scalia brims with confidence, even when he is bucking popular opinion. He felt no need, for example, to make any kind of apology in the 1989 case, *Texas v. Johnson,* that struck down anti-flag-desecration laws. It was a decision that riled conservatives especially and prompted Kennedy to write a concurring opinion lamenting having to make a decision he did not like.

Scalia, displaying a libertarian streak, simply signed onto an opinion by Justice William J. Brennan, Jr., usually his polar opposite, stating that flag burning is protected by the First Amendment.

In person, Scalia's boldness also attracts notice.

Says Synar, "His Italian background, his gregariousness and his willingness to be seen at public functions make him seem more human than the rest of the court."

In 1985, Synar went before Scalia, who was then on the U.S. Court of Appeals for the District of Columbia, in a case that challenged the constitutionality of the Gramm-Rudman anti-deficit law.

"He was the dominant personality in that case," Synar said of Scalia's questioning in *Bowsher v. Synar,* which eventually went to the Supreme Court.

Scalia has voted to uphold state restrictions on abortion. In the 1989 *Webster v. Reproductive Health Services* ruling, he chastised O'Connor for waffling on the issue and said her position "cannot be taken seriously."

Scalia rebuked O'Connor for upholding the Missouri abortion restrictions at issue but avoiding consideration of the constitutionality of *Roe v. Wade,* the

1973 ruling that made abortion legal nationwide. Her vote is now seen as the swing vote on sustaining or reversing *Roe.*

"Of the four courses we might have chosen today—to reaffirm Roe, to overrule it explicitly, to overrule it sub silentio, or to avoid the question—the last is the least responsible," Scalia chided.

The effect, he said, seemed to be "that the mansion of constitutionalized abortion law, constructed overnight in *Roe v. Wade,* must be disassembled doorjamb by doorjamb, and never entirely brought down, no matter how wrong it might be."

Supreme Court Justice Antonin Scalia has a message for Congress: In writing laws, say what you mean in the statute itself. Do not expect the courts to search for congressional intent in committee reports, floor speeches and other artifacts of legislative history.

Few members of Congress are aware that Scalia's narrow approach to interpreting federal laws appears to be gaining strength on the high court.

If they were, says Sen. Arlen Specter, R-Pa., "there would be a lot of resentment about it."

That is because for the past half century, the Supreme Court and the rest of the federal judiciary have used an array of legislative materials as a guide to what Congress intended to accomplish in a particular law.

It is not only judges who look to committee reports and other materials to determine what a statute means. Lawmakers themselves seldom read the bills they pass; they rely on committee reports or other staff-generated documents for their own understanding of what they are approving.

"If the Supreme Court is developing a different point of view on legislative intent and legislative history, we need to know about it," says Robert W. Kastenmeier, D-Wis., chairman of the House Judiciary Subcommittee on Courts, Intellectual Property and the Administration of Justice.

Kastenmeier has scheduled a hearing April 19 on how the federal courts interpret statutes. Even though Scalia's approach does not command a consistent majority on the Supreme Court, Specter and many legal authorities say it merits attention.

"I think Justice Scalia is a powerhouse and not a flash in the pan," Specter said. "He's a very astute jurist with a powerful intellect. He's young and is going to be there a long time, presumably."

Scalia is 54, the second youngest jurist on the court. He was appointed in 1986 by Ronald Reagan, after having been a judge for four years on the U.S. Court of Appeals for the District of Columbia.

In the view of some judges who differ with Scalia's view of legislative history, scrutiny is overdue.

U.S. Appeals Court Judge Patricia M. Wald wrote in a recent law review article that "by its silence on the issue of how its statutes are to be interpreted, [Congress] is missing a major arena of action in the separation of powers theater."

Shifting Balance of Power?

Read in the most dramatic terms, some lawyers and judges say, the result of this debate could affect the balance of power among the three branches.

Unless a court turns to extra-statutory materials, it must either rely on its own interpretation of what an ambiguous statute means or adopt an executive branch construction.

The Supreme Court, under a theory spelled out in the 1984 ruling *Chevron v. Natural Resources Defense Fund,* already defers to an agency's interpretation of a statute unless there is clear evidence of a contrary congressional intent.

Now, "the textualists are on the march," says Wald, chief judge for the District of Columbia Circuit.

Wald served with Scalia before his elevation to the Supreme Court. A Carter appointee, she is among those who say that a disregard for legislative history necessarily gives the executive branch the upper hand.

"For, if the clarity of Congress' will must be discerned solely from the text [of a statute], without access to legislative history, there will be fewer cases where judges can confidently decide what that is, and more cases will be decided by the executive under the . . . principle that where Congress has not spoken precisely to the issue, the executive's interpretation trumps the court's," Wald said in her article that appeared in the 1989 winter issue of *American University Law Review.*

Scalia's view, however, is making inroads. In a 5–4 ruling Feb. 21 in *Sullivan v. Everhart,* the court, led by Scalia, ruled that the secretary of Health and Human Services (HHS) did not have to give needy Social Security or welfare recipients a chance to appeal when the government offset an underpayment of benefits with overpayments from years earlier.

If Scalia and others in the majority had considered legislative history, argued dissenting Justice John Paul Stevens, they would have known that Congress did not mean for HHS to deny the needy a chance to persuade the government to waive its claim to the overpayment. Stevens criticized Scalia for giving the secretary "kingly power to rewrite history," by deferring to HHS's interpretation of statutes governing Social Security overpayments.

"The net effect of these distortions of statutory language is to defeat clear congressional intent," Stevens said.

Other critics of the Scalia approach suggest that because Republicans have held the presidency for 18 of the past 22 years, and GOP appointees make up more than half the federal bench, the judiciary is inclined to favor the executive branch at the expense of the Democratically controlled Congress.

Scalia's View

Yet, intimations of partisanship are absent from Scalia's opinions. His criticism of the use of legislative history is based more on philosophical concerns than on practical considerations.

He would reject suggestions that he is trying to augment the power of the executive by denying weight to legislative history. Indeed, he thinks the executive branch benefits from the practice of picking and choosing which elements of legislative history to rely on in enforcing a law.

Scalia declined to be interviewed on the record, but a close reading of his opinions and conversations with those familiar with his thinking indicate that his point is twofold. First, he believes that legislative history is not a legitimate measure of congressional will. And second, he thinks a reliance on the committee reports of today can actually prevent the Congress of tomorrow from nudging the executive branch into a modern interpretation of a law still on the books.

When judges rely on legislative history materials, he believes, they are not so much favoring today's Congress over today's executive as they are favoring members and staff who may well have left Congress.

Constitutionally speaking, in Scalia's view, judges owe deference only to language that a majority of Congress has approved and the president, by his signature, has endorsed.

He believes that materials outside the four corners of a statute carry no authority. They are to be consulted, if at all, much as one might check a dictionary—to ascertain possible meanings for a particular provision.

He also suspects that a committee report may not accurately reflect the sense of Congress on a particular issue because the panels usually are made up of members who have a special interest in the subject and arguably do not represent the interest of the general population or the Congress as a whole.

He has noted that members often speak on the floor about creating legislative history—a fiction he believes is written to influence future court interpretations.

Scalia's approach was supported in a 123-page document produced by the Justice Department's Office of Legal Policy in January 1989.

The report noted that when the president signs a bill, he is approving the language of the bill, not the entire Congressional Record.

"Filling in statutory gaps effectively adds language to the statute and is therefore a legislative function that is properly beyond the constitutional power of judges," the report said.

The report has not been adopted by Attorney General Dick Thornburgh, a spokesman says, and Thornburgh does not have a position on the use of legislative history in statutory interpretation.

Making a Difference

The debate is more than theoretical; it can affect the way laws are applied. In the court's last term, for instance, the use of legislative history helped shape a ruling that a federal law imposing certain requirements on advisory committees did not apply to the American Bar Association (ABA) panel that screens judicial nominees for the present.

In that case, *Public Citizen v. Department of Justice,* Justice William J. Brennan, Jr., said, "Reliance on the plain language of FACA (the Federal Advisory Committee Act) alone is not entirely satisfactory."

Brennan, writing for the majority, said "Read unqualifiedly, it [the statute] would extend FACA's requirements to any group of two or more persons, or at least any formal organization, from which the president or an executive agency seeks advice. We are convinced that Congress did not intend that result.

"A nodding acquaintance with FACA's purposes, as manifested by its legislative history and as recited in Section 2 of the act, reveals that it cannot have been Congress' intention, for example, to require the filing of a charter, the presence of a controlling federal official, and detailed minutes any time the president seeks the views of the NAACP before nominating commissioners to the Equal Employment Opportunity Commission, or asks the leaders of an American Legion Post he is visiting for the organization's opinion on some aspect of military policy."

Supreme Court Split

While the approach identified with Scalia—whom Justice Byron R. White calls "very engaging and persuasive" on the issue—is practiced by only a small minority of federal judges, it appears to be gaining support from other justices.

There is no consensus. But Justice Anthony M. Kennedy, the court's newest and youngest member, has at times declined to examine legislative history. To a lesser degree, so have Chief Justice William H. Rehnquist and Justices Sandra Day O'Connor and White.

Declining to say whether he agreed with the practice, White summed up Scalia's approach for the ABA at its annual meeting last August: "He has often said that courts should not refer to legislative history at all where the statutory test is clear enough. And he prefers, where ambiguity exists, to look to the text, the structure and purpose of the law rather than become involved in the legislative history."

In declining to be interviewed on the record for this story, Scalia did say that White had fairly characterized his position.

Usually in the other camp, actively searching for legislative intent in secondary materials, are Justices Brennan, Thurgood Marshall, Harry A. Blackmun and Stevens.

This split parallels the ideological divide that emerged on the court in its last '89 term: five conservative justices against four liberal justices.

The general conservative-liberal split could stem from the fact that conservatives, who believe in judicial restraint, do not consider the result of a statutory interpretation. The more liberal justices believe that the interpretation should produce a desirable result for society.

The latter group tends to examine as many materials as possible to determine what good Congress was seeking to accomplish by its statute.

Whose Intent Is It?

Scalia's concern about the judiciary's reliance on secondary materials to ascertain congressional intent emerged while he was serving on the D.C. Circuit.

He said in a concurrence in the 1985 *Hirschey v. Federal Energy Regulatory Commission,* "I think it is time for courts to become concerned about the fact that routine deference to the detail of committee reports, and the predictable expansion in that detail which routine deference has produced, are converting a system of judicial construction into a system of committee-staff prescription."

Four years later, on the Supreme Court, he said in a concurrence in *Blanchard v. Bergeron,* that he doubted that more than a few congressmen read the committee reports the court majority had relied on.

He concluded, "What a heady feeling it must be for a young staffer, to know that his or her citation [in a committee report] can transform [it] into the law of the land, thereafter dutifully to be observed by the Supreme Court itself."

Public interest groups—and members of Congress themselves—acknowledge that the legislative record can be misleading at times.

It is not unusual to find provisions in committee reports that broadly expand, or contradict, statute language. When a member cannot get an amendment to a bill adopted, he sometimes bargains to insert his sentiments in report language.

The *Congressional Record* publishes written statements from members as if they were made on the floor, when the member never left his office, and staged colloquies often attempt to give a bill a particular "spin" that might conflict with the majority view.

Scalia has suggested in opinions and has said publicly that members are not aware of what goes into a committee report and that lobbyists often draft the language.

But members and their aides insist that reports are written under scrutiny from committee chairmen.

A senior aide on the Senate Armed Services Committee said, "In this committee, every item of bill language and every item of report language is briefed by the chairman and ranking members and available to all members before we mark up [a bill]."

He added, "The first thing I was told when I came to this committee was 'No free-lancing.' "

In Defense of Congress

Scalia suggests that when the judiciary gives weight to committee reports, it allows Congress to unconstitutionally delegate its responsibility to staff. But defenders of Congress say the enormousness of government requires elected officials to delegate responsibility. They point out that the staff makes key executive branch decisions and that law clerks write Supreme Court opinions.

Furthermore, Specter says, members of Congress are more likely to read a committee report than the bill itself. The prose of a report is easier to understand, and, because a bill usually amends an existing statute, it is impossible to follow without referring to the U.S. Code.

"I think when justices disregard that kind of material [legislative history], it is just another way to write their own law," he says.

U.S. Appeals Court Judge Abner J. Mikva, a Carter appointee who served in the House as an Illinois Democrat in 1969–73 and 1975–79, says that federal judges generally do not understand the legislative process.

Mikva says of his former colleague on the D.C. Circuit, "With all respect to Justice Scalia, he really has not had the exposure to the legislative process that I wish he had had."

Mikva insists that committee reports offer "the most reliable record in measuring what Congress intended," although he acknowledges that they have been used for "political horsetrading and individual ego trips."

He says, "Every once in a while, a staff member goes berserk," injecting unauthorized material in a report, "but that doesn't happen very often."

Members defending themselves against complaints that their handiwork is ambiguous say it is difficult to write explicit statutes.

Rep. Don Edwards, D-Calif., for example, says the complexity of the legislative and regulatory process defies precision. If Congress had to spell out in statutes all circumstances under which a measure would apply, he explains, it would have to rewrite laws almost monthly to address changing circumstances.

"The courts are supposed to allow the laws to evolve," says Edwards, chairman of the House Judiciary Sub-committee on Civil and Constitutional Rights. "We expect judges and our colleagues and the regulators to learn more about what our intentions are."

Mikva says the legislative process is necessarily "inexact" and that words, by their nature, are fluid.

"The deeper argument here is how do you feel about pluralism, the inefficiencies of popular government," he says. "If you really trust popular government, the ups and downs, false starts, then you ought to look to legislative history, no matter how inexact it is."

A Wake-Up Call to Congress

Wald said in her article that she wondered whether and how hard Congress would fight back.

One reason the issue has not elicited more congressional attention is that, overall, the courts still are interpreting statutes the way Congress wants them construed.

Says House Legal Counsel Steven R. Ross, "Congress' goal is not to have committee reports and floor debates cited in court opinions. It's to have statutes interpreted as they were intended. There has not been an outbreak of courts' refusing to apply the law."

Nonetheless, from all corners of the legal establishment, there are calls for members to begin paying attention to the trend.

Last year the Congressional Research Service (CRS) issued a report to help members determine how best to influence judicial interpretations of legislation.

"If there is a trend in recent Supreme Court interpretations of statutes," CRS said, "it is toward increased emphasis on statutory text."

In a recent update, George Costello, a legislative lawyer with the CRS American Law Division, pointed out the two "fundamentally different approaches" on the Supreme Court to interpreting statutes.

"We now see a situation in which the court's willingness to resort to legislative history at all depends in large measure upon which justice writes the court's opinion," Costello said in the January–February report. "This fact alone counsels caution in attempts to achieve legislative goals through legislative history rather than through statutory language."

Separately, an effort is under way to get members to be more attuned to how the work of the judiciary affects Congress. It is an outgrowth of a colloquium by the Brookings Institution and the Governance Institute in 1987.

The Governance Institute, a small organization interested in separation of powers issues, is trying to create a process that would relay court opinions that raise statutory ambiguities or other problems to relevant congressional committees so that members become aware of the courts' difficulty in interpreting federal statutes.

The Federal Courts Study Committee, a mixed legislative-judicial advisory panel, which for the past year has been looking at problems in the federal courts, is expected to include among its final recommendations due out April 2 the creation of an office in the judiciary to focus on problems of writing and reading statutes.

The Last Word

The Supreme Court does not have the final say.

If Congress objects to the way a court has interpreted a federal statute, it can enact legislation reversing the decision.

This occurred a number of times in the 1980s. In 1982, when Congress approved a law (PL 97-205) extending the enforcement section of the 1965 Voting Rights Act, it repudiated a court ruling in *City of Mobile v. Bolden,* that had required proof of an intent to discriminate to establish a violation of the law.

It took four years for Congress to pass the legislation mandating a broader scope for anti-discrimination laws, largely because the measure (PL 100-259) became bogged down by tangential abortion and church-state issues.

Efforts are now under way to counter several rulings from the 1988–89 court term.

A bipartisan coalition is seeking to modify or repudiate six decisions that narrowed laws against job discrimination.

The Senate Labor and Human Resources Committee has approved a bill to counter a ruling that allows employers to discriminate against older workers in employee-benefit plans.

And members are moving to reassert that states are liable for failing to meet the needs of students under the Education of the Handicapped Act.

Their efforts respond to *Dellmuth v. Muth,* in which the court held that Congress had failed to state clearly that it intended states to be liable for failing to provide disabled students the "free, appropriate" education guaranteed by the federal law.

Despite arguments by dissenting justices that Congress obviously intended to override the states' usual 11th Amendment immunity from lawsuits, the five-member majority insisted that the act's language "does not evince an unmistakably clear intention."

So the Senate last November passed S 1824, which would expressly abrogate state immunity. The bill is pending in a House committee.

Kastenmeier, who is setting up a hearing on how courts interpret statutes, says he wants both the Congress and the federal bench to know more about how the other operates.

"We in the Congress have to reassure anyone—the courts and others looking to see what law is—that the legislative history is reliable, that the practices do lead to reliable interpretation," he says.

He says members should be concerned that skepticism about their work may be building. He said he is uncertain about the consequences of increased support for the Scalia approach, but adds, "It is thought that there may be some ideological undertones, that this is a new form of judicial activism, to defy the legislative branch."

Says Kastenmeier, "Congress should not be the last to know."

THE
BUREAUCRACY

Chapter
Seven

The bureaucracy is usually thought of as consisting of hordes of civil servants whose greatest interest is in job security and who spend their lives in eight-hour days engaged in routine matters, never taking a chance, hoping to reach retirement safely. Whatever ripples bureaucrats are supposed to cause on the political scene are generally thought to go no further than the invention of ingenious ways of increasing red tape and regulations that irritate the public. Bureaucrats are seldom pictured in the grandiose terms that are used to describe presidents, members of Congress, Supreme Court justices, and the leaders of parties and pressure groups. The bureaucracy and the people that serve within it may not seem as dynamic and forceful as the charismatic leaders that populate the political scene elsewhere, but the personalities and styles of bureaucratic leaders have had a profound effect on the political system and public policy over the years.

The great size and diversity of the bureaucracy, and the multifarious functions it performs, allow many kinds of personalities to be effective. There is greater movement into and out of the bureaucracy from the private sector than is the case with other governmental branches. The infusion of new personalities into the bureaucracy may cause changes in methods of operation and may cause different policies to be adopted or emphasized. There is a constant struggle in the administrative branch between defenders of the status quo and incoming or even permanent members of the bureaucracy who wish to innovate. The personality of bureaucrats goes a long way toward explaining such conflicts.

Contrasting personalities and styles are readily observable throughout the bureaucracy. There is the cautious bureau chief, who over the years has developed careful relations with the chairmen of the congressional committees that have jurisdiction over his agency. He will not make a move without consulting them and may have developed close personal friendships with them. Other administrative officials may pay only token attention to Congress, going to Capitol Hill only when it is absolutely necessary. Some officials may try to cultivate power relationships within the bureaucracy, whereas others may seek public acclaim and outside support. Some officials, when dissatisfied with policies that they see being implemented by the White House or by their agency, may resign in protest, making their dissatisfaction known to the press and the public. Other bureaucrats in the same position will try to change the policy from within and if they resign will keep their discontent to themselves, knowing that

297

in some agencies a public attack on the bureaucratic establishment will close the doors to future employment there. Differing bureaucratic personalities will result in a wide variety of styles, including playing it safe, playing an external or internal power game, becoming a bureaucratic politician, and seeking power and status through expertise. The positive and negative character attributes of administrators at all levels of the bureaucracy greatly affect government.

CERTAINLY NO ONE WOULD have predicted, when J. Edgar Hoover was born in 1895 in Washington to a family of undistinguished civil servants, that he would become one of the most powerful men in the federal bureaucracy. His base was the Federal Bureau of Investigation within the Justice Department, which was created in 1906 and expanded during World War I. In 1924 Attorney General Harlan Fiske Stone, who was shortly to join the Supreme Court, appointed Hoover to be the FBI's acting director.

Hoover had been working as a lawyer in the Justice Department when he became an assistant in 1918 to the director of a newly created General Intelligence Division, which had been assigned the task of compiling information on alleged radicals. During this period, A. Mitchell Palmer, the attorney general, used the bureau to carry out the infamous "Palmer Raids" on radicals throughout the country. Thousands of people, particularly new immigrants, were arrested without warrants and thrown into seamy jail cells. Most were eventually released, although some noncitizen anarchists were deported. The raids brought the Bureau of Investigation into disrespect in many quarters of the country. When President Warren G. Harding assumed office, a new director of the bureau was appointed, William J. Burns, who had once been head of the Secret Service, and had established the William J. Burns National Detective Agency in 1909 after his retirement. As a private detective he had been convicted of a misdemeanor charge after illegally entering a New York law office. Sanford J. Ungar notes, however, that to the Harding administration the conviction

> seemed to be taken as a qualification rather than as a blot on his record, and it became widely known that Bureau men, under Burn's leadership, randomly wiretapped, broke into offices, and shuffled through personal files, and kept tabs on people's private lives. The most likely targets were "enemies"—persons who criticized [Attorney General] Daughtery, the Department of Justice, and the Bureau of Investigation; Senators who asked too many questions; and other competing governments.[1]

The bureau continued to be deeply involved in political activities under the directorship of Burns, and attacks were launched on alleged radicals within and without government. When Democratic Senator Burton J. Wheeler of Montana attacked corruption in the Justice Department after his election in 1922, the bureau used every device possible to discredit him, including supplying information to the Republican National Committee on the senator's alleged radicalism, spying on his Washington home, and attempting to lure him into a compromising situation with a woman. But the bureau was not to stop there. It even aided the Justice Department in securing an indictment against Wheeler from a federal grand jury in Montana for influence peddling. The attempt by the bureau to frame Wheeler failed, and the senator was acquitted.

When Calvin Coolidge assumed the presidency after the death of Harding, he replaced Attorney General Daughtery, who had been implicated in the Teapot

---

[1]Sanford J. Ungar, *F.B.I.* (Boston: Atlantic-Little, Brown, 1976), p. 45.

Dome scandals, with Harlan Fiske Stone. Burns was forced to resign. It was Stone who chose Hoover to clean up the bureau. When Stone called Hoover into his office in May of 1924 to offer him the job, the following exchange took place:

> Hoover said, "I'll take the job, Mr. Stone, on certain conditions."
> "What are they?" the Attorney General asked.
> "The Bureau must be divorced from politics and not be a catchall for political hacks. Appointments must be based on merit. Second, promotions will be made on proved ability and the Bureau will be responsible only to the Attorney General," Hoover replied brashly.
> As this account has it, Stone was delighted with the terms and said, "I wouldn't give it to you under any other conditions. That's all. Good day."[2]

With that, J. Edgar Hoover become director of the Bureau of Investigation, and was to turn the FBI into one of the most politically oriented agencies of government under the guise of maintaining political neutrality at all costs and operating solely as a highly efficient federal police force.

Hoover proceeded cautiously after taking over the Bureau of Investigation, but soon he was to involve it in extensive public relations to fortify its image. Both he and the bureau were to become invincible in the minds of both the public and Congress. The agency was always treated with extreme favoritism by most senators and congressmen. Within the bureau, Hoover tried to rule over every detail, and he was to develop a cult of personality that has never been seen in the bureaucracy before or since. In the end J. Edgar Hoover became more powerful in many ways than the presidents he served. During the Nixon years, he single-handedly vetoed a White House-sponsored plan to establish extensive surveillance using the FBI, because he felt that it would not serve his purposes, but the president's. Hoover had for many years used the FBI for political surveillance.

In the following selection, we see how complete Hoover's domination was. For many years the FBI was run on the basis of Hoover's supposed strengths. In this selection Ungar shows that bureau operations equally reflected Hoover's many weaknesses.

[2]Ibid., p. 48.

32

Sanford J. Ungar
THE KING:
J. EDGAR HOOVER

FBI Director Clarence M. Kelley came to the office of Senator James O. Eastland (D., Miss.), chairman of the Senate Judiciary Committee, one day in June 1974 for a little ceremony in which Eastland presented Kelley with the first copy of a handsome black volume in memory of J. Edgar Hoover, containing *Memorial Tributes in the Congress of the United States and Various Articles and Editorials Relating to His Life and Work.* The following exchange occurred, as Kelley sought to turn a rather stiff and formal occasion into a relaxed and social one:

> KELLEY: "Senator, there's an *awful* lot about J. Edgar Hoover in this book."
>
> EASTLAND: "Chief Kelley, there's an awful lot about J. Edgar Hoover that ain't in this book."

There is a treasury of jokes about J. Edgar Hoover in FBI folklore, stories that agents tell each other during long, uneventful surveillances while they wait for things to happen and that assistant directors use to cheer each other up in moments of exasperation. In one, the director is at the beach with his constant companion, Clyde Tolson. Tolson agitatedly scans the shoreline back and forth and finally says with a sigh of relief, "Okay, Boss. The coast is clear. Now you can practice walking on the water." Another tale has it that Hoover and Tolson, as they became older, decided to check into the cost and availability of cemetery plots. When Tolson reported back to him on the high price, Hoover, a notorious cheapskate, was outraged. "Never mind, Clyde," he declared. "You buy yours. But I'll just rent a crypt. I don't plan to be there for more than a few days anyway." Yet another related that whenever Tolson became depressed or dispirited, which was apparently often, the director would seek to cheer him up by saying, "Clyde, why don't you transfer somebody?" If that didn't do the trick, Hoover would escalate the suggestion: "Go ahead, fire someone." And if Tolson still complained that this didn't help, the director would add, "Fire him with prejudice"—a device that made it nearly impossible for the victim to find another job. Only then, went the story, did Tolson feel better.

Such bizarre fantasies conjure up the image of a man who regarded himself as infallible and godlike and who exercised arbitrary and sometimes inexplicable control over thousands of lives. J. Edgar Hoover had a degree of authority and prerogative seldom seen in democratic governments. The longer he stayed in power, the greater these prerogatives became and the more inconceivable it became that he might ever be removed; the phenomenon seemed at times to grow out of the medieval notion of the divine right of kings. Indeed, some suggested that, in times of trouble, the elevation of Hoover was just what the country needed, and his friend, Senator Joseph McCarthy of Wisconsin, tried more than once in the 1950s to launch Hoover-for-President boomlets.

But Hoover disavowed any such ambition. He was content to stay where he was, ruling over a limited but significant realm—an agency that he had salvaged from the depths of scandal and raised to the heights of honor and influence. The director turned away other job offers—to become national baseball commissioner or head of the Thoroughbred Racing Association. Hoover put his own distinct imprint on the FBI and then turned himself into an institution. It became a tradition—and a necessity for those who sought to advance through the ranks—to say what the director wanted to hear. By definition, it was right. It also became a tradition, as one FBI official put it, "that you do what the director says without really agreeing with him." Hoover's words and acts were converted into legends, and some of them came out sounding as stiff and unreal or as difficult to believe as those of such other authoritarian leaders as Chairman Mao Tse-tung of the Chinese Communist party. If an attorney general or a president made him angry, the director could just threaten to resign, and that was usually enough to bring the offender back into line. No president could afford to lose him.

Reflecting on the reverence that came to be accorded Hoover, Clarence Kelley, his successor, says, "His most casual remark [to a member of the FBI leadership] would be turned into a point of philosophy. They would even go out and document it and build it up, so it could aid them at a future time."

This treatment could be taken to laughable extremes. Once asked how he got along so well with the director, Sam Noisette, Hoover's black retainer who was an "honorary agent," replied, "It's easy. . . . If it's snowing and blowing outside and the director comes in and says it's a beautiful, sunny day, it's a beautiful, sunny day. That's all there is to it."

John Edgar Hoover—he abbreviated his name when he learned of a namesake who had large debts—was born the third child of an obscure family of civil servants in Washington on the first day of 1895. His father, like his father before him, worked for the Coast and Geodetic Survey, and his brother, Dickerson N. Hoover, Jr., became inspector general of the Steamboat Inspection Service in the Department of Commerce. In high school Hoover distinguished himself as a good student, a debater (overcoming an early childhood stutter and arguing, on occasion, in favor of American annexation of Cuba and against women's suffrage), and a member of the cadet corps. He had to work for anything he obtained after his high school graduation in 1913, and while studying law at night at George Washington University he had a daytime job, for thirty dollars a month, as an indexer at the Library of Congress.

After obtaining two degrees, a bachelor's and a master's of law, and passing the District of Columbia bar exam, he went to work in 1917 as a law clerk in the Justice Department. As Jack Alexander noted in a unique and intimate 1937 profile of Hoover in *The New Yorker,* from his earliest days in the department,

> Certain things marked Hoover apart from scores of other young law clerks. He dressed better than most, and a bit on the dandyish side. He had an exceptional capacity for detail work, and he handled small chores with enthusiasm and thoroughness. He constantly sought new responsibilities to shoulder and welcomed chances to work overtime. When he was in conference with an official of his department, his manner was that of a young man who confidently expected to rise. His superiors were fully impressed, and so important did they consider his services that they persuaded him to spend the period of the [First] World War at his desk.

Rise he did. By 1919, at the age of 24, Hoover became a special assistant attorney general in charge of the General Intelligence Division of the Bureau of Investigation. In that position, he was responsible for assessing the threat to the United States from communists and other revolutionaries, and the information he developed became essential background for the "Red raids" conducted by Attorney General A. Mitchell Palmer in 1920. Few of the ten thousand persons arrested and detained in the raids were ever convicted under the wartime Sedition Act, but Hoover was successful in his personal efforts before a Labor Department tribunal to have at least three well-known figures deported: radicals Emma Goldman and Alexander Berkman as well as Ludwig Martens, the unofficial representative in the United States of the new Soviet government. Hoover became an assistant director of the Bureau of Investigation under Director William J. Burns during the presidency of Warren G. Harding; but his patience and freedom from association with the Harding scandals were rewarded when after his exchange with Coolidge's new attorney general, Harlan Stone, about the need to keep politics out of the Bureau, Stone named Hoover its acting director at age 29.

Before and after he took over the troubled Bureau of Investigation in 1924, Hoover was something of a mystery man in Washington. He kept very much to himself, living in the house where he was born and caring for his mother, the descendant of Swiss mercenary soldiers and a strong disciplinarian, until her death in 1938. But although he remained close to her, Hoover apparently shunned the rest of his family. His sister Lillian fell upon hard times, but got no help from him. "J. E. was always accessible if we wanted to see him, but he didn't initiate contacts with his family," said Margaret Fennell, his niece to interviewer Ovid Demaris. Indeed, even Hoover's most persistent admirers and defenders within the FBI complained occasionally that the absence of any family devotion on his own part contributed to his lack of compassion toward or understanding of strong family men who worked for him. "Hoover couldn't have a family-type feeling toward anyone," observed one agent long stationed in New York; "a man who has never been a father cannot think like a father." The wife of a former assistant director of the FBI said that "the man just had no feeling at all for families." There was a certain paradox to this attitude, as Hoover expected his married agents to be loyal family men.

Hoover's coldness to his own family could not be readily explained by a busy schedule of other commitments and associations. For a time, especially in the 1930s, he was seen frequently with well-known writers and other friends on the New York nightclub circuit; and sometimes he went with bachelor friends to baseball games and other sports events (he was occasionally joined on excursions to watch the Washington Senators in the 1950s by then Vice President Richard M. Nixon); but Hoover generally turned away all other social engagements, unless they involved official business at the Justice Department. There was little socializing in the top ranks of the bureau itself, and relations between Hoover and his associates were intentionally kept on a businesslike level. The only woman in the director's life, it was often said, was Shirley Temple, his favorite actress and then a child. His most frequent and celebrated diversion, especially as he became older, was horse races, where he generally placed small, losing bets and sometimes presented trophies in the winner's circle.

The replacement for family, and eventually for everyone else, in Hoover's celibate life was Clyde A. Tolson, a native of Missouri who came to Washington at the age of 18 to work as a clerk in the War Department. He eventually became confidential secretary to Secretary of War Newton D. Baker and two successors, but after getting a law degree in night school at George Washington University, he joined the bureau in 1928. He originally planned to move on to practice law in Cedar Rapids, Iowa, where he once attended business college for a year. But for reasons that were never entirely clear, Tolson rose quickly and was soon working at the Director's side. Hoover and Tolson became so close that, as Don Whitehead put it in his history, "They have even reached the point where they think alike." They also came to spend a great deal of time together, including, on most days, lunch at a restaurant and dinner at one or another's home. When Hoover appeared at an official function, Tolson was invariably a few steps behind and to the right of him, almost like a courtier carrying a king's cloak. As associate director, a title Hoover finally gave him in 1947, Tolson was in effect the director's chief of staff and his mouthpiece. He chaired the bureau's executive conference of assistant directors. Many of Hoover's attitudes and opinions, his wrath or his satisfaction, were transmitted through Tolson, who, as the years went on, seemed to do very little thinking or acting on his own. Tolson would invariably write his comments on a memorandum in pencil rather than in pen, so that he could change them to conform with the director's point of view if necessary. If the executive conference voted unanimously on a matter but Hoover was later found to disagree,[1] Tolson would take it upon himself to solicit unanimity for the "correct" position, and he usually got it. Long-time bureau officials, asked to list Tolson's contributions and innovations to the service, are generally unable to come up with any. And even to those who worked for years near his office, he remained an enigma. Efforts to fraternize with him were turned away abruptly, and any other bureau executive presumptuous enough to try to join him and the director for their ritual daily lunch at Harvey's restaurant or the Mayflower Hotel risked disciplinary action or some more subtle punishment.

Tolson's only known diversion was to dream up obscure inventions, and he actually obtained patents on a few, including a mechanism to open and close windows automatically. Hoover usually agreed to try out Tolson's inventions, either in the bureau or at home.

According to the persistent gossip in Washington for decades, Hoover and Tolson were homosexuals; and—according to this interpretation—their attempt to repress and conceal their relationship helped explain the bureau's vigilant, even hysterical bias against men of that sexual orientation. In fact, any such relationship between the two was never acknowledged or discovered. As one former ranking official put it, "If it was true, they were never caught. And you know how we feel in the bureau: you are innocent until proven guilty." Another debunked the rumors about their relationship on the basis of the fact that Hoover "liked to crack jokes about sex."

Tolson was always the more sickly of the two men, and whenever he fell ill, he would move into Hoover's home to be nursed back to health by the director's servants. When Hoover died suddenly in May 1972 Tolson was grief-stricken, and after going through the formality of being acting director of the FBI for about twenty-four hours, he announced his retirement. But for a few token items and sums of money willed to others, Hoover left all of his worldly possessions—an estate valued at half a million dollars—to Clyde Tolson. Tolson, increasingly ill, closed himself up in Hoover's home and declined to talk with anyone, even most of his former bureau colleagues. He died on April 14, 1975, at the age of 74, passing most of the fortune on to other loyal bureau folk.

From all accounts, of those who knew Hoover and those who studied him, the director was a cold and self-indulgent man. His expressions of warmth were few and far between and private—friendship with neighborhood youths whom he invited into his house; a gift of a beagle pup to replace one that died which had belonged to his neighbors in the 1950s, Senator and Mrs.

---

[1]The director's famous euphemism was to say, "I approve the minority view."

Lyndon B. Johnson; offers to pay a hospital bill for one of the children of Assistant Director Cartha D. DeLoach. But according to one official who was sometimes the beneficiary of such largess from Hoover, "He extracted a pound of flesh for every ounce of generosity," especially from those who worked for him. From them he expected repayment in the form of intensified loyalty and utter obeisance. From someone like Johnson he wanted political capital; from other neighbors he seemed to require only respect and deference. Seldom did his gestures seem to be motivated simply by unselfishness or humanitarian concern toward others.

Hoover moved only once in his life—after his mother's death in 1938, from the family home in Seward Square on Capitol Hill to a large red-brick house that he bought on 30th Place in Northwest Washington, near Rock Creek Park. There he built a huge collection of antiques, art objects, and pictures, mostly of himself with other famous people. According to his neighbors, the position of each item, once settled upon, remained the same year after year. Each time a new president was elected, Hoover would move a photograph of himself with that president into a place of particular prominence in the entrance hall. Some of the art objects were fine and valuable, but others, it was discovered when they were auctioned after his death, were peculiar items like an eight-sided basket made of popsicle sticks; a wooden stork from the old Stork Club, one of the director's favorite New York nightclubs; a salt shaker with a nude woman on the side; and other assorted bric-a-brac. Hoover's house was impeccably well kept (he had a fear of insects and germs and kept an ultraviolet light in the bathroom) and his Kentucky bluegrass front lawn was the pride of the neighborhood until it was replaced with artificial Astro Turf shortly before his death.

He was a man of habit, leaving the house and returning at precisely the same hour every day. He always ate cottage cheese and grapefruit for lunch. If he ever had serious health problems, beyond an ulcer condition, they were a carefully guarded secret; and he did not even like it to be known that in his later years he took a nap in the office for about two hours each afternoon. Hoover did not smoke, and he took only an occasional drink of bourbon, preferably Jack Daniels, with water.

His life was the FBI and there were few diversions from it. The director did have pretenses of being a religious man. (As a high school student he sang in a Presbyterian church choir and taught a Sunday school class, and at one point, according to his biographers, he considered becoming a minister.) But one man who worked closely with Hoover for many years claimed in an interview that the Bible on his desk was really just "a prop" and that the director exploited organized religion and famous preachers and evangelists for his own and the FBI's selfish purposes. Despite his extraordinary power and exposure, in the eyes of most of his associates Hoover seemed to remain a man of small dimensions who never became sophisticated or graceful. He was prejudiced and narrow-minded, overtly biased against black people ("As long as I am director, there will never be a Negro special agent of the FBI," he was often heard to say in the years before Attorney General Robert F. Kennedy exerted pressure on him to change that policy), distrustful of other minority groups, and intolerant of women in any but subservient positions. Always somewhat defensive and insecure about his own education, Hoover had a notorious distrust of people who had gone to Harvard and other Ivy League universities; he claimed that they had little knowledge of the real world. He was embarrassingly susceptible to manipulation through flattery or fulsome praise and sometimes hopelessly out of touch with the realities of changing times. He was, above all, a lonely man.

When Hoover first took over the bureau, he was little known and seldom noticed. When he was appointed to the job, *Time* magazine remarked only that he was distinguished by "an unusually accurate and comprehensive memory," but most of the press merely ignored him. It was almost five years, in fact, before he ever achieved a distinction symbolic to Washington bureaucrats, mention in the *Congressional Record.* A Democratic congressman from Texas, Thomas L. Blanton, took the floor of the House of Representatives in early 1929 to compliment Hoover for "the high character of the splendid work they are doing" at the bureau. Four years later, during a budget debate, Congressman John McCormack (D., Mass.)—later Speaker of the House and always one of Hoover's staunchest supporters—praised the bureau as "a credit to the federal government" and the director as "a brilliant young man . . . one of the finest public officials in the service of the federal government."

But before long, once he had consolidated power and genuinely improved the agency, Hoover determined to go public, to build a reputation for the bureau and to construct what came to be a cult around himself. This took the form initially of an anticrime "crusade," a zealous effort to awaken the citizenry to the threat and the consequences of lawlessness and to the need to cooperate with the authorities. The wisdom and invincibility of the "G-men" (a name that gangster George "Machine-Gun" Kelly allegedly gave the bureau agents, who had previously been known mostly as "the Feds") were trumpeted in comic strips; children wore G-man pajamas to bed and took G-man machine guns out to play. Alongside the easy, mass-appeal aspects of the crusade, however, there was also a loftier pitch for the federal police efforts, the development of a philosophy that gave the bureau coherence and lasting importance. The director came to have the image of an expert, a sage, almost of a saint come to deliver the nation from the forces of evil—even if he had never been out on the street working a case.

Hoover was hardly a scholar, nor was he a particularly literate man. He had made an early effort to "understand" the radical forces in the country, holding long arguments in his Justice Department office, for example, with Emma Goldman and others he had deported during the Palmer Raid era. But he soon abandoned any such dialogue and effort to understand and turned to the attack. Apart from the most important reports crossing his desk, he was said to read very little, and one of the best stories about the director was that not only had he not written the books published under his name, but he hadn't even bothered to read them. His letters often bordered on incoherence, especially in his last years, and sometimes what semblance of logic and rationality they had came from "corrections" mercifully made by close aides like Louis Nichols and Cartha DeLoach or Hoover's lifelong secretary, Helen Gandy. The director was notorious for his mispronunciation of words that he used often, such as communist ("cominist") and pseudo ("swaydo"), a term he generally put in front of "intellectual" or "liberal" as an expression of contempt; but it was taboo for anyone who intended to have a bright future in the bureau to correct him on such matters.

Most of Hoover's vocabulary was graphic and quotable, and some of it was crude. Criminals were generally "rats" of one form or another and those who failed to keep them in jail were "yammerheads." One of the greatest threats to the nation came from "venal politicians." Those who criticized him might be diagnosed, as columnist Westbrook Pegler was, as suffering from "mental halitosis." The press, for that matter, was full of "jackals." In a speech before the Washington, D.C., chapter of the Society of Former Special Agents of the FBI in 1971, he attacked the "few journalistic prostitutes" who could not appreciate the FBI; in that same appearance, one of his last major public addresses, he insisted that the FBI had no intention of compromising its standards "to accommodate kooks, misfits, drunks and slobs." "It is time we stopped coddling the hoodlums and the hippies who are causing so much serious trouble these days," he declared; "let us treat them like the vicious enemies of society that they really are regardless of their age."

Whatever the level of the discourse, Hoover found respectable forums and outlets for his ghostwritten elegies on law and order. He appeared regularly, for example, in the *Syracuse Law Review.* His treatise there on juvenile delinquency in 1953, replete with footnotes, advised the reader:

> Of primary importance in the child's early environment is a wholesome family life. A happy home which glows with morality provides a healthy atmosphere for the growing child. During the years of accelerated character development, the child quickly learns from observing his parents. As the language of his parents becomes his language, so the cleanliness of body and soul displayed by them exerts early influence on him. The child who is confronted with paternal strife, immorality, and unhappiness in the home must look beyond the family circle if he is to develop orderly, wholesome ideals. Too often the child does not find proper guidance when it is not provided in the home.

The same article advised that it was a bad idea for both parents in a family to be employed, that poolrooms and other "hangouts" bred juvenile delinquency, and warned that "law enforcement agencies in various parts of the

United States are required to adhere to restrictions which hamper policy efficiency . . . the tendency to discount juvenile crime and to assure an overly protective attitude toward the juvenile offender is dangerous." And there were generally a few words on behalf of the old virtues:

> Truthfulness is one of the strongest characteristics of good citizenship. All criminals are liars; their lives are patterned after the deceit which they reflect in both word and deed. Certainly each parent must insist of his children that they be truthful in their every word. A child should be disciplined more severely when he attempts to hide his misconduct behind a lie than when he is guilty of misconduct alone. That truthfulness can best be learned in the everyday association between the child and his parent is self-evident. Likewise the father who is caught in a lie hardly can demand the truth from his child.

Eleven years later, he was back in the same law review on the same subject, with some rather strident warnings:

> There is a growing possibility that Nikita Khrushchev will never be forced to make good his boast of burying us—we may save him the trouble by doing it ourselves through the dissipation of the youth of our country. . . . The moral deterioration in our people is another basic cause for the large juvenile involvement in criminal activity. . . . Either we solve the problem or we may well go down!

In his prime, Hoover gave frequent speeches, and he had something to say about nearly everything:

Corruption: "One of the worst degenerative forces in American life during the past fifty years has been corruption in public office. Corrupt politicians make venal politics, and right-thinking citizens know there is but one answer and one remedy. Corruption must be eradicated. . . . Few communities in the land are free from contamination of the syndicated leeches who masquerade behind the flattering term—'politician.'" (National Fifty Years in Business Club, Nashville, May 20, 1939.)

American Home Life: "When the home totters, a nation weakens. Every day it is my task to review the histories of scores who obey only the laws of their own choosing. Always the one thing that stands out is a lack of moral responsibility and any feeling of religious conviction. . . . While we fight for religious freedom, we must also fight the license sought by the atheist and those who ridicule, scoff and belittle others who would seek spiritual strength." (Commencement exercises, St. John's University Law School, Brooklyn, June 11, 1942.)

Loyalty: "In our vaunted tolerance for all peoples the Communist has found our 'Achilles' heel.' The American Legion represents a force which holds within its power the ability to expose the hypocrisy and ruthlessness of this foreign 'ism' which has crept into our national life—an 'ism' built and supported by dishonor, deceit, tyranny and a deliberate policy of falsehood. . . . We are rapidly reaching the time when loyal Americans must be willing to stand up and be counted. The American Communist party . . . has for its purpose the shackling of America and its conversion to the Godless, Communist way of life." (Annual convention of the American Legion, San Francisco, September 30, 1946.)

Hoover was even sought out by *Parents' Magazine* in 1940 for remarks on "The Man I Want My Son to Be." His answer:

> I would want him to be intelligent, not necessarily possessed of learning derived from reading, but equipped to face the world with a self-reliant resourcefulness that would enable him to solve, in the majority of instances, the problems of human existence. . . . I would want him to realize that nothing in life can be truly gained without paying the equivalent price and that hard, intensive work is necessary.

There were subjects, perhaps, that Hoover, with his accumulation of influence and credibility, could have profitably addressed himself to, but did not. For example, he never wrote or spoke about the need to control the distribution of handguns. Instead, in sensationalized accounts written for *American Magazine* under his byline by Courtney Ryley Cooper, with titles like "Gun-Crazy," he seemed to lend some romanticism to such groups as the "Brady Gang . . . the gun-craziest gang of desperadoes ever to fall to the lot of the Federal Bureau of Investigation to blast into extinction."

The director did not hesitate to pronounce his views on other issues of national controversy. He bitterly opposed the visit to this country of Nikita Khrushchev in 1959 (although he would later endorse President Nixon's voyages to Moscow and Peking). He frequently spoke out against the parole system, which he felt was administered by "sob sisters" with irresponsible leniency. "It is time that we approached the parole problem with a little more common sense," Hoover proclaimed in 1939; "it is time that sound practical businesslike methods supersede the whims of the gushing, well-wishing, mawkish sentimentalist. . . . The guiding principle, the basic requirement, the sole consideration in judging each and every individual case in which parole may be administered, should be the protection of the public."

Hoover often made decisions about people and chose his friends on the basis of their conformity with his own ideological attitudes. He was delighted, for example, when federal judge Irving Kaufman in New York gave death sentences to Julius and Ethel Rosenberg, who were convicted of espionage in his courtroom for the alleged leak of U.S. atomic secrets to the Soviet Union. Kaufman and Hoover became fast friends. Whenever the judge went to visit his son at college in Oklahoma, he was chauffeured by agents from the Oklahoma City Field Office; and even into the 1970s, after Hoover was gone, the FBI did special favors for Kaufman, by then chief judge of the U.S. Court of Appeals for the Second Circuit. Just a phone call from the judge to the New York Field Office, complaining about a group that was demonstrating outside his courthouse, was enough to launch a preliminary bureau investigation of the group.

With the help of his publicity-conscious lieutenants, Hoover cultivated his own image as the fearless enemy of every criminal, so effective in his job as to be loathed by them all. The director always behaved as if there were an imminent danger to his life. He would put his hat on one side of the rear-window ledge in his chauffeured limousine and then sink down in the corner of the other side, on the assumption that any would-be assassin would fire at the hat first. He and Tolson always sat against the wall in a restaurant so they could see anyone approaching them. And whenever Hoover traveled out of town, he invariably had a large retinue of agents from the nearest field office on duty to protect him. On one occasion, Hoover became alarmed over the origin of suspicious stains that appeared on the floor of his limousine. He ordered the FBI lab to do tests on the carpet. The conclusion: The stains came from a package of bones that he had taken home from a banquet for his dog. As former agent Joseph L. Schott has reported in his light-hearted memoir of life in the bureau, *No Left Turns,* after an incident in California during which Hoover was jostled uncomfortably during a left-hand turn of his car, he issued a strict order of procedure: There would henceforth be no left turns. His drivers would have to learn to chart their routes accordingly.

Occasionally the director was criticized—for example, by Senator Kenneth McKellar of Tennessee in 1936—for having little, if any, experience himself in the investigation and detection of crime and for never having made an arrest. As one sympathetic Hoover biographer, Ralph de Toledano, puts it, after McKellar's criticism "Hoover was boiling mad. He felt that his manhood had been impugned." In response, he staged a dramatic trip to New Orleans and supposedly led the raiding party to capture a member of the "Barker gang," Alvin Karpis. Later, thanks to arrangements made by his friend, columnist Walter Winchell, he repeated the performance in New York for the capture of rackets boss Louis "Lepke" Buchalter. Such gestures grabbed headlines and calmed his critics. It was only years later that it became known that Hoover strolled into both situations after all danger was past and that he played a purely symbolic role.

Many of those who worked closely with the director privately resented his comfortable daily schedule. While he took an interest in all the important matters before the bureau, says one longtime aide, he "never lost sleep"— neither from working around the clock nor from worrying about the progress on cases. While his agents logged the required "voluntary overtime," he usually left the office on schedule at 4:45 P.M. There was a standing order not to call him at home after 9 P.M. He handled bureau affairs in a routine and businesslike manner, apparently leaving most of the stresses and strains to

others. Nonetheless, Hoover showed unusual leadership abilities and maintained the undying loyalty of almost everyone in the FBI for nearly half a
century. He managed to persuade underlings that he cared deeply about their
careers, and there are thousands of people still in the FBI who, like Special-
Agent-in-Charge Arnold C. Larson of Los Angeles, attribute their success in
life to such inspirational personal advice from Hoover as "Set your goals high.
Go to college. Better yourself. Don't remain a clerk forever." Anyone in the
bureau who ever had a personal audience with the director remembers it in
intimate detail, even if it consisted merely, as it often did, of listening to a
Hoover monologue on the evils of communism or the misdeeds of politicians.
There was competition among some people to the very end to offer proof of
their closeness to the director; one ex-bureau official, John P. Mohr, asserts
that he was the first to be notified of Hoover's death, and John J. Rooney, the
New York congressman who supervised the FBI budget for many years,
boasted that he was the only member of Congress at the gravesite after
Hoover's funeral.

Hoover was often arbitrary and unreasonable, especially with those jock-
eying for his favor, but they seldom resisted his way of doing things. "There
was a constant desire on your part to please him," explained one man who
worked at it for some thirty years. "You wanted to obtain that praise from
him, that letter of commendation, that incentive award. When you did, you
had a great sense of pride in it. It gave you a feeling of exhilaration; you had
accomplished something. He had an ability to keep you at arm's length, yet
make you want to work your guts out for him. . . . I rebelled at the idea of
working through fear, but I did it anyway. This was my niche. I have always
wondered whether the fear was necessary, whether it might have been better
to rule on the basis of mutual respect. But it is hard to fight success."

Working for the FBI and for Hoover meant, above all, submitting to
discipline and regimentation that sometimes exceeded the military in its
severity and lack of compassion. During the Prohibition era, taking a single
alcoholic drink was grounds for being fired, if it were discovered. Hoover
assumed the right to set standards for his agents' personal lives, and the
sexual taboos, for example, were absolute. Not only would young unmarried
male and female clerks be dismissed if it were learned that they had had illicit
sexual relations, but the same punishment would be dealt to a fellow clerk
who knew about any such indiscretion and failed to report it. The rules
persisted, at least for agents, well after Hoover's death, and as late as mid-
1974 Director Clarence Kelley approved the transfer and demotion to street-
agent status for the special-agent-in-charge of the Salt Lake City Field Office
because of his alleged amorous adventures.

Cars had to be kept bright and shiny, and agents were to wear conservative
suits and white shirts—even though such uniform characteristics often gave
them away and made them less effective at their work. Coffee drinking on
the job was forbidden, especially at FBI headquarters, and some veterans still
tell of "Black Friday," in the 1950s, when a large number of agents were

caught drinking coffee in the Justice Department cafeteria after the deadline hour of 9 A.M. and severely punished. The official justification for such harsh standards was that Hoover wanted all his men to have "an unblemished reputation." As one official explained it, "The FBI name was to be so good that whenever an agent went before a jury, he would be believed."

Sometimes Hoover was simply mean; when he discovered that one agent's wife had an alcohol problem and his son was in trouble with drugs, he exiled the family to a small resident agency far away, apparently out of concern that the bureau would be embarrassed if the agent remained where he was stationed. The director was so angered when he heard that another agent had indiscreetly said he was willing to serve "anywhere but New York or Detroit" that he made a personal effort to guarantee that the man's entire career was spent in those two cities. The no-mistake concept that Hoover constantly preached caused the bureau to lose some valuable people to other agencies. William V. Broe, for example, was an up-and-coming supervisor when one minor error in a report that came to the director's attention brought him a cut in pay and a transfer. Broe decided he could not afford to accept the punishment and instead resigned and went to the Central Intelligence Agency, where he rose to one of its top positions.

One of the most-publicized disciplinary excesses involved agent Jack Shaw of the New York Field Office, who was taking graduate courses at the John Jay College of Criminal Justice under FBI auspices. Shaw wrote a letter to one of his professors, in part defending the bureau but also criticizing Hoover for concentrating on "dime-a-dozen" bank robbers and neglecting organized crime, and for a "sledgehammer" approach to public relations, among other matters; foolishly, Shaw had the letter typed in the office secretarial pool and its contents became widely known. Hoover, when the matter reached him, sent Shaw a telegram accusing him of "atrocious judgment" and transferring him to the Butte, Montana, Field Office, despite the fact that his wife was dying of cancer. When Hoover learned that the Shaw letter had been stimulated in the first place by remarks critical of the bureau by one of Shaw's professors, he also ordered that no more agents were to attend the John Jay College or any other educational institution where the FBI was not held in appropriate esteem. Shaw sued for reinstatement, and on behalf of agents' freedom of speech, but ultimately dropped his efforts to return to the bureau and settled for damages of $13,000. He eventually came back into the Justice Department after Hoover died, first working for the Office of National Narcotics Intelligence, then the Drug Enforcement Administration, and eventually the department's Office of Management and Finance.[2]

Hoover had some extraordinary fetishes. His dislike for sweaty or moist palms was rumored to be so extreme that some desperate agents with hands

[2]The bureau can bear a long grudge on its late director's behalf, however. When it issued passes in 1975 authorizing access to the new FBI building for certain Justice Department personnel, it excluded Shaw.

that tended to perspire were nearly driven to seek medical or psychiatric assistance in advance of an occasion when they were expected to shake hands with the director. Jay Robert Nash, in *Citizen Hoover*, tells of an incident in which Hoover, meeting with a new agents class, stared repeatedly at one man in the group who had a sallow complexion. The reason was that the man had been wounded in the face during wartime combat, and plastic surgery had been only partially successful; but Hoover didn't like his men to look that way, and so the prospective new agent, who had previously done well during the training course, was told that he had failed a critical examination. The director also instituted a stringent "weight-control program" which followed a life insurance company chart and went well beyond the actual restrictions within which men would be able to perform their jobs effectively. But resourceful individuals sometimes found their way around the rules, and on occasion the nation's number one G-man was easily fooled. Kenneth Whittaker, for example, later special-agent-in-charge of the Miami Field Office, once found himself overweight in advance of a scheduled interview with Hoover. He solved the problem by buying a suit and shirt that were too big for him—to create the impression that he had lost weight, rather than gained it—and personally thanked the director for "saving my life" with the weight requirements. In another instance a man slated to be assigned to one of the bureau's overseas offices was hesitant to keep an appointment with the director because he had gone bald since their last meeting and Hoover did not like to promote bald men. Thinking ahead, and with the help of some clever colleagues, the man wrote to Hoover saying he felt that it would be selfish and unfair to take up the director's precious time just before his annual appearance before the House Appropriations Committee. Hoover agreed and appreciated the man's sacrifice. When the agent later had to visit Hoover on his return from the overseas post, he brought the director a gift large enough to distract his attention from his offensive hairless scalp.

Gifts to Hoover—and sometimes to Tolson—were the clue to many dramatic promotions and rapid advances within the FBI ranks. One up-and-coming man had especially good luck after giving the director a custom-made Persian rug with the initials JEH woven into the center. After a time, major gifts to Hoover from the top leadership were, in effect, informally required on such occasions as his birthday and the yearly anniversary of his appointment as director. Each time his choice, usually things for the home, would be communicated through Tolson, and then the assistant directors would chip in the appropriate amount of money to try to find the item wholesale through bureau contacts. On Hoover's last bureau anniversary before his death, his forty-seventh on May 10, 1971, his aides spent almost two hundred dollars on a trash compacter obtained through an FBI friend at the RCA Whirlpool Corporation. Sometimes, if Hoover was not particularly fond of a gift, he would not hesitate to give it to someone else in the bureau, even though the recipient might have seen it the first time around. It saved him money. On one occasion, office assistant Sam Noisette was surprised and pleased to receive an expensive pair of cuff links from his boss; then he discovered that they were engraved with JEH on the back.

In order to believe that he looked good himself, the director often needed to hear that others looked bad. Some of his men played up to that need. In an FBI memorandum that became available to Justice Department officials during a court case in the 1960s, an assistant director, James H. Gale, described to Hoover a meeting with the attorney general, in this case Nicholas B. Katzenbach—Gale wrote that the attorney general "squirmed" in his chair and "turned pale" during the discussion; when they later shook hands, the assistant director said, the attorney general's hand was "cold and clammy." On another occasion Hoover returned from a meeting at the White House with President Truman and was furious—the director had quoted a passage from the Bible and Truman had insisted he was misquoting and had corrected him. Back at the bureau, Hoover wanted the matter researched. As it turned out, the director was wrong; but his aides twisted the context and presented their findings to Hoover so that it was the president who seemed foolish.

Others found different routes to favor with the director. One, Robert Kunkel, spent years as a clerk under the tutelage of Hoover's influential secretary Helen Gandy; she was generally considered to be responsible for his becoming an agent and, eventually, a special-agent-in-charge (although he also gained some leverage by giving good stock market tips to the director). John F. Malone, long the special-agent-in-charge in Los Angeles and later the assistant-director-in-charge in New York, is another bureau executive who became close to Hoover, in part because of the friendship he developed with bandleader Lawrence Welk, whose television program was one of the director's favorites.

Even those who admired Hoover's style and tolerated some of his excesses had difficulty with his more irrational and extreme acts. He tended, for example, to go overboard in trying to correct abuses or avoid controversy. After the Central Intelligence Agency was exposed in the late 1960s for having funded the National Student Association and other university groups, the director for a time withdrew authorization for anyone in the FBI to contact anyone on any campus, a ruling that made it difficult for agents to handle some routine inquiries. Eventually he relented. When Hoover declared in 1969 that agents were forbidden to fly on Trans World Airlines, because a TWA pilot had criticized the FBI's handling of a hijacking crisis, agents simply ignored the order because, as aides had tried to point out to Hoover, there were some air routes covered only by TWA. (In connection with the same incident, Hoover wrote to the president of the airline and, apparently drawing upon confidential files, told of the pilot's earlier "difficulties in the Air Force.") When Hoover was dissatisfied with the cooperation of the Xerox Corporation in the investigation that followed the theft and distribution of documents from the bureau's Media, Pennsylvania, Resident Agency, he sought to have all Xerox photocopying machines removed from all FBI offices and replaced with another brand; that plan was canceled only when assistant directors persuaded him that the change would be cumbersome, time-consuming, and expensive.

It required considerable bureau resources to build and nourish the desired public interest in Hoover. A "correspondence section" handled the replies to incoming mail that sought personal information about the director, ranging from his favorite recipe for apple turnovers to how he ate his steak and what color neckties he preferred. Sometimes the correspondence was handled in a laughable, almost cynical way. Once, for example, a two-page letter was drafted explaining why Hoover's favorite hymn was "When the Roll Is Called up Yonder." When the director saw the draft, he changed his mind and ordered up a new one giving his choice as "Rock of Ages." The correspondence section merely substituted the name of one hymn for the other and sent the letter out, with the explanation for the choice left the same.

One of the major occasions for pronouncements of wisdom from the director was his annual trip to Capitol Hill to justify the bureau's budget request before the House Appropriations Committee. (He testified only occasionally before the parallel Senate committee.) The transcripts of these sessions read smoothly and show Hoover first giving an eloquent statement and then responding with impressive clarity to every question posed by his congressional interrogators. Bureau officials familiar with the closed-door committee meetings, however, say that quite a lot of work went into sprucing up the public version of the transcripts; one told it this way: "There would be serious mistakes every time he appeared, especially before the House committee. The director would recite the facts concerning particular cases, and he might have them all wrong, even providing false information about individuals. Sometimes he would be completely off base, especially when he attempted to answer the congressmen's questions. . . . So we would always get the record back the next day, and we would work almost around the clock for three or four days to straighten it out. The job was controlled by John Mohr in the Administrative Division. We would take out the garrulous crap and replace it with perfect language and grammar. When the record came out [publicly], it would be beautiful; it had to be, because Hoover would issue it to everyone on the FBI mailing list. . . . The congressmen were proud to be part of it all, and most of them probably didn't even notice the difference."

But some of the Hoover statements were impossible to take out or doctor up, especially if some of the legislators had immediately latched on to them for their own purposes. The story is told of the occasion in the late 1940s when the director was asked how much crime cost the country each year and he answered, off the top of his head, twenty-two billion dollars. Back at headquarters later, in trying to justify the figure, the best anyone could come up with was eleven billion. But the public record was left to stand, of course, since Hoover's word was assumed to be gospel. That figure was used blindly for years until finally someone wrote in and asked why, in light of the increase in crime, its cost to the nation never changed. From that time on, the bureau began raising the estimate slightly each year.

These slips and quirks were not publicly known, however, and even had they been revealed, they would have posed no serious threat to Hoover's position. He had himself locked securely in place and employed foolproof techniques for keeping himself there. One was to let it be widely known, or at least believed, that his men in the field were collecting juicy tidbits about political figures, unrelated to pending cases but submitted for Hoover's personal interest and, if necessary, his use. Francis Biddle, one of President Franklin Roosevelt's attorney generals with whom Hoover got along well, wrote in his memoirs that the director, in private sessions with him, displayed an "extraordinarily broad knowledge of the intimate details of what my associates in the cabinet did and said, of their likes, their weaknesses and their associations." Such information was stored in special locked file cabinets in Hoover's inner office. Access was permitted to only about ten Hoover lieutenants through Miss Gandy. The director's personal files included some political dynamite—allegations about the extramarital affairs of President Roosevelt and his wife Eleanor, the inside story about an undersecretary of state believed to be a homosexual and his alleged attempt to seduce a porter during a train ride to Tennessee, incidents from Richard Nixon's years as vice president, and the early escapades of John F. Kennedy. The files grew thicker and more significant all the time, because whenever someone entered the running for president, Hoover would have any records on him in the bureau's general files pulled out, updated, and transferred to his office. What use Hoover made of any particular file is a matter of speculation; but what is now clear is that the implicit threat to use them was always there. It was one way of instilling in politicians a special kind of loyalty toward the FBI: fear of what Hoover might have on them and could choose to reveal. What became of each of Hoover's controversial private files after his death is still a subject of some mystery and concern. Miss Gandy and Tolson are each believed to have taken some with them when they left the bureau, and others were moved into the office of W. Mark Felt, who became acting associate director under Acting Director L. Patrick Gray, 3d, and were later inherited by Associate Director Nicholas Callahan. Many of the files are unaccounted for and were probably shredded before Hoover died or shortly after.

Attorney General Edward H. Levi, testifying before the House Judiciary Subcommittee on Civil Rights and Constitutional Rights on February 27, 1975, announced an inventory of the 164 files that had been made available to him from the associate director's office. Classified as Official and Confidential material or marked OC, they included "many routine, mundane and totally innocuous materials," Levi said; but he also acknowledged that at least forty-eight of the folders contained "derogatory information concerning individuals," including members of Congress. It seemed clear that some of the most important OC files were missing—and that there was probably another entire set of delicate Hoover files, perhaps labeled Personal and Confidential, that were missing and were never made available to the attorney general at all. Miss Gandy later admitted destroying the "personal" files.

Another of Hoover's successful techniques was to calculate carefully his relationships with those in power. As one former associate noted, the director had "many of the attributes of a genius. He could identify people's foibles and weaknesses and play upon them cleverly." He was not particularly fond of the Kennedy brothers, but the brother he liked least was Robert, who sought to assert unprecedented control over the FBI when he became his brother's attorney general. (One irritant, according to those in the Justice Department in the early 1960s, was Kennedy's personal comportment; Hoover felt that he desecrated the hallowed halls of the Justice Department by strolling around in his shirtsleeves and by bringing his dog to the office.) Hoover knew of, and exploited, Lyndon Johnson's distrust of Robert Kennedy, and immediately after John Kennedy's assassination the director virtually suspended communication with the attorney general. He replaced a Kennedy intimate, Courtney Evans, as White House liaison with a Johnson favorite, Cartha D. DeLoach. Hoover's antennae were excellent and helped him move quickly to keep up with any realignment of power.

Whatever the complaints about Hoover, most observers generally praised him for keeping the bureau honest and above the temptation of corruption to which so many other law enforcement agencies succumbed. But it has become clear that the director himself did not measure up to the rigorous standards of honesty and avoidance of conflict of interest that he set for others. In an agency where a man could be severely disciplined for taking an office car home overnight without special permission, it was a little difficult to reconcile and justify the fact that the director had five bulletproof limousines, each worth about $30,000, at his service—two in Washington and one each in Los Angeles, New York, and Miami—and that he regularly used them for personal business, like trips to the racetrack or on his vacations with Tolson. The vacations, in Florida or southern California, were never officially called vacations but "inspection trips"—meaning that Hoover would drop in at a field office or two each time and shake hands. That was enough for him to charge the whole trip to the government.

In Miami Hoover stayed free at a hotel owned by Meyer Schine, who admitted in congressional testimony that he also had ties with big-name bookmakers. (Schine's son, G. David, was counsel to Senator Joseph McCarthy's investigating subcommittee, along with Roy Cohn.) In La Jolla, California, his stays at the Hotel Del Charro were at no cost, courtesy of the owners, millionaire Texas businessmen Clint Murchison and Sid Richardson. Sometimes they had elaborate parties in La Jolla in Hoover's honor, flying in specially prepared chili from Texas for the occasion; the bills that were never presented to Hoover and Tolson ran into the thousands of dollars. Murchison and Richardson gained control of a nearby racetrack that Hoover frequented; some of the profits from it were supposed to be channeled to a newly established charitable foundation, but prominent members of the foundation board soon quit when they found that this was not happening. Both of these Hoover friends came under investigation in the mid-1950s in connection with a controversial proxy fight to win control of the New York Central Railroad, and it was learned years later that Richardson, who had extensive oil holdings, made payments to Robert Anderson while Anderson was serving as President Eisenhower's secretary of the treasury and was in a position to influence national oil policy. By means that were never publicly known, Hoover himself amassed substantial oil, gas, and mineral leases in Texas and Louisiana—they were valued at $125,000 at the time of his death—alongside his other valuable investments. All the while the director was growing rich, he never hesitated to accept free accommodations wherever he traveled.

His annual visit to the West Coast became one of the most important events on Hoover's calendar. If the invitation to stay at the Del Charro did not arrive on schedule, the SAC in San Diego was asked to nudge it along. One year the field office there was sent into a frenzy because it had neglected to stock the hotel's freezer with the director's favorite ice cream. When he asked for it upon arrival, the SAC had to call the ice cream manufacturer to open his plant at night in order to satisfy Hoover's needs. A stenographer from the field office was then dressed up as a waitress and dispatched to the Del Charro to serve the ice cream to Hoover and Tolson.

The director eagerly used the extensive and sometimes expert facilities of the bureau for his own personal whim and benefit. He was reluctant, ostensibly for security reasons, to permit outside workmen in or near his home, so it was the FBI laboratory that performed such duties as building a porch or installing new appliances. The lab was sent in on one occasion because Hoover was impatient with how long it took his television set to start up. The problem was solved by rigging the unit so that it was always on; he just had to turn it up to get the picture. Unknown to Hoover, this just meant that the tubes burned out and had to be changed often—at government expense. Sometimes the lab's assignments nearly resulted in disaster, as on the occasion Hoover decided that he wanted a new toilet installed. But the director did not like the new one, because it was too low, and he demanded the old one back. Fortunately, the technicians were able to reclaim it from a junk heap after a search.

In his earliest days at the bureau, Hoover had steadfastly and emphatically declined to profit from the G-man boom, turning back the honoraria when he gave speeches and declining to endorse cigarettes or other commercial products. But as time passed he became avaricious. When the Freedoms Foundation, a conservative organization based in Valley Forge, Pennsylvania, twice gave him its gold medal and five-thousand-dollar award, it called ahead to the director's aides, pointing out that it was customary for the recipient of the award to donate the money back to the foundation. Both times Hoover refused and said he intended to keep the money for himself. Perhaps the most profitable transactions, however, involved the books published under Hoover's name, especially the enormously successful *Masters of Deceit,* subtitled *The Story of Communism in America and How to Fight It.* The book was written primarily by agent Fern Stukenbroeker, a bureau researcher on subversive groups, but the substantial royalties were divided five ways—one-fifth each to Hoover; Tolson; Assistant-to-the-Director Louis B. Nichols; William I. Nichols (no relation to Louis), editor and publisher of *This Week* magazine, who helped to market the book; and the FBI Recreation Association—which permitted the director to contend that the profits were going to the hardworking FBI personnel. Hoover aides urged that Stukenbroeker be rewarded for his efforts with an incentive award. Hoover balked, but agreed after a dispute; however, he knocked the amount down from five hundred dollars to two hundred and fifty. Later, when Warner Brothers wanted to launch a television series about the FBI, Hoover's condition was that the film studio purchase the movie rights to *Master of Deceit.* His price was seventy-five thousand dollars. As the deal was being closed, the director suddenly got cold feet and worried whether he would be subjecting himself to criticism. He sent Cartha DeLoach to President Johnson to discuss the situation, and Johnson gave his confidential approval. The television series, with Efrem Zimbalist, Jr., as the star, got off to a successful start. Hoover pocketed the money and later left it to Clyde Tolson.

When J. Edgar Hoover died suddenly on May 2, 1972, the news was initially kept from the agents for about three hours; the day began like any other in the bureau, early and busily. When the word finally came out, it was greeted with a combination of shock and relief. Some felt comfort, for Hoover's sake, that he had died painlessly and in the job rather than suffering the indignity of replacement after forty-eight years; others looked ahead to the opportunity, at last, for a review and reconsideration of the FBI and its roles. Many were oblivious to the turmoil Hoover was leaving behind, and few sensed the trouble ahead.

That night, hundreds of agents and former agents, some traveling from far away, gathered at a funeral home in Washington to pay their respects to the director. One who came from out of town later recalled the scene this way: "They had washed his hair, and all the dye had come out. His eyebrows, too. He looked like a wispy, gray-haired, tired little man. There, in the coffin, all the front, all the power, and the color had been taken away."

The next day his body lay in state in the rotunda of the United States Capitol and Hoover was eulogized by Chief Justice Warren E. Burger as "a man who epitomized the American dream of patriotism, dedication to duty, and successful attainment." A day later, in the National Presbyterian Church, President Nixon added his own tribute: "He was one of those individuals who, by all odds, was the best man for a vitally important job. His powerful leadership by example helped to keep steel in America's backbone and the flame of freedom in America's soul." He was buried not at Arlington National Cemetery but, in accordance with his instructions, at the Congressional Cemetery in the Capitol Hill section of Washington, with members of his family.

On the first anniversary of Hoover's death—a day that one can imagine Hoover would have wanted to be elaborately noted—there was no ceremony because the FBI was in disarray. On the second anniversary, Director Clarence M. Kelley led the assistant directors in a solemn, private wreath-laying ceremony at the director's grave. For the faithful, that made things seem a little better again.

FBI DIRECTOR J. EDGAR HOOVER became a legend in his own time. He was the paradigm of the bureaucratic politician, building an empire that transcended and circumvented the formal lines of authority that placed the FBI under the attorney general. Presidents did not attempt to fire Hoover, as some of them would have liked, nor did powerful members of Congress ask for the director's resignation. They did not love Hoover, but feared him and respected his power.

The bureaucracy is highly political at every level, but especially at the top. Those who make the bureaucracy a life-long career must play a particularly astute political game if they want to maintain and expand the power they have attained. Civil Service laws protect the lowly bureaucrat, but not the ambitious one who has achieved a policymaking position by moving up from within the bureau.

Outside political appointees, such as cabinet secretaries, must also be skilled in making their voices heard at the White House, on Capitol Hill, and within their own departments. Unlike their bureau chiefs and many of their principal aides, however, cabinet secretaries usually have a firm base outside of the bureaucracy to which they happily return if trouble overwhelms them. When President Jimmy Carter fired Joseph Califano, his secretary of Health, Education, and Welfare, Califano simply returned to his prosperous Washington law practice where he reportedly makes $1.5 million a year, a sharp contrast to his $60,000-per-year salary as secretary. There are others like Califano, such as Caspar Weinberger, Reagan's defense secretary, and John Connally, former Texas governor and treasury secretary under Nixon, who move in and out, all the time maintaining their reputations for power.

By contrast with the Califanos of the political world, those who have chosen to make the bureaucracy a permanent career must construct barriers against the winds of political change, or learn to bend with them. Those who stay in power often use their entrepreneurial talents to build empires that are immune from outside attack. Others learn to serve, or appear to serve, their master of the moment. The entrepreneurs, such as J. Edgar Hoover and Admiral Hyman Rickover, often become public figures because of their ability to cultivate and manipulate the press. But there are largely invisible bureaucrats as well who eschew publicity and remain in power by making themselves indispensable to their chiefs.

The following selection depicts both the entrepreneurial, often flamboyant holders of bureaucratic power and those that quietly stay at the top by effectively adjusting to constant political change.

33

Jonathan Alter
THE POWERS
THAT STAY

What's hard, at the political level [of the bureaucracy], is *staying* in—figuring out how to avoid these four-year dry spells when all you can do is write op-ed pieces, agonize over lunch dates, and decide which boring law firm or think tank to bide your time in while waiting for a chance to get back to the action. The real survivors don't have to worry that they're not so terrific at picking which obscure former governor will win the Iowa caucuses. Why sweat it? They're still in.

How does this group of high-wire performers do it? Well, most of the survivors themselves aren't of much help beyond a grunt or two and the startling revelations that they "worked hard" or "just outlived 'em." Like other great con men, they can't ever admit their secrets, for if they do—confessing to "gambits" and "techniques"—it's a good bet they've just taken the first step toward permanent retirement. That's because success in this slippery game is determined by whether they have come to believe their own cons, and whether they've so adroitly melded their personalities, instincts, and accomplishments that they fool everybody, even themselves.

But taking that as a given, there are basically two ways of surviving in the government: Call them "ring kissing" and "empire building." Ring kissing is based on the model practiced by low-level civil servants and other prostrate subordinates throughout American society, but at the high levels we're talking about, it must be perfected to an art form. This requires that the aspiring survivor perform all sorts of tasks that convince his superiors (and potential future superiors) that he is indispensable. By making the boss look good, or by simply doing the boss's bidding, the imaginative ring kisser can collect a government check practically forever.

Empire building, by contrast, doesn't require the help of superiors at all. In fact, the best empire builders have prevailed over active opposition from presidents, cabinet secretaries, and others who would prefer they hang up their spikes. They survive by carving out independent power bases that are stronger than normal lines of authority, and by developing constituencies on Capitol Hill and in the press that help them to pursue their own goals. Because these goals are their own and not simply a divining of what the boss wants, the empires often take on a momentum that translates into longevity for the people who build them.

Ring kissers, you may have guessed, are by far the more common breed. In fact, most government officials planning a career in survival are only dimly aware that another model exists. This is their loss, for the very greatest of Washington players—the sultans of survival—have rejected supplication as a technique. The career of Hyman Rickover certainly testifies to that. He served in the navy for more than sixty years, at least half of them under chiefs of naval operations who would have preferred he stay submerged for good after one of his sea trials. Or consider J. Edgar Hoover. Almost every president and attorney general he served under during his forty-eight-year career as director of the FBI disliked him, but when he left the bureau, it was on his back. These masters may have been exceptions, but the skills they plied contain some useful lessons about how to complete lengthy service in the U.S. government—and how to do it without acting like a toady.

Shanghai Log Cabins

To get a sense of the real difference between the two kinds of survival, let's look at a few examples of people who fall into the ring-kissing category, who fit the conventional image of how a "Washington survivor" is supposed to behave.

The man believed by himself and some others to be Washington's "ultimate survivor" is Joseph Laitin, a public affairs officer who survived at a high level from Kennedy to Johnson to Nixon to Ford to Carter. Laitin's aim was to serve his "client," as he put it, the point being that clients tend to appreciate good service and respond with job security. His biggest client was Lyndon Johnson, and his idea of serving him—in fact, the principal Joe Laitin accomplishment of the years he spent as deputy White House press secretary—was to feed the president gossip. When LBJ went to the ranch, he'd call Laitin frequently at about 11 to hear scuttlebutt on reporters traveling to Texas. Johnson felt particularly unfriendly toward one reporter for the old *New York Herald Tribune,* and Laitin was only too happy to regale the boss with tales of the reporter's after-hours activities. "At first I told true stories about him," Laitin has proudly recounted on several occasions, "but then I began making them up. I think the president knew I was making them up, but he loved it just the same."

That story, pathetic as it is, has been trotted out for years as testimony to Laitin's uncanny ability to survive. Of course, "serving the client" can also take the form of genuinely helping the boss, and Laitin was good at that, too. So good, in fact, that the Ford and Carter White Houses got angry at him because he made his clients, James Schlesinger under Ford and Michael Blumenthal under Carter, look good in the press at the expense of the president.

Take the time Treasury Secretary Blumenthal flew out to the Far East for meetings. As assistant secretary for public affairs, Laitin went too, fulfilling the classic survivalist dictum that you should always travel with the boss. (The logic, now a bit dated, being that if you and the chief happen upon certain naughty diversions, it makes it hard for him ever to fire you.) Anyway,

Laitin, employing his gift, suddenly insisted that Blumenthal visit Shanghai, where the new treasury secretary had lived as a boy after escaping Nazism. "That's your log cabin," Laitin told him. Blumenthal made the trip and came away with enormous publicity, not to mention respect for Laitin. Was Laitin providing good information to the public about economic issues? That didn't matter to Blumenthal. Was the large section of the department for which he was responsible well run? That didn't matter either.

So Laitin, like countless other ring kissers, could hardly be blamed for sensing that all that really matters in surviving is pleasing those above you. As for subordinates, according to this model of survival they aren't especially relevant. That explains why reporters tend to like Laitin as a person and as a professional (in part because he leaked a lot), while a number of former subordinates show a decided lack of enthusiasm on the subject of their old chief. If Laitin was known around press haunts as a guy who never forgot the name of an important reporter or government official, at Treasury he spent so much time on the phone and out to lunch that he is said not to have known even the names of two of the secretaries in his own office. A few years earlier, while at the FAA, he walked into the office of one of his top staffers one day and the secretaries remarked that they had never even *seen* him before. But why should they have? Laitin wasn't building an empire; he was building a reputation—for service to superiors.

As you can imagine, such reputations don't often depend heavily on a person's beliefs. Like most public affairs officers—indeed, like most ring kissers who bounce from agency to agency—Laitin was not much of a policy man. To come across as one is considered bad form for survivors choosing this mode, the obvious reason being that the more closely associated you are with a particular policy, the worse off you'll be when administrations change. (The new guard can usually tell the difference between those who make policy and those who just mouth it.) On the other hand, if you don't identify with the administration at least partially, you could be out before the next election. So there's a balance to be struck.

A man who has spent the better part of a lifetime striking that balance is Dwight Ink, who for thirty years was a top manager at a half-dozen different agencies. Ink was a competent manager as managers go, but his greatest skill, according to several people who worked with him, was appearing neither too partisan nor too facelessly neutral. The latter is the way most career civil servants play it, and that's why few rise to be super bureaucrats at a political level. Ink was different. Whether he was at the AEC, or HUD, or OMB he could subtly—and without really saying anything—convey a sympathy with the prevailing political ideology, then just as effortlessly shed those few calculated ounces of conviction when bosses or administrations changed.

"If he knew what the secretary wanted, he'd help you get it," recalls Charles Haar, a Harvard law professor who was an assistant secretary of HUD in the late 1960s when Ink was assistant secretary for administration. "But he'd never move anything too fast; the instinct was for more paper, more copies, more dotted i's and crossed t's rather than for getting something done." The reason for that, as Haar and others have noted, is that getting something done too fast might have put him in a vulnerable position, and that kind of vulnerability is what the ring-kissing survivalist fears most.

Like many other administrators who endure for years, Ink is smart, hardworking, and competent; that's his reputation, and it's one reason he gets tapped so frequently. The problem with the definition lies with that word "competence." More often than not, the word has come to mean a peculiarly calibrated type of bureaucratic performance that doesn't have much to do with commitment to goals. While sometimes sharing and acting upon the boss's goals, subordinates too often substitute for genuine aims the kind of "managerial" efficiencies that so many administrators mistakenly believe can be separated from issues of policy.

Thus, just as Joe Laitin never cared much about the politics of his clients as long as they sold briskly and reflected well on the salesman, so Dwight Ink never cared much about the prevailing philosophy of government as long as it allowed him to "do the job," whatever that meant. Given that, it was no big surprise when Ink accepted Reagan's offer last year to come out of retirement and coordinate the dismantling of the Community Services Administration, snuffing out some of the very same programs he once helped create while working at HUD. It wasn't that Ink had decided on long reflection that the programs didn't work. He simply did what good ring kissers believe they are supposed to do. He did what he was told.

Wind Sniffing

Now, in some ways it's a little unfair to single out Laitin and Ink. After all, they simply responded to the same ground rules for survival that most other upper-level bureaucrats, including many still in the government, subscribe to. Take William Heffelfinger of the Department of Energy. Reagan is planning to put DOE out of its misery, and Heffelfinger, as assistant secretary for management and administration, will do the bulk of the honors (the secretary, James Edwards, is a deferential sort of tooth puller). The fact that Heffelfinger held a similar job under Carter when the department was *created* passes in Washington without notice. After all, the standard response goes, these are bureaucrats we're talking about, and they're supposed to be "professionals."

Heffelfinger's hard-nosed—many call it brutal—style of management is said to be the only reason he survives at all. A congressional subcommittee learned in 1978 that during his many earlier government incarnations he had falsified his resume by adding degrees and awards he never received, and had destroyed public documents, among other vices. When a man can undergo a full-scale congressional investigation and still get reappointed—and the reason he can get the new job is that he has a reputation for cracking the whip and otherwise pleasing whoever is boss—the legend of this route to survival grows stronger. This is true despite the fact that Heffelfinger does not appear to act like a timid ring kisser. He yells and screams and tries to be a "tough" manager who gets things done. Depending on whom you talk to, that may even be true. The point, though, is that he furthers the impression that the best strategy for getting ahead in the government is to do others' bidding rather than your own. Heffelfinger may have missed out on other survivalist secrets—a clean nose, for instance—but he remembered the one about sniffing the wind to catch the drift of one's superiors.

The current master of that art is Frank Carlucci, a hard-working, bright, former foreign service officer, ambassador, deputy director of the Office of Economic Opportunity, deputy director of OMB, deputy CIA director, and now deputy secretary of defense. Carlucci's legendary budget-cutting abilities, like those of his current boss, Cap (nee "the Knife") Weinberger, were dulled considerably once it became clear what *Weinberger's* boss—the president—really thought about defense spending. The quickness of Carlucci's response to Reagan's concerns about leaks testifies to this uncanny meteorological ability that is so often believed to be essential for ring-kissing survival. Carlucci embraced and implemented the order that lie detector tests be administered to senior defense officials. And like the good soldier he is, went first.

Ultimately, the lie detectors may prove far more destructive to Reagan than the leaks. As high-ranking Carter administration officials can attest, nothing so quickly breaks down basic loyalty to a president as this particular brand of faith in one's trustworthiness. But more to the point, the lie detectors prove once and for all that Carlucci belongs among the ring kissers. He apparently considers it a productive day's work to have humiliated colleagues and subordinates in order to keep the boss happy.

Persuasion by Polar Water

Of course in his heart of hearts, Frank Carlucci probably doesn't like ring kissing very much. In his line of work, ambition is not easily sublimated, and people who know him say that his will to survive is developing into a will to conquer. What Carlucci may be learning is that conquering can assure surviving, and that it makes some sense to develop empire-building skills, which in Washington means contacts in the press and on the Hill. These contacts are not meant to make your boss look good (the survival technique of a Laitin) but to make *you* look good, and to hell with your boss.

The greatest empire builder of recent years is Admiral Hyman G. Rickover, who as a captain after World War I came up with an idea—nuclear submarines—and in the next thirty-five years proceeded to shape almost every aspect of the U.S. Navy: training, technology, surface ships, and so forth. The way he did it is a fascinating story, but equally interesting is the way he got away with it without losing his job.

It was in 1952 that Rickover first realized the classic ring-kissing route wouldn't work for him. He had already beaten the odds and made great progress on the development of the first nuclear submarine (it was eventually finished many years ahead of schedule), but that year a navy selection board passed him over for promotion from captain to rear admiral for the second time. Whether it was because of his Jewish background or simply that he already nettled navy brass, his career appeared over. Up to then, two rejections meant automatic retirement.

But Rickover was smart enough to know that if he could create enough interest outside the navy, he might have a fighting chance after all. In part because he had a sexy project (though it really wasn't much more newsworthy that year than a lot of what goes on in government today), he caught the attention of the press, particularly a young Pentagon correspondent for *Time* named Clay Blair. Blair knew a good story when he saw one, and Rickover knew how to be cooperative—he even lent the use of his office and his wife's editing skills for the book Blair eventually wrote about him. In later years, once safely ensconced, Rickover shunned reporters. But when it counted he played them masterfully, especially those journalists like Edward R. Murrow whom he knew could endow him with some of their own respectability.

Meanwhile, he wasted no time meeting the right people on the Hill. The year before the promotion controversy he happened to have been seated on an airplane next to a young politician named Henry Jackson. They became friends, and along with Representative Sidney Yates, Jackson led the charge that forced the navy to make Rickover a rear admiral, notwithstanding the selection board's decision. Rickover reached the mandatory retirement age for all navy personnel in 1963, but until last year (when at age eighty-one he almost sank a submarine while at the controls) he continually had been granted special two-year extensions, a biennial event that caused untold teeth gnashing among his superiors.

Why did Congress admire Rickover so much? Part was clever flattery. He took members on submarine rides, wrote them hundreds of handwritten notes while on historic sea trials (who wouldn't save a letter with the dateline, "At Sea, Submerged"?), and brought back "polar water" as gifts for their offices. But most important, according to his recent biographers, Norman Polmar and Thomas B. Allen, was a peculiar "chemistry" he developed with many congressmen that made them believe they actually were involved with the building of the world's first nuclear-powered submarine and, later, with the creation of a nuclear navy. That chemistry—a critical element in any kind of empire building—is really just the reflection of an ability to accomplish goals.

The fact that Congress and the press respond best to tangible achievement—as opposed to loyal ring kissing—has not always been a positive thing for the country. Just because reporters and congressmen can see it, touch it, and report it back home, doesn't mean the rest of us need it, as Rickover's success in winning support for a poorly conceived weapon like the Trident submarine suggests. But if this kind of congressional behavior can bring us bad weapons and wasteful pork barrel projects, it can also bring out the best in government employees—the desire to create and produce, and the understanding that if you do a good enough job in those areas, forces outside the bureaucracy will help you survive.

Rickover should be particularly inspirational to budding empire builders because he proves that rank plays no role in such survival. He was a *fourth-echelon* officer (as deputy commander for nuclear propulsion, Naval Ships System Command, he reported to the chief of naval materiel, who reported to the chief of naval operations, who reported to the president). That's not to say he didn't use what position he did have, but in Rickover's case this meant an additional position *outside* of the navy, at the Atomic Energy Commission (and later at the Department of Energy).

Many powerful survivors have donned two hats before—Richard J. Daley was both mayor of Chicago and chairman of the powerful party committee that slated candidates for mayor of Chicago—but Rickover elevated it into an art form. Admiral Elmo Zumwalt, who despised Rickover for upstaging him when Zumwalt was chief of naval operations, recalls that when a navy request irked Rickover, his standard practice was to reply on AEC stationery, which allowed him to distribute the copies of his position to congressional friends without going through the navy chain of command.

It was that chain of command that drove Rickover to distraction. Acting solicitous toward Congress and the press was one thing, the point being that it helped you accrue more autonomy for yourself. But performing like that every day for your boss was quite another (although Rickover expected it of his much-abused staff). "What was fatal to [General Wilhelm] Keitel [chief of Hitler's combined general staff] was not his weaknesses," Rickover lectured a congressional committee during one of his more than 150 formal appearances on the Hill, "but his virtues—the virtues of a subordinate." Among such regrettable virtues, Rickover believed, was a conception of the chain of command as something that entitled a bureaucrat to someday win perquisites. As far as he was concerned, such niceties had nothing at all to do with power and survival.

So where Frank Carlucci tends to want the best office space available, Rickover worked for thirty years out of a converted ladies room with no rug and flaking yellow plasterboard; where William Heffelfinger dines most afternoons at the likes of Le Provencal, Rickover had canned soup, cottage cheese, and skimmed milk at his desk; and where Joe Laitin, while assistant secretary of defense, bragged that he sat ahead of the generals in a motorcade, Rickover rarely wore a uniform and was indifferent to the idea of a fourth star. After all, he reasoned, what did organization charts have to do with building and keeping an empire?

Passport to Perpetuation

Now, not everybody in the government can, or should, think like Hyman Rickover. If they did, we'd have a country of anarchists and ulcers. But the fact remains that in almost any realm—military or civilian—chain of command tends to impede action. The best empire builders recognize this and risk angering others in the hierarchy who believe individual initiative is a threat. Their power *and* their survival depend on a base outside the normal line of authority.

The greatest practitioner of this art was J. Edgar Hoover. When Hoover took over the FBI in 1924, it was a weak, corrupt, politicized, highly ineffective agency. When he died in 1972, the same thing might have been said. But in between, the FBI was, in the words of Victor Navasky, editor of the *Nation* and hardly a Hoover admirer, the "least corruptible, most sophisticated investigative agency in the world." Hoover revolutionized the science of crime detection—legitimate crime detection—by sponsoring innovation in lab work and training and by creating a high standard of performance for his agents.

The point is not to absolve this racist redbaiter of his crimes—against Martin Luther King, Jr., Jean Seberg, and the Constitution in general—but simply to make it clear that Hoover could not rely solely on his survivalist wits. If his cagey bureaucratic abilities had not been underlain by a strong conviction on the part of outsiders that he was doing something good, he wouldn't have made it.

But accomplishment, as any government official should know, takes you only so far. Like Rickover, Hoover undertook a major effort to cultivate the press, particularly columnist Walter Winchell, and the Congress, particularly Representative John J. Rooney, who for twenty-five years oversaw the FBI's budget. Equally important, he cultivated a public image, by using gimmicks like the Ten Most Wanted List and a long-running television series. Efrem Zimbalist, Jr., may be reluctant to star in the TV version of "The FDA" (co-starring special agent James Beard?), but that doesn't mean heads of government agencies less dramatic than the FBI cannot borrow some of the imagination Hoover used to create a public constituency for his programs.

You don't have to be as famous as Rickover or Hoover in order to use such skills. Consider the case of a woman named Frances Knight, who ran the passport office at the state department for more than twenty years, largely over the objections of most of the secretaries of state she saw come and go. These men resented her fiefdom but were essentially powerless to do anything about it. (Finally, in 1977, the state department succeeded in turning the passport office into what the career people always wanted—a place to let foreign service officers punch their tickets while waiting for another overseas assignment.)

Knight was controversial, but she realized that controversy, because it keeps the press interested, can be the stuff of survival, even for those in seemingly modest positions. She also understood that the press and Congress respond best if they are fed and cared for. When Drew Pearson called one Christmas Eve to say he needed fifteen passports right away, she hustled down to the office. When a congressman had a problem with a constituent's passport, she took care of it within hours, an ability that members of Congress still recall with awe.

These survival skills, applied on the Hill and in the press, should not necessarily make us feel more cynical about the way the government works. As it happens, Knight often would extend the same service to anyone (airline clerks at international terminals across the country had her home phone number). But even if she hadn't such cultivation of outside sources of power isn't objectionable in itself. What is objectionable is the use of such networks solely for the purpose of surviving. When the aim instead is survival as a way of accomplishing admirable goals—even if the goal is simply running an efficient passport office—well, then even the most dubious survival techniques can be put to good use.

To demonstrate the point, let's look at the most base and contemptible of those techniques, namely, Hoover's use of blackmail. The conversation with a congressman usually went something like this:

"Hello, congressman. Edgar Hoover here. Terribly sorry to hear about this unfortunate matter."

"What do you mean?"

"Well, we've had some reports that have come into our field office in your district. Frankly, I personally find them very difficult to believe. The whole thing just doesn't sound like you. But I just wanted to alert you to the fact that some reports have indeed been filtering into the bureau."

"What reports?"

"Believe me, congressman, this matter will be kept in strictest confidence between us. I've instructed the field office to route all the details of your case straight to the Director."

Whatever the congressman's little embarrassment—a drunken visit to a whorehouse, a son who happened to be a homosexual—Hoover knew how to use it to his advantage. The strategy, which didn't have to be employed too often to be effective, worked equally well with presidents. Hoover's reappointment was John Kennedy's first order of business after his election, and even after a feud broke out between Hoover and his nominal boss, Robert Kennedy (during which the director instructed tour guides at the FBI building to point out that he had become head of the bureau the year before the attorney general was born), JFK never even considered his removal. How could he? Hoover knew certain, uh, details about Kennedy's personal life. If William Sullivan, longtime number three man at the bureau, is to be believed, Hoover used this strategy even on Nixon of all people, after he and Bebe Rebozo were spotted in the company of a particular Chinese woman during trips to Hong Kong in the mid-1960s. By the early 1970s, Nixon, once a big Hoover booster, wanted him fired too, but like other presidents, he subscribed to Lyndon Johnson's memorable judgment that given the permeability of the administration's tent, it made more sense to have Hoover inside pissing out.

Honorable Blackmail

It doesn't require a deep sensitivity to fine moral distinctions to see that Hoover's form of persuasion constituted the most reprehensible form of survivalism imaginable. But if you think about it a moment, you might realize that Hoover's blackmail, sans the prurient details, can be surprisingly instructive, especially to people who, unbelievable as it sounds, want to do good with their government service.

Suppose you hope to improve your program or agency, and that such improvement demands a certain level of performance from your boss. To the extent that you let the boss know that you are cognizant of what is wrong in this program or agency, and to the extent that he knows you care enough to do something about it, you have created in him a dependency not unlike that felt by presidents toward Hoover. This assumes, of course, that the boss is aware that you have attended to the fundamental empire-building duties of making contacts on the Hill and in the press that might allow you to make good on the implied threat of revelation, and it assumes that you have the guts to use those contacts. If the boss believes that you really are willing and able to go public, then he's more likely to want you inside his tent. That means you now have a powerful ability to pursue your own vision of how your agency or program should be run. Your boss, respecting this new power, will provide you more autonomy, which, assuming you maintain those essential outside contacts, could be the beginning of your own empire.

But what's remarkable is that even if you have no designs on an empire—even if you like your boss so much that you might be characterized as a ring kisser—you still can play a form of this game. In fact, the most effective user of constructive blackmail is the person who admires his superior, who wants to believe the best about him, who hopes that the boss soon realizes that his subordinates and all of the people who believe in his program will be disappointed if he doesn't shape up. What this really involves is a genuine, sincere version of what Hoover was disingenuously saying on the telephone to that congressman. It is an unconscious, unspoken way of playing not on the boss's fear of being exposed, but on his sense of guilt—guilt that he will disillusion those who share his goals.

Naturally, the only way the ring kisser can inspire that very positive form of guilt is if he does indeed share those goals. And if he does share them, he might not be such an objectionable ring kisser after all. Harry Hopkins (FDR's aide) and D. B. Hardeman (Sam Rayburn's aide) are examples of this better breed. Because they believed in what their bosses were trying to do, they shared in their bosses' accomplishments. Conversely, when ring kissers do not believe in what their superiors are trying to do—when they are simply determined to outlast them—then they do not share in their major accomplishments, except in the sense that they feel a little battered for having endured the long ride. Joe Laitin showed a keen sensitivity to this point when he admitted to the *Los Angeles Times* last year after his luck finally ran out that "I can't point to one thing I've accomplished, but my blood is all over this town for fighting for what I believe is right." What was "right," of course, was simply survival itself.

So the determining factor is not which strategy you choose to employ, but what you want to employ those survivalist techniques *for.* If survival is an end in itself, then none of the gambits are worthy of our respect. On the other hand, if survival is used as the means to genuine accomplishment, then ring kissing, currying favor with Congress and the press, even blackmail have their place when done constructively. That doesn't make all survival techniques equal in morality or even in plain tastefulness, but it can hook them to some larger purpose. The best survivors—the ones we all should learn something from—have made this essential connection.

A SELF-DESCRIBED NEO-MARX-
ist and left-wing liberal in college, a graduate student in the-
ology, Ronald Reagan's budget director
David Stockman changed careers and
soon changed his ideas when he went to
Washington as a congressional staffer in
the early 1970s. While a divinity student
at Harvard, Stockman through mutual acquaintance came under the spell of the
charismatic Daniel Patrick Moynihan,
who then was a government professor on
leave in Washington as a top adviser to
President Richard M. Nixon. Although
the professor was a Democrat, Nixon
sought his recognized expertise on the
pressing welfare reform issue. During
weekends when Moynihan returned to
Cambridge, he regaled Stockman with
Washington stories that fascinated the
younger man, who as a result caught
Potomac fever on the banks of the
Charles River.

Always the ideologue, Stockman became more convinced than ever of the
correctness of his new views when he
shifted from the far left end of the political spectrum to the right. Unlike many
ideologues, Stockman was also a skillful
politician, winning his first congressional
race in southern Michigan by 61 percent
of the vote. He had changed to the conservative side slightly ahead of the nation,
but soon found that his philosophy represented an emerging political majority.

In Congress Stockman was part of a
brain trust that New York congressman
Jack Kemp had formed to advise him on
economic theory. Stockman, always a
person who quickly absorbed every idea
in sight, soon became a leading propo-
nent of "supply-side" economics, which
Kemp and his group had proposed as a
panacea to solve the nation's problems.
The theory simply stated that taxes
should be cut to promote private sector
demands and at the same time reduce
substantial federal expenditures, especially subsidies. Stockman became a
modern-day Adam Smith, proclaiming
that the best government is the one
which governs least.

The highly visible Congressman Stockman soon came to the attention of Ronald Reagan's presidential campaign in
1980. Reagan's media adviser, David
Gergen, asked Stockman to coach Reagan for the upcoming debates. Stockman
impressed Reagan's team with his knowledge of economics and his Grand Doctrine. After Reagan's election Stockman
gave up his congressional seat to become
the president's new budget director.

In the following selection Stockman
depicts his role in shaping the Reagan
Revolution—which could just as accurately have been called the Stockman
Revolution—which led to massive tax
cuts but failed, because of political considerations, to produce corresponding reductions in federal expenditures.

34

David Stockman
THE TRIUMPH
OF POLITICS

Somewhere in all this there was an inauguration.

We were about to become a government . . . finally. Since the election, we had just been a loose group of people bumping into each other in rented rooms.

Senator Mark Hatfield, chairman of the inaugural, had the highminded notion that everyone seated behind the President on the West Front of the Capitol should wear morning coats. At first I thought it was just an inconvenience; but that morning I understood that Hatfield was right. It helped to create the extraordinary and grave sense that something new was starting. I would be dishonest if I said I didn't get a little choked up when the President, looking out over a crowd of almost ten thousand in the direction of the west from which he had come, said: "Let us, together, make a new beginning."

My new office was in the Executive Office Building, the French Renaissance-style building next to the White House that looks something like an elaborate wedding cake. It is the most stately office building in the world, with immensely long corridors of black and white marble. If you look closely at the floor, you can see cochleate fossils, little spiral creatures that lived millions of years ago. Their fate became to be trodden on by presidents, vice-presidents, secretaries of state and war, admirals, generals, bureaucrats, and buffoons.

My three deputies and I did some gaping that first full day in our new quarters. My office alone was about the size of the gymnasium of my junior high school. It took some getting used to.

We did notice something distressing that first day. The office, cavernous though it was, was filthy.

The General Services Administration, which among other things sees to the cleaning of government offices, has several levels of bureaucratic cleanliness. Level One, for instance, would mean that your office got vacuumed every day. Level Five meant it only got cleaned once a week—something like that.

As head of the Carter White House's administrative staff, Hugh Carter, also known as "Cousin Cheap," had decided to save money by opting for Level Five. It looked as though he'd opted for Level Twenty. When I picked up my phone, it almost slipped out of my hand it was so greasy.

One of my deputies shook his head. Another, who never passed up a wisecrack, said, "The reason it's greasy is they spent the last four months of the campaign handing out pork."

As a cabinet officer I was eligible for the perk of eating in the Executive White House Mess right next to the Situation Room.

Executive Mess privileges were, next to access to the president, the ne plus ultra of White House status. It sounded good. But once we kicked the congressional politicians in the shins, I could never get out from under the daily crises. So I had to eat at my desk, only getting to the mess during congressional recesses. When you consider how often they took them, though, I wasn't exactly deprived.

As I started work in my new office, I began fully to comprehend how ill-prepared I was for the job ahead. The realization came late, but these realizations always do: the new ship's captain, biographer, or architect seldom, I suppose, feels truly inadequate to his task until it is too late. What lay ahead for me had nothing to do with the elegant theories of my Grand Doctrine; it was all planning, processing, negotiating, deciding, and leading. And I had no experience in any of it.

The one consolation was that the six hundred OMB career staff were dedicated anti-bureaucrats. They weren't in the business of giving things away. They were in the business of interposing themselves between the federal Santa Claus and the kids and saying, "Whoa . . ."

Governance, I was learning, consisted not so much of a tidal wave but of endless, smaller waves of angry Lilliputians. By Saturday afternoon, January 24, the first wave had arrived.

Just before the inaugural, the President had approved, in principle, a series of symbolic "first day" directives designed to show that we would "hit the ground running" and come out slugging the federal monster. Among these were an across-the-board hiring freeze, a 15 percent cutback in agency travel budgets, a 5 percent cutback in consulting fees, and a freeze on buying any more furniture, office machines, and other such equipment.

Within hours of the first full day I was swamped with urgent demands as to the meaning of these "directives." Did the travel cut apply to FBI agents on their way to apprehending a felon? Did the equipment freeze cover the blood-circulating machines essential to coronary bypass surgery? How did the hiring freeze impact the guy promised a federal job in Washington on February 1 who had already moved there from Utah? My staff and I held a desultory debate on it all and ended up exempting as much as we included.

Maddening as these problems were, they were insignificant compared to some of the other things that were fast piling up on my desk, already cluttered with paperwork driven by the February 18 launch date. Following his own naive plan for cabinet government, Ed Meese had scheduled a full cabinet meeting with the president for *each day of the first week* to continue the review of my budget cuts.

It was a mixed blessing. I was reluctant to put on the table any important items I hadn't already worked out with the relevant cabinet member. But my staff had not yet had time to write up all the easy, non-controversial cuts. We had scores of budget line items that you could table without fear of provoking an outburst, such as killing government publications on how to grow a tomato. We had to scramble all week to find enough of these "safe" items to fill Meese's cabinet agenda while the "big ticket" spending-cut and economic forecast items receded further and further.

By Friday, the cabinet was understandably restless. For several days it had been forced to sit uselessly around the table mouthing non sequiturs while I ran the show. When I walked in on Friday morning, four or five of them, including Jim Edwards of Energy and Mac Baldrige of Commerce, were huddled in a corner grousing about "Stockman's high-handedness."

I grinned sheepishly. I thought they were probably offended by the fact that their briefing papers were still warm from the OMB Xerox machines. We just didn't have time to get the papers to the cabinet members before they saw them at these meetings.

Sensing a revolt was brewing, I hauled the box of black briefing books for that day out into the hall near the Oval Office. With the help of a few staffers, I began frantically removing all the items I thought might cause any controversy whatsoever. I'd already heard enough incorrect and erroneous ideas from the cabinet that week to recognize that not all of my new colleagues were in the vanguard of the supply-side revolution. Some of them, in fact, sounded like partisans of the other side.

One of the "safe" items I had left in their books, however, was a brief paper recommending an immediate presidential action: The total elimination of oil price and allocation controls. It was so central to our free market approach that I hadn't imagined anyone would object.

I was wrong. Jim Edwards, dentist and former governor of South Carolina, did. He began with a noisy fuss about "moving too fast," then built up a good head of steam declaiming that oil decontrol was a "complex" matter, that consumers wouldn't "like" it, and that the President himself might be blamed for "higher gasoline prices." He also needed "tools" to deal with future shortages and worried about small refineries losing their access to "cheap," federally allocated crude oil.

As I listened to this claptrap, I thought, "Dentist, extract thyself." Decontrol should have happened six years ago, and here he was saying he hadn't even studied it yet. The Secretary of Energy was missing a point— like the entire free market doctrine on which administration policy was based.

At the same Friday meeting, the cabinet had pounced on another of the "safe" items I had left in their briefing books—a requirement that all cabinet agencies clear any new regulations they proposed through the OMB so that

OMB could do a stringent cost-benefit analysis of them. Sweeping deregulation was another pillar of the supply-side platform.

"What kind of bureaucracy are you building up over at OMB?" Secretary of Transportation Drew Lewis demanded. I was flabbergasted. This "regulatory budgeting"—that is, central, systematic review of new regulations—had become an article of faith among conservative critics of the regulatory superstate. He had the equation upside down.

These were the early warning signals. I was faced with cabinet colleagues who were ill-schooled in even the basic tenets of the Reagan Revolution. Most were carrying their own do-it-yourself policy formulation kits. Hence, I could see that getting the program out the front door of the White House might involve a struggle for which there was no time.

The next morning over scrambled eggs I told [*Washington Post* national news editor] Greider: "It'll be the people in the Executive Office versus the cabinet departments like it always is. The cabinet secretaries are getting domesticated by their people, by their permanent bureaucracies."

My anxiety was compounded by another factor. To be efficient about the budget item-cutting process, the OMB staff and I had created four categories of budget reductions. We had labelled them A through D. "A" consisted of items that would each save a billion dollars or more per year, whereas "D" consisted of tiny programs—small "nicks," as we called them—that each amounted to savings of $25 million per year or less.

Each list was accompanied by a towering stack of papers explaining and justifying every proposed cut. I knew there were tens of billions of dollars of desperately needed and philosophically justifiable savings to be gleaned from this awesome pile. But I also saw that the level of detail and the complexity of the numbers were mind-boggling.

The OMB staff papers recommended savings in Uncle Sam's two separate black lung programs, three different veterans' pension programs, and half a dozen small, overlapping nutrition programs. There were also savings to be harvested from two separate airline subsidies, five different programs to pump taxpayer money into the railroads, and a half dozen mechanisms each for distributing subsidized credit to farmers and small business. The options went on and on.

How was I going to get through all this, I wondered; how would there be time to explain, defend, and get all this approved by everyone in the White House? Thus by the end of the first week I confessed to Greider that the process was already out of control and that I was asphyxiating in paper:

> Well the inauguration disrupted everything. It's just been organized chaos. We're getting the paper done at 9 A.M. and I'm rushing into the Cabinet Room at 10 and giving the briefings because that's as fast as it can get processed.
>
> Now at my desk over at OMB literally I have a stack of options papers, I'm not kidding, it's two feet high and I'm going through those things, having them

revised, modified, rewritten and churned back into the process as quickly as I can but I just can't get ahead of the curve. . . .

With less than three weeks left before our self-imposed deadline, a drastic shortcut had to be taken. I settled on two expedients: using something called "budget plugs," and forming a budget-cutting committee that would be able to make an end-run around both the cabinet and the White House.

The budget plugs were placeholders for decisions we would now have to make after the program was launched on February 18. Since we didn't yet know exactly how much the defense budget would be in the out-years, we would insert an estimate with an asterisked line below saying: "Exact future defense spending to be determined." Likewise, we would insert in the budget a ballpark estimate of what we expected to save once every single one of the thousands of domestic programs had been reviewed.

Together, the plugs and the committee would tame the chaos sufficiently to allow the president to make his February 18 speech to the Congress. An impressively thick "White Paper" chock-a-block with details and apparent precision would give the impression that the economic program was being launched with utter coherence and admirable preparation. In fact, my expedients saw to it that critical loose ends were left unresolved everywhere. They ensured that the whole fiscal plan was embedded with contradictions and booby-trapped with hidden pressures. . . .

Suddenly remembering that I was tempting the national news editor of *The Washington Post* with more explosive information than someone in his position might be expected to keep to himself, I reminded Greider that we were off the record.

"If you tell your guys about this shit, I'll have 160 people calling the White House," I told him.

Greider smiled. "You will anyway," he said.

Two things were certain about the events after February 7. The first was that as we went into the final ten days, the President of the United States was not even given the slightest warning that his economic policy revolution was bursting at its fiscal seams. I'd made perfunctory status reports at a couple of cabinet meetings. For all practical purposes, however, he'd been out of the loop completely since inauguration week. . . .

There was an indecent irony to this two-week gap in the President's economic policy log. His architect had been frenetically designing a fiscal house of cards for the New Order. Meanwhile, the President had been busily trying to persuade the agog congressional Republicans to support an emergency increase in the debt ceiling to keep the old order solvent. They were kicking and screaming al the idea. But he told them once his new economic plan was enacted, they'd never, ever have to do it again.

"This is the last time I will ever ask you to do this," he declared, with the air of a parent asking a son to take his dateless sister to the prom. And as far as he knew, it was the last time. What he couldn't know was that he would end up raising the national debt by more than all of his predecessors combined.

The second certainty was that the final week of White House deliberation on the economic plan gave a new definition to the concept of chaos—leaving the notion of confusion with no remaining worlds to conquer.

Symptomatic of this is that we did not have a final economic forecast and final estimate of the budget gap until the *last day for decisions.* The promised additional 1984 savings needed for a balanced budget might be $30 billion, $40 billion, $50 billion. We'd find out at the end.

Still, someone might have asked some basic questions. How many congressional horses do you need to cut $40 billion more—on top of the black book full of cuts already proposed? How many horses do we actually have?

This essential political feasibility question was never asked. Our team had no serious legislative experience or wisdom. Most of them had no comprehension of the numbers, and I didn't really care. Mowing down the political resistance was the whole purpose of the Reagan Revolution.

Moreover, you couldn't even grab that "future savings" number, stick it up in the wind, and see which way it pointed. The number bounced up and down and all over the lot during the last five days.

The OMB numbers-crunchers were already working around the clock, but we were trying to remake a $700 billion budget in two or three weeks. Decisions were being made, unmade, modified, and revised by the hour. There was thus a traffic jam of numbers flowing into the OMB central computer.

I had invented a one-page budget scoresheet to keep everyone posted on the numbers. I knew what it meant, almost. But it was beyond reason to believe anyone else could have.

Nevertheless, on Tuesday, February 10, a full cabinet meeting was held to update the President and his team on the budget plan that had to be locked in and finished by Friday.

The scoresheet showed 1984 revenues after the tax cut, and total outlays after the defense increase but before any domestic spending cuts. The difference between those two numbers was the starting budget gap—$129 billion.

The rest of the table was supposed to tell you how much of the $129 billion we had already saved and how much we had left to go. But that's where everything got complicated. Both the haste and my expedience had given rise to four different categories of savings numbers.[1]

---

[1]Approved savings, Budget Working Group—$71 billion; pending savings, Budget Working Group—$9 billion; expected additional savings from small programs and accounts (March revisions)—$15 billion; remaining savings to be identified—$34 billion.

If you squinted hard enough at this complicated scoresheet, you could see something important: We were four days from D-Day; yet we had only $71 billion in firm savings in the bank, or just over *half* of what it took to get a balanced budget. The other three categories were either still up in the air or just air.

But no one squinted hard at the scoresheet or maybe even looked at all. No one said, "Now just where are you going to get the $58 billion savings in the last three categories? Name names. Kick some tail! Gore some oxen! Slay some sacred cows right here on the cabinet table!"

To be sure, I went over the numbers and tried to convey the meaning.

"We can make it add up, but what remains to be cut," I told them, "is nearly as big as what we've already cut. The additional cuts will be far tougher than anything we've already agreed upon."

There was no dissent. The cabinet apparently figured there was room in the Reagan Revolution for the Russell Long caveat: "Don't cut you, don't cut me, cut the guy behind the tree."

The President nodded. "We're here to do whatever it takes," he said. He would make this statement over and over in the future. It was his mantra.

In effect, the President was letting his fiscal architect develop his economic policy revolution for him. He was taking my plan on faith alone, having no reason to suspect that the numbers wouldn't add up.

If there were no questions or dissent at the cabinet meeting, however, there was something much worse: confusion. A number of the cabinet officers complained that the administration was getting a "black eye" because of the proposed social cuts. I tried to calm them by pointing to the Chapter Two cuts.

"Barge operators, dairy farmers, general aviation, big oil," I said, rattling off the list, "they're all going to take their hit too."

Warming to our defense, I then began to tick off a number of so-called social programs that we hadn't cut a dime out of. Social Security, Medicare, veterans' benefits, Head Start, Supplemental Security Income for the poor, disabled, and elderly, summer jobs programs for ghetto youth. But—crucial point—it wasn't that we intended to spare those programs; they would have to be cut too if the whole fiscal plan was to work. It was simply that we hadn't yet got around to cutting them.

My own facility for rattling off lists proved to be my undoing. Before I had finished my recitation, there was a clamor around the table.

"That's great!" someone said. "We've got to get this out."

Ed Meese immediately threw in that he thought it was a swell idea. I should "get with" him, press Secretary Jim Brady, and Dave Gergen right after the meeting to work out a press announcement for the next day.

The whole point of the cabinet meeting had been to inform them we would need *$58 billion in additional cuts.* But—in part through my carelessness—they were now about to fence off enormous chunks of the budget and say, in effect, "See, we haven't touched these!" We were turning into The Gang That Couldn't Cut Straight.

When we huddled after the meeting, I warned Meese and the others, "We can't imply that they're exempted from cuts entirely." At best, I said, we can say we're not going to cut the "basic benefits" in these areas. "That doesn't exempt them from serious reform."

Meese then declared an on-the-spot compromise. The "sacred cows" list would include the five I had mentioned plus two more for good measure: low-income school lunches and veterans' disability benefits.

I left the Cabinet Room thinking that the "basic benefits" proviso gave me all the running room I would need when time came to lower the ax. But it was a meaningless proviso.

The lead in the next day's *New York Times* story showed exactly what kind of damage had been done:

> President Reagan's abrupt announcement yesterday sparing seven basic social programs from budget cuts . . .

The fact was these seven programs accounted for $240 billion of baseline spending—more than 40 percent of the domestic budget. And we had just neatly built a fence around them. Henceforth people would have these newspaper clippings in our face over and over.

The next day, Wednesday, brought another bombshell.

Up to now, the President had remained almost entirely passive. At a meeting that day we brought up the Chapter Two tax expenditure proposals, starting with the oil depletion allowance. All of a sudden, the President became animated. Our proposal unleashed a pent-up catechism on the virtues of the oil depletion allowance, followed by a lecture on how the whole idea of "tax expenditures" was a liberal myth.

"The idea implies that the government owns all your income and has the right to decide what you can keep," said the President. "Well, we're not going to have any of that kind of thinking round here."

Having rendered 40 percent of the budget immune from cutting on Tuesday, Wednesday the entire tax code was put off limits.

When I met with Greider to tell him that my Chapter Two cuts—the ones I had so triumphantly said would sail through the White House—had been discarded, I was somewhat sheepish and awed. I told him that an unexpected, and adamant, Ronald Reagan had risen to the occasion. What I didn't tell him because I still didn't realize it myself was that my whole plan was now in big trouble.

> The President has a very clear philosophy. A lot of people criticize him for being short on the details, but he knows when something's wrong. He just jumped

all over my tax proposals . . . he doesn't believe in tax expenditures. We didn't even bring up the other proposals. When we got shot down so fast on the depletion allowance, I figured, "Well, this is futile."

By Friday, February 13, when we met for a wrap-up session, the scoresheet showed that we had backed ourselves into a tight corner. Itemized 1984 deficit reductions would total about $70 billion. The "future savings to be proposed" would now amount to a negative $50 billion. That was a bigger number than everything then in the budget except defense, Social Security, and interest.

Defense had gotten cockeyed, too. To satisfy the White House staff clamor for defense cuts, I essentially conjured up a mirage. The February 18 budget would now show $6 billion in "defense savings" as part of the $70 billion cut total for 1984. Over five years, the new defense savings number was $28 billion.

But I had to keep my agreement with Weinberger, too. So I just raised the pre-Reagan baseline by $28 billion, added Weinberger's increase, then subtracted the new "defense savings." This two-sided bookkeeping entry left Weinberger happy and everyone else confused. It was only symptomatic.

After the plan had been signed off on Friday, the numbers kept moving all weekend. The exhausted and frantic OMB professional staff struggled to catch up. When I came into the office on Sunday morning, Dale McComber, the *numero uno* of federal budgeteers, was still chained to his desk. He'd been there all night. Dale was scratching his head; he wasn't impressed by the madness that had gone on—and it still didn't add up.

Due to final technical reestimating, the itemized savings proposals had shrunk down to $64 billion. Fortunately, the total budget gap for 1984 had come down, too. Still, to get the budget to balance in 1984, we'd have to put a negative $44 billion in the "future savings" line.

McComber then reminded me that Marty Anderson and the whole White House senior staff had been adamant. The "future savings" plug couldn't be bigger than $30 billion. A bigger number might raise "credibility" problems.

"So what am I supposed to do now," I complained. "The first phase of the show is over."

The collapse of the tax loophole component of Chapter Two had been the culprit. So, I quickly created a second "future savings" plug, worth about $13 billion in 1984. This was to represent what we thought might be saved in the next package of "cats and dogs" to be forwarded to Congress in March. I buried it way down at the bottom of the white paper appendix table. If you had a magnifying glass, you could read it.

Had I been a standard policymaker and not an ideologue with a Grand Doctrine for changing the whole complexion of American government, I would have panicked at this point and said, "This won't work." To close a $44 billion budget gap *after* already cutting the budget by $64 billion would have involved nothing less than trench-style political warfare. But I had my own agenda. Four weeks of nonstop budget cutting, congressional briefings, press interviews, and Washington show stopping had given me an exaggerated sense of power.

I knew that the remaining $44 billion gap was huge. I remembered it was probably going to end up even larger, due to our cockeyed economic forecast. But I saw in this only the potential leverage it provided to further my Grand Doctrine, not its danger to the nation's finances.

The $44 billion in future budget cuts would become a powerful battering ram. It would force Congress to shrink the welfare state. It would give me an excuse to come back to them again and again.

The misdirected and corrupt politicians of the Second Republic would be hammered into the new servants of the public good. This wasn't arrogance of the normal sort; it was grandiosity of the historical variety.

Three days later the President stood before a joint session of the Congress and unveiled his plan for economic prosperity to the country.

"Can we," he said, "who man the ship of state, deny that it is somewhat out of control? Our national debt is approaching one trillion dollars. . . . Have they [the Democrats] an alternative which offers a better chance of balancing the budget, reducing and eliminating inflation . . . are they suggesting that we can continue on the present course without coming to a day of reckoning?"

Those were our beliefs. But, to extend the president's rhetorical line of question in hindsight, was the ship sailing with an accurate chart?

A profound question about the chart's accuracy was actually buried between the lines of the very first page of our white paper. On a five-year basis, our giant tax cut and big defense buildup cost nearly $900 billion. Our domestic spending cuts, including the $44 billion magic asterisk, came to only about half that.

So how could you worsen the budget by $900 billion, cut it by $450 billion, and still come out with a balanced budget? The answer was buried in Murray Weidenbaum's visceral computer. We were peering into the veil of the economic future. We were betting the fiscal house of the United States on our ability to predict the precise shape and composition of a $4 trillion economy all the way out to 1986.

One single number that didn't appear in the white paper might have made a profound difference. It blared out a clear message: *Murray, go slap it again. Your first answer doesn't compute.*

If you projected the *inherited* budget policy, Carter's mess, the one which had brought us to "a day of reckoning," as the President said that night, with our Rosy Scenario economic forecast, what did you get? That was the missing number: a *$365 billion surplus* over five years.

With Rosy Scenario, the old, 1970s tax and spending policy would have projected out over five years to produce an unprecedented surplus without cutting a dime of domestic spending. That's what a mechanical computation of the numbers would have shown.

But how could that have been? The politicians had spent two decades revving up the welfare state. There hadn't been a budget surplus in twelve years. Spending was out of control, everyone agreed.

The answer was this: Rosy Scenario, why, she was an economic heart-throb. Touch her hand to the deficit-ridden federal budget and the surpluses never stopped.

The idea that we were actually inheriting a huge budget surplus was just plain . . . haywire. Still, that was what our numbers assumed.